Stephen Pettitt

Philharmonia Orchestra:

Complete Discography
1945-1987

Travis & Emery Music Bookshop

Philharmonia Orchestra: Complete Discography 1945-1987

First edited and published, John Hunt 1987.

Republished Travis & Emery 2009.

Publisher's note - This title was originally published with another title, so the pagination started at page 142.

Published by
Travis & Emery Music Bookshop
17 Cecil Court, London, WC2N 4EZ, United Kingdom.
(+44) 20 7240 2129
neworders@travis-and-emery.com

ISBN Hardback: 978-1-906857-15-8 Paperback: 978-1-906857-16-5

Introduction
Stephen J Pettitt

This volume chronicles the work of the Philharmonia (and New Philharmonia) Orchestra in the recording studio from July 1945 to the middle of 1987. It should serve as a useful companion to my history of the Philharmonia Orchestra, published by Robert Hale in September 1985 to celebrate the orchestra's fortieth anniversary.

From 2 July 1945 the first recordings for the EMI group of companies were on a casual basis, that is by letter agreement per session or group of sessions. From June 1946 the Philharmonia had an exclusive contract with Columbia, which also entitled it to record for the sister companies HMV, Parlophone and, later, Capitol. This contract was renewed until March 1964, when Walter Legge suspended the Philharmonia; a few outstanding engagements were fulfilled, the last on 8 November 1964. The orchestra had already re-formed as the New Philharmonia, under its own management, and secured a new contract with EMI in the summer of 1964. This was non-exclusive and expired in 1972, from when further engagements were made by letter agreement, per job, as had those for the other major record companies since 1964.

In order to link the orchestra's recording work with its concert activities, introductory linking commentary has been added at the beginning of the listing for crucial years in the Philharmonia's history.

Most recordings of extended works (Symphonies, concertos, operas, and so on) were spread over periods of days or even longer, and there exist discrepancies between the recording sheets of EMI and the orchestra's own ledgers, not to mention the diaries of individual orchestra members. It must therefore be born in mind that work included in the published recording may not have taken place on every one of the dates stated, some sessions or parts thereof being devoted to tests or being later rejected by the artists or technical staff.

To the orchestra's official recordings have been added, for the sake of completeness, the handful of existing live recordings undertaken and published illicitly without the approval of the artists (these include performances by Callas, Flagstad, Furtwängler, Giulini, Klemperer and Toscanini).

I have had enormous help from several individuals whom I must thank here: Mr E.Lawrence, formerly of EMI's Hayes factory, helped at the beginning and was followed by Mrs Ruth Edge of EMI Archives; Richard Bradburn, Anthony Locantro and John Watson at EMI International Classical Division were very helpful, as were Derek Lewis of the BBC Gramophone Library, Miss Julie Denton and Miss Alina Dadlez of Decca Records, Bill Salthouse of Reader's Digest, Miss Elizabeth Wells of the British Library National Sound Archive and Christopher Bishop and his staff at the Philharmonia Orchestra. John Hunt and I will be most grateful to anyone else who can point out any inaccuracies or omissions, which we shall hope to incorporate into a later, second edition of the discography.

Stephen J. Pettitt

PHILHARMONIA ORCHESTRA
A Record of Achievement 1945-1985
Stephen J Pettitt
FOREWORD BY HRH THE PRINCE OF WALES

This new appraisal, incorporating recent archival discoveries, is published to coincide with the fortieth anniversary celebrations of Britain's best loved and most prestigious symphony orchestra.

Since its foundation in 1945, the cream of classical musicians have worked with the Philharmonia, including Toscanini, Richard Strauss, Karajan and Klemperer.

Stephen Pettitt reveals the politics behind the public face of the orchestra and points to a new era of success with the appointment of Giuseppe Sinopoli as Principal Conductor.

Royal 8vo 228pp
30 illus. £17.95

Available from bookshops,
or in case of difficulty from:
Robert Hale Ltd.,
45/47 Clerkenwell Green
London EC1R 0HT
Tel. 01-251 2661

The Discography

1945

When Walter Legge first conceived the idea of the Philharmonia Orchestra, he had hoped that it would form the pit orchestra for Covent Garden Opera when he and Sir Thomas Beecham resumed control after the war. By July 1945 that possibility had vanished, and Legge decided to form the Philharmonia anyway, using his position as a record producer with EMI to launch it with some recordings. For the British Council he was already planning to record Purcell's "Dido and Aeneas", and he insisted on using the strings of the RAF Symphony Orchestra, which he described as "the best in the country for the purpose". Twenty-four players from the RAF were engaged and given the name "Philharmonia String Orchestra". On 2 July 1945 some preliminary recordings were made at EMI's Abbey Road studios, and two days later the "Dido and Aeneas" recording was begun.

Even though in the early weeks the Philharmonia was being used primarily to accompany, its quality was soon noticed by the critics, and in October 1945 Alec Robertson wrote in "Gramophone":

"The orchestra, making here a first appearance, is evidently a body to be reckoned with. We shall hear more of it."

On 27 October 1945 Legge presented the Philharmonia before the public for the first time, in a Mozart concert in Kingsway Hall conducted by Sir Thomas Beecham. One newspaper commented:

"The most promising of the concert ventures that are springing up this autumn began yesterday at the Kingsway Hall. It had the benefit of a threefold formula that seems to spell success - first, a new orchestra of "hand-picked" players; secondly, an all-Mozart programme; third, Sir Thomas Beecham.

"It (the orchestra) played well, at times exceedingly well. The best part was the execution of the notes, which was precise beyond normal professional competence."

1945

2 July 1945, Abbey Road

J.C.Bach Sinfonia in B flat	Susskind	Columbia unpublished
Wolf Italian Serenade	Susskind	Columbia DX 1236

4, 5 & 6 July 1945, Abbey Road

Purcell　　　　　　　　　Lambert　　　　　　　　　　　HMV C 3471/2/3/4/5/6/7
Dido and Aeneas　　　　　Chorus　　　　　　　　　　　　(Auto C 7628/9/30/1/2/3/4)
　　　　　　　　　　　　　Hammond, Baillie, Coates,　　Excerpt: EMI HLM 7142
　　　　　　　　　　　　　Fullerton, Patriss,
　　　　　　　　　　　　　Hobson, Ripley, T.Jones,
　　　　　　　　　　　　　Noble

10 August 1945, Kingsway Hall

Handel Every valley; Comfort ye (Messiah)	W.Braithwaite Nash	HMV C 3454 HMV 7EG 8681
Handel Lo, sits here.....Love in her eyes (Acis and Galatea)	W.Braithwaite Nash	HMV 7EG 8681

22 August 1945, Friends' Meeting House, Euston Road

Bach Orchestral Suite No 2	Susskind	Columbia unpublished
Tartini Concertino (arr. Jacob)	Susskind Kell	Columbia unpublished

25 August 1945, Abbey Road

Elgar Sea Pictures	Miles Ripley	HMV unpublished
German O Peaceful England (Merrie England)	Miles Ripley	HMV C 3490

30 & 31 August 1945, Friends' Meeting House, Euston Road

Tchaikovsky Piano Concerto No 1	Weldon Moiseiwitsch	HMV C 3466/7/8/9/70 (Auto C 7623/4/5/6/7)

31 August 1945, Friends' Meeting House, Euston Road

Mendelssohn Scherzo (A Midsummer Night's Dream)	Weldon	HMV unpublished

12 October 1945, Abbey Road

Purcell Chaconne for strings	Lambert	Columbia DX 1230
Bartok Six Rumanian Dances	Lambert	Columbia DX 1221
Grieg Two Elegaic Melodies	Lambert	Columbia unpublished
Ole Bull Shepherds Away (arr. Svendsen)	Lambert	Columbia unpublished
Walton Death of Falstaff; Touch her soft lips (Henry V)	Walton	HMV C 3480 HMV ALP 1375 EMI ED 29 07151

21 November 1945, Abbey Road

Sibelius Violin Concerto	Susskind Neveu	HMV DB 6244/5/6/7 (Auto DB 9007/8/9/10) HMV ALP 1479 EMI RLS 749* EMI 29 08241

1946

The Philharmonia Orchestra was registered as a company on 14 January 1946, and Joan Ingpen, who administered the orchestra, immediately began negotiating a recording contract with EMI. This was signed on 7 June 1946 with Columbia, but with it the right to record also for HMV. It was for only twenty sessions per annum, but at this time EMI had access to both RCA Victor and the US Columbia labels. Full royalties on record sales were only payable on recordings featuring the orchestra alone, and it can be seen from the discography that these were relatively small in number.

In order to tide the Philharmonia over these early days Legge used his contacts in the film business to engage the orchestra for film recordings at Ealing and Denham Studios in particular (although only those recordings which were issued in disc form are to be found in the discography).

1946

17 January 1946, Kingsway Hall

Handel How beautiful are the feet (Messiah)	Jacques Baillie	Columbia unpublished
Handel Come unto him (Messiah)	Jacques Baillie	EMI RLS 714*
Haydn On mighty pens (The Creation)	Jacques Baillie	Columbia unpublished

18 January 1946, Kingsway Hall

Handel So shall lute and harp (Judas Maccabaeus)	Jacques Baillie	Columbia unpublished
Mozart Exsultate, jubilate	Jacques Baillie	Columbia unpublished (recording incomplete)

19 January 1946, Kingsway Hall

Mascagni Easter Hymn (Cavalleria Rusticana)	Susskind Chorus Hobson, Ripley	Columbia unpublished
Wagner Senta's Ballad (The Flying Dutchman)	Susskind Hobson	Columbia unpublished

24 January 1946, Kingsway Hall

Borodin In the Steppes of Central Asia	Lambert	Columbia DX 1449
Glinka Jota (Caprice brillant)	Lambert	Columbia unpublished

30 January 1946, Kingsway Hall

Rimsky-Korsakov Skaska	Lambert	Columbia DX 1485/6
Dvorak The Peasant a Rogue, Overture	Susskind	Columbia unpublished
Dvorak Scherzo Capriccioso	Susskind	Columbia unpublished (recording incomplete)

8 February 1946, Abbey Road

Handel
Why do the nations ?;
The people in darkness
(Messiah)
    Miles
    N.Walker
    Columbia unpublished

Mendelssohn
It is enough (Elijah)
    Miles
    N.Walker
    Columbia unpublished

Haydn
With joy the impatient
husbandman
(The Seasons)
    Miles
    N.Walker
    Columbia unpublished

18 February 1946, Abbey Road

Gluck
Che farò (Orfeo ed Euridice)
    Miles
    Ripley
    HMV unpublished

Elgar
Sea Slumber Song
(Sea Pictures)
    Miles
    Ripley
    HMV unpublished

Butterworth
Banks of Green Willow
    Miles
    HMV C 3491

25 February 1946, Abbey Road

Donizetti
Down her pale cheek
(L'Elisir d'amore)
    Susskind
    Nash
    HMV C 3492

Gounod
'Tis love, 'tis love
(Romeo and Juliet)
    Susskind
    Nash
    HMV C 3492

Gounod
Lend me your aid
(The Queen of Sheba)
    Susskind
    Nash
    HMV unpublished

26 February 1946, Abbey Road

Marcello
Oboe Concerto
    Cameron
    L.Goossens
    Columbia unpublished

Scarlatti
Canzonetta and Polonaise
(Oboe Concerto)
    Cameron
    L.Goossens
    Columbia unpublished

27 February 1946, Abbey Road

Verdi
How wondrous..oh, folly
(La Traviata)
    Susskind
    Hammond
    HMV C 3486

Puccini
That your mother should
take you (Madam Butterfly)
    Susskind
    Hammond
    HMV unpublished

Puccini
Oh, you've no notion
(La Fanciulla del West)
    Susskind
    Hammond
    EMI HLM 7042

12 March 1946, Abbey Road

Weber Der Freischütz, Overture	Susskind	Columbia DX 1244
Weber Ruler of the Spirits, Overture	Susskind	Columbia DX 1262

27 March 1946, Abbey Road

Mozart Horn Concerto No 2	Susskind Brain	Columbia DX 1365/6 EMI RLS 7701*
Bach Double Violin Concerto	Susskind Grumiaux, Pougnet	Columbia DX 1276/7

28 & 29 March 1946, Abbey Road

Rawsthorne Symphonic Studies	Lambert	HMV C 3542/3/4 HMV CLP 1056 EMI MFP 2069

29 March 1946, Abbey Road

Rawsthorne Street Corner, Overture	Lambert	HMV C 3502
Bliss Phoenix March	Lambert	HMV C 3518

5 April 1946, Abbey Road

Weber Softly sighs (Der Freischütz)	Whitehead Hammond	HMV unpublished (recording incomplete)

15 April 1946, Abbey Road

Weber Softly sighs (Der Freischütz)	Tausky Hammond	HMV C 3510
Weber Ocean, thou mighty monster (Oberon)	Tausky Hammond	HMV C 3493

28 May 1946, Abbey Road

Elgar Sea Pictures	Weldon Ripley	HMV C 3498/3499/3500 (Auto C 7638/7639/7640)
Haydn Hark, what I tell thee (The Spirit's Song)	Weldon Ripley	HMV C 3500 EMI HLM 7145

4 June 1946, Abbey Road

Beethoven Egmont, Overture	Galliera	Columbia DX 1273
Verdi La Forza del Destino, Overture	Galliera	Columbia unpublished (recording incomplete)
Wagner Tannhäuser, Overture	Galliera	Columbia unpublished

5 June 1946, Abbey Road

Falla The Three-Cornered Hat, Suite	Galliera	Columbia DX 1258/9

5 & 7 June 1946, Abbey Road

Beethoven Piano Concerto No 4	Dobrowen Schnabel	HMV DB 6303/4/5/6 (Auto DB 9032/3/4/5) HMV COLH 4

6 June 1946, Abbey Road

Beethoven Piano Concerto No 2	Dobrowen Schnabel	HMV DB 6323/4/5/6 (Auto DB 9099/9100/1/2) HMV COLH 2

11 & 12 June 1946, Abbey Road

Vaughan Williams Flos Campi	Boult BBC Chorus Primrose	HMV DB 6353/4/5 (Auto DB 9112/2/3) EMI EH 29 12761

19 June 1946, Kingsway Hall

Clarke Trumpet Voluntary	Weldon Mortimer	Columbia unpublished
Haydn On mighty pens (The Creation)	Weldon Baillie	Columbia DX 1392 EMI RLS 714* EMI RLS 7703*
Handel From mighty kings (Judas Maccabaeus)	Weldon Baillie	Columbia unpublished

19 June 1946, Abbey Road

Haydn Trumpet Concerto	Weldon Mortimer	Columbia DX 1535/6
Bach Aria, Jauchzet Gott in allen Landen (Cantata No 51)	Weldon Baillie	Columbia unpublished

22 June 1946, Abbey Road

Bartok Two Portraits	Lambert Szigeti	Columbia LX 1531 EMI HLM 7016

24 & 25 June 1946, 6 May 1947 and 3 February 1948, Abbey Road

Tchaikovsky Symphony No 4	Dobrowen	HMV C 3809/10/11/12/13 (Auto C7736/37/38/39/40)

25 June 1946, Abbey Road

Mussorgsky Dance of the Persian Slaves (Khovantschina, orch. Rimsky-Korsakov)	Dobrowen	HMV unpublished

26 June 1946, Westminster Central Hall

Beethoven Symphony No 5	Dobrowen	HMV unpublished

27 June 1946, venue unknown

Puccini None shall sleep; Weep no more (Turandot)	W.Braithwaite McHugh	HMV unpublished
Puccini Strange harmony; When the stars were brightly shining (Tosca)	W.Braithwaite McHugh	HMV DB 2234 Columbia SEG 7756

27 & 28 June, Abbey Road

Haydn Symphony No 104 "London"	Dobrowen	HMV C 3515/6/7 (Auto C 7645/6/7)

1 July 1946, Abbey Road

Ravel Piano Concerto in G	Bernstein, cond. & sol.	Victor 12-0226/7/8

22 & 23 July 1946, Abbey Road

Walton Viola Concerto	Walton Primrose	HMV DB 6309/10/11 (Auto DB 9036/7/8) Imprimatur IMP 6 EMI EH 29 12761

30 July 1946, Watford Town Hall

Dvorak Scherzo Capriccioso	Susskind	Columbia unpublished

10 August 1946, Abbey Road

Bach Concerto in D minor	Susskind H.Cohen	Columbia DX 1312/3/4 (Auto DX 8242/3/4) EMI HLM 7148

16, 17 & 18 August 1946, Abbey Road

Brahms Violin Concerto	Dobrowen Neveu	HMV DB 6415/6/7/8/9 (Auto DB 9126/7/8/9/30) HMV COLH 80 EMI RLS 749* EMI 29 08241

18 August 1946, Abbey Road

Chausson Poème	Dobrowen Neveu	HMV ALP 1520 EMI RLS 749* EMI 2C 051 03982

20 August 1946, Abbey Road

Strauss Don Juan	Galliera	Columbia DX 1356/7

21 August 1946, Abbey Road

Stravinsky The Firebird, Suite (1919)	Galliera	Columbia DX 1757/8/9 (Auto DX 8382/3/4)

24 August 1946, Abbey Road

Delius Piano Concerto	Lambert Moiseiwitsch	HMV C 3533/4/5 (Auto C 7648/49/50) World Records SH 224

26 August 1946, Abbey Road

Berlioz Rêverie et caprice	Lambert Szigeti	Columbia LX 946 EMI HQM 1224 Discocorp BWS 715

27 & 28 August and 12 & 13 October 1946, Abbey Road

Walton Incidental Music to the film of Shakespeare's Henry V, plus speeches	Walton Chorus Olivier	HMV C 3583/4/5/6 (Auto C 7678/79/80/81) HMV ALP 1375

(additional session on 13 November 1946, conducted by Roy Douglas)

28 September 1946, Abbey Road

Neapolitan Songs: Rondino al nido (De Crescenzo); Core 'ngrato (Cardillo)	F.Patane Infantino	HMV DB 2335
Neapolitan Songs: Sunnanne a Pusilleco (Campese); Torna a Surriento (De Curtis)	F.Patane Infantino	HMV DB 2314

10 & 13 November 1946, Abbey Road

Schubert Symphony No 8 "Unfinished"	Kletzki	Columbia LX 1222/3/4 (Auto LX 8690/1/2)

13 & 14 November 1946, Abbey Road

Tchaikovsky Symphony No 5	Kletzki	Columbia LX 969/70/1/2/3/4 (Auto LX 8541/2/3/4/5/6) American Columbia RL 3036

19 November 1946, Abbey Road

Handel Sound an alarm (Judas Maccabaeus)	W.Braithwaite Nash	HMV C 3550
Leoncavallo Prologue (I Pagliacci)	W.Braithwaite Hargreaves	HMV unpublished

20 November 1946, Abbey Road

Chopin Piano Concerto No 2	Kletzki Malcuzynski	Columbia LX 1013/4/5/6 (Auto LX 8571/2/3/4) Columbia 33CX 1066

9 December 1946, Abbey Road

Borodin No rest, no peace (Prince Igor)	W.Braithwaite Hargreaves	HMV C 3561
Saint-Saëns Softly awakes my heart (Samson et Dalila)	W.Braithwaite Ripley	HMV unpublished

12 December 1946, Abbey Road

Donizetti O luce di quest' anima (Linda di Chamonix)	W.Braithwaite Ribetti	HMV C 3587
Verdi Caro nome (Rigoletto)	W.Braithwaite Ribetti	HMV C 3587
Ponce Estrellita	W.Braithwaite Ribetti	HMV unpublished

13 & 14 December 1946, Abbey Road

Mendelssohn Violin Concerto	Galliera Grumiaux	Italian Columbia GQX 11126/7/8/9

14 December 1946, Abbey Road

Stravinsky Introduction (The Firebird, 1919 Suite)	Galliera	Columbia DX 1757

ROYAL ALBERT HALL
Manager: C. S. TAYLOR

Sunday, 19th October

RICHARD STRAUSS

conducts a concert of his own works with

THE PHILHARMONIA ORCHESTRA
(*Leader:* Thomas Carter)

•

Don Juan. *Symphonic Poem*
Sinfonia Domestica
Burleske, for Piano and Orchestra
Soloist: Alfred Blume
Rosenkavalier Waltzes. (Symphonic Version, 1946)

•

Wednesday, 29th October, at 8 p.m.

RICHARD STRAUSS

will appear with

THE BBC SYMPHONY ORCHESTRA
(*Leader:* Paul Beard)

conducting Till Eulenspiegel. *Symphonic Poem*

The concert will be repeated in the Third Programme on October 30th, at 9 p.m.

1947

A real scoop for the Philharmonia was getting the composer Richard Strauss to conduct them in a concert of his works during his visit to London in October 1947. The orchestra had already recorded "Don Juan" with Alceo Galliera, and the First Horn Concerto and the Oboe Concerto with Dennis Brain and Leon Goossens respectively. In the programme for the 19 October concert Josef Krips wrote:

"The Philharmonia is the first English orchestra with which I have worked, and I can only say it is a first-class body of musicians. The strings, like the wind, are artists of the highest class, who naturally fulfil the desires of the most exacting conductors.

"Most of all, this orchestra has heart: heart combined with ability, talent and discipline are the essential qualities of this orchestra. London should be proud of its Philharmonia Orchestra."

1947

2 January 1947, Abbey Road

Mozart Per pietà (Così fan tutte)	Collingwood Cross	Columbia DX 1353
Smetana Our dream of love (The Bartered Bride)	Collingwood Cross	EMI RLS 707*

20 & 21 January 1947, Abbey Road

Brahms Piano Concerto No 1	Cameron Arrau	HMV DB 6596/7/8/9/6600/1 (Auto DB 9251/2/3/4/5/6)

29 January 1947, Abbey Road

Puccini Do you know, my sweet (Madama Butterfly); Oh, you've no notion (La Fanciulla del West)	W.Braithwaite Hammond	HMV B 9747
Wagner Elsa's Dream (Lohengrin); Elisabeth's Greeting (Tannhäuser)	W.Braithwaite Hammond	HMV C 3562

24 February 1947, Kingsway Hall

Debussy Prélude à l'après-midi d'un faune	Galliera	Columbia DX 1381

24, 25 & 26 February and 1 March 1947, Kingsway Hall

Dvorak Symphony No 9 "From the New World"	Galliera	Columbia DX 1399/1400/1/2/3 (Auto DX 8275/6/7/8/9)

18 March 1947, Abbey Road

Gounod Ballad of the King of Thule; Jewel Song (Faust)	W.Braithwaite Hammond	HMV C 3674
Verdi Heaven, my father (Aida)	W.Braithwaite Hammond Llewelyn	HMV C 3735 EMI HQM 1186

19 March 1947, Kingsway Hall

Berners Nicholas Nickleby, Film Music	E.Irving	Columbia DX 1362

24, 25 & 27 March 1947 and 3 February 1948, Abbey Road

Tchaikovsky The Nutcracker, Suite	Malko	HMV C 3835/6/7 (Auto C 7744/5/6) Victor LBC 1007

25 March 1947, Abbey Road

Khatchaturian Lullaby; Dance of the Young Maidens (Gayaneh)	Malko	HMV C 3572

26 & 27 March 1947, Abbey Road

Tchaikovsky Symphony No 6 "Pathétique"	Malko	HMV C 3630/1/2/3/4/5 (Auto C 7697/8/9/7700/01/02) Victor LBC 1002

28 March 1947, Abbey Road

Tchaikovsky 1812 Overture	Malko	HMV C 3617/8 Victor LBC 1014

19 April 1947, Abbey Road

Haydn Violin Concerto in C	Susskind Goldberg	Parlophone R 20558/59/60 (Auto SW 8098/99/8100) Parlophone PMA 1007

22 April 1947, Kingsway Hall

D.Scarlatti Oboe Concerto (arr.Bryan)	Susskind L.Goossens	Columbia DX 8347/8

23 April 1947, Kingsway Hall

Marcello Oboe Concerto	Susskind L.Goossens	Columbia DX 1389/90

24 & 25 April 1947, Abbey Road

Beethoven Piano Concerto No 5 "Emperor"	Susskind Matthews	Columbia DX 1462/3/4/5 (Auto DX 8308-8312) American Columbia RL 3037

25 April 1947, Abbey Road

Saint-Saëns Piano Concerto No 2	Cameron Moiseiwitsch	HMV C 3588/89/90 (Auto C 7682/3/4)

29 & 30 April and 1 May 1947, Abbey Road

Brahms Piano Concerto No 2	Dobrowen Solomon	HMV C 3610/1/2/3/4/5 (Auto C 7688/89/90/1/2/3) EMI XLP 30093 EMI SLS 5094* EMI 1C 147 03081/2M*

2, 5, 7 & 9 May 1947, Abbey Road

Medtner Piano Concerto No 2	Dobrowen Medtner	HMV DB 6559/60/61/62/63 (Auto DB 9191/2/3/4/5) Melodiya M10 41171/2

2 & 6 May 1947 and 3 February 1948, Abbey Road

Beethoven Leonore No 3, Overture	Dobrowen	HMV unpublished

6, 7 & 26 May 1947, Abbey Road

Tchaikovsky Serenade for strings	Dobrowen	HMV C 3751/2/3/4 (Auto C 7722/3/4/5)

8 May 1947, Abbey Road

Fauré Pavane	Sargent Chorus	Columbia DX 1369

9 May 1947, Abbey Road

Wagner Die Meistersinger, Act 1 Prelude	Dobrowen	HMV C 3926/7 Victor LBC 1048

10, 13, 26 & 28 May 1947, Abbey Road

Medtner Piano Concerto No 3	Dobrowen Medtner	HMV DB 6718/19/20/21/22 (Auto DB 9259/60/61/62/63) Melodiya D 06501-2 Melodiya M10 41173/4

13 May 1947, Abbey Road

Vaughan Williams Loves of Joanna Godden, Film Music	E.Irving	Columbia DX 1377

21 May 1947, Kingsway Hall

Strauss Horn Concerto No 1	Galliera Brain	Columbia DX 1397/8 EMI RLS 7701*

22 May 1947, Kingsway Hall

Wagner Tannhäuser, Overture	Galliera	Columbia unpublished

26 May 1947, Abbey Road

Liadov Berceuse	Dobrowen	HMV C 3754

27 & 28 May 1947, Abbey Road

Beethoven Piano Concerto No 5 "Emperor"	Galliera Schnabel	HMV DB 6692/3/4/5/6 (Auto DB 9326/27/28/29/30) HMV COLH 5

30 & 31 May 1947, Abbey Road

Beethoven Piano Concerto No 3	Dobrowen Schnabel	HMV COLH 3

3 June 1947, Abbey Road

Weber Oberon, Overture	Susskind	HMV/Columbia unpublished
Liszt Hungarian Rhapsody No 2	Susskind	HMV/Columbia unpublished (recording incomplete)

24 July 1947, Abbey Road

Berners Les Sirènes, Film Music	E.Irving	Columbia DX 1542

27 August 1947, Kingsway Hall

Dyson Wyf of Bathe (The Canterbury Pilgrims)	Sargent Baillie	EMI HQM 1015
Haydn With joy the impatient husbandman (The Seasons)	Sargent N.Walker	Columbia unpublished
Haydn Now heaven in fullest glory (The Seasons)	Sargent N.Walker	Columbia DX 1407

27 & 28 August 1947, Kingsway Hall

Dvorak Where art thou ? (The Spectre's Bride)	Sargent Baillie	Columbia DX 1471

28 August 1947, KIngsway Hall

Elgar The sun goeth down (The Kingdom)	Sargent Baillie	Columbia DX 1443 EMI HQM 1015

1 September 1947, Abbey Road

Leoncavallo Prologue (I Pagliacci)	Collingwood Hargreaves	HMV C 3995 EMI RLS 707*

1 & 13 September 1947, Abbey Road

Puccini Sola perduta abbandonata (Manon Lescaut)	Collingwood Hammond	HMV C 3720
Giordano La mamma morta (Andrea Chenier)	Collingwood Hammond	HMV C 3720 EMI HQM 1186

13 September 1947, Abbey Road

Puccini In quelle trine morbide (Manon Lescaut)	Collingwood Hammond	HMV B 9705 EMI RLS 29 00143*

13 September 1947 and 21 February 1948, Abbey Road

Leoncavallo How fierce he looked (I Pagliacci)	Collingwood Hammond	HMV C 3725

15 & 23 September 1947, Kingsway Hall

Strauss Oboe Concerto	Galliera L.Goossens	Columbia DX 1444/5/6 (Auto DX 8301/2/3) HMV CLP 1698 World Records SH 243

16 September 1947, Abbey Road

Mozart Still Susanna delays.... Vanished are ye (The Marriage of Figaro)	Susskind Baillie	HMV DB 2444
Mozart God of Love (The Marriage of Figaro)	Susskind Baillie	HMV/Columbia unpublished
Grieg Last Spring	Susskind	Columbia unpublished

16 & 17 September 1947, Abbey Road

Rachmaninov Rhapsody on a theme of Paganini	Susskind Rubinstein	HMV DB 6556/7/8 (Auto DB 9188/89/90) EMI 1C 137 1544273*

17 September 1947, Abbey Road

Mozart Porgi amor; Dove sono (Le Nozze di Figaro)	Susskind Steber	HMV unpublished
Charpentier Depuis le jour (Louise)	Susskind Steber	HMV DB 6514
Bizet Je dis que rien (Carmen)	Susskind Steber	HMV DB 6514

18 & 19 September 1947, Abbey Road

Grieg Piano Concerto	Galliera Lipatti	Columbia LX 1029/30/31/32 (Auto LX 8579/80/81/82) Columbia 33C 1040 EMI XLP 30072 EMI HLM 7046 EMI 1C 197 53780-86M* EMI 2C 051 43321

20 September 1947, Abbey Road

Liszt Piano Concerto No 2	Susskind Malcuzynski	Columbia LX 1071/2/3 (Auto LX 8605/6/7) Columbia 33CX 1106

23 September 1947, Kingsway Hall

Mussorgsky Scene 5 Prelude, Khovantschina	Galliera	Columbia unpublished
Franck Les Eolides	Galliera	Columbia DX 1507

23 & 24 September 1947, Kingsway Hall

Strauss Horn Concerto No 2	Galliera Brain	Columbia unpublished (recording incomplete)

25 September 1947, Abbey Road

Verdi Ritorna vincitor (Aida)	J.Krips Welitsch	Columbia LB 65 EMI HLM 7006 World Records SH 289 EMI 101 2671
Verdi Qui Radames verrà..... o fresche valle (Aida)	J.Krips Welitsch	Columbia unpublished

26 September 1947, Abbey Road

Mozart E Susanna non vien... Dove sono (Le Nozze di Figaro)	J.Krips Cebotari	HMV DA 1875 Victor LCT 1115 EMI 1C 147 29118-9M* Preiser PR 9860
Humperdinck Sandman's song; Evening prayer (Hänsel und Gretel)	J.Krips Schwarzkopf, Seefried	Columbia LX 1037 EMI RLS 763*
Mozart In quali eccessi..Mi tradi (Don Giovanni)	J.Krips Schwarzkopf	Columbia LX 1210 EMI RLS 763*

26 & 27 September 1947, Abbey Road

Humperdinck Dance Duet (Hänsel und Gretel)	J.Krips Schwarzkopf, Seefried	Columbia LX 1036/7 EMI RLS 763*

27 September 1947, Abbey Road

Mozart Giunse alfin il momento ...Deh vieni, non tardar (Le Nozze di Figaro)	J.Krips Seefried	Columbia unpublished
Mozart Ach, ich fühl's (Die Zauberflöte)	J.Krips Seefried	Columbia LX 1145 EMI 29 12363*

29 September, 1 & 6 October and 1 November 1947, Abbey Road

Medtner Piano Concerto No 1	Weldon Medtner	HMV DB 6900/1/2/3/4 (Auto DB 9379/80/81/82/83) Melodiya D 16313-4 Melodiya M10 41169-70

29 & 30 September 1947, Abbey Road

Saint-Saëns Cello Concerto No 1	Susskind Fournier	HMV DB 6602/3

7 October 1947, Abbey Road

Johann Strauss Die Fledermaus, Overture	J.Krips	Columbia DX 1707

8 October 1947, Abbey Road

Mozart Et incarnatus est (Mass in C minor)	J.Krips Berger	HMV DB 6536 Victor LM 6130
Mozart Tiefe Stille rings um mich ...Frühlingslüfte (Idomeneo)	J.Krips Berger	HMV DB 6617 EMI 1C 137 46104/5M*
Nicolai The Merry Wives of Windsor, Overture	J.Krips	Columbia DX 1484
Johann & Josef Strauss Pizzicato-Polka	J.Krips	Columbia DB 2485 American Columbia RL 3056

10 October 1947, Abbey Road

Mozart Piano Concerto No 25	J.Krips E.Fischer	HMV DB 6604/5/6/7 (Auto DB 9287/88/89/90) Victor LHMV 1004 Turnabout THS 65094 EMI 2C 061 01408 EMI 2C 051 43326
Johann Strauss Tales from the Vienna Woods, Waltz	J.Krips	Columbia DX 1503
Johann Strauss father Radetzky March	J.Krips	Columbia DB 2485

11 October 1947, Abbey Road

Wagner Lohengrin, Act 1 Prelude	Kletzki	Columbia LX 1153 American Columbia RL 3060
Wagner Lohengrin, Act 3 Prelude	Kletzki	Columbia LX 1161 American Columbia RL 3060
Verdi Caro nome (Rigoletto)	J.Krips Berger	HMV unpublished
Mozart Martern aller Arten (Entführung aus dem Serail)	J.Krips Berger	HMV DB 6616 EMI 1C 047 28556 EMI 1C 137 46104/5M*

11 & 13 October 1947, Abbey Road

Beethoven Coriolan, Overture	Kletzki	Columbia unpublished

13 October 1947, Abbey Road

Beethoven Leonore No 3, Overture	Kletzki	Columbia LX 1069/70

16 October 1947, Abbey Road

Brahms Tragic Overture	Kletzki	Columbia LX 1251/2 American Columbia RL 3060
Wagner Der fliegende Holländer, Overture	Kletzki	Columbia LX 1160/1 American Columbia RL 3060

26 October 1947, Abbey Road

Bixio Roads through the forest; One night with you	Hollingsworth Martini	HMV DA 1882

30 November 1947, Abbey Road

Cilea Lamento di Federico (L'Arlesiana)	Erede Di Stefano	HMV DB 6580 EMI RLS 756*
Thomas Ah non credevi (Mignon)	Erede Di Stefano	HMV DB 6618 EMI RLS 756*

30 November and 6 December 1947, Abbey Road

Donizetti Una furtiva lagrima (L'Elisir d'amore)	Erede Di Stefano	HMV unpublished

6 December 1947, Abbey Road

Puccini E lucevan le stelle (Tosca)	Erede Di Stefano	HMV DB 6580 EMI RLS 756*

11 December 1947, Abbey Road

Massenet   Erede   HMV DB 6868
Ah dispar, vision (Manon)   Di Stefano   EMI RLS 756*

Massenet   Erede   HMV unpublished
Il sogno (Manon)   Di Stefano

22 December 1947, Kingsway Hall

Clarke   Weldon   Columbia unpublished
Trumpet Voluntary   Mortimer

The Maharaja of Mysore's Musical Foundation

By MARTIN COTTON

In October 1946, Compton Mackenzie, editor of *The Gramophone*, was a guest of the 28 year-old Maharaja of Mysore. The Maharaja expressed a desire to help financially in the recording of music which might not otherwise be available, particularly the works of Nicolas Medtner, at that time living in Hampstead and supported by a pension from the Maharaja. Walter Legge, already famous for his conception and production of the Hugo Wolf Society series of recordings for EMI in the thirties, was invited to Mysore by the Maharaja, where an agreement was reached to record, at the Maharaja's expense, a conspectus of Medtner's music and a large range of other works. This offer could hardly have come at a better time for Legge, who had just formed the Philharmonia, initially as a recording orchestra, and was looking for ways of supplementing its income from royalties. After a second visit to Mysore, it was also arranged that the Philharmonia Concert Society, a non-profit-making organisation run by Legge to promote concerts by the Philharmonia, Philharmonia String Quartet, and other artists, should receive a grant of £10,000 per year from the Maharaja. So from its very beginning, the Maharaja of Mysore's Musical Foundation had close links with the Philharmonia. As events turned out, it was the only orchestra used for recordings sponsored by the Foundation.

A committee of advisers set up for the Medtner recordings included Legge, Compton Mackenzie, Christopher Stone, Benno Moiseiwitsch and Fred Smith (of Rimington, Van Wyck Ltd, the London record dealers) with the assistance of Captain S.T. Binstead, the Maharaja of Mysore's Commissioner in the UK. In May 1947, Medtner himself, then 67, agreed to take part in the projected recordings. Between then and the end of the year, the material for the Medtner Society's three albums was recorded. Each album consisted of seven twelve-inch 78 r.p.m. discs, and included one of Medtner's three piano concertos and a selection of piano music and songs, with the composer at the piano.

The Maharaja of Mysore was not responsible only for the Medtner Society albums. During 1949 and early 1950, several other works were recorded under his auspices. A list of these appeared in an article in *The Gramophone* in April 1950 and included Balakirev's *First Symphony*; Bartok's *Music for Strings, Percussion and Celeste*; Roussel's *Fourth Symphony* (conducted by Karajan); and Skriabin's *Piano Concerto* (Solomon, Philharmonia conducted by Dobrowen). The last of these recordings unaccountably never appeared, but the others were issued during the sixteen months following the announcement. The main purpose of the article, however, was to announce a competition to decide the works to be recorded under a five-year plan approved by the Maharaja. A list of over 120 titles was printed, from which the entrants had to select, in order of preference, the twenty they personally would most like to see recorded, and the twenty they felt would be most welcome to the musical public in general. The list of works (then mostly unrecorded) comes as a surprise to modern eyes. Included are: Bartok's piano concertos; Bruckner's symphonies; Bach's *Christmas Oratorio*; Berg's *Violin Concerto*; Moussorgsky's *Boris Godunov*; Schoenberg's *Five Orchestral Pieces* and concertos, as well as some symphonies by Mahler and other pieces whose recorded availability is now taken for granted. Also on the list were a few works less well known today — *Birulki* by Lyadov; *Canzones Castilianas* by Salos; and Egon Wellesz's *Symphony*, for example.

One of the judges of the competition was Walter Legge, and, with his position with both EMI and the Philharmonia, it is certain that no other record company or orchestra would have been involved in recording the chosen works. In fact, despite the publication of the results of the competition, nothing came of the project, owing to the sudden decline in finances of the Maharaja of Mysore. After Indian independence, in common with all Indian princes, he found his property being seized by the new government (the grant to the Philharmonia Concert Society had been halved to £5,000 after one year, and, at the end of three years, stopped altogether, owing to the "malign intervention of the late Krishna Menon" in Legge's words), and by the end of 1950, he was unable to finance any new recordings. Such recordings as subsequently appeared had all been made earlier. The last to be issued, in January 1952, is possibly the greatest curiosity of all — Artur Schnabel's *Rhapsody for Orchestra* (conducted by Paul Kletzki), an essay in a thickly scored, atonal, romantic idiom which would never have been committed to disc had it not been for the financial backing of the Maharaja of Mysore.

1948

Herbert von Karajan was one of Walter Legge's greatest "discoveries" and since 1946 had been working with Legge and the Vienna Philharmonic Orchestra on a series of recordings. In April 1948 Karajan came to London to record the Schumann Piano Concerto with the Philharmonia and Dinu Lipatti, and to make his British début with the Philharmonia in the Royal Albert Hall on 11 April.

Karajan was interested in the Philharmonia, and Legge realised that money was needed to hold the best players in the orchestra and to promote an international series of concerts that would attract conductors like Karajan to work regularly with it in London. Within a year help came from an unexpected source, the Maharaja of Mysore.

1948

3 January 1948, Abbey Road

Alfano Tu vedi (Don Juan); Mascagni O amore (L'Amico Fritz)	Zamboni Gigli	HMV DA 1937
Scarlatti O cessate; Mazziotti Ritorno	Zamboni Gigli	HMV unpublished

3 February 1948, Abbey Road

Berlioz Le carnaval romain, Overture	Dobrowen	HMV C 3709

14 February 1948, Abbey Road

Sibelius Finlandia	Malko	HMV C 3767
Liadov Baba Yaga	Malko	HMV C 3974

19 & 23 February and 4 March 1948, Abbey Road

Borodin Symphony No 2	Malko	HMV C 3971/2/3/4 (Auto C 7781/2/3) Victor LBC 1024

20 February 1948, Abbey Road

Gounod The hour is late (Faust)	Susskind Hammond, Nash, Brannigan	HMV C 3724/5 EMI RLS 707*

21 February 1948, Abbey Road

Puccini Non la sospiri (Tosca)	Susskind Hammond, Nash	HMV B 9705
Verdi Ingemisco (Requiem Mass)	Susskind Nash	HMV B 9705

10 March 1948, Abbey Road

Grieg Eros	W.Braithwaite Flagstad	HMV DA 1979
Grieg En svane	W.Braithwaite Flagstad	HMV DA 1979 EMI HQM 1057 EMI 1C 147 01491/2M*
Grieg Fra Monte Pincio	W.Braithwaite Flagstad	HMV unpublished

14 March 1948, Abbey Road

Falla Vivan los que rien; Alli està riyendo (La vida breve)	Robinson De los Angeles	HMV DB 6702
Mozart Voi che sapete (Le Nozze di Figaro)	Robinson De los Angeles	HMV unpublished

25 & 27 March 1948, Abbey Road

Rachmaninov Piano Concerto No 3	Galliera Malcuzynski	Columbia unpublished

26 March 1948, Abbey Road

Wagner Brünnhilde's Immolation (Götterdämmerung)	Furtwängler Flagstad	HMV DB 6792/3/4 (Auto DB 9323/4/5) Victor LHMV 1024 EMI 1C 147 01491/2M* EMI 2C 051 03855 EMI EX 29 12273*

28 & 30 March 1948, Abbey Road

Franck Symphony in D minor	Galliera	Columbia DX 1629/30/31/32/33 (Auto DX 8340/41/42/43/44)

31 March 1948, Abbey Road

Wagner Isolde's Narration and Curse (Tristan und Isolde)	Dobrowen Flagstad, Höngen	HMV DB 6748/9 EMI HQM 1138 EMI 1C 147 01491/2M* EMI EX 29 12273* EMI 29 10373*

1 April 1948, Abbey Road

Wagner Liebestod (Tristan und Isolde)	Dobrowen Flagstad	EMI EX 29 12273* EMI 29 10373*
Wagner Allmächtige Jungfrau (Tannhäuser)	Dobrowen Flagstad	HMV DB 6795 EMI 1C 147 01491/2M* EMI EX 29 12273* EMI 29 10373*

3 April 1948, Abbey Road

Grieg Ved Rundarne	W.Braithwaite Flagstad	HMV DA 1992
Grieg Den Sarede	W.Braithwaite Flagstad	HMV DB 21020 EMI 1C 147 01491/2M*
Grieg En Drom	W.Braithwaite Flagstad	HMV DB 21020 EMI HQM 1057 EMI 1C 147 01491/2M*

8 April 1948, Denham Studios

Walton Hamlet, Music for the film	Mathieson	HMV C 3755/6/7 HMV ALP 1375

9 & 10 April 1948, Abbey Road

Schumann Piano Concerto	Karajan Lipatti	Columbia LX 1110/11/12/13 (Auto LX 8624/5/6/7) Columbia 33C 1001 EMI XLP 30072 EMI HLM 7046 EMI 1C 197 53780-86M* EMI 2C 051 03713

12 April 1948, Abbey Road

Mozart Ah, tis gone (The Magic Flute)	W.Braithwaite Schwarzkopf	EMI ALP 143 5501
Verdi What madness (La Traviata)	W.Braithwaite Schwarzkopf	Columbia LX 1079

15 April 1948, Kingsway Hall

Bach Cantata No 82	Susskind Hotter	Columbia unpublished

20 April 1948, Abbey Road

Litolff Scherzo (Concerto Symphonique No 4)	Susskind Lympany	HMV C 3763 EMI HLM 7179 Imprimatur IMP 5
Beethoven German Dances Nos 11 & 12	Susskind	Columbia unpublished

24 April 1948, Abbey Road

Wagner Like Death's dark shadow ....O Star of Eve (Tannhäuser)	W.Braithwaite Llewelyn	HMV C 3952
Gounod Even bravest heart (Faust); Bizet Toreador's song (Carmen)	W.Braithwaite Llewelyn	HMV C 3800

26 April 1948, Abbey Road

Eugene Goossens Oboe Concerto	Susskind L.Goossens	Columbia DX 1578/9

27 April 1948, Abbey Road

Liszt Hungarian Fantasia	Susskind Solomon	HMV C 3761/2 (Auto C 7688/9) EMI SLS 5094* World Records SH 125 Turnabout THS 65108 EMI RLS 701*

5 May 1948, Abbey Road

Weber Wie nahte mir der Schlummer (Der Freischütz)	Susskind Welitsch	Columbia LX 1090 EMI HLM 7006 World Records SH 289 EMI 101 2671
Puccini Vissi d'arte (Tosca)	Susskind Welitsch	Columbia LB 82 EMI HLM 7006 World Records SH 289 EMI 101 2671

8 & 29 May 1948, Abbey Road

Beethoven Violin Romance in F	Erede De Vito	HMV DB 6727

14 & 29 May 1948, Abbey Road

Vitali Chaconne (arr. Respighi)	Erede De Vito	HMV DB 6936/7

22 May 1948, Abbey Road

Tchaikovsky Tatiana's Letter Scene (Eugene Onegin)	Susskind Welitsch	Columbia LX 1108/9 Columbia 33C 1011 EMI HLM 7006 World Records SH 289 EMI 101 2671

24 May 1948, Kingsway Hall

Sibelius En Saga	Kletzki	Columbia LX 1307/8/9 (Auto LX 8729/30/31)

25 & 26 May 1948, Abbey Road

Mozart Piano Concerto No 9	Susskind Kraus	Parlophone SW 8104/5/6

26 & 28 May 1948, Kingsway Hall

Mozart Exsultate, jubilate	Susskind Schwarzkopf	Columbia unpublished

27 May 1948, Kingsway Hall

Wagner Siegfried Idyll	Kletzki	Columbia LX 1296/7
Grieg Varen	Susskind Flagstad	HMV DA 1904 Victor LM 99
Gluck Che farò senza Euridice (Orfeo ed Euridice)	Susskind Flagstad	HMV DB 6913 EMI HQM 1057 EMI 1C 147 01491/2M* EMI 29 02061

28 & 31 May 1948, Kingsway Hall

Bach Cantata No 51	Susskind Schwarzkopf	Columbia unpublished

29 May 1948, Abbey Road

Grieg Fra Monte Pincio	W.Braithwaite Flagstad	HMV DA 1905 Victor LM 99
Purcell Thy hand, Belinda.... When I am laid in earth (Dido and Aeneas)	W.Braithwaite Flagstad	HMV DB 6913 EMI HQM 1057 EMI 1C 147 01491/2M*
Grieg Guten (orch. Gunstrom)	W.Braithwaite Flagstad	HMV DA 1992 Victor LM 99

30 May 1948, Abbey Road

Bach Violin Concerto in E	Susskind Goldberg	Parlophone SW 8108/9/10 Parlophone PMA 1007

31 May 1948, Kingsway Hall

Brahms Hungarian Dance No 5	Kletzki	Columbia LX 1252 American Columbia RL 3091
Brahms Hungarian Dance No 6	Kletzki	International Columbia LCX 12 American Columbia RL 3091
Sibelius Valse triste	Kletzki	Columbia LX 1309 American Columbia RL 3091

4 June and 23 September 1948, Kingsway Hall

Handel Organ Concerto in B flat (arr. Wood)	Susskind Thalben-Ball	HMV C 3814/5/6

5 June 1948, Abbey Road

Mascagni Mother, you know (Cavalleria Rusticana); Verdi Ma dall' arido (Un Ballo in Maschera)	Susskind Hammond	HMV C 3771

8 June 1948, Abbey Road

Leoncavallo What? Thou? (I Pagliacci)	Susskind Hammond, Hargreaves	HMV C 3923/4

15 June 1948, Abbey Road

Puccini Nulla silenzio (Il Tabarro)	Erede Inghilleri	HMV C 3772
Puccini Perchè (Il Tabarro)	Erede Tegani, Inghilleri	HMV C 3772
Verdi Alzati...Eri tu (Un Ballo in Maschera)	Erede Inghilleri	HMV B 9712

17 & 18 June 1948, Abbey Road

Mozart Piano Concerto No 20	Susskind Schnabel	Victor LHMV 1012 Turnabout THS 65046 EMI 2C 051 43166 EMI EX 29 00723*

18 & 19 June 1948, Abbey Road

Mozart Piano Concerto No 24	Susskind Schnabel	Victor LHMV 1012 Turnabout THS 65046 EMI 2C 051 43166 EMI EX 29 00723*

22 June 1948, Abbey Road

Wagner Blick' ich umher.... O du mein holder Abendstern (Tannhäuser)	Erede Rothmüller	HMV C 3790
Puccini Tre sbirri (Tosca)	Erede Rothmüller	HMV C 4019

3 July 1948, Abbey Road

Bizet Agnus Dei	W.Braithwaite Flagstad	HMV DB 6791
Handel Ombra mai fù (Serse)	W.Braithwaite Flagstad	HMV DB 6791 EMI 1C 147 01491/2M* EMI 29 02061
Handel (attrib.) Dank sei Dir, Herr	W.Braithwaite	HMV unpublished

1 September 1948, Pinewood Studios

Bax Oliver Twist, Film music	Mathieson H.Cohen	Columbia DX 1515/7

20 September 1948, Abbey Road

Handel Let the bright seraphim (Samson)	Collingwood Ritchie	HMV unpublished
Hook (arr. Franklin) Hush every breeze (Pink String and Sealing Wax)	Collingwood Ritchie	HMV B 10017

22 September 1948, Abbey Road

Szymanowski Violin Concerto No 1	Fitelberg Uminska	Parlophone SW 8101/2/3

1 October 1948, Abbey Road

Rachmaninov Rhapsody on a theme of Paganini	Sargent C.Smith	Columbia DX 1608/9/10 (Auto DX 8334/5/6)

3 October 1948, Abbey Road

Mendelssohn Piano Concerto No 1	Kubelik Lympany	HMV C 3838/9 Victor LHMV 1025 EMI HLM 7179

4 October 1948, Abbey Road

Bruch Violin Concerto No 1	Kubelik Haendel	HMV C 3802/3/4 (Auto C 7733/4/5) Victor LBC 1013

5, 7, 8 & 9 October 1948, Abbey Road

Dvorak Symphony No 8	Kubelik	HMV C 3852/3/4/5/6 (Auto C 7750/1/2/3/4) HMV ALP 1064

13 & 16 October 1948, Abbey Road

Beethoven	Kubelik	Columbia LX 1312/3/4/5
Piano Concerto No 1	Gieseking	EMI 3C 153 52425-31M*

18 & 19 October 1948, Abbey Road

Dvorak	Kubelik	HMV DB 6887/88/89/90/91
Cello Concerto	Fournier	(Auto DB 9397/8/9/9400/01)

5 & 8 November 1948, Abbey Road

Ippolitov-Ivanov	Malko	HMV C 3936/7
Caucasian Sketches		Victor LBC 1019

6 November 1948, Abbey Road

Glinka	Malko	HMV C 3878
Jota Aragonesa		
Mussorgsky Gopak;	Malko	HMV C 3828
Rimsky-Korsakov		
Flight of the bumble bee		

8 November 1948, Abbey Road

Glinka	Malko	HMV C 3949
Valse-Fantasie		
Glière	Malko	HMV C 3828
Russian Sailors' Dance		
(The Red Poppy)		

26 November 1948, Abbey Road

Donizetti	Gennai	HMV DA 1910
In questo semplice modesto	Carosio	
asilo (3etley)		

1 & 2 December 1948, Kingsway Hall

Bizet	Sargent	Columbia DX 1605/6
L'Arlésienne, Suite No 2		

2 December 1948, Kingsway Hall

Elgar	Sargent	Columbia DX 1561
Pomp and Circumstance		American Columbia RL 3042
Marches Nos 1 and 4		
Wagner	Sargent	Columbia DX 1607
Das Rheingold, Prelude;		
Die Walküre, Ride of the		
Valkyries		

9 December 1948, Abbey Road

Tchaikovsky Marche slave	Sargent	Columbia DX 1574
Borodin Nocturne (arr. Sargent)	Sargent	Columbia DX 1618 American Columbia RL 3042

22 December 1948, Abbey Road

Rimsky-Korsakov Dance of the Tumblers; Introduction, Sadko	Collingwood	HMV C 3840
Elgar Chanson de matin; Chanson de nuit	Collingwood	HMV C 3858

23 December 1948, Abbey Road

Rachmaninov Piano Concerto No 1	Sargent Moiseiwitsch	HMV C 3932/3/4 (Auto C 7769/70/71)

30 December 1948, Abbey Road

Vaughan Williams Scott of the Antarctic, Film music	E.Irving Ritchie	HMV C 3834
Thomas Raymond, Overture	E.Irving	HMV unpublished

1949

Walter Legge returned from Mysore in July 1949 with a guarantee of £10,000 per annum for the Philharmonia Concert Society. This enabled him to engage Manoug Parikian and Max Salpeter as joint leaders, to offer the lavish series of London concerts listed opposite, and to begin a regular association with Karajan by recording works under the Maharaja's Foundation.

Philharmonia Concert Society

(President : H.H. THE MAHARAJA OF MYSORE)

at the

ROYAL ALBERT HALL

(Manager - C. S. TAYLOR)

EVENINGS at 7.30 P.M.

EIGHT ORCHESTRAL CONCERTS

PHILHARMONIA ORCHESTRA

(Founder and Hon. Artistic Director : WALTER LEGGE)

Leaders : MANOUG PARIKIAN and MAX SALPETER

Programmes subject to alteration

SERIES A

November 25th, Friday
BEETHOVEN Symphony No. 9
Conductor : HERBERT von KARAJAN
Soloists : SCHWARZKOPF, WATSON, LUDWIG, CHRISTOFF
B.B.C. CHORAL SOCIETY
(Chorusmaster : LESLIE WOODGATE)

February 20th, Monday
MOZART Symphony No. 39 E flat
No. 40 G minor
Motet : Jubilate Esultate
(Jupiter) Symphony No. 41 C major
Conductor : RAFAEL KUBELIK
Soloist : ELISABETH SCHWARZKOPF

April 27th, Thursday
SCHNABEL Rhapsody
(First European Performance)
BEETHOVEN Violin Concerto in D
MOUSSORGSKY-RAVEL Pictures at an Exhibition.
Conductor : PAUL KLETZKI
Soloist : YEHUDI MENUHIN

May 11th, Monday
BACH Concerto for pianoforte A minor
Concerto for pianoforte, violin and flute
Concerto for two pianos C major
Concerto for three pianos
Conductor and Soloist : EDWIN FISCHER
Soloists : DENIS MATTHEWS
MAX SALPETER
GARETH MORRIS

SERIES B

December 2nd, Friday
ROUSSEL Symphony No. 4
BARTOK Pianoforte Concerto No. 3
TCHAIKOWSKY Symphony No. 6 in B minor
Conductor : HERBERT von KARAJAN
Soloist : DINU LIPATTI

February 2nd, Thursday
BRAHMS Variations on a theme of Haydn
MEDTNER Concerto No. 3
BEETHOVEN Symphony No. 7
Conductor : ALCEO GALLIERA
Soloist : NICHOLAS MEDTNER

April 13th, Thursday
SCHUBERT Unfinished Symphony
CHOPIN Concerto No. 2
FRANCK Variations Symphoniques
BALAKIREV Symphony No. 1 in C
Soloist : ALFRED CORTOT
Conductor : SIR ADRIAN BOULT

May 22nd, Monday
WAGNER Meistersinger Prelude
Siegfried Idyll
STRAUSS 4 Orchestral Songs
(First performance in Europe)
WAGNER Tristan Prelude and Liebestod
Goetterdaemmerung Siegfried's Rhine Journey
Closing Scene
Conductor : WILHELM FURTWAENGLER
Soloist : KIRSTEN FLAGSTAD

2,500 SUBSCRIPTION - TICKETS UNDER 5/- PER CONCERT

Subscription Tickets, Series A and B (each 4 Concerts). Unreserved : 7/-, 13/-, 18/-, 27/-, 39/-, 46/-, 55/-.
Single Tickets available from November 4th onwards : 2/6, 3/6, 5/-, 7/6, 10/6, 12/6, 15/-, 21/-.
From all Agents. For further information on Subscription Tickets write to : The Secretary, Philharmonia Concert Society, 42/43, Cranbourn Street, W.C.2. Telephone : Gerrard 1172. Subscription Booking opens October 3rd. Booking Office open : Monday to Friday 9 a.m. to 7 p.m. Saturday 9 a.m. to 12.30.

1949

6 January 1949, Abbey Road

Verdi Pace pace, mio dio (La Forza del Destino); Morro, ma prima in grazia (Un Ballo in Maschera)	W.Braithwaite Hammond	HMV C 3879
Ponchielli Suicidio (La Gioconda)	W.Braithwaite Hammond	HMV C 3901 EMI HQM 1186
Cilea Troppo, signori (Adriana Lecouvreur)	W.Braithwaite Hammond	HMV unpublished
Grainger Molly on the shore; Mock Morris	W.Braithwaite	HMV DB 2572 American Columbia RL 3042
Grainger Handel in the Strand	W.Braithwaite Lush	Columbia DX 1660 American Columbia RL 3042
Traditional arr. Grainger Londonderry Air	W.Braithwaite	Columbia DX 1660 American Columbia RL 3042

13 January 1949, Abbey Road

Lambert The Rio Grande	Lambert BBC Chorus Ripley, Greenbaum	Columbia DX 1591/2 Columbia 33SX 1003 EMI HQM 1078
Lambert Aubade Héroique	Lambert	Columbia unpublished

14 January 1949, Abbey Road

Lambert Horoscope, Ballet Suite	Lambert	Columbia DX 1567/8 Columbia 33SX 1003 EMI HQM 1078
Liszt orch. Jacob and arr. Lambert Apparitions, Ballet Suite	Lambert	Columbia DX 1560 & 1568

20 January 1949, Abbey Road

Puccini Vissi d'arte (Tosca)	Robinson Sladen	HMV B 9755 EMI RLS 707*
Puccini O mio babbino caro (Gianni Schicchi)	Robinson Sladen	HMV B 9755
Dvorak Biblical Songs Nos 3 & 8	Robinson Thomas	HMV B 9746

21 January and 12 February 1949, Abbey Road

Addinsell　　　　　　　　　　Mathieson　　　　　　　　　Columbia DX 1551
Passionate Friends,
Ballet Music from the film

Easdale　　　　　　　　　　　Mathieson　　　　　　　　　Columbia unpublished
The Pimpernel Waltz

12 February and 20 July 1949, Abbey Road

Easdale　　　　　　　　　　　Mathieson　　　　　　　　　Columbia DX 1597/8
The Red Shoes,
Music from the film

22 February 1949, Abbey Road

Mendelssohn　　　　　　　　　Mudie　　　　　　　　　　　HMV C 3850
Is not his word like a　　　 Noble
fire?; It is enough (Elijah)

26 & 27 April 1949, Abbey Road

Rachmaninov　　　　　　　　　Kletzki　　　　　　　　　　Columbia LX 1352/3/4/5/6
Piano Concerto No 3　　　　　 Malcuzynski　　　　　　　　(Auto LX 8767/68/69/70/71)
　　　　　　　　　　　　　　　　　　　　　　　　　　　　　 Columbia 33CX 1161

9 May 1949, Abbey Road

Puccini　　　　　　　　　　　 Susskind　　　　　　　　　 HMV unpublished
Si, mi chiamano Mimi　　　　　De los Angeles
(La Bohème)

Massenet　　　　　　　　　　　Susskind　　　　　　　　　 HMV DB 6994
Je ne suis que faiblesse　　　De los Angeles
...Adieu, notre petite
table (Manon)

Turina　　　　　　　　　　　　Susskind　　　　　　　　　 HMV DA 1929
Saeta; Poema No 3　　　　　　 De los Angeles
(Cantares)

11 May 1949, Abbey Road

Mozart　　　　　　　　　　　　Susskind　　　　　　　　　 HMV unpublished
Voi che sapete　　　　　　　　De los Angeles
(Le Nozze di Figaro)

Granados　　　　　　　　　　　Susskind　　　　　　　　　 HMV unpublished
La Maja y el Ruiseñor　　　　 De los Angeles
(Goyescas)

12 May 1949, Abbey Road

Gounod Il était un roi de Thulé; O Dieu! que de bijoux! (Faust)	Susskind De los Angeles	HMV DB 6938
Mozart Porgi amor (Le Nozze di Figaro)	Susskind De los Angeles	HMV DB 6994 EMI 29 05583*

18, 26, 27 & 28 May 1948, Abbey Road

Borodin Prince Igor, Overture	Dobrowen	HMV C 3979/80

19 May 1949, Abbey Road

Mussorgsky Death of Boris (Boris Godunov, orch. Rimsky-Korsakov)	Dobrowen Covent Garden Chorus Christoff, Schwarzkopf	HMV DB 21097 HMV BLP 1003 EMI 1C 147 03336/7M* EMI RLS 735*

20 May 1949, Abbey Road

Mussorgsky Farewell & Prayer of Boris (Boris Godunov, orch. Rimsky-Korsakov)	Dobrowen Christoff	HMV DB 6935 HMV BLP 1003 EMI 1C 147 03336/7M* EMI RLS 735*
Mussorgsky I have attained the highest power (Boris Godunov, orch. Rimsky-Korsakov)	Dobrowen Christoff	HMV DB 6948 EMI 1C 147 03336/7M* EMI RLS 735*
Boito Ave signor (Mefistofele)	Dobrowen Christoff	HMV DB 21047 EMI 1C 147 03336/7M* EMI RLS 735*

21 May 1949, Abbey Road

Massenet En fermant les yeux (Manon); Puccini E lucevan le stelle (Tosca)	Susskind Schock	HMV B 9868 EMI 29 12013*
Puccini Non piangere Liu; Nessun dorma (Turandot)	Susskind Schock	EMI 29 12013*

23 & 24 May 1949, Abbey Road

Scriabin Piano Concerto	Dobrowen Solomon	HMV unpublished

25 May 1949, Abbey Road

Johann Strauss Voices of Spring, Waltz	Susskind Berger	HMV DB 6954
Verdi Caro nome (Rigoletto)	Susskind Berger	HMV unpublished
Borodin Polovtsian March (Prince Igor)	Dobrowen	HMV C 3980
Wagner Entry of the Guests (Tannhäuser)	Dobrowen	HMV C 3927

26, 27 & 28 May 1949, Abbey Road

Tchaikovsky Piano Concerto No 1	Dobrowen Solomon	HMV C 3996/7/8/9 (Auto C 7776/7/8/9) HMV CLP 1001 EMI SLS 5094*

28 May 1949, Abbey Road

Verdi Ella giammai m'amò (Don Carlo)	Dobrowen Christoff	HMV unpublished
Scarlatti Oboe Concerto (arr.Bryan)	Susskind L.Goossens	Columbia DX 8347/8

1 June 1949, Abbey Road

Vivaldi Oboe Concerto op 8 no 9	Susskind L.Goossens	Columbia DX 8367/8

1 June 1949 and 1 September 1952, Abbey Road

Bach Oboe Concerto (arr. Tovey)	Susskind L.Goossens	HMV CLP 1656 World Records SH 243

4 June 1949, Abbey Road

Wagner Todesverkündigung (Die Walküre)	Böhm Flagstad, Svanholm	HMV DB 6962/3 EMI HQM 1138 EMI 1C 147 01491/2M* EMI EX 29 12273* EMI 29 10373*

5 June 1949, Abbey Road

Wagner O sink hernieder, Nacht der Liebe (Tristan und Isolde)	Böhm Flagstad, Svanholm Shacklock	HMV DB 21112/3/4 Victor LM 1151 EMI 1C 147 01491/2M* EMI EX 29 12273* EMI 29 10373*

9 June 1949, Abbey Road

Bach Violin Concerto in A minor	Bernard Varga	Columbia DX 1586/7
Beethoven Violin Romance No 1	Bernard Varga	Columbia DX 1615

13 June 1949, Abbey Road

Bellini Sediziose voci.... Casta diva (Norma)	Susskind Covent Garden Chorus Hammond	EMI HLM 7042
Verdi Son giunta.... Madre pietosa vergine (La Forza del Destino)	Susskind Covent Garden Chorus Hammond	HMV DB 21019 EMI HQM 1186

14 June 1949, Abbey Road

Cilea Troppo, signori (Adriana Lecouvreur)	Susskind Hammond	HMV C 3901 EMI HQM 1186
Leoncavallo Minuet and Harlequin's Serenade (I Pagliacci)	Susskind Hammond, Nash	HMV C 3924
Catalani Ebben? Ne andrò lontana (La Wally)	Susskind Hammond	HMV DB 21580 HMV ALP 1076

20 June 1949, Kingsway Hall

Franck Symphonic Variations	Susskind Lympany	HMV C 7784/5 HMV CLP 1002 EMI HLM 7179 Imprimatur IMP 5
Turina Rapsodia sinfonica	Susskind Lympany	HMV C 3913 HMV DB 4306 Victor LHMV 1025 Imprimatur DIMP 2

26 June 1949, Abbey Road

Verdi
Giovanna D'Arco, Overture
Markevitch
HMV C 3965

26 June 1949, Abbey Road and 30 June and 8 July 1949, Kingsway Hall

Verdi
Act 3 Ballet Music
(Macbeth)
Markevitch
HMV C 7937/8

30 June 1949, Kingsway Hall

Verdi
Aida, Prelude
Markevitch
HMV C 7937

30 June and 8 July 1949, Kingsway Hall

Verdi
La Forza del Destino,
Overture
Markevitch
HMV C 3920

20 July 1949, Abbey Road

Easdale
Minuet
(The Scarlet Pimpernel)
Mathieson
Columbia unpublished

21 July 1949, Abbey Road

Donizetti
Ardon gl'incensi
(Lucia di Lammermoor);
Benedict
Carnevale di Venezia
W.Braithwaite
Del Pozo
HMV C 3967
World Records Australia
RO 5417

Rodrigo
4 Madrigales amatorios
W.Braithwaite
Del Pozo
HMV unpublished

26 August 1949, Abbey Road

Mendelssohn
Calm Sea and Prosperous
Voyage, Overture
Kubelik
HMV C 7836/7

26 August and 17 September 1949, Abbey Road

Dvorak
Scherzo Capriccioso
Kubelik
HMV C 7822/3
HMV DB 4316/7

15 & 16 September 1949, Abbey Road

Beethoven Violin Concerto	Kubelik Haendel	HMV C 4126/27/28/29/30/31 (Auto C 7979/80/81/82/83/84) Victor LBC 1003 Toshiba EAC 60230-39*

4 October 1949, Abbey Road

Donizetti Quanto bella (L'Elisir D'Amore); Puccini Nessun dorma (Turandot)	Robinson Gigli	HMV DB 21138 EMI RLS 732*
Chopin arr. Glinski Omaggio a Bellini; Inno alla Patria	Robinson Gigli	EMI RLS 732*

21 October 1949, Abbey Road

Franck Symphonic Variations	Weldon Casadesus	Columbia LX 8800/1
Handel Samson, Overture	Weldon	Columbia DX 1731

18, 21 & 22 November 1949, Kingsway Hall

Balakirev Symphony No 1	Karajan	Columbia LX 1323/4/5/6/7/8 (Auto LX 8746/7/8/9/50/51) Columbia 33CX 1002 Toshiba EAC 37020-38* EMI XLP 60001 EMI RLS 7715*

22 & 28 November 1949, Kingsway Hall

Roussel Symphony No 4	Karajan	Columbia LX 1348/49/50/51 (Auto LX 8763/4/5/6) French Columbia FCX 163 Toshiba EAC 37020-38* EMI XLP 60003

28 November 1949, Kingsway Hall

Verdi Ella giammai m'amò (Don Carlo)	Karajan Christoff	HMV DB 21007 EMI 1C 147 03336/7M* EMI RLS 735*
Mussorgsky Varlaam's Song (Boris Godunov)	Karajan Christoff	HMV DB 21097 HMV BLP 1003 EMI 1C 147 03336/7M* EMI RLS 735*
Gounod Serenade (Faust)	Karajan Christoff	HMV unpublished

29 & 30 November 1949, Kingsway Hall

Bartok Music for Strings, Percussion and Celesta	Karajan	Columbia LX 1371/2/3/4 (Auto LX 8781/2/3/4) American Columbia ML 4456 Toshiba EAC 37020-38*

3 December 1949, Abbey Road

Mussorgsky Pimen's Monologue (Boris Godunov)	Malko Christoff	HMV DA 1938 EMI 1C 147 03336/7M* EMI RLS 735*
Boito Son lo spirito che nega (Mefistofele)	Malko Christoff	HMV DB 21047 EMI 1C 147 03336/7M* EMI RLS 735*

1950

14 February 1950, Abbey Road

Handel Markevitch HMV C 7852/3
Concerto Grosso in D   HMV DB 4308/9
op 6 no 5   French HMV FBLP 1057

15 February 1950, Abbey Road

Weber Markevitch HMV C 4018
Invitation to the Dance   Victor LBC 1028
(orch. Berlioz)

21 February 1950, Kingsway Hall

Rossini Galliera Columbia DX 1690
Il Barbiere di Siviglia,
Overture

21, 24 & 25 February 1950, Kingsway Hall

Beethoven Galliera Columbia DX 1697/98/99/
Symphony No 7   1700/1
   (Auto DX 8359/60/61/62/63)
   American Columbia RL 3035

25 February 1950, Kingsway Hall

Rossini Galliera Columbia DX 1690
La Gazza Ladra, Overture

6 March 1950, Abbey Road

Wagner Fistoulari HMV DB 21095
Dich teure Halle De los Angeles EMI 1C 187 30183/4*
(Tannhäuser);   EMI 29 05583*
Einsam in trüben Tagen
(Lohengrin)

7 March 1950, Abbey Road

Granados Fistoulari HMV DB 21069
La Maja y el Ruiseñor De los Angeles
(Goyescas)

14 March 1950, Abbey Road

Verdi Urna fatale del mio destino (La Forza del Destino); Vanne!... Credo in un dio crudel (Otello)	Robertson Gobbi	HMV DB 21071 EMI 1C 187 01549/50M* EMI RLS 738*
Mozart Non piu andrai (Le Nozze di Figaro)	Robertson Gobbi	HMV DA 1693 EMI 1C 187 01549/50M* EMI RLS 738*
Mozart Aprite un po' quegli occhi (Le Nozze di Figaro)	Robertson Gobbi	HMV DA 1693 EMI 1C 187 01549/50M*

22 March 1950, Kingsway Hall

Waldteufel Les Patineurs, Waltz	Lambert	Columbia DX 1674 Columbia 33S 1006
Waldteufel Estudiantina, Waltz	Lambert	Columbia DX 1693 Columbia 33S 1006

22 & 24 March 1950, Kingsway Hall

Bach Cantata No 82	Bernard Hotter	Columbia LX 1290/91/92 (Auto LX 8719/20/21) EMI 1C 147 01633/4M* EMI 29 02071

23 March 1950, Abbey Road

Tchaikovsky Suite No 3	Malko	HMV C 4058/59/60 (Auto C 7826/7/8) Victor LBC 1024 (Variations only)
Mussorgsky Gopak	Malko	HMV C 3991
Glazunov Introduction (The Seasons)	Malko	HMV C 7874

24 March 1950, Kingsway Hall

Suppé Pique Dame, Overture	Lambert	Columbia DX 1746
Suppé Morning, Noon and Night in Vienna, Overture	Lambert	Columbia DX 1665 American Columbia RL 3054

25 March 1950, Abbey Road

Glazunov Winter (The Seasons)	Malko	HMV C 7875
Thomas Raymond, Waltz	Malko	HMV C 3991

27 March 1950, Abbey Road

Albinoni Oboe Concerto op 7 no 6	Susskind L.Goossens	Columbia DX 1753
Albinoni Oboe Concerto op 7 no 3 (first movement only)	Susskind L.Goossens	Columbia DX 8368

29 & 30 March 1950, Kingsway Hall

Davies Solemn Melody; Handel Largo (Serse)	Weldon	Columbia DX 1681
Handel Minuet (Berenice); Boccherini Minuet (Quartet op 13 no 5)	Weldon	Columbia DX 1670

23 & 24 April 1950, Abbey Road

Schnabel Rhapsody for Orchestra	Kletzki	Columbia LX 8843/4

24 & 25 April 1950, Abbey Road

Tchaikovsky Capriccio italien	Kletzki	Columbia LX 8736/7

4 May 1950, Abbey Road

Rimsky-Korsakov Song of the Viking Guest (Sadko)	Dobrowen Christoff	HMV DB 21127 EMI 1C 147 03336/7M* EMI RLS 735*
Mussorgsky Dositheus' aria (Khovantachina, arr. Rimsky-Korsakov)	Dobrowen Christoff	HMV DB 21207 Victor LHMV 1033 EMI 1C 147 033336/7M* EMI RLS 735*

5 May 1950, Abbey Road

Borodin How are you, Prince? (Prince Igor)	Dobrowen Christoff	HMV DB 21262 HMV BLP 1003 EMI 1C 147 03336/7M* EMI RLS 735*

6 May 1950, Abbey Road

Charpentier Depuis le jour (Louise)	Dobrowen Schwarzkopf	EMI RLS 763* EMI 154 6133*
Puccini Donde lieta uscì (La Bohème)	Dobrowen Schwarzkopf	Columbia unpublished

7 & 11 May 1950, Abbey Road

Martinu
Concerto for two string
orchestras, piano and
timpani

Kubelik

HMV C 7911/12/13

8 May 1950, Abbey Road

Borodin
Galitzky's aria
(Prince Igor)

Dobrowen
Christoff

HMV DB 21127
HMV BLP 1003
EMI 1C 147 03336/7M*
EMI RLS 735*

Mascagni
Cherry Duet
(L'amico Fritz)

Dobrowen
Hammond, Schock

HMV DB 21098
EMI 1C 147 28963/4M*
EMI 29 12013*

Giordano
Vicino a te...La nostra
morte (Andrea Chenier)

Dobrowen
Hammond, Schock

HMV DB 21260
EMI 1C 147 28963/4M*
EMI 29 12013*

10 May 1950, Abbey Road

Mendelssohn
Scherzo (A Midsummer
Night's Dream)

Kubelik

HMV C 7836
HMV ALP 1049

Berlioz
Hungarian March;
Dance of the Sylphs
(La Damnation de Faust)

Kubelik

HMV C 4031

Dvorak
Legend No 10

Kubelik

HMV C 7822
HMV DB 4317/4328

Verdi
Willow Song and Ave Maria
(Otello)

Susskind
Hammond, Sinclair

HMV unpublished

12 May 1950, Abbey Road

Mozart
Crudele....non mi dir
(Don Giovanni);
Misera, dove son?,
Concert aria

W.Braithwaite
Hammond

EMI HLM 7042

13 May 1950, Abbey Road

Rossini
Sombre forêt (William
Tell)

W.Braithwaite
Hammond

HMV unpublished

Massenet
Celui dont la parole
(Hérodiade)

W.Braithwaite
Hammond

EMI HLM 7042

15 & 16 May 1950, Abbey Road

Bach Concerto in E BWV 1053	E.Fischer, cond. & sol.	HMV unpublished

16 May 1950, Abbey Road

Bach Concerto in C BWV 1064	E.Fischer, cond. & sol. R.Smith, Matthews	HMV DB 21180/81/82 (Auto DB 9573/4/5) HMV ALP 1103 EMI 29 06261M

22 May 1950, Royal Albert Hall (live recording of final rehearsal)

Strauss Vier letzte Lieder	Furtwängler Flagstad	Ed Smith Records EJS 432 Fonit Cetra LO 501 Turnabout TV 34830 Fonit Cetra FE 41*

26 May and 13 October 1950, Abbey Road)

Prokofiev Peter and the Wolf	Markevitch Pickles	HMV C 4046/7/8 Victor LBC 1015 HMV DLP 1001 EMI XLP 30064

12 June 1950, Abbey Road

Vaughan Williams Song of the Road (Hugh the Drover); German English Rose (Merrie England)	Robertson Johnston	Columbia DX 1668
Cardillo Catari, Catari	Robertson Johnston	Columbia unpublished

19 & 20 June 1950, Abbey Road

Tchaikovsky Violin Concerto	Susskind Heifetz	HMV DB 21228/29/30/31 HMV BLP 1012

21 June 1950, Abbey Road

Beethoven Violin Romances in G and F	Susskind Heifetz	HMV unpublished

22 & 23 June 1950, Abbey Road

Lalo Symphonie Espagnole	Susskind Heifetz	HMV unpublished

25 June 1950, Abbey Road

Bach Erbarme dich (St Matthew Passion)	Susskind Flagstad	HMV DB 21237 EMI HQM 1057 EMI 1C 147 01491/2M* EMI 29 02051

26 & 27 June 1950, Abbey Road

Walton Violin Concerto	Walton Heifetz	HMV DB 21257/8/9 HMV BLP 1047

14 July 1950, Abbey Road

Mozart Ein Mädchen oder Weibchen (Die Zauberflöte); Donne mia la fate (Così fan tutte)	Robertson Rothmüller	HMV C 4054
Giordano Nemico della Patria? (Andrea Chenier)	Robertson Rothmüller	HMV C 4019

6 August and 6 October 1950, Kingsway Hall

Bach Cantata No 51	Gellhorn Schwarzkopf	Columbia LX 1334/5/6 (Auto LX 8756/7/8) American Columbia ML 4792 Seraphim 60013 EMI 154 6133*

10 August 1950, Abbey Road

Tchaikovsky Lebt wohl (The Maid of Orleans)	Collingwood Jurinac	EMI HQM 1024
Tchaikovsky Lisa's aria (Pique Dame)	Collingwood Jurinac	HMV unpublished

6, 7 & 8 September 1950, Abbey Road

Song of Songs; Ah, sweet mystery of life	Fistoulari Peerce	HMV DA 2010
Torna a sorrento	Fistoulari Peerce	HMV DA 1962
Sylvia; O sole mio; Mattinata; La danza; When you and I were young; Silver threads among the gold; Valencia; Amapola; Schubert Serenade	Fistoulari Peerce	HMV unpublished

11 September 1950, Abbey Road

Smetana Wiegenlied (The Kiss)	W.Braithwaite Jurinac	HMV unpublished
Smetana Endlich allein..... wie fremd und tot (The Bartered Bride)	W.Braithwaite Jurinac	HMV DB 21136 EMI HQM 1024 EMI 1C 047 01444M

14 September 1950, Kingsway Hall

Waldteufel Pomona, Waltz	Lambert	Columbia DX 1713 Columbia 33S 1006
Waldteufel Sur la plage, Waltz	Lambert	Columbia DX 1755 Columbia 33S 1006

22 September 1950, Abbey Road

Mozart In uomini, in soldati; Una donna a quindici anni (Così fan tutte)	Susskind Noni	HMV DA 1986
Verdi Volta la terra; Saper vorreste (Un Ballo in Maschera)	Susskind Noni	HMV DA 1954

24 September 1950, Abbey Road

Verdi Di provenza il mar (La Traviata); Pari siamo (Rigoletto)	Susskind Gobbi	HMV DB 21227 EMI 1C 187 01549/50M* EMI RLS 738*

27 September 1950, Kingsway Hall

Walton Façade, Ballet Suite	Lambert	Columbia DX 1734/5/6 (Auto 8734/5/6) Columbia 33SX 1003
Chabrier Ballabile (orch.Lambert)	Lambert	Columbia DX 1736

29 September and 7 October 1950, Abbey Road

Wagner Prelude and Liebestod (Tristan und Isolde)	Dobrowen	HMV C 4111/12/13

29 September and 6 October 1950, Abbey Road

Mussorgsky Khovantschina, Act 1 Prelude	Dobrowen	HMV unpublished

3 October 1950, Abbey Road

Paganini Violin Concerto No 2	Fistoulari Menuhin	HMV DB 9588/89/90/91 HMV BLP 1018 Toshiba EAC 60230-39*

4 October 1950, Kingsway Hall

Bellini Ah! non credea mirarti (La Sonnambula); Donizetti Quel guardo il cavaliere (Don Pasquale)	Fistoulari Del Pozo	HMV C 4237

5 October 1950, Kingsway Hall

Traditional Song of the Volga Boatmen; Mussorgsky Song of the Flea (orch.Rimsky-Korsakov)	Dobrowen Christoff	HMV DB 21305 EMI 1C 147 033336/7M* EMI RLS 735*
Rimsky-Korsakov The Prophet	Dobrowen Christoff	EMI RLS 735*

6 & 7 October 1950, Abbey Road

Rimsky-Korsakov Russian Easter Festival Overture	Dobrowen	HMV C 7916/7

11 & 12 October 1950, Kingsway Hall

Debussy Trois Nocturnes (1. Nuages 2. Fêtes 3. Sirènes)	Galliera Glyndebourne Festival Chorus (No 3 only)	Columbia 33S 1002 Columbia DX 1754 (No 1 only) Columbia DX 1782 (No 2 only)

12 & 13 October 1950, Kingsway Hall

Debussy La Mer	Galliera	Columbia DX 1726/7/8 (Auto DX 8369/70/71) American Columbia RL 3055

13 October 1950, Abbey Road

Bach Mein gläubiges Herze (Cantata No 68)	Gellhorn Schwarzkopf	Columbia LX 1336 American Columbia ML 4792

14 October 1950 and 27 January 1951, Kingsway Hall

Brahms Haydn Variations (St Antoni Chorale)	Markevitch	HMV C 7856/7 Victor LBC 1010

18 October 1950, Abbey Road

Puccini Donde lieta uscì (La Bohème)	Galliera Schwarzkopf	Columbia LB 110 EMI RLS 763* EMI 154 6133*
Puccini Signore, ascolta (Turandot)	Galliera Schwarzkopf	Columbia LB 110 EMI RLS 763*
Puccini Un bel dì, vedremo (Madama Butterfly)	Galliera Schwarzkopf	Columbia LX 1370 EMI RLS 763* EMI 154 6133*

19 October 1950, Abbey Road

Verdi Addio del passato (La Traviata)	Galliera Schwarzkopf	Columbia LX 1370 EMI RLS 763*
Beethoven Ach wär' ich schon (Fidelio)	Galliera Schwarzkopf	Columbia LX 1410
Bizet Je dis que rien ne m'épouvante (Carmen)	Galliera Schwarzkopf	Columbia LX 1410 EMI ALP 143 5501

20 October 1950, Abbey Road

Respighi Brazilian Impressions	Galliera	Columbia unpublished

9 December 1950, Abbey Road

Glazunov Ruses d'amour	Malko	HMV C 7875
Tchaikovsky The Voyevode, Intermezzo	Malko	HMV C 4060
Glinka Oriental Dances (Russlan and Ludmilla)	Malko	HMV C 4196

18 December 1950, Kingsway Hall

Handel Ombra mai fù (Serse); Gluck Che farò (Orfeo)	Robertson Watson	Columbia DX 1721
Verdi Stride la vampa (Il Trovatore); Re dell' abisso (Un Ballo in Maschera)	Robertson Watson	Columbia DB 2912

20 December 1950, Abbey Road

Beethoven			Sargent			HMV C 4160/1/2/3
Piano Concerto No 3		Moiseiwitsch		(Auto C 7904/5/6/7)
						Victor LBC 1012

1951

8 January 1951, Abbey Road

Verdi Pace, pace, mio Dio (La Forza del Destino); D'amor sull'ali rose (Il Trovatore)	W.Braithwaite Menkes	HMV unpublished
Verdi Ritorna vincitor (Aida)	W.Braithwaite Menkes	HMV C 4078

24 January 1951, Abbey Road and 27 January 1951, Kingsway Hall

Tchaikovsky The Nutcracker, Suite	Markevitch	HMV C 4133/4/5 (Auto C 7885/6/7) Victor LBC 1015

26 January 1951, Kingsway Hall

Verdi Luisa Miller, Overture	Markevitch	HMV C 4097
Verdi La Battaglia di Legnano, Overture	Markevitch	HMV C 4181

19 & 20 February 1951, Abbey Road

Beethoven Piano Concerto No 5 "Emperor"	Furtwängler E.Fischer	HMV DB 21315/6/7/8/9 (Auto DB 9661/2/3/4/5) HMV ALP 1051 EMI HLM 7027 EMI 29 00021 EMI RLS 29 00013* Toshiba CC35-3167

6 March 1951, Kingsway Hall

Gluck O Diana, dea spietate (Iphigenie in Aulis)	Fistoulari Christoff	EMI RLS 735*
Verdi Chi mai vegg'io!.... L'offeso ognor, signori (Ernani)	Fistoulari Christoff	HMV DB 21424 EMI 1C 147 03336/7M* EMI RLS 735*

7 March 1951, Abbey Road

Verdi Celeste·Aida (Aida)	Mudie Johnston	Columbia unpublished
Mascagni You here, Santuzza (Cavalleria Rusticana)	Mudie Shuard, Johnston	Columbia DX 1748 EMI RLS 707*

24 April 1951, Kingsway Hall

Puccini In questa reggia (Turandot)	Robinson Hammond	HMV DA 1988 EMI HQM 1186 EMI RLS 29 00143*

3 May 1951, Royal Festival Hall (live recording of the inaugural concert, with the Royal Festival Orchestra, comprising members of the five London orchestras)

Bourgeois All people that on earth	Dykes Bower Royal Festival Choir	HMV DB 21273
Purcell Soul of the world	Boult Royal Festival Choir	HMV DB 21273
Handel Zadok the Priest	Boult Royal Festival Choir	HMV DA 1980
Elgar Pomp and Circumstance, March No 1	Boult	HMV DA 1981
Vaughan Williams Serenade to Music	Boult Royal Festival Choir	HMV DA 7040/1 EMI ED 29 10921
Handel Hallelujah Chorus; Amen Chorus (Messiah)	Sargent Royal Festival Choir	HMV DB 21274

11 May 1951, Abbey Road

Vieuxtemps Violin Concerto No 4	Susskind Menuhin	HMV DB 21307/8/9 HMV BLP 1005

16 May 1951, Kingsway Hall

Massenet Il est doux, il est bon (Hérodiade)	Robinson Hammond	HMV unpublished

201

20 May 1951, Abbey Road

Verdi
Ah! fors' è lui....
Sempre libera
(La Traviata)

Fistoulari
Carosio

HMV DB 21306

Bellini
Oh! Quante volte
(I Capuletti ed i Montecchi)

Fistoulari
Carosio

HMV DB 21336

23 May and 14, 15 & 16 June 1951, Kingsway Hall

Rimsky-Korsakov
Scheherazade

Stokowski

HMV ALP 1339
Stokowski Society LS 12

26 & 27 May 1951, Abbey Road

Haydn
Cello Concerto in D
(arr. Gevaert)

Kubelik
Fournier

HMV DB 21448/49/50
(Auto DB 9743/4/5)
Victor LHMV 1043

27 May 1951, Abbey Road

Mozart
Idomeneo, Overture

Kubelik

HMV DB 21465
HMV ALP 1109

Verdi
Ave Maria (Otello)

Fistoulari
Carosio

HMV 7ER 5162

Massenet
Ebben (Manon)

Fistoulari
Carosio

HMV DB 21336

5 June 1951, Kingsway Hall

Rossini
Ils s'éloignent enfin!...
Sombre forêt
(William Tell);
Massenet
Pleurez mes yeux (Le Cid)

Robinson
Hammond

EMI HLM 7042

6 & 11 June 1951, Kingsway Hall

Grieg
Piano Concerto

Karajan
Gieseking

Columbia LX 1503/4/5/6
(Auto LX 8888/89/90/91)
Columbia 33C 1003
EMI 1C 147 01363M
EMI 3C 153 52425-31M*
Toshiba EAC 37001-19*

7 June 1951, Kingsway Hall

Franck Symphonic Variations	Karajan Gieseking	Columbia LX 8937/8 American Columbia ML 4536 EMI 1C 147 01363M Toshiba EAC 37001-19*

8 & 9 June 1951, Kingsway Hall

Beethoven Piano Concerto No 5 "Emperor"	Karajan Gieseking	International Columbia LCX 5008/9/10/11/12 Columbia 33CX 1010 EMI 3C 153 52425-31M* Toshiba EAC 37001-19*

9 & 11 June 1951, Kingsway Hall

Beethoven Piano Concerto No 4	Karajan Gieseking	Columbia LX 1443/4/5/6 (Auto LX 8831/2/3/4) Columbia 33C 1007 EMI 3C 153 52425-31M* Toshiba EAC 37001-19*

10 June 1951, Kingsway Hall

Mozart Piano Concerto No 23	Karajan Gieseking	Columbia LX 1510/1/2/3 (Auto LX 8894/5/6/7) Columbia 33C 1012 EMI 3C 153 52425-31M* Toshiba EAC 37001-19*

12, 13 & 14 June 1951, Abbey Road

Wagner Heil dir, Sonne (Siegfried)	Sebastian Flagstad, Svanholm	HMV BLP 1035 EMI HQM 1138 EMI 1C 047 01149M EMI EX 29 12273* EMI 29 10373*

14 June 1951, Abbey Road

Wagner Zu neuen Taten (Götterdämmerung)	Sebastian Flagstad, Svanholm	EMI EX 29 12273* EMI 29 10373*

15 June 1951, Abbey Road

Wagner Einsam in trüben Tagen (Lohengrin)	Weigert Varnay	Columbia LX 1535 EMI 1C 047 01373M
Wagner Ich sah das Kind (Parsifal)	Weigert Varnay	Columbia LX 1560 EMI 1C 047 01373M

16 June 1951, Abbey Road

Wagner
Dich, teure Halle
(Tannhäuser)
    Sebastian
    Varnay
    Columbia LX 1535
    EMI 1C 047 01373M

Wagner
Mild und leise
(Tristan und Isolde)
    Sebastian
    Varnay
    Columbia LX 1417
    EMI 1C 047 01373M

29 June 1951, Abbey Road

Wagner
Zu neuen Taten
(Götterdämmerung)
    Weigert
    Flagstad, Svanholm
    HMV unpublished

Wagner
Helle Wehr! Heilige Waffe!
(Götterdämmerung)
    Weigert
    Flagstad, Svanholm
    EMI EX 29 12273*
    EMI 29 10373*

3 July 1951, Abbey Road

Granados
Goyescas, Intermezzo;
Meyerbeer
Coronation March
(Le Prophète)
    Weldon
    Columbia DX 1801

Massenet
Méditation (Thais)
    Weldon
    Parikian
    Columbia DX 1792

Leopold Mozart
Toy Symphony
(Cassation in G)
    Weldon
    Columbia DX 1784

Bach
Sheep may safely graze
(The Wise Virgins,
arr. Walton)
    Weldon
    Columbia DB 3164
    Columbia 33SX 1032

Ippolitov-Ivanov
Procession of the Sardar
(Caucasian Sketches)
    Weldon
    Columbia DX 1792
    Columbia 33SX 1032

6 July 1951, Kingsway Hall

Wagner
O Gnade! Höchstes Heil!
(Parsifal)
    Dobrowen
    Weber
    Columbia LX 1442
    EMI 1C 177 00933/4M*

Wagner
Titurel, der fromme Held
(Parsifal)
    Dobrowen
    Weber
    Columbia LX 1441
    EMI 1C 177 00933/4M*

Wagner
Gar viel und schön
(Tannhäuser)
    Dobrowen
    Weber
    German Columbia LWX 449
    EMI 1C 177 00933/4M*

Wagner
Mein Herr und Gott
(Lohengrin)
    Dobrowen
    Weber
    Columbia unpublished

7 July 1951, Kingsway Hall

Verdi Mia madre aveva una povera ancella...Salce, salce (Otello)	Dobrowen Martinis	Columbia LX 1520 Preiser PR 9855
Verdi Ave Maria (Otello)	Dobrowen Martinis	Columbia LX 1463 Preiser PR 9855
Tchaikovsky Polonaise and Waltz (Eugene Onegin)	Dobrowen	HMV C 4190

9 July 1951, Kingsway Hall

Verdi Ecco l'orrido campo.... Ma dell' arido stelo (Un Ballo in Maschera)	Dobrowen Martinis	Columbia LX 1548 Preiser PR 9855
Verdi Pace, pace, mio Dio! (La Forza del Destino)	Dobrowen Martinis	Preiser PR 9855
Mozart Le Nozze di Figaro, Overture	Dobrowen	HMV unpublished
Grieg Symphonic Dance No 1	Dobrowen	HMV C 4142

10 July 1951, Kingsway Hall

Verdi Ritorna vincitor! (Aida)	Dobrowen Martinis	Columbia LX 1536 Preiser PR 9855
Verdi O patria mia (Aida)	Dobrowen Martinis	Columbia LX 1463 Preiser PR 9855

11 August 1951, Abbey Road

Bach Violin Concerto in A minor	Susskind Goldberg	Parlophone SW 8140/1

13 August 1951, Abbey Road

Mozart Violin Concerto No 5	Susskind Goldberg	Parlophone unpublished

14 August 1951, Abbey Road

Mozart Violin Concerto No 3	Susskind Goldberg	Parlophone PMA 1003 Toshiba EAC 60230-39*

15 August 1951, Abbey Road

Mozart Violin Concerto No 4	Susskind Goldberg	Parlophone PMA 1003 Toshiba EAC 60230-39*

16 August 1951, Abbey Road

Mozart Dalla sua pace (Don Giovanni)	Susskind Midgeley	HMV unpublished
Massenet En fermant les yeux (Manon)	Susskind Midgeley	HMV DB 21358

30 & 31 August 1951, Abbey Road

Rimsky-Korsakov May Night, Overture	Fistoulari	Parlophone PMC 1031 EMI XLP 30031
Reznicek Donna Diana, Overture; Nicolai The Merry Wives of Windsor, Overture; Wolf-Ferrari Susanna's Secret, Overture	Fistoulari	Parlophone unpublished

1 & 2 September 1951, Abbey Road

Dvorak Symphony No 7	Kubelik	HMV ALP 1075

4 September 1951, Abbey Road

Haydn Trumpet Concerto in E flat	Kubelik Jackson	HMV unpublished
Smetana The Bartered Bride, Overture and Furiant	Kubelik	HMV DB 21463 HMV ALP 1049
Smetana Dance of the Comedians (The Bartered Bride)	Kubelik	HMV unpublished

5 September 1951, Kingsway Hall

Mussorgsky Night on Bare Mountain	Kletzki	Columbia LX 8951/2
Berlioz Béatrice et Bénédict, Overture	Kletzki	Columbia LX 1529 Columbia 33CX 1003 EMI XLP 30014

6 September 1951, Kingsway Hall

Berlioz Benvenuto Cellini, Overture	Kletzki	Columbia LX 8935/6 Columbia 33CX 1003 EMI XLP 30014
Berlioz Les francs juges, Overture	Kletzki	Columbia LX 8926/7 Columbia 33CX 1003 EMI XLP 30014

7 September 1951, Kingsway Hall

Berlioz Le corsair, Overture	Kletzki	Columbia LX 1533 Columbia 33CX 1003 EMI XLP 30014
Glinka Russlan and Ludmilla, Overture	Kletzki	Columbia LX 8951
Brahms Hungarian Dance No 1	Kletzki	Columbia LX 8926
Brahms Hungarian Dances Nos 2 & 3	Kletzki	Columbia LX 8936

12 & 13 September 1951, Abbey Road

Brahms Symphony No 2	Kubelik	HMV unpublished

15 September 1951, Abbey Road

Wagner Tatest du's wirklich? (Tristan und Isolde)	Schüchter Weber	Columbia LX 8892/3 EMI 1C 177 00933/4M*

16 September 1951, Abbey Road

Wagner Tot denn alles (Tristan und Isolde)	Schüchter Weber, Schwarzkopf	Columbia LX 8892 EMI 1C 177 00933/4M*
Wagner Das schöne Fest (Die Meistersinger von Nürnberg); Mein Herr und Gott (Lohengrin)	Schüchter Weber	Columbia unpublished

24 September 1951, Abbey Road

Tchaikovsky Adieu forêts (The Maid of Orleans)	Susskind Tourel	Columbia unpublished
Saint-Saëns Printemps qui commence (Samson et Dalila)	Susskind Tourel	Columbia LX 1555

25 September 1951, Abbey Road

Saint-Saëns Mon coeur s'ouvre à ta voix (Samson et Dalila)	Susskind Tourel	Columbia LX 1555
Bizet Habañera (Carmen); Puccini Musetta's Waltz Song (La Bohème)	Susskind Tourel	Columbia LX 1507

12 October 1951, Abbey Road

Mendelssohn Symphony No 4 "Italian"	Cantelli	HMV unpublished

13 October 1951, Abbey Road

Tchaikovsky Romeo and Juliet	Cantelli	HMV DB 21373/4/5 HMV ALP 1086 World Records SH 287

16 October 1951, Abbey Road

Wagner Siegfried Idyll	Cantelli	HMV DB 9746/7 HMV ALP 1086 World Records SH 287

17, 18 & 19 October 1951, Abbey Road

Walton Symphony No 1	Walton	HMV ALP 1027 EMI SLS 5246*

19 October 1951, Abbey Road

Walton Scapino, Overture	Walton	HMV DB 21499 EMI ED 29 07151

26 October 1951, Abbey Road

Bellini Ah, per sempre (I Puritani); Verdi Gran Dio! (Ernani)	W.Braithwaite Silveri	Columbia LX 1509
Bizet Toreador's Song (Carmen); Borodin No sleep, no rest (Prince Igor)	W.Braithwaite Silveri	Columbia LX 1530

29 October 1951, Abbey Road

Milhaud Piano Concerto No 1; Honegger Piano Concertino	Fistoulari Jacquinot	MGM E 3041

6 November 1951, Kingsway Hall

Berlioz Hungarian March (La Damnation de Faust); Mendelssohn War March of the Priests (Athalie)	Weldon	Columbia DX 1818 American Columbia RL 3042

6 & 8 November 1951, Kingsway Hall

Humperdinck Dream Pantomime (Hänsel und Gretel)	Weldon	Columbia DX 1811

8 November 1951, Kingsway Hall

Mascagni Cavalleria Rusticana, Intermezzo	Weldon	Columbia DX 1807 Columbia 33SX 1032

9 November 1951, Kingsway Hall

Tchaikovsky Waltz (The Sleeping Beauty)	Weldon	Columbia DX 1807 Columbia 33SX 1032
Offenbach Orpheus in the Underworld, Overture	Weldon	Columbia DX 1823

10 November 1951, Abbey Road

Handel Dall' ondoso periglio (Giulio Cesare)	Weldon Hotter	Columbia LX 1538 EMI 1C 147 01633/4M*
Handel Soll ich in Mamres Segens Au'n (Joshua); Wie willig trägt mein Vaterherz (Samson)	Weldon Hotter	Columbia LX 1516 EMI 1C 147 01633/4M*

12 & 13 November 1951, Abbey Road

Stravinsky Le sacre du printemps	Markevitch	HMV CLP 1003 EMI MFP 2043

14 November 1951 and 11 & 13 September 1952, Abbey Road

Prokofiev Markevitch Columbia 33CX 1049
Symphony No 1 "Classical" EMI XLP 30001

14 November 1951 and 13 September 1952, Abbey Road

Falla Markevitch Columbia 33CX 1049
The Three-Cornered Hat, EMI XLP 30001
Ballet Suite (Miller's Dance also on
 33CX 1198)

28 November 1951, Kingsway Hall

Mendelssohn Susskind Columbia unpublished
The Hebrides, Overture

Mozart Susskind Columbia DX 8405
Le Nozze di Figaro,
Overture

28, 29 & 30 November 1951, 26 & 29 April and 5 & 8 May 1952, Kingsway Hall

Beethoven Karajan Columbia 33CX 1035
Symphony No 7 World Records SM 143-149*
 EMI SLS 5053*
 Toshiba EAC 37001-19*

30 November and 1 December 1951, Kingsway Hall

Handel Karajan Columbia unpublished
The Water Music, Suite

1 December 1951, 28 & 29 November 1952 and 21 & 22 July 1953, Kingsway Hall

Bartok Karajan Columbia 33CX 1054
Concerto for Orchestra Toshiba EAC 37020-38*

1 December 1951 and 28 & 29 July 1952, Kingsway Hall

Sibelius Karajan Columbia 33CX 1047
Symphony No 5 Toshiba EAC 37020-38*

3 December 1951, Kingsway Hall

Strauss Karajan Columbia LX 8920/1
Don Juan Columbia 33CX 1001
 Toshiba EAC 37020-38*
 EMI RLS 7715*

4 December 1951, Kingsway Hall

Strauss Karajan Columbia LX 8908/9
Till Eulenspiegel Columbia 33CX 1001
 Toshiba EAC 37020-38*
 EMI RLS 7715*

5 December 1951, Kingsway Hall

Bizet Carmen, Intermezzi; Leoncavallo I Pagliacci, Intermezzo; Mascagni Cavalleria Rusticana & L'Amico Fritz, Intermezzi; Wolf-Ferrari The Jewels of the Madonna & The School for Fathers, Intermezzi	Schüchter	Parlophone PMD 1022

6 December 1951, Kingsway Hall

Rimsky-Korsakov Capriccio Espagnol	Schüchter	Parlophone PMC 1003

6 & 7 December 1951, Kingsway Hall

Ippolitov-Ivanov Caucasian Sketches	Schüchter	Parlophone PMC 1003

7 December 1951, Kingsway Hall

Tchaikovsky Marche slave	Schüchter	Parlophone PMC 1003
Mussorgsky Persian Dance (Khovantschina, arr. Rimsky-Korsakov)	Schüchter	Columbia DX 1862
Beethoven March (Egmont)	Schüchter	Parlophone unpublished

1952

Since 1950 the Philharmonia Orchestra had been owned personally by Walter Legge, and it was managed from offices in the Ibbs and Tillett building in Wigmore Street by Jane Withers. In 1952 the EMI recording contract was renewed for thirty sessions per annum, twenty sessions per annum to be without soloist. In reality the number of annual sessions regularly exceeded the contractual minimum, and the income from royalties on record sales enabled the orchestra to survive without outside subsidy.

Legge also felt confident enough to take the Philharmonia on its first European tour in May 1952, and it was as a result of this tour that Toscanini was persuaded to come to London to conduct the Philharmonia in a pair of unforgettable Brahms concerts.

ROYAL ALBERT HALL

Manager: C. S. Taylor

PHILHARMONIA
ORCHESTRA

Founder and Artistic Director: WALTER LEGGE
Leader: MAX SALPETER

DR. WILHELM
FURTWÄNGLER

KIRSTEN
FLAGSTAD

SCHUMANN: Manfred Overture
SCHUMANN: Symphony No. 4
RAVEL: Rhapsodie Espagnol

INTERVAL

WAGNER: Five Wesendonck Songs
WAGNER: Closing Scene from Götterdämmerung

Thursday, April 24, 1952

Management: IBBS & TILLETT LTD., 124 WIGMORE STREET, W.1

EUROPEAN TOUR

May 11th - May 31st 1952

PHILHARMONIA
ORCHESTRA
Founder and Artistic Director: WALTER LEGGE

and

HERBERT VON

KARAJAN

May	12	PARIS	Palais de Chaillot
	13	PARIS	Palais de Chaillot
	14	BERNE	Casino
	15	GENEVA	Victoria Hall
	16	ZURICH	Tonhalle
	17	BASLE	Musiksaal-Casino
	18	TURIN	Conservatorio
*	19	MILAN	La Scala (Opening Concert of the Season)
*	20	MILAN	La Scala
*	22	VIENNA	Musikverein (International Music Congress)
*	23	VIENNA	Musikverein (International Music Congress)
	24	LINZ	Turnhalle
	26	MUNICH	Deutsches Museum
	27	HAMBURG	Musik Halle
	29	BERLIN	Titania Palast
	30	BERLIN	Titania Palast

* The Concerts marked with an asterisk are already sold out

The Philharmonia Orchestra

conducted by

Arturo Toscanini

1st VIOLINS
Manoug Parikian, } *Joint*
Max Salpeter, } *Leaders*
Jack Kessler, *Sub-Leader*
Jessie Hinchliffe
William Monro
Marie Wilson
Nathan Comras
Hans Geiger
Peter Mountain
Ernest Scott
Arthur Davison
Derek Collier
Ivor McMahon
Alfred Davis
Michael Jones
Norman Chapple

2nd VIOLINS
David Wise, *Principal*
Gerald Emms
Rowland Sirrell
Charles Verney
Frank Bilbe
Jean Lefevre
Kathleen Sturdy
Ernest Rutledge
Denis Brown
Kathleen Tierney
Pierrette Galeone
Michael Freedman
Hugh Maguire
Colin Sauer
Neville Marriner
Felix Kok

VIOLAS
Herbert Downes, *Principal*
Maurice Loban
Bernard Davis
Anne Wolfe
Roy Patten
Leo Birnbaum
Muriel Tookey
Samuel Rosenheim
Lance Lange
Lindo Southworth
Kenneth Essex
Maurice Meek
Vincent Groves
Margo Slebbing

'CELLOS
Raymond Clark, *Principal*
Alexander Kok
David Ffrangcon-Thomas
John Holmes
Tom Hill
Peter Beavan
Norina Semino
Nelson Cooke
Jem Marchant
Maurice Westerby
Jacques Piretti
Ambrose Gauntlett

DOUBLE BASSES
James Edward Merrett, *Principal*
Adrian Beers
Gerald Brooks
Desmond Wrench
Geoffrey Clark
John Honeyman
James Bateson
Samuel Sterling
Victor Wright
Herbert Howarth

FLUTES
Gareth Morris, *Principal*
Ronald Gillham
George Crozier

PICCOLO
Arthur Ackroyd

OBOES
Sidney Sutcliffe, *Principal*
Stanley Smith
Peter Newbury
Peter Graeme

CLARINETS
Frederick Thurston, *Principal*
Archie Jacob
Bernard Walton
Wilfred Hambleton

BASSOONS
Cecil James, *Principal*
Paul Draper
William Waterhouse

CONTRA BASSOON
Peter Parry

HORNS
Dennis Brain, *Principal*
Neill Sanders
Edmund Chapman
Alfred Cursue
Aubrey Thonger

TRUMPETS
Harold Jackson, *Principal*
Dennis Clift

TENOR TROMBONES
Stanley Brown, *Principal*
John Ashby
Arthur Wilson

BASS TROMBONE
Frederick Mansfield

TUBA
Philip Catelinet

TIMPANI
James Bradshaw

PERCUSSION
Harry Eastwood
Cecil Norrington

Outstanding Recordings of the

Philharmonia Orchestra

ON THE

New

Columbia

Long Playing

33⅓ R.P.M. RECORDS

CONDUCTED BY HERBERT VON KARAJAN

"Till Eulenspiegel" and "Don Juan"— *R. Strauss* - - - - 33CX1001

Symphony in C major— *Balakirev (Recorded under the auspices of the Maharaja of Mysore's Musical Foundation)* - - - - - - 33CX1002

CONDUCTED BY PAUL KLETZKI

Overtures by Berlioz: "Le Corsaire", "Benvenuto Cellini",
"Béatrice et Bénédict", "Les Francs Juges" - - - - - 33CX1003

CONDUCTED BY ALCEO GALLIERA
with Members of the Glyndebourne Festival Chorus

Nocturnes— *Debussy* - - - - - - - 33SI002

Available in October, together with other fine Columbia Long Playing 33⅓ r.p.m. Records. Full details at all Record Dealers.

COLUMBIA *the finest name on record*

COLUMBIA GRAPHOPHONE COMPANY LIMITED HAYES, MIDDLESEX

1952

15 January 1952, Kingsway Hall

Verdi Willow Song and Ave Maria (Otello)	Tausky Hammond	HMV DB 21558

15 & 17 January 1952, Kingsway Hall

Verdi Tu che la vanità (Don Carlo)	Tausky Hammond	HMV DB 21510

17 January 1952, Kingsway Hall

Verdi O patria mia (Aida)	Tausky Hammond	HMV 7R 172
Offenbach Elle a fui, la tourturelle (Les Contes d'Hoffman)	Tausky Hammond	EMI HLM 7042

21 January 1952, Abbey Road

Wagner Der fliegende Holländer, Overture	Malko	HMV C 4176 Victor LBC 1048
Glinka Oriental Dances (Russlan and Ludmilla)	Malko	HMV C 4196
Tchaikovsky Entry of the Lilac Fairy and Bluebird Pas de Deux (The Sleeping Beauty)	Malko	HMV C 4205
Tchaikovsky Rose Adagio and Pas de Deux for Puss in Boots (The Sleeping Beauty)	Malko	HMV C 4212

22 January 1952, Royal Festival Hall

Mussorgsky Night on Bare Mountain	Malko	HMV C 7914/5

23 January 1952, Kingsway Hall

Tchaikovsky 'twill soon be midnight (The Queen of Spades);	Tausky Hammond	HMV DB 21451
Dvorak O Silver Moon (Rusalka)	Tausky Hammond	HMV DB 21451 EMI HQM 1186 EMI RLS 29 00143*
Rossini Sombre forêt (William Tell)	Tausky Hammond	HMV DB 21549

24 January 1952, Abbey Road

Tchaikovsky
Dance of the Maids of
Honour and Pas de
Caractère for
Red Riding Hood
(The Sleeping Beauty)   Malko   HMV C 4258

Mussorgsky   Malko   HMV C 7914
Khovantschina, Prelude Act 4
(orch. Rimsky-Korsakov)

4 February 1952, Abbey Road

Grieg   Fistoulari   Parlophone PMD 1025
Peer Gynt, Suite No 1;
Norwegian Dances

16 February 1952, Abbey Road

Mendelssohn   Kubelik   HMV ALP 1049
Nocturne & Wedding March
(A Midsummer Night's Dream)

16 & 17 February 1952, Abbey Road

Mendelssohn   Kubelik   HMV ALP 1049
A Midsummer Night's Dream,
Overture

17 February 1952, Abbey Road

Smetana   Kubelik   HMV unpublished
The Bartered Bride,
Overture

Mozart   Kubelik   HMV DB 9753
Die Entführung aus dem   HMV ALP 1109
Serail, Overture

Gluck   Kubelik   HMV DB 9753/4
Iphigenia in Aulis,
Overture (rev. Wagner)

Smetana   Kubelik   HMV DB 21464
Dance of the Comedians   HMV ALP 1049
(The Bartered Bride)

18 & 19 February 1952, Kingsway Hall

Brahms   Schwarz   HMV BLP 1028
Double Concerto   De Vito, Baldovino

22 February 1952, Abbey Road

Brahms Academic Festival Overture	Schüchter	Columbia DX 8405/6

23 February 1952, Abbey Road

Beethoven Coriolan, Overture	Schüchter	Columbia DX 1841
Mendelssohn The Hebrides, Overture	Schüchter	Columbia DX 1835

25 February 1952, Abbey Road

Nicolai The Merry Wives of Windsor, Overture	Schüchter	Columbia DX 1827
Suppé Poet and Peasant, Overture	Schüchter	Columbia unpublished

3 March 1952, Abbey Road

Tippett Concerto for Double String Orchestra	Goehr	HMV C 7926/7/8 HMV CLP 1056 EMI MFP 2069

15, 27 & 28 March 1952, Abbey Road

Purcell Dido and Aeneas	Jones Mermaid Singers Flagstad, Schwarzkopf, Mandikian, McNab, Rex, Pollak, Lloyd, Hemsley	HMV ALP 1026 World Records SH 117 EMI 2C 051 03613

(Recording ledgers make it clear that the Philharmonia Orchestra participated in this recording under the name of "The Mermaid Orchestra", but that they did not take part in several live performances recorded previously by EMI in the Mermaid Theatre.)

17 March 1952, Abbey Road

Mozart Madamina (Don Giovanni)	Schüchter Christoff	HMV DA 2080 EMI 1C 147 03336/7M* EMI RLS 735*

18 March 1952, Abbey Road

Verdi O tu Palermo (I Vespri Siciliani) Glinka They guess the truth (A Life for the Tsar)	Schüchter Christoff	EMI RLS 735*

19 March 1952, Abbey Road

Rimsky-Korsakov O vain illusion of glory and grandeur (The Legend of the Invisible City of Kitezh); Tchaikovsky Gremin's aria (Eugene Onegin)	Schüchter Christoff	HMV DB 21626 EMI 1C 147 03336/7M* EMI RLS 735*

8 April 1952, Abbey Road

Parry Jerusalem; Arne Rule Britannia	Sargent Royal Choral Society	HMV C 4213
God Save the Queen (arr. Elgar)	Sargent Royal Choral Society	HMV B 10484

8 April 1952, Kingsway Hall

Donizetti Una furtiva lagrima (L'Elisir d'Amore); Meyerbeer O Paradis (L'Africaine)	Tausky Midgeley	HMV DB 21501
Verdi La donna è mobile; Questa o quella (Rigoletto)	Tausky Midgeley	HMV unpublished

10 & 15 April 1952, Abbey Road

Liszt Piano Concerto No 1	Fistoulari Cherkassky	HMV DB 9763/4 HMV BLP 1013

18 April 1952, Kingsway Hall

Wagner Die Frist ist um (Der fliegende Holländer)	Schüchter Björling	Columbia LX 1562 Columbia 33C 1035

19 April 1952, Kingsway Hall

Wagner Senta's Ballad (Der fliegende Holländer)	Schüchter Covent Garden Chorus Rysanek	Columbia LX 1573 Columbia 33C 1035 EMI 1C 147 29150/1M*

19 & 21 April 1952, Kingsway Hall

Wagner Wie aus der Ferne (Der fliegende Holländer)	Schüchter Rysanek, Björling	Columbia 33C 1035 EMI 1C 147 29150/1M*

21 April 1952, Kingsway Hall

Strauss Das war sehr gut, Mandryka (Arabella)	Schüchter Rysanek	Columbia LX 1559 EMI 1C 147 29150/1M*

22 April 1952, Abbey Road

D'Albert Ich weiss nicht, wer mein Vater war (Tiefland)	Schüchter Rysanek	Columbia LX 1559 EMI 1C 147 29150/1M*
Weber Ozean, du Ungeheuer (Oberon)	Schüchter Rysanek	Columbia unpublished

26 April and 31 July 1952, Kingsway Hall

Handel The Water Music, Suite	Karajan	Columbia LX 8945/6 Columbia 33CX 1033 Toshiba EAC 37001-19*

28 April & 2 May 1952, Kingsway Hall and 28 & 29 May 1955, Abbey Road

Mozart Divertimento No 15 K287	Karajan	Columbia 33CX 1511 Toshiba EAC 37001-19*

1 & 8 May, 25 & 31 July 1952 and 19 June 1953, Kingsway Hall

Tchaikovsky Symphony No 5	Karajan	Columbia 33CX 1133 Toshiba EAC 37020-38*

3 & 5 May 1952, Kingsway Hall

Stravinsky Jeu de cartes	Karajan	French Columbia FCX 163 Toshiba EAC 37020-38* EMI XLP 60003

5 & 7 May and 26, 28 & 31 July 1952, Kingsway Hall

Brahms Symphony No 1	Karajan	Columbia 33CX 1053 Toshiba EAC 37020-38*

4 June 1952, Kingsway Hall

Handel Organ Concerto op 4 no 2	Schüchter Jones	HMV DLP 1037 EMI SMVP 8034

4 & 5 June 1952, Kingsway Hall

Handel Organ Concerto op 4 no 4	Schüchter Jones	HMV DLP 1037 EMI SMVP 8034

6 & 7 June 1952, Kingsway Hall

Handel	Schüchter	HMV DLP 1052
Organ Concerto op 7 no 2	Jones	EMI SMVP 8034

7 June 1952, Kingsway Hall

Handel	Schüchter	HMV DLP 1052
Organ Concerto op 7 no 4	Jones	EMI SMVP 8034

7 June 1952, Abbey Road and 1 September 1952, Kingsway Hall

Vaughan Williams Oboe Concerto	Susskind L.Goossens	World Records SH 243
Bach Oboe Concerto in A	Susskind L.Goossens	Columbia unpublished (recording incomplete)

9, 10, 11, 12, 13, 14, 16, 17, 18, 19, 20, 21 and 23 June 1952, Kingsway Hall

Wagner Tristan und Isolde	Furtwängler Covent Garden Chorus Flagstad, Thebom, Suthaus, Fischer-Dieskau, Greindl, E.Evans, Schock, Davies	HMV ALP 1030/1/2/3/4/5 EMI RLS 684 EMI EX 29 06843 EMI CDS 747 3228 Excerpts: EMI HQM 1235 (Act 3 Prelude on HMV DB 21585)

23 June 1952, Kingsway Hall

Wagner Immolation Scene (Götterdämmerung)	Furtwängler Flagstad	HMV ALP 1016 EMI HQM 1057 EMI 1C 147 01149M EMI 2S 10373*

24 & 25 June 1952, Kingsway Hall

Mahler Lieder eines fahrenden Gesellen	Furtwängler Fischer-Dieskau	HMV ALP 1270 EMI XLP 30044 EMI 100 8981 EMI CDC 747 6572

25 June and 1 September 1952, Kingsway Hall

Borodin Prince Igor, Suite	Susskind	Parlophone PMD 1023

1 July 1952, Kingsway Hall

Mozart Batti batti, o bel Masetto (Don Giovanni)	Pritchard Schwarzkopf	Columbia LB 145 Columbia 33CX 1069 World Records T 583 EMI 2C 051 43222 EMI CDC 747 9502
Mozart Voi che sapete (Le Nozze di Figaro)	Pritchard Schwarzkopf	Columbia 33CX 1069 World Records T 583 EMI 2C 051 43222 EMI CDC 747 9502

1 & 4 July 1952, Kingsway Hall

Mozart Porgi amor (Le Nozze di Figaro)	Pritchard Schwarzkopf	Columbia 33CX 1069 World Records T 583 EMI 2C 051 43222 EMI RLS 763*

2 July 1952, Kingsway Hall

Mozart Vedrai carino (Don Giovanni)	Pritchard Schwarzkopf	Columbia LB 145 Columbia 33CX 1069 World Records T 583 EMI 2C 051 43222 EMI CDC 747 9502
Mozart Non so più (Le Nozze di Figaro)	Pritchard Schwarzkopf	Columbia 33CX 1069 World Records T 583 EMI 2C 051 43222 EMI CDC 747 9502
Mozart Giunse alfin il momento ..Deh vieni, non tardar (Le Nozze di Figaro)	Pritchard Schwarzkopf	Columbia 33CX 1069 World Records T 583 EMI 2C 051 43222 EMI RLS 763* EMI CDC 747 9502

4 July 1952, Kingsway Hall

Mozart Giunse alfin il momento ..Deh vieni, non tardar (Le Nozze di Figaro)	Pritchard Schwarzkopf	Columbia unpublished
Mozart Crudele?...Non mi dir (Don Giovanni)	Pritchard Schwarzkopf	Columbia 33CX 1069 World Records T 583 EMI 2C 051 43222 EMI CDC 747 9502

5 July 1952, Kingsway Hall

Mozart Crudele?...Non mi dir (Don Giovanni); Ach, ich fühl's (Die Zauberflöte)	Pritchard Schwarzkopf	Columbia unpublished

7 July 1952, Kingsway Hall

Berlioz Kletzki Columbia LX 1574
Le carnaval romain, EMI XLP 30014
Overture

7 & 9 July 1952, Kingsway Hall

Schubert Kletzki Columbia 33CX 1157
Rosamunde, Incidental Music EMI XLP 30041
(Overture, Entr'actes 1 & 2,
Ballet Music 1 & 2, Minuet)

8 & 10 July 1952, Kingsway Hall

Tchaikovsky Kletzki Columbia 33CX 1164
Serenade for Strings EMI MFP 2045

10 July 1952, Kingsway Hall

Bizet Kletzki Columbia unpublished
L'Arlésienne, Suite No 1

15 July 1952, Abbey Road

Tchaikovsky Fistoulari Parlophone PMC 1014
Romeo and Juliet

16 & 21 July 1952, Abbey Road

Tchaikovsky Fistoulari Parlophone PMC 1014
Hamlet

29, 30 & 31 July 1952, Kingsway Hall

Sibelius Karajan Columbia LX 1593
Finlandia Columbia 33CX 1047
 Toshiba EAC 37020-38*

31 July and 1 December 1952, Kingsway Hall

Tchaikovsky Karajan Columbia LX 1599 & 1602
The Nutcracker, (excerpts only)
Ballet Suite Columbia 33CX 1033
 Toshiba EAC 37020-38*

1 August 1952, Abbey Road

Verdi Tu sul labbro dei veggenti (Nabucco)	Benintende-Neglia Rossi-Lemeni	EMI 3C 053 01738
Verdi Infelice!...Infin, che un brando vindice (Ernani)	Benintende-Neglia Rossi-Lemeni	HMV ALP 1099 EMI 3C 053 01738
Gounod Vous qui faites l'endormie (Faust)	Benintende-Neglia Rossi-Lemeni	HMV DA 2050 HMV ALP 1074 EMI 3C 053 03249

2 August 1952, Abbey Road

Mozart Madamina (Don Giovanni)	Benintende-Neglia Rossi-Lemeni	HMV ALP 1074 EMI 3C 053 03249
Mozart Deh vieni alla finestra; Finch' han dal vino (Don Giovanni)	Benintende-Neglia Rossi-Lemeni	HMV DB 21573

3 August 1952, Abbey Road

Verdi O tu Palermo (I Vespri Siciliani)	Benintende-Neglia Rossi-Lemeni	HMV ALP 1099 EMI 3C 053 01738
Bellini Vi ravviso (La Sonnambula)	Benintende-Neglia Rossi-Lemeni	HMV DB 9779 HMV ALP 1074 EMI 3C 053 03249
Mozart Non più andrai (Le Nozze di Figaro)	Benintende-Neglia Rossi-Lemeni	HMV DB 21573

4 August 1952, Abbey Road

Glinka They guess the truth (A Life for the Tsar)	Benintende-Neglia Rossi-Lemeni	HMV DB 21559 HMV ALP 1074 EMI 3C 053 03249
Borodin I hate a dreary life (Prince Igor, orch. Rimsky-Korsakov)	Benintende-Neglia Rossi-Lemeni	HMV unpublished

5 August 1952, Abbey Road

Borodin I hate a dreary life (Prince Igor, orch. Rimsky-Korsakov)	W.Braithwaite Rossi-Lemeni	HMV DB 21559 HMV ALP 1074 EMI 3C 053 03249
Bellini Ite sul colle; Guerrieri...Ah, del Tebro (Norma)	W.Braithwaite Covent Garden Chorus Rossi-Lemeni	HMV ALP 1074 EMI 3C 053 03249

6 August 1952, Abbey Road

Gounod Le veau d'or (Faust)	Fistoulari Covent Garden Chorus Rossi-Lemeni	HMV DA 2050 HMV ALP 1074 EMI 3C 053 03249

6 & 7 August 1952, Abbey Road

Verdi Oh, chi piange?.... Del futuro nel buio discerno (Nabucco)	Fistoulari Covent Garden Chorus Rossi-Lemeni	HMV DB 21610 HMV ALP 1099 EMI 3C 053 01738
Verdi Sperate, o figli... D'Egitto là sui lidi (Nabucco)	Fistoulari Covent Garden Chorus Rossi-Lemeni	HMV ALP 1099 EMI 3C 053 01738

7 August 1952, Abbey Road

Verdi Come notte a sol fulgente (Nabucco)	Fistoulari Covent Garden Chorus Rossi-Lemeni	HMV DB 21610 HMV ALP 1099 EMI 3C 053 01738
Verdi Il santo nome di Dio (La Forza del Destino)	Fistoulari Covent Garden Chorus Hammond, Rossi-Lemeni	HMV DB 9779/80 HMV ALP 1099 EMI 3C 053 01738

3, 4 & 5 September 1952, Kingsway Hall

Brahms Piano Concerto No 1	Kubelik Solomon	HMV ALP 1172 EMI 1C 147 03081/2M* EMI SLS 5094*

5 September 1952, Kingsway Hall

Mendelssohn The Fair Melusine, Overture	Kubelik	HMV unpublished
Mozart Die Zauberflöte, Overture	Kubelik	HMV ALP 1109

6 September 1952, Abbey Road

Mozart Don Giovanni; La finta giardiniera, Overtures	Kubelik	HMV ALP 1109
Mozart La Clemenza di Tito, Overture	Kubelik	HMV DB 21556 HMV ALP 1109
Mozart Der Schauspieldirektor, Overture	Kubelik	HMV DB 21548 HMV ALP 1109

7 September 1952, Abbey Road

Mozart Le Nozze di Figaro, Overture	Kubelik	HMV DB 21548 HMV ALP 1109
Mozart Così fan tutte, Overture	Kubelik	HMV DB 21556 HMV ALP 1109

9 September 1952, Kingsway Hall

Mozart Dove sono (Le Nozze di Figaro)	Pritchard Schwarzkopf	Columbia 33CX 1069 World Records T 583 EMI 2C 051 43222 EMI RLS 763*

9, 10 & 16 September 1952, Kingsway Hall

Mozart In quali eccessi..Mi tradi (Don Giovanni)	Pritchard Schwarzkopf	Columbia unpublished

10 & 16 September 1952, Kingsway Hall

Mozart Zeffiretti lusinghieri (Idomeneo)	Pritchard Schwarzkopf	Columbia 33CX 1069 World Records T 583 EMI 2C 051 43222 EMI CDC 747 9502

11 & 13 September 1952 and 8 June 1954, Abbey Road

Britten Young Person's Guide to the Orchestra	Markevitch Pears	Columbia 33CX 1175 EMI XLP 30064

12 September 1952, Abbey Road

Chabrier Fête polonaise (Le roi malgré lui)	Markevitch	Columbia 33CX 1273
Dukas L'apprenti sorcier	Markevitch	Columbia 33CX 1049 EMI XLP 30001

14 & 15 September 1952, Abbey Road

Rossini/Respighi La boutique fantasque	R.Irving	HMV DLP 1032

15 & 16 September 1952, Kingsway Hall

Mozart Exsultate, jubilate	Pritchard Schwarzkopf	Columbia unpublished

15 & 20 September 1952, Abbey Road

Gounod Faust, Ballet Music	R.Irving	HMV C 7932/3

19 September 1952, Abbey Road

Strauss Burleske	Fistoulari Jacquinot	Parlophone PMC 1005
Liszt Totentanz	Fistoulari Jacquinot	Parlophone PMD 1026

22 September 1952, Abbey Road

Dohnanyi Variations on a Nursery Song	Fistoulari Jacquinot	Parlophone PMC 1005
Rimsky-Korsakov Piano Concerto	Fistoulari Jacquinot	Parlophone PMD 1026

29 September 1952, Royal Festival Hall (live recording)

Brahms Tragic Overture; Symphony No 1; Symphony No 2	Toscanini	Toscanini Society ATS 1030-3* Turnabout THS 65027/8/9/30* Fonit Cetra LO 511* Fonit Cetra DOC 52* Hunt Productions CD 524*

1 October 1952, Royal Festival Hall (live recording)

Brahms Haydn Variations (St Antoni Chorale); Symphony No 3; Symphony No 4	Toscanini	Toscanini Society ATS 1030-3* Turnabout THS 65027/8/9/30* Fonit Cetra LO 511* Fonit Cetra DOC 52* Hunt Productions DC 524*

(Toscanini Society and Turnabout issues also include the British National Anthem, which was performed at the beginning of each concert)

3 October 1952, Kingsway Hall

Gruber Silent night, holy night (arr. Salter); Traditional The First Nowell (arr.Salter)	Pritchard Covent Garden Chorus Hampstead Parish Church Choir Schwarzkopf	Columbia LB 131
Traditional O come all ye faithful (arr. Salter)	Pritchard Covent Garden Chorus Hampstead Parish Church Choir Schwarzkopf	Columbia unpublished

9 & 31 October 1952, Royal Festival Hall

Schumann Carnaval, Ballet Music (arr. Jacob)	R.Irving	HMV CLP 1013

13 & 20 October 1952, Abbey Road

Bach Brandenburg Concerto No 5	E.Fischer, cond. & sol.	HMV ALP 1084 Toshiba GR 2213 EMI 29 06261M

22 October 1952, Royal Festival Hall

Rossini La Gazza Ladra, Overture	Cantelli	HMV unpublished

24 & 28 October 1952, Royal Festival Hall

Tchaikovsky Symphony No 6 "Pathétique"	Cantelli	HMV ALP 1042 World Records SHB 52*

25 October 1952, Royal Festival Hall

Ravel Pavane pour une infante défunte	Cantelli	HMV DB 21553 HMV ALP 1207 EMI XLP 30092

3, 4 & 5 November 1952, Kingsway Hall

Beethoven Piano Concerto No 4	Cluytens Solomon	HMV BLP 1036 EMI XLP 30020 EMI SLS 5026*

3, 5 & 6 November 1952, Kingsway Hall

Beethoven Piano Concerto No 2	Cluytens Solomon	HMV BLP 1024 EMI MFP 2067 EMI SLS 5026*

7 November 1952, Kingsway Hall

Chabrier	Cluytens	HMV unpublished
España		

10 November 1952, Abbey Road

Liszt	Fistoulari	Parlophone PMD 1019
Les Préludes; Mazeppa		

12 November 1952, Abbey Road

Rimsky-Korsakov	Fistoulari	Parlophone PMD 1028
The Snow Maiden, Suite;		
Baba Yaga; Skaska		

18 November 1952, Kingsway Hall

Turina	Schüchter	Parlophone PMD 1018
Danzas fantàsticas;		
Granados		
Danzas españoles		

19 & 24 November and 1 December 1952, Kingsway Hall

Tchaikovsky	Karajan	Columbia 33CX 1065
Swan Lake, Ballet Suite		Toshiba EAC 37020-38*

19 November and 31 December 1952, Kingsway Hall

Dohnanyi	Schüchter	Parlophone PMC 1017
Ruralia Hungarica, Suite		EMI MFP 2042

20, 21 & 22 November and 1 December 1952, Kingsway Hall

Beethoven	Karajan	Columbia 33CX 1046
Symphony No 3		World Records SM 143-149*
"Eroica"		EMI SLS 5053*
		Toshiba EAC 37001-19*

23, 28, 29 & 30 November 1952 and 16 July 1953, Abbey Road

Bach	Karajan	Columbia 33CX 1121/2/3
Mass in B minor	Schwarzkopf, Höffgen,	World Records T 854/5/6
(Arias only)	Gedda, Rehfuss	EMI RLS 746
		EMI 29 09743

(Choruses recorded in Vienna on 2, 3, 4, 5 & 7 November 1952, with Vienna Singverein and Orchestra)

24 November and 1 December 1952, Kingsway Hall

Tchaikovsky	Karajan	Columbia 33CX 1065
The Sleeping Beauty,		Toshiba EAC 37020-38*
Ballet Suite		

25 November and 1 December 1952, Kingsway Hall, 6 November 1954 and 28 & 29 May 1955, Abbey Road

Mozart Symphony No 35 "Haffner"	Karajan	Columbia 33CX 1511 Toshiba EAC 37001-19*

3 December 1952, Kingsway Hall

Handel I know that my redeemer liveth (Messiah); Gluck Divinités du Styx (Alceste)	Fistoulari Flagstad	HMV unpublished

4 December 1952, Kingsway Hall

Rimsky-Korsakov Tsar Sultan, Suite	Dobrowen	Columbia 33SX 1010 EMI XLP 30003

5 December 1952, Kingsway Hall

Rimsky-Korsakov Le Coq d'Or, Suite	Dobrowen	Columbia 33SX 1010 EMI XLP 30003

6 December 1952, Kingsway Hall

Saint-Saëns Bacchanale (Samson et Dalila)	Dobrowen	Columbia DX 1898

15 & 16 December 1952 and 30 March 1953, Kingsway Hall

Grieg Holberg Suite	Fistoulari	HMV ALP 1570

16 December 1952, Kingsway Hall

Wolf-Ferrari The Jewels of the Madonna, Intermezzo	Fistoulari	HMV unpublished

17, 18 & 21 December 1952 and 5 January 1953, Abbey Road

Rimsky-Korsakov Scheherazade	Dobrowen	Columbia 33SX 1007

22 & 23 December 1952, Abbey Road

Schumann Piano Concerto	Schwarz Hess	HMV BLP 1039 EMI HQM 1014

23 December 1952, Abbey Road

Weber   Schwarz   HMV C 4208
Euryanthe, Overture   HMV CLP 1022

31 December 1952 and 1 January 1953, Kingsway Hall

Kodaly   Schüchter   Parlophone PMC 1017
Hary Janos, Suite   EMI MFP 2042

1953

2 January 1953, Abbey Road

Bruch Violin Concerto No 1	Susskind Varga	Columbia 33SX 1017

3 January 1953, Abbey Road

Mozart Violin Concerto No 1	Susskind Varga	Columbia 33SX 1017

8 January 1953, Abbey Road

Tchaikovsky Suite No 4 "Mozartiana"	Fistoulari	Parlophone PMC 1028 EMI XLP 30031

9 January 1953, Abbey Road

Tchaikovsky The Slippers, Suite	Fistoulari	Parlophone PMC 1028

13 January 1953, Abbey Road

Mozart Piano Concerto No 14	Cameron Horsley	HMV CLP 1012 EMI XLP 30004

14 January 1953, Abbey Road

Dohnanyi Variations on a Nursery Song	Sargent C.Smith	Columbia 33SX 1018

19 January 1953, Kingsway Hall

Rossini La Scala di Seta, Il Signor Bruschino and La Cenerentola, Overtures	Galliera	Columbia 33SX 1006 EMI MFP 2031

20 January 1953, Kingsway Hall

Rossini L'Italiana in Algeri, Overture	Galliera	Columbia DX 1910 Columbia 33SX 1006 EMI MFP 2031
Rossini William Tell, Overture	Galliera	Columbia 33SX 1006 EMI MFP 2031

21 January 1953, Kingsway Hall

Rossini Semiramide, Overture	Galliera	Columbia 33SX 1006 EMI MFP 2031
Verdi La Traviata, Act 1 Prelude	Galliera	Columbia DX 1890 Columbia 33SX 1009

21 & 22 January 1953, Kingsway Hall

Verdi Aida, Prelude	Galliera	Columbia 33SX 1009

22 January 1953, Kingsway Hall

Verdi La Traviata, Act 3 Prelude	Galliera	Columbia DX 1890 Columbia 33SX 1009
Verdi Nabucco, Overture	Galliera	Columbia DX 1904 Columbia 33SX 1009
Verdi La Forza del Destino, Overture	Galliera	Columbia 33SX 1009

23 January 1953, Kingsway Hall

Verdi I Vespri Siciliani, Overture	Galliera	Columbia 33SX 1009

23 & 24 January 1953, Kingsway Hall

Tchaikovsky Capriccio italien	Galliera	Columbia 33SX 1013 EMI MFP 2087

24 January and 10 & 11 April 1953, Kingsway Hall

Liszt Les Préludes	Galliera	Columbia 33SX 1013 EMI MFP 2087

28 January 1953, Kingsway Hall

Beethoven Coriolan, Overture	Malko	HMV C 4232 HMV DLP 1061
Beethoven Leonore No 3, Overture	Malko	HMV DLP 1061
Hérold Zampa, Overture	Malko	HMV C 4227 HMV DLP 1069 EMI MFP 2034

29 January 1953, Kingsway Hall

Borodin Prince Igor, Suite	Malko	HMV DLP 1092
Beethoven Prometheus, Overture	Malko	HMV DLP 1061

30 & 31 January 1953, Kingsway Hall

Tchaikovsky Symphony No 4	Malko	HMV CLP 1045

31 January 1953, Abbey Road

Handel O thou that tellest glad tidings (Messiah)	Weldon Deller	HMV C 4222 EMI HLM 7234
Handel He was despised (Messiah)	Weldon Deller	HMV B 10682 EMI HLM 7234

2 & 3 February 1953, Abbey Road

Rachmaninov Piano Concerto No 2	Malko Lympany	HMV CLP 1007 EMI MFP 2035

3 February 1953, Abbey Road

Mendelssohn Capriccio brillant	Malko Lympany	HMV C 4241 HMV CLP 1007 EMI MFP 2035 EMI HLM 7179

6 February 1953, Kingsway Hall

Tchaikovsky 1812, Overture	Malko	HMV DLP 1069 EMI MFP 2034

6, 7 & 9 February 1953, Kingsway Hall

Brahms Piano Concerto No 1	Rieger Malcuzynski	Columbia 33CX 1048

7 & 10 February 1953, Abbey Road

Bach Brandenburg Concerto No 2	E.Fischer	HMV ALP 1084 Toshiba GR 2213

17 February 1953, Abbey Road

Mozart Piano Concerto No 21	Menges Lympany	HMV CLP 1038

25 & 27 February and 2 & 6 March 1953, Kingsway Hall

Brahms Violin Concerto	Schwarz De Vito	HMV ALP 1104 EMI ENC 110 EMI MFP 2003

28 February and 1 March 1953, Abbey Road

Chopin Piano Concerto No 2	Kletzki Malcuzynski	Columbia 33CX 1066

2 & 4 March 1953, Abbey Road

Liszt Piano Concerto No 2	Susskind Malcuzynski	Columbia 33CX 1106

7 March 1953, Abbey Road

Liszt Hungarian Rhapsody No 2	Weldon	Columbia DX 1886 Columbia 33SX 1032
Suppé Light Cavalry, Overture	Weldon	Columbia DX 1873 Columbia 33SX 1032

9 March 1953, Abbey Road

Dvorak Carnaval, Overture	Collingwood	Columbia DX 1881
Borodin In the Steppes of Central Asia	Collingwood	Columbia DX 1879
Weinberger Polka and Fugue (Schwanda the Bagpiper)	Collingwood	Columbia DX 1885
Beethoven Turkish March (The Ruins of Athens)	Collingwood	Columbia unpublished

10 March 1953, Abbey Road

Mussorgsky Night on Bare Mountain (orch. Rimsky-Korsakov)	Susskind	Parlophone PMC 1018 EMI MFP 2049
Mussorgsky Prelude, Dance of the Persian Slaves and Entr'acte Act 4 (Khovantschina, orch. Rimsky-Korsakov)	Susskind	Parlophone PMC 1018 EMI MFP 2049

11 March 1953, Abbey Road

Mussorgsky Introduction and Gopak (Sorotchinsky Fair, orch. Liadov)	Susskind	Parlophone PMC 1018 EMI MFP 2049
Mussorgsky Intermezzo in B minor; Scherzo in B flat major (orch. Rimsky-Korsakov)	Susskind	Parlophone PMC 1018 EMI MFP 2049
Mussorgsky The Capture of Kars, Triumphal March (orch. Rimsky-Korsakov)	Susskind	Parlophone PMC 1018 EMI MFP 2049

12 March 1953, Abbey Road

Mussorgsky Introduction, Polonaise and March (Boris Godunov, orch. Rimsky-Korsakov)	Susskind	Parlophone unpublished

13 March 1953, Kingsway Hall

Beethoven Ah perfido !	Susskind Hammond	HMV BLP 1073

14 March 1953, Kingsway Hall

Mozart Misera, dove son ?	Susskind Hammond	HMV ALP 1076
Bruch Ave Maria (Das Feuerkranz)	Susskind Hammond	HMV ALP 1076 EMI HQM 1186

16 March 1953, Kingsway Hall

Weber Und ob die Wolke (Der Freischütz)	Susskind Hammond	HMV ALP 1076

16 & 17 March 1953, Kingsway Hall

Massenet Je suis encore tout étourdie; Adieu, notre petite table (Manon)	Susskind Hammond	HMV ALP 1076

17 March 1953, Kingsway Hall

Massenet L'amour est une vertu rare (Thais)	Susskind Hammond	HMV ALP 1076
Korngold Glück, das mir verblieb (Die tote Stadt)	Susskind Hammond	HMV DB 21625

18 March 1953, Kingsway Hall

Walton Orb and Sceptre, Coronation March	Walton	Columbia LX 1583 Columbia 33C 1016 EMI HQM 1006 EMI SLS 5246*
Walton Crown Imperial, Coronation March	Walton	Columbia 33C 1016 EMI HQM 1006 EMI SLS 5246*

18 & 21 March 1953, Kingsway Hall

Walton Portsmouth Point, Overture	Walton	Columbia 33C 1016 EMI HQM 1006 EMI SLS 5246*
Bach Sheep may safely graze (The Wise Virgins, arr. Walton)	Walton	Columbia 33C 1016

25 March 1953, Kingsway Hall

Cilea Poveri fiori (Adriana Lecouvreur)	Susskind Hammond	HMV ALP 1076 EMI RLS 29 00143*
Boito L'altra notte (Mefistofele)	Susskind Hammond	HMV DB 21625
Saint-Saens O beaux pays (Etienne Marcel)	Susskind Hammond	HMV BLP 1073

30 March and 27 July 1953, Kingsway Hall

Grieg Elegiac Melody No 1 "Heart's Wounds"	Fistoulari	HMV ALP 1570

30 March 1953 and 7 December 1954, Kingsway Hall

Grieg Holberg Suite	Fistoulari	HMV 7ER 5172 HMV ALP 1570

1 April 1953, Kingsway Hall

Berlioz D'amour l'ardente flamme (La Damnation de Faust)	Susskind Hammond	HMV BLP 1073
Verdi O patria mia (Aida)	Susskind Hammond	HMV DB 21580
Bach Violin Concerto in A minor	Boult Menuhin	HMV unpublished

2 April 1953, Kingsway Hall

Mendelssohn Violin Concerto in D minor	Boult Menuhin	HMV ALP 1085
Vivaldi Violin Concerto in C "Il Piacere"	Boult Menuhin	Victor LHMV 16

7 & 8 April 1953, Kingsway Hall

Beethoven Violin Concerto	Furtwängler Menuhin	HMV ALP 1100 Seraphim 60135 EMI CDC 747 1192

8 & 9 April 1953, Kingsway Hall

Beethoven Violin Romance No 2	Furtwängler Menuhin	HMV ALP 1135 EMI HLM 7015 EMI 2C 153 52540-51*

9 April 1953, Kingsway Hall

Beethoven Violin Romance No 1	Furtwängler Menuhin	HMV ALP 1135 EMI HLM 7015 Seraphim 60135 EMI 2C 153 52540-51*

9 April 1953, Abbey Road

Verdi Pace, pace, mio Dio (La Forza del Destino); Bellini Ah non credea mirarti (La Sonnambula)	Sivieri R.Gigli	HMV DB 21619
Donizetti Prendi, per me sei libera (L'Elisir d'Amore); Massenet Adieu, notre petite table (Manon)	Sivieri R.Gigli	HMV unpublished

10 April 1953, Kingsway Hall

Massenet En fermant les yeux (Manon)	Galliera Gedda	Columbia LX 1614 Columbia 33CX 1130
Massenet Pourquoi me réveiller? (Werther)	Galliera Gedda	Columbia 33CX 1130
Bizet Je crois entendre encore (Les Pêcheurs de Perles)	Galliera Gedda	Columbia LX 1614 Columbia 33CX 1130 EMI 1C 137 78233/4/5/6*

10 & 11 April 1953, Kingsway Hall

Gounod Ah, lève-toi soleil (Roméo et Juliette)	Galliera Gedda	Columbia 33CX 1130

11 April 1953, Kingsway Hall

Donizetti Una furtiva lagrima (L'Elisir d'Amore)	Galliera Gedda	Columbia 33CX 1130
Flotow Ach so fromm (Martha)	Galliera Gedda	Columbia LX 1617 Columbia 33CX 1130
Cilea E la solita storia (L'Arlesiana)	Galliera Gedda	Columbia 33CX 1130 EMI SLS 5250* EMI 1C 137 78233/4/5/6*

11, 13, 14 & 15 April 1953, Kingsway Hall

Rossini arr. Respighi La Boutique Fantasque	Galliera	Columbia 33S 1009

12 April 1953, Abbey Road

Schubert Symphony No 8 "Unfinished"	Schwarz	HMV CLP 1022

13 April 1953, Kingsway Hall

Auber Du pauvre seul ami fidèle (La Muette de Portici)	Galliera Gedda	Columbia 33CX 1130 EMI SLS 5250* EMI 1C 137 78233/4/5/6*
Donizetti Spirto gentil (La Favorita)	Galliera Gedda	Columbia 33CX 1130

13 & 14 April 1953, Kingsway Hall

Tchaikovsky Lensky's aria (Eugene Onegin)	Galliera Gedda	Columbia 33CX 1130

14 April 1953, Kingsway Hall

Ponchielli Cielo e mar (La Gioconda)	Galliera Gedda	Columbia 33CX 1130
Verdi Parmi veder le lagrime (Rigoletto)	Galliera Gedda	Columbia LX 1617 Columbia 33CX 1130

16, 17, 18 & 21 April 1953, Kingsway Hall

Lehar The Merry Widow	Ackermann BBC Chorus Schwarzkopf, Loose, Gedda, Kunz, Niessner, Kraus, Schmidinger	Columbia 33CX 1051/2 EMI SXDW 3045 Excerpts: Columbia LX 1597 Columbia 33CX 1712

17 April 1953, Kingsway Hall

Lortzing Auch ich war ein Jüngling (Der Waffenschmied); O Sancta Justitia (Zar und Zimmermann)	Ackermann Kunz	German Columbia C 70407 EMI 1C 147 03580/1M*

17, 19 & 20 April and 28 June 1953, Kingsway Hall

Lehar The Land of Smiles	Ackermann BBC Chorus Schwarzkopf, Loose, Gedda, Kunz, Kraus, Kent, Mattoni	Columbia 33CX 1114/5 EMI SXDW 3044 Excerpts: Columbia 33CX 1712

21 April 1953, Kingsway Hall

Lortzing Fünftausend Thaler (Der Wildschütz)	Ackermann Kunz	Columbia LB 143 German Columbia C 70407 EMI 1C 147 03580/1M*

25 April 1953, Abbey Road

Liszt Hungarian Rhapsodies Nos 3 and 6	Schwarz	HMV CLP 1033 EMI MFP 2044

26 April 1953, Abbey Road

Liszt Hungarian Rhapsody No 1	Schwarz	HMV C 4259 HMV CLP 1033 EMI MFP 2044

27, 28 & 30 April and 2 May 1953, Abbey Road

Dvorak Slavonic Dances (complete)	Malko	HMV CLP 1019/20

28 April and 1 May 1953, Abbey Road

Grieg Lyric Suite	Malko	HMV CLP 1020

1 May 1953, Abbey Road

Liszt Hungarian Rhapsody No 2	Schwarz	HMV C 4259 HMV CLP 1033 EMI MFP 2044
Weber Oberon, Overture	Malko	HMV C 4240 HMV DLP 1069
Haydn Serenade; Boccherini Minuet	Malko	HMV 7EP 7067
Glazunov Polka (Les Vendredis)	Malko	HMV DLP 1092

2 May 1953, Abbey Road

Liadov Eight Russian Folksongs	Malko	HMV DLP 1092
Gounod Judex (Mors et Vita); Delibes Pas de Naila (La Source)	Malko	HMV C 4261
Mendelssohn Bees' Wedding & Spring Song (Songs without Words)	Malko	HMV C 4246

4 & 5 May 1953, Kingsway Hall

Tchaikovsky Swan Lake, excerpts	R.Irving	HMV CLP 1018

13 May 1953, Abbey Road

Handel Alma del gran Pompeo (Giulio Cesare)	Weldon Deller	HMV C 4222 EMI HLM 7234
Handel Mad Scene (Orlando)	Weldon Deller	HMV unpublished

15 & 21 May 1953, Kingsway Hall

Schumann Symphony No 4	Cantelli	HMV BLP 1044 EMI ENC 122 EMI XLP 30030 World Records SH 315 EMI 29 05761

21 & 22 May 1953, Kingsway Hall

Brahms Symphony No 1	Cantelli	HMV ALP 1152 EMI ENC 116 EMI XLP 30023 World Records SH 314

11 & 12 June 1953, Kingsway Hall

Arnold Homage to the Queen, Suite	R.Irving	HMV CLP 1011

12 June 1953, Kingsway Hall

Arnold English Dances	R.Irving	HMV CLP 1172

15 & 16 June 1953, Kingsway Hall

Wagner Tannhäuser, Overture and Venusberg Music (Paris version)	Kletzki	Columbia 33CX 1129

16 & 23 June 1953, Kingsway Hall

Ippolitov-Ivanov Caucasian Sketches	Kletzki	Columbia 33CX 1167

19 & 23 June 1953, Kingsway Hall

Wagner Tristan und Isolde, Prelude and Liebestod	Kletzki	Columbia 33CX 1129

20 June and 15 July 1953, Kingsway Hall

Beethoven Coriolan, Overture	Karajan	Columbia 33CX 1227 EMI SLS 5053* Toshiba EAC 37001-19*
Beethoven Egmont, Overture	Karajan	Columbia 33CX 1136 EMI SLS 5053* Toshiba EAC 37001-19*

23 June 1953, Kingsway Hall

Ravel Bolero	Kletzki	Columbia 33CX 1164 EMI MFP 2045

24 June 1953, Kingsway Hall

Smetana The Bartered Bride, Overture	Kletzki	Columbia LX 1594 Columbia 33CX 1164 EMI MFP 2045
Barber Adagio for Strings	Kletzki	Columbia LX 1595

27, 29 & 30 June and 1, 2 & 16 July 1953, Kingsway Hall

Humperdinck Hansel and Gretel	Karajan Loughton High School Choir Bancroft's School Choir Schwarzkopf, Grümmer, Ilosvay, Schürhoff, Felbermayer, Metternich	Columbia 33CX 1096/7 World Records OC 187/8 EMI SLS 5145 Excerpts: Columbia 33CX 1819 World Records OH 189

30 June and 8 & 9 October 1953, Kingsway Hall

Elgar Enigma Variations	Weldon	Columbia 33SX 1024 EMI MFP 2093

2 & 3 July 1953, Kingsway Hall

Strauss Tod und Verklärung	Karajan	EMI 2M 055 43228 EMI RLS 7715*

4, 8, 10 & 16 July 1953, Kingsway Hall

Tchaikovsky Symphony No 4	Karajan	Columbia 33CX 1139 Toshiba EAC 37020-38*

6 & 7 July 1953, Kingsway Hall

Sibelius Symphony No 4	Karajan	Columbia 33CX 1125 Toshiba EAC 37020-38*

9 & 10 July 1953, Kingsway Hall

Beethoven Symphony No 6 "Pastoral"	Karajan	Columbia 33CX 1124 World Records SM 143-149* EMI SLS 5053* Toshiba EAC 37001-19*

13 & 14 July 1953, Kingsway Hall

Beethoven Leonore No 3, Overture	Karajan	Columbia 33CX 1136 EMI SLS 5053* Toshiba EAC 37001-19*

14 & 15 July 1953, Kingsway Hall

Sibelius Tapiola	Karajan	Columbia 33CX 1125 Toshiba EAC 37020-38*

16 & 17 July 1953, Kingsway Hall

Ravel Rapsodie espagnole	Karajan	Columbia 33CX 1099 Toshiba EAC 37020-38*

17 July 1953, Kingsway Hall

Chabrier España	Karajan	Columbia 33CX 1335 Toshiba EAC 37020-38*

20, 21 & 22 July 1953, Kingsway Hall

Debussy La Mer	Karajan	Columbia 33CX 1099 Toshiba EAC 37020-38*

21 July 1953, Kingsway Hall

Waldteufel The Skaters' Waltz	Karajan	Columbia 33CX 1335 Toshiba EAC 37020-38*
Sousa The Stars and Stripes Forever & El Capitan, Marches	Karajan	Columbia unpublished

17, 18 & 19 August 1953, Kingsway Hall

Berg Violin Concerto	Kletzki Gertler	Columbia 33C 1030

22 & 23 August 1953, Abbey Road

Mozart Piano Concerto No 25	Rosbaud Gieseking	Columbia 33CX 1235

23 August 1953, Abbey Road

Mozart Piano Concerto No 20	Rosbaud Gieseking	Columbia 33CX 1235

24 & 25 August 1953, Kingsway Hall

Schumann Piano Concerto	Karajan Gieseking	Columbia 33C 1033 EMI 1C 047 01401M EMI 3C 153 52425-31M* Toshiba EAC 37001-19*

25 August 1953, Kingsway Hall

Mozart Symphony No 41 "Jupiter"	Karajan	Columbia unpublished (recording probably incomplete)

26 August 1953, Kingsway Hall

Mozart Piano Concerto No 24	Karajan Gieseking	Columbia 33CX 1526 EMI 3C 153 52425-31M* Toshiba EAC 37001-19*

26, 27 & 28 August 1953, Kingsway Hall

Beethoven Symphony No 5	Karajan	Columbia unpublished

7 & 8 September 1953, Kingsway Hall

Mozart Piano Concerto No 15	Ackermann Solomon	HMV ALP 1194 EMI RLS 726*

8 & 9 September 1953, Abbey Road

Schumann Piano Concerto	Ackermann Moiseiwitsch	HMV CLP 1008

9, 10 & 21 September 1953, Abbey Road

Grieg Piano Concerto	Ackermann Moiseiwitsch	HMV CLP 1008

10 September 1953, Abbey Road

Smetana The Moldau (Má Vlast)	Ackermann	Columbia 33C 1042

12 & 13 September 1953, Abbey Road

Bartok Violin Concerto No 2	Furtwängler Menuhin	HMV ALP 1121 EMI 2C 051 01322

14 September 1953, Kingsway Hall

Holst Weldon Columbia 33S 1100
St Paul's Suite EMI XLP 30049

14 & 15 September 1953, Kingsway Hall

Bach Bernard HMV BLP 1046
Double Violin Concerto Menuhin, De Vito Toshiba EAC 60230-39*
in D minor

25 September 1953, Watford Town Hall

Strauss Ackermann Columbia 33CX 1107
Vier letzte Lieder Schwarzkopf EMI RLS 751*
  EMI 10 38651

26 September 1953, Watford Town Hall

Strauss Ackermann Columbia 33CX 1107
Capriccio, Closing Scene Schwarzkopf EMI RLS 751*
  EMI 10 38651

1 October 1953, Kingsway Hall

Verdi Galliera EMI 29 10753*
Madamigella Valery?... Schwarzkopf, Panerai
Pura siccome un angelo...
Dite alle giovine
(La Traviata)

Leoncavallo Galliera Columbia 33C 1052
Prologue (I Pagliacci); Panerai
Giordano
Nemico della patria
(Andrea Chenier)

2 October 1953, Kingsway Hall

Verdi Galliera Columbia 33CX 1305
Pari siamo; Figlia! Mio Dobbs, Panerai
padre; Chi è mai...
Lassù in cielo
(Rigoletto)

Verdi Galliera Columbia 33CX 1305
Caro nome (Rigoletto); Dobbs
Bellini
Ah! non credea mirarti
(La Sonnambula)

Verdi Galliera Columbia 33C 1052
Il balen del suo sorriso Panerai
(Il Trovatore)

3 October 1953, Kingsway Hall

Rimsky-Korsakov Hymn to the sun (Le Coq d'Or)	Galliera Dobbs	Columbia 33CX 1305
Verdi Di Provenza il mar (La Traviata); Rossini Largo al factotum (Il Barbiere di Siviglia)	Galliera Panerai	Columbia 33C 1052

3 & 6 October 1953, Kingsway Hall

Delibes Sous le ciel étoilé; Les fleurs me paraissent plus belles; Pourquoi dans les grands bois (Lakmé)	Galliera Dobbs	Columbia 33CX 1305

5 October 1953, Kingsway Hall

Verdi Ave Maria (Otello)	Galliera Schwarzkopf	Columbia unpublished

6 October 1953, Kingsway Hall

Massenet Obéissons...Profitons de la jeunesse (Manon)	Galliera Dobbs	Columbia 33CX 1305
Verdi Credo in un dio crudel; Era la notte (Otello)	Galliera Panerai	Columbia 33C 1052

7 & 8 October 1953, Kingsway Hall

Dvorak Symphony No 9 "From the New World"	Galliera	Columbia 33SX 1025

9 October 1953, Kingsway Hall

Elgar Pomp and Circumstance, March No 1	Weldon	Columbia 33SX 1024 EMI MFP 2093

9 October and 6 November 1953, Kingsway Hall

Elgar Cockaigne, Overture	Weldon	Columbia 33SX 1024 EMI MFP 2093

12 & 13 October 1953, Abbey Road

Tchaikovsky Piano Concerto No 1	Galliera Anda	Columbia 33CX 1156

13, 14 & 15 October 1953, Abbey Road

Rachmaninov Piano Concerto No 2	Galliera Anda	Columbia 33CX 1143

15 October 1953, Abbey Road

Wolf-Ferrari Il segreto di Susanna, Overture	Galliera	Columbia unpublished

6 November 1953, Kingsway Hall

Elgar Pomp and Circumstance, March No 4	Weldon	Columbia 33SX 1024 EMI MFP 2093

10 November 1953, Abbey Road and 23 November 1953, Kingsway Hall

Britten Variations on a theme of Frank Bridge	Karajan	Columbia 33CX 1159 Toshiba EAC 37020-38* EMI XLP 60002

11 November 1953, Abbey Road and 23 November 1953, Kingsway Hall

Vaughan Williams Fantasia on a theme by Thomas Tallis	Karajan	Columbia 33CX 1159 Toshiba EAC 37020-38* EMI XLP 60002

12, 13 & 23 November 1953, Kingsway Hall

Mozart Horn Concertos Nos 1, 2, 3 and 4	Karajan Brain	Columbia 33CX 1140 EMI ASD 1140 Toshiba EAC 37001-19* EMI 2C 051 00414

12, 13 & 23 November 1953 and 7 July 1955, Kingsway Hall

Beethoven Symphony No 2	Karajan	Columbia 33CX 1227 World Records SM 143-149* EMI SLS 5053* Toshiba EAC 37001-19*

13 & 16 November 1953, Kingsway Hall

Beethoven Symphony No 4	Karajan	Columbia 33CX 1278 World Records SM 143-149* EMI SLS 5053* Toshiba EAC 37001-19*

13 November 1953 and 19 & 20 May 1955, Kingsway Hall

Beethoven Symphony No 8	Karajan	Mono version Columbia 33CX 1391/2* Toshiba EAC 37001-19* Stereo version World Records SM 143-149* EMI SLS 5053* Toshiba EAC 37001-19*

17 & 18 November 1953, Abbey Road

Mozart Sinfonia Concertante for Winds in E flat	Karajan Sutcliffe, James, Walton, Brain	Columbia 33CX 1178 Toshiba EAC 37001-19* EMI XLP 60004 EMI RLS 7715*

18 November 1953, Abbey Road

Mozart Serenade No 13 "Eine kleine Nachtmusik"	Karajan	Columbia 33CX 1178 Toshiba EAC 37001-19*

21 November 1953, Kingsway Hall

Beethoven Symphony No 1	Karajan	Columbia 33CX 1136 World Records SM 143-149* EMI SLS 5053* Toshiba EAC 37001-19*

25 November 1953, Abbey Road

Berlioz Le carnaval romain, Overture	Schüchter	Parlophone PMC 1022

26 November 1953, Abbey Road

Kabalevsky Colas Breugnon, Suite	Schüchter	Parlophone PMC 1007
Berlioz Le corsair, Overture	Schüchter	Parlophone PMC 1022
Berlioz Hungarian March, Dance of the Sylphs and Dance of the Will-o-the-Wisps (La Damnation de Faust)	Schüchter	Parlophone PMC 1022

27 November 1953, Abbey Road

Prokofiev
The Gamblers, Suite
Schüchter
Parlophone PMC 1007

Berlioz
Trojan March (Les Troyens)
Schüchter
Parlophone PMC 1022

2 & 3 December 1953, Abbey Road

Khachaturian
Violin Concerto
E.Goossens
I.Oistrakh
Columbia 33CX 1141
EMI MFP 2050

1954

1954 was a golden year for the Philharmonia. Walter Legge had succeeded in getting the Lucerne Festival organisers to engage the orchestra for all the symphony concerts that summer. The orchestra also played at Aix-en-Provence and Edinburgh, and in October they toured Europe again with Karajan.

The Philharmonia was so busy that it had to turn down an opportunity to record "Die Walküre" with Furtwängler, who recorded it instead with the Vienna Philharmonic in October. Eight weeks later Furtwängler was dead.

The Philharmonia did make their first recordings with Otto Klemperer in October 1954. An earlier contract had been signed between Klemperer and EMI in May 1952, but was cancelled in July 1953 because Klemperer was a US citizen and his long absences from the USA caused the American Federation of Musicians to forbid him to record abroad. In 1954 he gave up his American citizenship and made a new contract with EMI. The recordings he made that autumn marked the beginning of an eighteen-year association which was soon to replace that of Karajan; the latter was, of course, to succeed Furtwängler in Berlin.

International Festival
of Music

August 8th - 29th

SYMPHONY CONCERTS
played by the
PHILHARMONIA ORCHESTRA

conducted by

ANDRE CLUYTENS	Dr. WILHELM FURTWANGLER
Dr. EDWIN FISCHER	HERBERT VON KARAJAN
FERENC FRICSAY	RAFAEL KUBELIK

Lucerne, the ideal holiday resort in Spring, Summer and Autumn offers you:

Excellent hotels for every budget, greatest variety of scenic excursions, favourite shops, cultural and sporting events of world fame

For information please apply to the Official Tourist Office
SCHWEIZERHOLQUAI 4, LUCERNE, SWITZERLAND

ROYAL FESTIVAL HALL
General Manager: T. E. Bean

PHILHARMONIA CONCERT SOCIETY
Artistic Director:
WALTER LEGGE

presents

PHILHARMONIA
ORCHESTRA
Leader: MANOUG PARIKIAN

HERBERT von KARAJAN

EDWIN FISCHER

PROGRAMME

BERLIOZ:	Symphonie Fantastique, Op. 14

INTERVAL

MOZART:	Piano Concerto No. 22 in E flat, K.482
MOUSSORGSKY-RAVEL:	"Tableaux d'une Exposition"

*Friday, October 15th, 1954
at 8 p.m.*

Management: IBBS & TILLETT LTD., 124 WIGMORE STREET, W.1

Philharmonia concerts were sometimes able to present artists in combinations not possible on disc because of the division of loyalties between Columbia and HMV

1954

6 January 1954, Kingsway Hall

Mozart	Pritchard	HMV ALP 1281
Violin Concerto No 5	Menuhin	

8 January 1954, Abbey Road

Saint-Saens	Markevitch	Columbia 33CX 1175
Le carnaval des animaux	Anda, Siki	

12 January 1954, Abbey Road

Busoni	Markevitch	Columbia 33CX 1273
Tanzwalzer		

12 January and 2 & 3 March 1954, Abbey Road

Liszt	Markevitch	Columbia 33CX 1273
Mephisto Waltz		

13 & 14 January 1954, Abbey Road

Bartok	Markevitch	HMV ALP 1588
Dance Suite		

26 January 1954, Kingsway Hall

Bliss	Bliss	Columbia 33CX 1205
Miracle in the Gorbals		EMI HQM 1009

27 & 28 January 1954, Kingsway Hall

Bliss	Bliss	Columbia 33CX 1205
Music for Strings		EMI HQM 1009

29 January and 12 February 1954, Kingsway Hall

Tchaikovsky	Kletzki	Columbia 33CX 1189
Manfred Symphony		EMI XLP 30015

3 February 1954, Kingsway Hall

Borodin	Kletzki	Columbia 33CX 1167
Symphony No 2		

4 & 5 February 1954, Kingsway Hall

Mendelssohn A Midsummer Night's Dream, Incidental Music	Kletzki BBC Chorus Cole, McLoughlin	Columbia 33CX 1174 EMI XLP 30025 Scherzo & Intermezzo: Columbia LX 1615 Nocturne: EMI RLS 7701*

15, 16 & 17 February 1953, Kingsway Hall

Brahms Violin Concerto	Kletzki Martzy	Columbia 33CX 1165

27 February 1954, Abbey Road

Haydn Gloria, Qui tollis & Quoniam (Nelson Mass)	Dykes Bower St Paul's Cathedral Choir	Columbia 33CX 1237
Mozart Ave verum corpus	Dykes Bower St Paul's Cathedral Choir	Columbia 33CX 1193

2 March 1954, Abbey Road

Sibelius Valse triste; Mozart German Dance No 3 (Three German Dances K605); Stravinsky Waltz (Suite No 2)	Markevitch	Columbia 33CX 1273

3 March 1954, Abbey Road

Weber Invitation to the Dance (orch. Berlioz)	Markevitch	Columbia 33CX 1197 EMI XLP 30007

3 March and 15 May 1954, Abbey Road

Chopin Mazurka (Les Sylphides, orch. Douglas)	Markevitch	Columbia 33CX 1198

3 & 15 March and 15 May 1954, Abbey Road

Berlioz Dance of the Sylphs (La Damnation de Faust); Saint-Saens Danse macabre	Markevitch	Columbia 33CX 1273

5 March 1954, Kingsway Hall

Wagner
Als du in kühnem Sange; Blick ich umher; O du mein holder Abendstern (Tannhäuser)   Schüchter / Fischer-Dieskau   HMV 7ER 5033

17 March 1954, Kingsway Hall

Mendelssohn
Ruy Blas;
Son and Stranger,
Overtures   Kletzki   Columbia SEL 1525

Mendelssohn
The Hebrides, Overture   Kletzki   Columbia unpublished

22 March 1954, Kingsway Hall

Mozart
Piano Concerto No 12   Schwarz / Matthews   Columbia 33SX 1031

22 & 23 March 1954, Kingsway Hall

Mozart
Piano Concerto No 14   Schwarz / Matthews   Columbia 33SX 1031

23 March and 1 April 1954, Kingsway Hall

Mozart
Piano Concerto No 23   Schwarz / Matthews   Columbia 33S 1039

1 April 1954, Kingsway Hall

Mozart
Piano Concerto No 27   Schwarz / Matthews   Columbia 33S 1032

23 April 1954, Abbey Road

Ravel
Daphnis et Chloe,
Suite No 2   Markevitch   Columbia 33CX 1197

24 April 1954, Abbey Road

Stravinsky
Russian Dance (Petrushka)   Markevitch   Columbia unpublished

25 & 27 April 1954, Abbey Road

Stravinsky
Petrushka: Nos 2, 3 & 8   Markevitch   Columbia 33CX 1199

27 & 29 April 1954, Abbey Road

Prokofiev   Markevitch   Columbia 33CX 1199
Le pas d'acier

27 & 29 April 1954, Kingsway Hall

Delibes   R.Irving   HMV CLP 1058
Sylvia, Ballet

28 April 1954, Abbey Road

Mozart   Malko   HMV CLP 1038
Piano Concerto No 12   Lympany

30 April 1954, Abbey Road

Rachmaninov   Malko   HMV CLP 1037
Piano Concerto No 1   Lympany

3 & 4 May 1954, Abbey Road

Mozart   E.Fischer, cond. & sol.   HMV BLP 1066
Piano Concerto No 20

4, 9 & 14 May 1954, Abbey Road

Beethoven   E.Fischer, cond. & sol.   HMV BLP 1067
Piano Concerto No 4   EMI RLS 29 00013*
                                                   EMI 29 09913*
(recording details suggest that the orchestra leader at these sessions, Manoug Parikian, directed the orchestra)

7 & 14 May 1954, Abbey Road

Beethoven   E.Fischer, cond. & sol.   HMV BLP 1063
Piano Concerto No 3   EMI RLS 29 00013*
(recording details suggest that the orchestra leader at these sessions, Manoug Parikian, directed the orchestra)

11 May 1954, Kingsway Hall

Bliss   Bliss   Columbia DX 1912
Welcome the Queen   EMI HLM 7093

12 May 1954, Abbey Road

Satie   Markevitch   Columbia 33CX 1197
Parade, Ballet Suite

13 May 1954, Abbey Road

Scarlatti Markevitch Columbia 33CX 1198
The Good-Humoured Ladies,
Ballet Suite
(arr. Tommasini)

13 & 15 May and 8 June 1954, Abbey Road

Tchaikovsky Markevitch Columbia 33CX 1198
Swan Lake, excerpts

18, 19, 20, 21, 26, 27, 28 & 31 May and 25 September 1954, Kingsway Hall

Johann Strauss Ackermann Columbia 33CX 1329/30
Der Zigeunerbaron Chorus EMI SXDW 3046
  Schwarzkopf, Köth, Seidl,
  Sinclair, Gedda,
  Burgsthaler-Schuster,
  Kunz, Prey, Ferenz,
  Schmiedinger, Stepanek,
  Paulik

21, 22, 26, 28 & 31 May 1954, Kingsway Hall

Johann Strauss Ackermann Columbia 33CX 1186/7
Wiener Blut Chorus EMI SXDW 3042
  Schwarzkopf, Köth, Loose,
  Norgerd, Gedda, Dönch,
  Kunz, Pernerstorfer,
  Stepanek

25, 26, 27, 28 & 31 May and 25 September 1954, Kingsway Hall

Johann Strauss Ackermann Columbia 33CX 1224/5
Eine Nacht in Venedig Chorus EMI SXDW 3043
  Schwarzkopf, Loose, Seidl,
  H.Ludwig, Norbert, Gedda,
  Klein, Kunz, Dönch,
  Stepanek, Diffring

1 June 1954, Kingsway Hall

Falla Cantelli HMV ALP 1207
The Three-Cornered Hat,
Ballet Suite

Dukas Cantelli HMV ALP 1207
L'apprenti sorcier   EMI XLP 30092

2 June 1954, Abbey Road

Dohnanyi R.Irving HMV CLP 1043
Suite for Orchestra

3 June 1954, Abbey Road

Tchaikovsky Hamlet, Fantasy Overture	R.Irving	HMV CLP 1043 EMI XLP 30036
Ravel Daphnis et Chloe, excerpts; Debussy Prélude à l'après-midi d'un faune	Markevitch	Columbia 33CX 1197

4 & 8 June 1954, Kingsway Hall

Debussy Le Martyre de Saint-Sébastien	Cantelli	HMV ALP 1228 EMI 2C 027 03758

8 June 1954, Abbey Road

Liadov Kikimora	Markevitch	Columbia 33CX 1199

8 & 9 June 1954, Kingsway Hall

Debussy Prélude à l'après-midi d'un faune	Cantelli	HMV ALP 1207 EMI XLP 30092

9, 10 & 11 June 1954, Kingsway Hall

Mozart Violin Concerto No 3	Sawallisch Martzy	Columbia unpublished

10 June 1954, Kingsway Hall

Bliss Song of Welcome	Bliss BBC Chorus Sutherland, J.Cameron	Columbia unpublished

10 & 11 June 1954, Kingsway Hall

Mendelssohn Violin Concerto	Sawallisch Martzy	Columbia unpublished

12, 14 & 15 June 1954, Kingsway Hall

Dvorak Symphony No 8	Sawallisch	Columbia 33SX 1034

15 June 1954, Kingsway Hall

Dvorak Scherzo Capriccioso	Sawallisch	Columbia 33SX 1034

24 June 1954, Abbey Road

Saint-Saens
Piano Concerto No 4
Tzipine
Johannesen
HMV CLP 1149

24 June 1954 and 14 June 1956, Abbey Road

Milhaud
Le Carnaval d'Aix
Tzipine
Johannesen
HMV CLP 1149

30 June and 1, 2, 5, 6 & 7 July 1954, Kingsway Hall

Strauss
Ariadne auf Naxos
Karajan
Schwarzkopf, Seefried,
Streich, Otto, Hoffman,
Felbermayer, Schock,
Neugebauer, Dönch, Unger,
Cuenod, Strauss, Kraus,
Prey, Ollendorff, Krebs
Columbia 33CX 1292/3/4
EMI RLS 760

7, 8, 9 & 21 July 1954, Kingsway Hall

Berlioz
Symphonie Fantastique
Karajan
Columbia 33CX 1206
World Records TP 625
Toshiba EAC 37001-19*
EMI RLS 7715*

13 July 1954 Kingsway Hall, 14, 15, 16, 17, 19, 20 & 21 July and 6 November 1954, Abbey Road

Mozart
Così fan tutte
Karajan
Chorus
Schwarzkopf, Merriman,
Otto, Simoneau,
Panerai, Bruscantini
Columbia 33CX 1262/3/4
World Records SOC 195/6/7
EMI 1C 147 01748/49/50M
EMI 1C 197 54200-8M*
EMI RLS 7709
Excerpts:
World Records OH 198

22 July 1954, Kingsway Hall

Bizet
Carmen, Act 4 Entr'acte;
Mascagni
L'Amico Fritz, Intermezzo;
Granados
Goyescas, Intermezzo;
Leoncavallo
I Pagliacci, Intermezzo
Karajan
Columbia 33CX 1265
Toshiba EAC 37020-38*

22 & 24 July 1954, Kingsway Hall

Puccini
Manon Lescaut, Intermezzo
Karajan
Columbia 33CX 1265
Toshiba EAC 37020-38*

23 July 1954, Kingsway Hall

Weinberger Polka (Schwanda the Bagpiper)	Karajan	Columbia 33CX 1335 Toshiba EAC 37020-38*
Massenet Méditation (Thais)	Karajan Parikian	Columbia 33CX 1265 Toshiba EAC 37020-38*
Verdi La Traviata, Act 3 Prelude; Offenbach Barcarolle (Les Contes d'Hoffmann); Mussorgsky Khovantschina, Act 4 Entr'acte (orch. Rimsky-Korsakov)	Karajan	Columbia 33CX 1265 Toshiba EAC 37020-38*

24 July 1954, Kingsway Hall

Mascagni Cavalleria Rusticana, Intermezzo; Kodaly Hary Janos, Intermezzo	Karajan	Columbia 33CX 1265 Toshiba EAC 37020-38*
Bizet Carmen, Acts 2 and 3 Entr'actes	Karajan	Columbia unpublished
Beethoven Consecration of the House, Overture	Karajan	Columbia unpublished (recording incomplete)

22 August 1954, Kunsthaus Lucerne (live recording)

Beethoven Symphony No 9 "Choral"	Furtwängler Lucerne Festival Chorus Schwarzkopf, Cavelti, Haefliger, Edelmann	Fonit Cetra LO 530* Discocorp RR 390 <u>Seven Seas K35Y 41</u>

13 & 14 September 1954, Kingsway Hall

Debussy La Mer	Cantelli	HMV ALP 1228 EMI 2C 027 03758

15 September 1954, Watford Town Hall

Puccini	Serafin	Columbia 33CX 1204
Si mi chiamano Mimi	Callas	EMI ALP 3799
(La Bohème);		EMI 2C 165 54178-88*
O mio babbino caro		EMI CDC 747 9662
(Gianni Schicchi);		
Signore, ascolta; Tu che		
di gel sei cinta (Turandot);		
In quelle trine morbide;		
Sola perduta abandonnata		
(Manon Lescaut)		

15 & 18 September 1954, Watford Town Hall

Puccini	Serafin	Columbia 33CX 1204
In questa reggia	Callas	EMI ALP 3799
(Turandot)		EMI 2C 165 54178-88*
		EMI CDC 747 9662

15 & 21 September 1954, Watford Town Hall

Puccini	Serafin	Columbia 33CX 1204
Donde lieta uscì	Callas	EMI ALP 3799
(La Bohème)		EMI 2C 165 54178-88*
		EMI CDC 747 9662

16 September 1954, Watford Town Hall

Puccini	Serafin	Columbia 33CX 1204
Un bel dì	Callas	EMI ALP 3799
(Madama Butterfly)		EMI 2C 165 54178-88*
		EMI CDC 747 9662

16 & 17 September 1954, Watford Town Hall

Puccini	Serafin	Columbia 33CX 1204
Con onor muore	Callas	EMI ALP 3799
(Madama Butterfly)		EMI 2C 165 54178-88*
		EMI CDC 747 9662

16 & 20 September 1954, Watford Town Hall

Puccini	Serafin	Columbia 33CX 1204
Senza mamma	Callas	EMI ALP 3799
(Suor Angelica)		EMI 2C 165 54178-88*
		EMI CDC 747 9662

17 September 1954, Watford Town Hall

Boito	Serafin	Columbia 33CX 1231
L'altra notte (Mefistofele)	Callas	EMI ALP 3824
		EMI 2C 165 54178-88*
		EMI CDC 747 2822

18 & 20 September 1954, Watford Town Hall

Giordano	Serafin	Columbia 33CX 1231
La mamma morta	Callas	EMI ALP 3824
(Andrea Chenier)		EMI 2C 165 54178-88*
		EMI CDC 747 2822

20 September 1954, Watford Town Hall

Cilea Io sono l'umile ancella; Poveri fiori (Adriana Lecouvreur); Catalani Ebben? Ne andrò lontana (La Wally)	Serafin Callas	Columbia 33CX 1231 EMI ALP 3824 EMI 2C 165 54178-88* EMI CDC 747 2822
Beethoven Abscheulicher (Fidelio)	Karajan Schwarzkopf	Columbia 33CX 1266 Toshiba EAC 37001-19* EMI RLS 7715*
Beethoven Ah perfido !	Karajan Schwarzkopf	Columbia 33CX 1278 Toshiba EAC 37001-19* EMI RLS 7715*

21 September 1954, Watford Town Hall

Rossini Una voce poco fà (Il Barbiere di Siviglia); Delibes Dov'è l'indiana bruna? (Lakmé); Meyerbeer Ombra leggiera (Dinorah); Verdi Mercè, dilette amiche (I Vespri Siciliani)	Serafin Callas	Columbia 33CX 1231 EMI ALP 3824 EMI 2C 165 54178-88* EMI CDC 747 2822

24 & 29 September 1954, Kingsway Hall

Rawsthorne Practical Cats (dialogue added later by Robert Donat)	Rawsthorne	Columbia 33C 1044

25 September 1954, Kingsway Hall

Smetana From Bohemia's Woods and Fields (Má Vlast)	Ackermann	Columbia 33C 1042

27, 28 & 29 September and 6 October 1954, Kingsway Hall

Strauss Arabella, excerpts	Matacic Schwarzkopf, Felbermayer, Gedda, Dickie, Berry, Metternich, Schlott, Pröglhöf	Columbia 33CX 1226 World Records OH 199 EMI 1C 037 03297M EMI RLS 751*

5 & 6 October and 24 November 1954, Kingsway Hall

Mozart Symphony No 41 "Jupiter"	Klemperer	Columbia 33CX 1257

7 October 1954, Kingsway Hall

Hindemith	Klemperer	Columbia unpublished
Horn Concerto	Brain	(recording incomplete)

7 & 8 October 1954, Kingsway Hall

Hindemith	Klemperer	Columbia 33CX 1241
Nobilissima Visione		

8 & 9 October 1954, Kingsway Hall

Mozart	Klemperer	Columbia 33CX 1257
Symphony No 29		

9 October 1954, Kingsway Hall

Brahms	Klemperer	Columbia 33CX 1241
Haydn Variations		
(St Antoni Chorale)		

12 & 13 October and 11 & 14 December 1954, Kingsway Hall

Bruckner	Matacic	Columbia 33CX 1274/5
Symphony No 4 "Romantic"		

4 November 1954, Abbey Road

Grieg	Menges	HMV CLP 1037
Piano Concerto	Lympany	EMI MFP 2064

5 November 1954, Kingsway Hall

Wagner	Karajan	Columbia 33CX 1335
Venusberg Music		Toshiba EAC 37020-38*
(Tannhäuser);		
Verdi		
Act 2 Ballet Music (Aida)		

6 November 1954, Kingsway Hall

Ponchielli	Karajan	Columbia 33CX 1335
Dance of the Hours		Toshiba EAC 37020-38*
(La Gioconda)		

8 November 1954, Kingsway Hall

Mussorgsky	Karajan	Columbia 33CX 1335
Dance of the Persian Slaves		Toshiba EAC 37020-38*
(Khovantschina, orch.		
Rimsky-Korsakov);		
Borodin		
Dance of the Polovtsian		
Maidens and Polovtsian		
Dances (Prince Igor)		

11 November 1954, Kingsway Hall

Leimer	Karajan	German Columbia WCX 1508
Piano Concerto in C minor	Leimer	Electrola SME 91793

11 & 12 November 1954, Kingsway Hall

Leimer	Karajan	German Columbia WCX 1508
Piano Concerto for the Left Hand	Leimer	Electrola SME 91793

13 & 14 November 1954, Abbey Road

Lalo	Martinon	Columbia 33CX 1246
Symphonie Espagnole	D.Oistrakh	EMI XLP 30109

15 & 16 November 1954, Abbey Road

Prokofiev	Menges	HMV ALP 1349
Piano Concerto No 2	Cherkassky	

16 November 1954, Abbey Road

Shostakovich	Menges	HMV ALP 1349
Piano Concerto No 1	Cherkassky	

17 November 1954, Kingsway Hall

Beethoven	Klemperer	Columbia 33CX 1270
Leonore No 1, Overture		EMI SLS 873*
		EMI EX 29 04573*

18 November 1954, Kingsway Hall

Beethoven	Klemperer	Columbia 33CX 1270
Leonore No 3;		EMI SLS 873*
Fidelio, Overtures		EMI EX 29 04573*

18 & 24 November 1954, Kingsway Hall

Beethoven	Klemperer	Columbia 33CX 1270
Leonore No 2, Overture		EMI SLS 873*
		EMI EX 29 04573*

19, 20, 22 & 23 November and 3 & 4 December 1954, Kingsway Hall

Bach	Klemperer	Columbia 33CX 1239/40
Orchestral Suites Nos 1, 2, 3 and 4		

24 & 27 November 1954, Kingsway Hall

Khachaturian   Khachaturian   Columbia 33C 1041
Gayaneh, Ballet Suite

26 & 27 November 1954, Kingsway Hall

Khachaturian   Khachaturian   Columbia 33CX 1303
Violin Concerto   D.Oistrakh

3 & 4 December 1954, Kingsway Hall

Khachaturian   Khachaturian   Columbia 33C 1043
In Memoriam

4 December 1954, Kingsway Hall

Khachaturian   Khachaturian   Columbia 33C 1043
Masquerade, Suite

6 December 1954, Kingsway Hall

Mozart   Pritchard   HMV ALP 1281
Violin Concerto No 4   Menuhin

7 December 1954, Kingsway Hall

Vieuxtemps   Fistoulari   HMV ALP 1241
Violin Concerto No 5   Menuhin

11 & 13 December 1954, Kingsway Hall

Balakirev   Matacic   Columbia 33CX 1280
Russia, Symphonic Poem   EMI XLP 30107

13 December 1954, Kingsway Hall

Balakirev   Matacic   Columbia 33CX 1280
Thamar, Symphonic Poem

14 December 1954, Kingsway Hall

Balakirev   Matacic   Columbia 33CX 1280
Islamey, Oriental Fantasy

15 & 16 December 1954, Kingsway Hall

Paganini   Matacic   Columbia 33CX 1281
Violin Concerto No 1   Rabin

16 & 17 December 1954, Kingsway Hall

Glazunov	Matacic	Columbia 33CX 1281
Violin Concerto	Rabin	

18 December 1954, Kingsway Hall

Balakirev	Matacic	Columbia 33CX 1420
Overture on Russian Themes		EMI XLP 30107

20 December 1954, Kingsway Hall

Mozart	Pritchard	HMV CLP 1061
Serenade No 6		
"Sernata notturna"		

20 & 21 December 1954, Kingsway Hall

Haydn	Pritchard	HMV CLP 1061
Symphony No 80		

21 December 1954, Kingsway Hall

Haydn	Pritchard	HMV CLP 1061
Notturno in C		
(arr. Geiringer)		

SUPERB LONG PLAYING RECORDS BY

Herbert von Karajan

AND THE

PHILHARMONIA ORCHESTRA

Fantasia on a theme by Thomas Tallis — *Vaughan-Williams* ; Variations on a theme of Frank Bridge — *Britten*	33CX1159
Concerto for Orchestra — *Bartók*	33CX1054
Symphony No. 5 in E flat major — *Sibelius* ; Finlandia — Symphonic Poem — *Sibelius*	33CX1047
Symphony fantastique — *Berlioz*	33CX1206
Rapsodie espagnole — *Ravel* ; La Mer — *Debussy*	33CX1099

These items will also be included in the repertoire of Herbert von Karajan and the Philharmonia Orchestra during their forthcoming tour of Canada and the United States.

COLUMBIA

33⅓ R.P.M. LONG PLAYING RECORDS

COLUMBIA GRAPHOPHONE CO., LTD., RECORD DIVISION, 8-11 GREAT CASTLE ST., LONDON, W.1

12 September 1955

Hearing that this splendid orchestra is making a tour of America with Herbert von Karajan, I send my best wishes and warmest regards to him and the members of the Philharmonia Orchestra. I am sure this tour of such prominent artists will prove a great success.

Jean Sibelius
Jean Sibelius

23 September 1955

The collaboration of the Philharmonia Orchestra of London and Austrian Herbert von Karajan has written a new and revolutionary chapter in the history of European music-making. From Shakespeare onwards Britain's supreme achievements in the arts have been the fruits of cross-fertilization of our nation's qualities with the finest flowers of the Continent. To my friend Herbert von Karajan and each individual member of the Philharmonia Orchestra I send my best wishes for every one of the concerts they play together in America.

William Walton

It is great news that the Philharmonia Orchestra is going to tour the U.S.A. I am certain that our American friends will enjoy hearing this wonderful orchestra under their remarkable conductor Herbert von Karajan as much as I have always done.

Benjamin Britten
Benjamin Britten.

1955

18 January 1955, Kingsway Hall

Suppé Light Cavalry, Overture	Kletzki	Columbia SEL 1529
Suppé The Beautiful Galathea, Overture	Kletzki	Columbia SEL 1603

18, 20 & 21 January 1955, Kingsway Hall

Hérold Zampa, Overture	Kletzki	Columbia SEL 1541

19 January 1955, Kingsway Hall

Josef Strauss Sphärenklänge, Waltz	Kletzki	Columbia SEL 1535
Nicolai The Merry Wives of Windsor, Overture	Kletzki	Columbia SEL 1541
Mussorgsky Dance of the Persian Slaves (Khovantschina, orch. Rimsky-Korsakov)	Kletzki	Columbia SEL 1542

20 & 21 January 1955, Kingsway Hall

Suppé Pique Dame, Overture	Kletzki	Columbia SEL 1542
Suppé Morning, Noon and Night in Vienna, Overture	Kletzki	Columbia SEL 1529
Glinka Kamarinskaya	Kletzki	Columbia SEL 1603
Weinberger Polka and Fugue (Schwanda the Bagpiper)	Kletzki	Columbia unpublished

2 & 5 February 1955, Abbey Road

Beethoven Piano Concerto No 1	Galliera Anda	Columbia 33CX 1302

7 February 1955, Kingsway Hall

Prokofiev   Malko   HMV CLP 1044
Symphony No 7   EMI SXLP 30437
    EMI CFP 4523

(First stereo recording made by EMI)

7 & 9 February 1955, Kingsway Hall

Prokofiev   Malko   HMV CLP 1060
The Love of Three   EMI MFP 2047
Oranges, Suite   EMI SXLP 30437
    EMI CFP 4523

9 & 11 February 1955, Kingsway Hall

Tchaikovsky   Malko   HMV CLP 1060
The Nutcracker, Suite   EMI MFP 2047
    EMI ESD 7115

11 February 1955, Kingsway Hall

Prokofiev   Malko   HMV CLP 1044
Symphony No 1 "Classical"   EMI SXLP 30437
    EMI CFP 4523

11, 17 & 18 March 1955, Abbey Road

Meyerbeer   Collingwood   HMV DLP 1115
Ombra leggiera (Dinorah);   Catley
Bizet
Sweet echo, come tune thy
lay (Fair Maid of Perth);
Verdi
Dearest name (Rigoletto);
Gounod
Waltz Song
(Roméo et Juliette);
Johann Strauss
Laughing Song; See me,
the village flirt
(Die Fledermaus)

15 March 1955, Kingsway Hall

Strauss   Galliera   Columbia 33CX 1328
Tod und Verklärung

15 & 16 March 1955, Kingsway Hall

Tchaikovsky   Galliera   Columbia 33CX 1328
Romeo and Juliet,
Fantasy Overture

16 & 17 March 1955, Kingsway Hall

Rimsky-Korsakov   Galliera   Columbia 33CX 1356
Capriccio espagnol

18 March 1955, Kingsway Hall

Verdi Collingwood HMV unpublished
Rigoletto, Catley, Dowling
Unspecified duet

18 & 19 March 1955, Kingsway Hall

Respighi Galliera Columbia 33CX 1339
Brazilian Impressions EMI MFP 2055

19 & 21 March 1955, Kingsway Hall

Respighi Galliera Columbia 33CX 1339
The Fountains of Rome EMI MFP 2055

22 & 23 March 1955, Kingsway Hall

Shostakovich Kurtz HMV ALP 1322
Symphony No 10 EMI HQM 1034

24 March and 8 June 1955, Kingsway Hall

Tchaikovsky Sargent HMV ALP 1372
Suite No 3

25 March 1955, Kingsway Hall

Shostakovich Kurtz HMV BLP 1080
The Age of Gold, EMI HQM 1026
Ballet Suite

25 March and 4 May 1955, Kingsway Hall

Barber Kurtz HMV BLP 1080
Souvenirs, Ballet Suite

6, 7 & 8 April 1955, Abbey Road

Borodin Galliera Columbia 33CX 1356
Symphony No 1 EMI XLP 30107

6, 8 & 9 April 1955, Abbey Road

Pizzetti Galliera Angel 35324
La pisanella

9 & 10 April 1955, Abbey Road

Schubert Galliera Columbia unpublished
Symphony No 5

10 April 1955, Abbey Road

Mozart	Galliera	Columbia unpublished
Nehmt meinen Dank	Schwarzkopf	

18, 19 & 20 April 1955, Kingsway Hall

Walton	Walton	Columbia 33CX 1313
Troilus and Cressida,	Schwarzkopf,	World Records OH 217
Scenes	Sinclair, Lewis	

20 April 1955 and 26 March 1957, Kingsway Hall

Walton	Walton	Columbia 33C 1054
Façade, Suites Nos 1 & 2		EMI HQM 1006
		EMI SLS 5246*

26, 27, 28, 29 & 30 April 1955, Kingsway Hall

Johann Strauss	Karajan	Columbia 33CX 1309/10
Die Fledermaus	Chorus	EMI RLS 728
	Schwarzkopf, Streich,	Excerpts:
	Gedda, Krebs, Kunz,	Columbia 33CX 1516
	Dönch, Christ, Majkut,	
	Böheim, Martinis	

7 & 8 May 1955, Abbey Road

Liszt	Ackermann	Columbia 33CX 1366
Piano Concerto No 1	Anda	

8 & 9 May 1955, Abbey Road

Liszt	Ackermann	Columbia 33CX 1366
Hungarian Fantasia	Anda	

9 May 1955, Abbey Road

Mozart	Ackermann	Columbia unpublished
Ch'io mi scordi di te ?	Schwarzkopf, Anda	

10 & 11 May 1955, Abbey Road

Mozart	Menges	HMV ALP 1316
Piano Concerto No 23	Solomon	EMI RLS 726*

11 & 12 May 1955, Abbey Road

Mozart	Menges	HMV ALP 1316
Piano Concerto No 24	Solomon	EMI RLS 726*

13 & 14 May 1955, Abbey Road

Beethoven	Menges	HMV ALP 1300
Piano Concerto No 5	Solomon	EMI SLS 5026*
"Emperor"		

15 May 1955, Abbey Road

Warlock Menges HMV 7EP 7063
Capriol Suite

Holst Menges HMV 7EP 7054
St Paul's Suite

17 & 18 May 1955, Kingsway Hall

Brahms Karajan Columbia 33CX 1349
Haydn Variations Toshiba EAC 37001-19*
(St Antoni Chorale)

17, 21, 23, 24 & 27 May 1955 and 18 June 1956, Kingsway Hall

Tchaikovsky Karajan Columbia 33CX 1377
Symphony No 6 Toshiba EAC 37020-38*
"Pathétique" EMI SXLP 30534

18 & 19 May 1955, Kingsway Hall

Schubert Karajan Columbia 33CX 1349
Symphony No 8 Toshiba EAC 37001-19*
"Unfinished" EMI SXLP 30513

20 May and 9 July 1955, Kingsway Hall

Johann & Josef Strauss Karajan Columbia 33CX 1393
Pizzicato Polka Toshiba EAC 37020-38*

24 & 25 May 1955, Kingsway Hall

Brahms Karajan Columbia 33CX 1355
Symphony No 2 Toshiba EAC 37020-38*
 EMI SXLP 30513

25 & 27 May and 7 July 1955, Kingsway Hall

Johann Strauss Karajan Columbia 33CX 1393
Künstlerleben, Waltz Toshiba EAC 37020-38*

26 & 27 May 1955, Kingsway Hall

Brahms Karajan Columbia 33CX 1362
Symphony No 4 Toshiba EAC 37020-38*
 EMI SXLP 30505

30 & 31 May 1955, Abbey Road

Beethoven Galliera Columbia 33CX 1333
Piano Concerto No 4 Arrau

16 & 17 June 1955, Abbey Road

Dvorak Cello Concerto	Sargent Tortelier	HMV ALP 1306 EMI XLP 30018/SXLP 30018

20 June 1955, Abbey Road

Chopin Autumn Leaves; Glazunov Bacchanale (The Seasons)	Kurtz	HMV ALP 1301
Rubinstein Melody in F	Kurtz	HMV unpublished

21 June 1955, Abbey Road

Tchaikovsky Adagio (Sleeping Beauty); Chopin Nocturne No 8; Lincke Gavotte (Glow Worm Idyll); Tchaikovsky Russian Dance (orch. Schmid)	Kurtz	HMV ALP 1301

21, 22 & 30 June 1955, Abbey Road

Verdi-Mackerras The Lady and the Fool, Ballet	Mackerras	HMV CLP 1059 EMI XLP 30006

21 June and 22 July 1955, Abbey Road

Saint-Saens The Swan (The Carnival of the Animals)	Kurtz	HMV ALP 1301

25 & 29 June 1955, Abbey Road

Fauré Fantasie	Schwarz Blumenthal	Columbia unpublished

27 & 29 June 1955, Abbey Road

Lipatti Piano Concertino	Schwarz Blumenthal	Columbia unpublished

30 June 1955, Abbey Road

Nicolai The Merry Wives of Windsor; Suppé The Beautiful Galathea, Overtures	Schwarz	Columbia SED 5550

4 & 5 July 1955, Kingsway Hall

Sibelius Symphony No 6	Karajan	Columbia 33CX 1341 Toshiba EAC 37020-38*

5 & 6 July 1955, Kingsway Hall

Sibelius Symphony No 7	Karajan	Columbia 33CX 1341 Toshiba EAC 37020-38* EMI SXLP 30430

6 July 1955, Kingsway Hall

Josef Strauss Delirien, Waltz	Karajan	Columbia 33CX 1393 Toshiba EAC 37020-38*

6, 8 & 9 July 1955, Kingsway Hall

Johann Strauss Tritsch-Tratsch Polka	Karajan	Columbia 33CX 1335 Toshiba EAC 37020-38*

7 July 1955, Kingsway Hall

Johann Strauss Emperor Waltz; Der Zigeunerbaron, Overture	Karajan	Columbia 33CX 1393 Toshiba EAC 37020-38*

7 & 8 July 1955, Kingsway Hall

Johann Strauss The Blue Danube, Waltz	Karajan	Columbia 33CX 1393 Toshiba EAC 37020-38*

8 July 1955, Kingsway Hall

Offenbach Orpheus in the Underworld, Overture; Johann Strauss father Radetzky March; Johann Strauss Thunder and Lightning Polka	Karajan	Columbia 33CX 1335 Toshiba EAC 37020-38*

9 July 1955, Kingsway Hall

Johann & Josef Strauss Pizzicato Polka	Karajan	Columbia 33CX 1393 Toshiba EAC 37020-38*
Chabrier Joyeuse marche; Suppé Light Cavalry, Overture	Karajan	Columbia 33CX 1335 Toshiba EAC 37020-38*
Reznicek Donna Diana, Overture	Karajan	Columbia unpublished (probably incomplete)

9 & 10 July 1955, Abbey Road

Mozart Clarinet Concerto	Karajan Walton	Columbia 33CX 1361 Toshiba EAC 37001-19* EMI XLP 60004

10 July 1955, Abbey Road

Mozart Minuet (Divertimento No 17)	Karajan	Columbia unpublished
Mozart Non più andrai (Le Nozze di Figaro)	Karajan Gobbi	Columbia unpublished
Mozart Là ci darem la mano (Don Giovanni)	Karajan Gobbi Soprano unidentified	Columbia unpublished

10 July 1955, Abbey Road and 10 & 11 October 1955, Kingsway Hall

Mozart Symphony No 39	Karajan	Columbia 33CX 1361 Toshiba EAC 37001-19*

15 & 16 July 1955, Kingsway Hall

Sibelius Symphony No 2	Kletzki	Columbia 33CX 1332 Columbia SAX 2280 EMI XLP 30061/SXLP 30061

18 & 19 July 1955, Kingsway Hall

Sibelius Symphony No 1	Kletzki	Columbia 33CX 1311

20 & 21 July 1955, Kingsway Hall

Sibelius Symphony No 3	Kletzki	Angel 35315
Sibelius En Saga	Kletzki	Columbia unpublished

24, 25, 26, 27, 28 & 29 July 1955, Musikvereinssaal, Vienna

Beethoven Symphony No 9 "Choral"	Karajan Vienna Singverein Schwarzkopf, Höffgen, Häfliger, Edelmann	Columbia 33CX 1391/2 World Records SM 143-149* EMI SLS 5053* Toshiba EAC 37001-19*

28 July 1955, Musikvereinssaal, Vienna

Mozart Ave verum corpus	Karajan Vienna Singverein	Columbia 33CX 1741 Columbia SAX 2389 EMI SLS 839* EMI SXLP 30161 Longanesi Periodici CGL 02

3, 4 & 6 August 1955, Kingsway Hall

Debussy Nuages and Fêtes (Nocturnes)	Cantelli	HMV BLP 1089 EMI XLP 30092

4 & 6 August 1955 and 28 May 1956, Kingsway Hall

Ravel Daphnis et Chloé, Suite No 2	Cantelli	HMV BLP 1089 EMI XLP 30092

8, 9, 12, 16 & 18 August 1955, Kingsway Hall

Brahms Symphony No 3	Cantelli	HMV BLP 1083 EMI XLP 30030 World Records SH 315 EMI 29 05761

12, 13 & 16 August 1955, Kingsway Hall

Mendelssohn Symphony No 4 "Italian"	Cantelli	HMV ALP 1325 World Records SH 290

13 & 14 August 1955, Abbey Road

Rachmaninov Piano Concerto No 2	Rignold Moiseiwitsch	HMV CLP 1094 World Records SH 380

14 & 15 August 1955, Abbey Road

Rachmaninov Rhapsody on a theme of Paganini	Rignold Moiseiwitsch	HMV CLP 1072 World Records SH 380

18 August 1955, Kingsway Hall

Mozart A Musical Joke	Cantelli	HMV ALP 1461 EMI XLP 30034 EMI 2C 027 03748 EMI RLS 7701*
Schubert Symphony No 8 "Unfinished"	Cantelli	HMV ALP 1325 World Records SH 290

4, 5 & 6 September 1955, Abbey Road

Beethoven Piano Concerto No 5 "Emperor"	Galliera Gieseking	EMI TCC2-POR 154 5949 (cassette only)

6 & 7 September 1955, Abbey Road

Beethoven Piano Concerto No 4	Galliera Gieseking	German Columbia SMC 91481 EMI TCC2-POR 154 5949 (cassette only)

9 September 1955, Abbey Road

School for Scandal, Incidental Music (Boyce Symphonies Nos 2, 4 and 5)	Jellinek	Columbia unpublished

15 September 1955, Abbey Road

Saint-Saens Cello Concerto	Menges Tortelier	HMV ALP 1336

16 September 1955, Abbey Road

Tchaikovsky Rococo Variations	Menges Tortelier	HMV ALP 1336

17 September 1955, Abbey Road

Fauré Elégie	Menges Tortelier	HMV ALP 1336

19 September 1955, Kingsway Hall

Arnold Tam O'Shanter, Overture; English Dances Nos 3 & 5	Arnold	Columbia SED 5529

22 September 1955, Kingsway Hall

Ibert Elizabethan Suite	Sargent Chorus Mandikian	HMV unpublished

23 September 1955, Kingsway Hall

Borodin Symphony No 2	Malko	HMV CLP 1075 EMI XLP 30010

24 September 1955, Kingsway Hall

Borodin Symphony No 3	Malko	HMV CLP 1075 EMI XLP 30010

29 & 30 September and 1 & 2 October 1955, Abbey Road

Vivaldi The Four Seasons	Giulini Parikian	Columbia 33CX 1365 EMI XLP 30058

2 October 1955 and 6 & 7 October 1956, Abbey Road

Bizet Jeux d'enfants	Giulini	Columbia 33CX 1518 Columbia SAX 2279 EMI XLP 30067/SXLP 30067

3 & 4 October and 17 December 1955, Kingsway Hall

Beethoven Symphony No 3 "Eroica"	Klemperer	Columbia 33CX 1346 EMI SLS 873* EMI EX 29 04573*

4, 5 & 6 October and 19 December 1955, Kingsway Hall

Beethoven Symphony No 7	Klemperer	Columbia 33CX 1379 EMI SLS 873* EMI EX 29 04573* EMI ED 29 13411

6 & 7 October and 19 December 1955, Kingsway Hall

Beethoven Symphony No 5	Klemperer	Columbia 33C 1051 EMI SLS 873* EMI EX 29 04573*

11 & 12 October 1955 and 18 June 1956, Kingsway Hall

Mussorgsky Pictures at an Exhibition	Karajan	Columbia 33CX 1421 Columbia SAX 2261 EMI SLS 5019* EMI SXLP 30445

23 November 1955, Abbey Road

Mozart Violin Concerto No 3	Ackermann Kogan	Columbia 33CX 1395
Ravel Tzigane	Ackermann Kogan	Columbia unpublished

23 & 24 November 1955, Abbey Road

Mozart Serenade No 13 "Eine kleine Nachtmusik"	Kempe	HMV BLP 1088
Mozart Symphony No 34	Kempe	HMV ALP 1471 EMI MFP 2082

25 November 1955, Abbey Road

Bach Double Violin Concerto in D minor	Ackermann Kogan Elisabeth Gilels	Columbia 33CX 1373

25 November 1955, Kingsway Hall

Bach Violin Concerto in E	Ackermann Kogan	Columbia 33CX 1373

25 & 26 November 1955, Kingsway Hall

Haydn Symphony No 100 "Military"	Ackermann	Columbia unpublished

26 November 1955, Kingsway Hall

Verdi Ma dall' arido stelo divulsa (Un Ballo in Maschera); O patria mia (Aida)	Curiel Hammond	HMV ALP 1407 EMI ENC 109 EMI MFP 2015 EMI RLS 29 00143*
Verdi Pace, pace, mio Dio (La Forza del Destino)	Curiel Hammond	HMV ALP 1407 EMI ENC 109 EMI MFP 2015

26 & 29 November 1955, Kingsway Hall

Verdi Ritorna vincitor ! (Aida)	Curiel Hammond	HMV ALP 1407 EMI ENC 109 EMI MFP 2015 EMI RLS 29 00143*
Verdi Morro ma prima in grazia (Un Ballo in Maschera); Tacea la notte placida; D'amor sull' ali rosee (Il Trovatore)	Curiel Hammond	HMV ALP 1407 EMI ENC 109 EMI MFP 2015

28 & 29 November 1955, Kingsway Hall

Rachmaninov Piano Concerto No 2	Ackermann Malinin	Columbia 33CX 1369

29 November 1955, Kingsway Hall

Tchaikovsky Sérénade mélancolique	Ackermann Kogan	Columbia unpublished
Verdi Addio del passato (La Traviata); Sul fil d'un soffio etesio (Falstaff)	Curiel Hammond	HMV ALP 1407 EMI ENC 109 EMI MFP 2015

1 December 1955, Kingsway Hall

Puccini Se sapeste (La Fanciulla del West)	Curiel Hammond	HMV BLP 1086
Puccini Con onor muore (Madama Butterfly)	Curiel Hammond	HMV unpublished

1 & 5 December 1955, Kingsway Hall

Puccini Senza mamma (Suor Angelica)	Curiel Hammond	HMV BLP 1086

4 December 1955, Abbey Road

Mozart Così fan tutte; Idomeneo; Die Zauberflöte; Le Nozze di Figaro, Overtures	Kempe	HMV BLP 1088

5 December 1955, Kingsway Hall

Puccini
Un bel dì (Madama Butterfly); O mio babbino caro (Gianni Schicchi); Si mi chiamano Mimì (La Bohème); Vissi d'arte (Tosca)

Curiel
Hammond

HMV BLP 1086

Puccini
Donde lieta uscì (La Bohème)

Curiel
Hammond

HMV unpublished

17 & 19 December 1955, Kingsway Hall

Brahms
Symphony No 1

Klemperer

Columbia unpublished
(recording incomplete)

20 & 21 December 1955, Kingsway Hall

Mendelssohn
Violin Concerto

Kletzki
Martzy

Columbia 33CX 1497

22 December 1955, Kingsway Hall

Beethoven
Violin Romances Nos 1 & 2

Kletzki
Martzy

Columbia 33CX 1497

ROYAL FESTIVAL HALL
(General Manager: T. E. Bean)

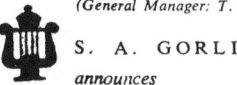 S. A. GORLINSKY
announces

SUNDAY, JULY 1st at 7.30 p.m.

FRIDAY, JULY 6th at 8 p.m.

GUIDO CANTELLI

conducting two performances

VERDI REQUIEM

with

Elisabeth Schwarzkopf
Ebe Stignani
Ferruccio Tagliavini
Giuseppe Modesti

Philharmonia Orchestra
Croydon Philharmonic Choir

Tickets: 42/-, 30/-, 21/-, 15/-, 10/-
BOOK NOW from Royal Festival Hall Box Office
(WAT 3191) and usual agents

MAGNIFICENT PERFORMANCES BY

Drawing by Milein Cosman

Otto Klemperer

and the

PHILHARMONIA ORCHESTRA

Variations on a theme by Haydn
(St. Antoni Chorale) — *Brahms*
Nobilissima Visione — Suite — *Hindemith*
33CX1241

Beethoven Overtures:
 "Fidelio" Act 1;
 "Leonore" Overtures Nos. 1, 2 and 3
33CX1270

Symphony No. 3 in E flat
("Eroica") — *Beethoven*
33CX1346

Symphony No. 5 in C minor — *Beethoven*
33C1051

Symphony No. 7 in A — *Beethoven*
33CX1379

Symphony No. 29 in A, K.201 — *Mozart*;
Symphony No. 41 in C ("Jupiter") K.551
— *Mozart*
33CX1257

The Bach Suites:
 No. 1 in C; No. 2 in B minor
 No. 3 in D (with Gareth Morris, flute)
 No. 4 in D
33CX1239-40

COLUMBIA

33⅓ r.p.m. Long Playing Records

COLUMBIA GRAPHOPHONE COMPANY LIMITED / RECORD DIVISION 8-11 GREAT CASTLE STREET LONDON. W.1

1956

5 January 1956, Kingsway Hall

Waldteufel	H.Krips	Columbia 33SX 1048
Estudiantina;		Columbia SCX 3251
Les patineurs, Waltzes		EMI XLP 30035/SXLP 30035
		EMI CFP 40305

5 & 6 January 1956, Kingsway Hall

Waldteufel	H.Krips	Columbia 33SX 1048
Les grenadiers, Waltz		Columbia SCX 3251
		EMI XLP 30035/SXLP 30035
		EMI CFP 40305

6 January 1956, Kingsway Hall

Waldteufel	H.Krips	Columbia 33SX 1048
Mon rêve; Pomona;		Columbia SCX 3251
España, Waltzes		EMI XLP 30035/SXLP 30035
		EMI CFP 40305

9 January 1956, Kingsway Hall

Suppé	H.Krips	Columbia 33SX 1053
Light Cavalry; Pique Dame;		Columbia SCX 3256
Poet and Peasant, Overtures		EMI XLP 30037/SXLP 30037

10 January 1956, Kingsway Hall

Suppé	H.Krips	Columbia 33SX 1053
Morning, Noon and Night		Columbia SCX 3256
in Vienna; Irrfahrt		EMI XLP 30037/SXLP 30037
ins Glück, Overtures		

11 January 1956, Kingsway Hall

Tchaikovsky	Matacic	Columbia 33CX 1420
Hamlet, Fantasy Overture		

11, 12, 13 & 16 January 1956, Kingsway Hall

Glazunov	Matacic	Columbia unpublished
Raymonda, Ballet		

12 & 13 January 1956, Kingsway Hall

Tchaikovsky	Matacic	Columbia 33CX 1420
The Tempest, Overture		

16 January 1956, Kingsway Hall

Bruckner Matacic Columbia unpublished
Scherzo in D minor

25 January 1956, Abbey Road

Britten Menges HMV CLP 1118
Piano Concerto Abram EMI HQM 1103
   EMI SLS 5080*

7 & 8 February 1956, Kingsway Hall

Rimsky-Korsakov E.Goossens HMV ALP 1490
Le Coq d'Or, Suite   HMV ASD 262
   EMI CFP 126

8 February 1956, Kingsway Hall

Balakirev E.Goossens HMV ALP 1490
Islamey, Oriental Fantasy   HMV ASD 262
   EMI CFP 126

13 February 1956, Kingsway Hall

Rimsky-Korsakov E.Goossens HMV ALP 1490
Russian Easter Festival,   HMV ASD 262
Overture   EMI CFP 126

13 & 14 February 1956, Kingsway Hall

Scriabin E.Goossens HMV ALP 1470
Poème de l'extase

14 & 15 February 1956, Kingsway Hall

Albeniz E.Goossens HMV ALP 1470
Iberia;
Scriabin
Rêverie

16 & 17 February 1956, Kingsway Hall

Dvorak Malko HMV CLP 1125
Symphony No 9   EMI MFP 2004
"From the New World"

17 & 18 February 1956, Kingsway Hall

Borodin Prince Igor; Glinka Russlan and Ludmilla, Overtures	Malko	HMV CLP 1110
Mendelssohn The Hebrides; Suppé Poet and Peasant, Overtures	Malko	HMV CLP 1110 EMI MFP 2034

20 & 22 February 1956, Kingsway Hall

Dvorak Symphonic Variations	Sargent	HMV ALP 1372 EMI XLP 20065/SXLP 20065

24 & 25 February 1956, Kingsway Hall

Taneiev Suite de concert	Malko D.Oistrakh	Columbia 33CX 1390 EMI SLS 5004*

27 February 1956, Kingsway Hall

Tchaikovsky The Tempest, Overture	Fistoulari	HMV ALP 1582 EMI SXLP 30101

29 February and 2 & 3 March 1956, Kingsway Hall

Brahms Double Concerto	Galliera D.Oistrakh, Fournier	Columbia 33CX 1487 Columbia SAX 2264 EMI SXLP 30185 EMI EMX 2035

1 March 1956, Kingsway Hall

Rimsky-Korsakov The Snow Maiden, Suite; Ivan the Terrible, Overture	Malko	HMV CLP 1110
Mendelssohn Ruy Blas, Overture	Malko	HMV CLP 1110 EMI MFP 2034

1 March and 27 July 1956, and 14 March 1957, Kingsway Hall

Glazunov Stenka Razin, Symphonic poem	Fistoulari	HMV ALP 1582 EMI SXLP 30119

5 March 1956, Abbey Road

Miaskovsky Cello Concerto	Sargent Rostropovitch	HMV ALP 1427

6 March 1956, Abbey Road

Saint-Saens Cello Concerto No 1	Sargent Rostropovitch	HMV ALP 1427

12 March 1954, Kingsway Hall

Sibelius Finlandia; Ponchielli Dance of the Hours (La Gioconda); Nicolai Merry Wives of Windsor; Mendelssohn The Hebrides, Overtures	Weldon	Columbia 33SX 1054 EMI MFP 2037

13 March 1956, Kingsway Hall

Grieg Peer Gynt, Suite No 1	Susskind	Columbia 33SX 1057 EMI SXLP 30105

14 March 1956, Kingsway Hall

Saint-Saens Danse macabre; Bacchanale (Samson et Dalila)	Weldon	Columbia 33SX 1054 EMI MFP 2037
Grainger Londonderry Air; Délibes Pizzicato (Sylvia)	Weldon	Columbia SED 5547

14 March, 18 & 19 April and 10 May 1956, Kingsway Hall

Tchaikovsky The Sleeping Beauty	Weldon	Columbia 33SX 1095/6 EMI CFPD 4458 Excerpts: EMI XLP 30012/SXLP 30012

15 March 1956, Kingsway Hall

Schumann Cello Concerto	Sargent Fournier	Columbia 33CX 1407 Columbia SAX 2282

16 March 1956, Kingsway Hall

Tchaikovsky Rococo Variations	Sargent Fournier	Columbia 33CX 1407 Columbia SAX 2282

25 March 1956, Abbey Road

Mozart Serenade No 13 "Eine kleine Nachtmusik"	Klemperer	Columbia 33C 1053 Columbia SBO 2751
Mozart Serenade No 6 "Serenata notturna"	Klemperer	Columbia 33CX 1438

26 March 1956, Abbey Road

Brahms Symphony No 3	Klemperer	Columbia unpublished (recording incomplete)

26 & 27 March 1956, Abbey Road

Beethoven Grosse Fuge	Klemperer	Columbia 33CX 1438 EMI SLS 873* EMI EX 29 03799* EMI ED 29 02711 EMI CDC 747 1862

27 March 1956, Abbey Road

Mozart Adagio and Fugue in C minor	Klemperer	Columbia 33CX 1438 Columbia 33CX 1948 Columbia SAX 2587 EMI SLS 5048* EMI EX 29 04823*

28 March 1956, Abbey Road and 26 July 1956, Kingsway Hall

Handel Concerto Grosso op 6 no 4	Klemperer	Columbia 33C 1053 Columbia SBO 2751 Columbia 33CX 5252 Columbia SAX 5252

19 April 1956, Kingsway Hall

God save the Queen (arr. Walton 1953); God save the Queen (arr. Walton 1955)	Weldon	Columbia unpublished

24 & 25 April 1956, Abbey Road

Mozart Concerto for Two Pianos	Galliera Haskil, Anda	Columbia 33CX 1403 EMI SXLP 30175 EMI 2C 051 00439

25 & 26 April 1956, Abbey Road

Bach Concerto in C BWV 1061	Galliera Haskil, Anda	Columbia 33CX 1403 EMI SXLP 30175 EMI 2C 051 00439

27 April 1956, Kingsway Hall

Weber Ozean, du Ungeheuer (Oberon)	Susskind Schwarzkopf	Columbia unpublished
Weber Und ob die Wolke (Der Freischütz); Wagner Dich teure Halle; Allmächt'ge Jungfrau (Tannhäuser)	Susskind Schwarzkopf	Columbia 33CX 1658 Columbia SAX 2300 EMI SXDW 3049*

27 & 28 April 1956, Kingsway Hall

Weber Wie nahte mir der Schlummer..Leise, leise (Der Freischütz)	Susskind Schwarzkopf	Columbia 33CX 1658 Columbia SAX 2300 EMI SXDW 3049*

28 April 1956, Kingsway Hall

Wagner Einsam in trüben Tagen (Lohengrin)	Susskind Schwarzkopf	Columbia 33CX 1658 Columbia SAX 2300 EMI SXDW 3049*

2 May 1956, Abbey Road

Prokofiev Piano Concerto No 1	Susskind Lympany	HMV CLP 1126 HMV CSD 1253 World Records ST 735

3 May 1956, Abbey Road

Prokofiev Piano Concerto No 3	Susskind Lympany	HMV CLP 1126 HMV CSD 1253 World Records ST 735

4 May 1956, Abbey Road

Rawsthorne Piano Concerto No 1	Menges Lympany	HMV CLP 1118 EMI HQM 1025 EMI SLS 5080*

9 May 1956, Kingsway Hall

Wagner Act 2 Scene 2 Euch Lüften, die mein Klagen (Lohengrin)	Susskind Schwarzkopf, Hoffman, Czerwenka	Columbia unpublished

11, 12 & 14 May 1956, Watford Town Hall and 15 May 1956, Abbey Road

Cornelius Der Barbier von Bagdad	Leinsdorf Chorus Schwarzkopf, Hoffman, Gedda, Unger, Jaresch, Christ, Prey, Wächter, Czerwenka	Columbia 33CX 1400/1 EMI 1C 147 01448/9M

(recording also includes, as an appendix, Mottl's orchestration of the Overture)

22, 23, 25 & 26 May 1956, Abbey Road

Orff Die Kluge	Sawallisch Schwarzkopf, Christ, Kuen, Cordes, Prey, Kusche, Frick, Wieter, Neidlinger	Columbia 33CX 1446/7 Columbia SAX 2257/8 Excerpts: Columbia 33CX 1810

26 May 1956, Abbey Road

Grieg Norwegian Dances	Susskind	Columbia 33SX 1057 EMI SXLP 30105

29, 30 & 31 May 1956, Kingsway Hall

Beethoven Symphony No 7	Cantelli	HMV ALP 1472 HMV ASD 254 EMI CFP 103 Seraphim 60038

31 May and 1, 4 & 5 June 1956, Kingsway Hall

Beethoven Symphony No 5	Cantelli	HMV unpublished (recording incomplete)

(Second movement published on HMV ALP 1535 "The Art of Guido Cantelli"; rehearsal sequences from the second, third and fourth movements published on Arturo Toscanini Society ATS-GC 1201/2/3/4/5/6*)

2 & 4 June 1956, Kingsway Hall

Mozart Symphony No 29	Cantelli	HMV ALP 1461 EMI ENC 122 EMI XLP 30034 EMI 2C 027 03748

8 June 1956, Abbey Road

Haydn Symphony No 104 "London"	Kempe	HMV ALP 1471 EMI MFP 2034

9 June 1956, Abbey Road

Sullivan Iolanthe; Ruddigore, Overtures	Mackerras	HMV 7EP 7037
Sullivan The Mikado; Yeomen of the Guard, Overtures	Mackerras	HMV unpublished

11, 12 & 13 June 1955, Hornsey Town Hall

Tchaikovsky Violin Concerto	Galliera Rabin	Columbia 33CX 1422 EMI MFP 2002

12 June 1956, Kingsway Hall

Mozart Symphony No 39	Kempe	HMV unpublished (recording incomplete)

12 & 13 June 1956, Hornsey Town Hall

Saint-Saens Havanaise	Galliera Rabin	Columbia 33CX 1597

13 June 1956, Hornsey Town Hall

Wolf-Ferari The School for Fathers, Intermezzo	Galliera	Columbia 33CX 1545

13 June 1956, Hornsey Town Hall and 25 January 1957, Kingsway Hall

Wolf-Ferrari Susanna's Secret, Overture	Galliera	Columbia 33CX 1545

18, 21, 22, 23, 25, 26, 27, 28 & 29 June 1956, Kingsway Hall

Verdi Falstaff	Karajan Chorus Schwarzkopf, Moffo, Merriman, Barbieri, Alva, Gobbi, Panerai, Zaccaria, Spataro, Ercolani	Columbia 33CX 1410/11/12 Columbia SAX 2254/5/6 EMI SLS 5037 EMI SLS 5211 Excerpts: Columbia 33CX 1939 Columbia SAX 2578

11 & 12 July 1956, Kingsway Hall

Dvorak Cello Concerto	Susskind Starker	Columbia 33CX 1477 Columbia SAX 2263 World Records ST 751 EMI CFP 40070

12 & 13 July 1956, Kingsway Hall

Dohnanyi Konzertstück	Susskind Starker	Columbia 33CX 1595 World Records ST 783

14 July 1956, Kingsway Hall

Milhaud Cello Concerto	Susskind Starker	Columbia 33CX 1425

16 & 17 July 1956, Kingsway Hall

Prokofiev Cello Concerto	Susskind Starker	Columbia 33CX 1425
Fauré Elégie	Susskind Starker	Columbia 33CX 1477 Columbia SAX 2263 World Records ST 751 EMI CFP 40070

19 July 1956, Kingsway Hall

Mozart Symphony No 36 "Linz"	Klemperer	Columbia 33CX 1786 Columbia SAX 2436 EMI SLS 5048* EMI EX 29 04823*

20, 23 & 24 July 1956, Kingsway Hall

Mozart Symphony No 38 "Prague"	Klemperer	Columbia 33CX 1486

21 & 23 July 1956, Kingsway Hall

Mozart Symphony No 40	Klemperer	Columbia 33CX 1457 Columbia SAX 2278

21 & 25 July 1956, Kingsway Hall

Beethoven Die Weihe des Hauses, Overture	Klemperer	Angel 35329 EMI EX 29 04573*

23 & 24 July 1956, Kingsway Hall

Mozart
Symphony No 39
Klemperer
Columbia 33CX 1486

25 July 1956, Kingsway Hall

Mozart
Symphony No 25
Klemperer
Columbia 33CX 1457
Columbia SAX 2278
Columbia 33CX 5252
Columbia SAX 5252
EMI SLS 5048*
EMI EX 29 04823*

27 July 1956, Kingsway Hall

Grieg
Elegaic Melody No 2
Fistoulari
HMV ALP 1570

27 July 1956 and 14 March 1957, Kingsway Hall

Borodin
Nocturne
(orch. Tcherepnin)
Fistoulari
HMV ALP 1582
EMI SXLP 30119

30 & 31 July 1956, Abbey Road

Chopin
Piano Concerto No 1
Galliera
Anda
Columbia 33C 1057
EMI TRI 33199

12 September 1956, Kingsway Hall

Bruch
Violin Concerto No 1
Susskind
Menuhin
HMV ALP 1669
HMV ASD 334
EMI SLS 5106*
EMI CDM 769 0032

13 & 14 September 1956, Kingsway Hall

Lalo
Symphonie espagnole
E.Goossens
Menuhin
HMV ALP 1571
HMV ASD 290
EMI SXLP 30277
EMI CFP 40364

16, 17 & 26 September 1956, Abbey Road

Beethoven
Piano Concerto No 1
Menges
Solomon
HMV ALP 1583
HMV ASD 294
EMI MFP 2067
EMI SLS 5026*

18, 19 & 24 September 1956, Abbey Road

Schumann	Menges	HMV ALP 1643
Piano Concerto	Solomon	HMV ASD 272
		EMI SLS 5094*
		EMI CFP 40255
		EMI EMX 2002

18, 19 & 26 September 1956, Abbey Road

Beethoven	Menges	HMV ALP 1546
Piano Concerto No 3	Solomon	HMV BSD 751
		World Records ST 540
		EMI SLS 5026*

20 September 1956, Abbey Road

Mozart	Blech	Capitol P 8362/SP 8362
Violin Concerto No 5	Milstein	

(Orchestra described on label and cover as "Festival Orchestra")

21 & 26 September 1956, Abbey Road

Bach	Blech	Capitol P 8362/SP 8362
Violin Concerto in	Milstein	
A minor		

(Orchestra described on label and cover as "Festival Orchestra")

22 September 1956, Abbey Road

Strauss	Sawallisch	Columbia 33CX 1491
Horn Concerto No 1	Brain	EMI HLS 7001
		EMI CDC 747 8342

22 & 23 September 1956, Abbey Road

Strauss	Sawallisch	Columbia 33CX 1491
Horn Concerto No 2	Brain	EMI HLS 7001
		EMI RLS 7701*
		EMI CDC 747 8342

25 & 26 September 1956, Abbey Road

Grieg	Menges	HMV ALP 1643
Piano Concerto	Solomon	HMV ASD 272
		EMI SLS 5094*
		EMI CFP 40255
		EMI EMX 2002

27, 28 & 29 September 1956, Kingsway Hall

Tchaikovsky	Giulini	Columbia 33CX 1523
Symphony No 2		Columbia SAX 2416
"Little Russian"		World Records ST 816
		EMI SXLP 30506

29 September and 8 October 1956, Kingsway Hall

Mussorgsky Night on Bare Mountain	Giulini	Columbia 33CX 1523 Columbia SAX 2416 World Records ST 816

1, 2 & 3 October 1956, Kingsway Hall

Stravinsky L'oiseau de feu, Suite	Giulini	Columbia 33CX 1518 Columbia SAX 2279 EMI XLP 30067/SXLP 30067

4 & 5 October 1956, Kingsway Hall

Haydn Symphony No 94 "Surprise"	Giulini	Columbia 33CX 1539

5, 7 & 8 October 1956, Kingsway Hall

Boccherini Symphony in C minor	Giulini	Columbia 33CX 1539

7 October 1956, Kingsway Hall

Boccherini Overture in D	Giulini	Columbia 33CX 1539

9 & 10 October 1956, Kingsway Hall

Ravel Ma Mère L'Oye, Suite	Giulini	Columbia 33CX 1518 Columbia SAX 2279 EMI XLP 30067/SXLP 30067

22 October 1956, Abbey Road

Gounod Faust, Ballet Music	Mackerras	HMV DLP 1177
Wolf-Ferrari Susanna's Secret; The School for Fathers, Overtures	Mackerras	HMV DLP 1193

22 October and 30 November 1956, Abbey Road

Wolf-Ferrari The School for Fathers, Intermezzo	Mackerras	HMV DLP 1193

23 October 1956, Abbey Road

Wolf-Ferrari The Jewels of the Madonna, Suite	Mackerras	HMV DLP 1193

24 October 1956, Abbey Road

Copland   Mackerras   HMV unpublished
Cuban Dance

Berlioz   Mackerras   HMV DLP 1168
Hungarian March; Dance of
the Sylphs; Minuet of the
Will 'o the wisps
(La Damnation de Faust);
Trojan March
(Les Troyens)

24 & 25 October 1956, Abbey Road

Mussorgsky   Mackerras   HMV DLP 1170
Gopak

25 October 1956, Abbey Road

Glinka   Mackerras   HMV DLP 1170
Russlan and Ludmilla,
Overture;
Rimsky-Korsakov
Flight of the bumble bee;
Glazunov
Concert Waltz;
Glière
Russian Sailor's Dance
(The Red Poppy)

26 October 1956, Abbey Road

Chabrier   Mackerras   HMV DLP 1177
Fête polonaise

Rimsky-Korsakov   Mackerras   HMV DLP 1170
Dance of the tumblers
(The Snow Maiden);
Ippolitov-Ivanov
Procession of the Sardar
(Caucasian Sketches)

27 October 1956, Abbey Road

Chabrier   Mackerras   HMV DLP 1177
España

Berlioz   Mackerras   HMV DLP 1168
Le carnaval romain,
Overture

29 & 30 October 1956, Kingsway Hall

Brahms   Klemperer   Columbia 33CX 1517
Symphony No 2   Columbia SAX 2362
                                                                 EMI ASD 2706
                                                                 EMI SLS 804*
                                                                 EMI SXLP 30238

29 & 31 October 1956 and 28 March 1957, Kingsway Hall

Brahms   Klemperer   Columbia 33CX 1504
Symphony No 1   Columbia SAX 2262
                                                                  EMI ASD 2705
                                                                 EMI SLS 804*
                                                                 EMI SXLP 30217

1 November 1956 and 28 & 29 March 1957, Kingsway Hall

Brahms   Klemperer   Columbia 33CX 1591
Symphony No 4   Columbia SAX 2350
                                                                 EMI ASD 2708
                                                                 EMI SLS 804*
                                                                 EMI SXLP 30214

2 November 1956, Kingsway Hall

Verdi   Mackerras   HMV DLP 1185
Luisa Miller; Nabucco;   EMI XLP 30019/SXLP 30019
La Forza del Destino,
Overtures

3 November 1956, Kingsway Hall

Verdi   Mackerras   HMV DLP 1185
Alzira, Overture   EMI XLP 30019/SXLP 30019

5 November 1956, Kingsway Hall

Brahms   Galliera   Columbia 33CX 1487
Tragic Overture   Columbia SAX 2264
                                                                  EMI SXLP 30185

5 & 6 November 1956, Kingsway Hall

Catalani   Galliera   Columbia 33CX 1545
Dance of the water sprites
(Loreley)

6 November 1956, Kingsway Hall

Catalani   Galliera   Columbia 33CX 1545
La Wally, Acts 3 & 4
Preludes

Bizet   Galliera   Columbia 33CX 1663
Carmen, Suite   Columbia SAX 2303
                                                EMI CFP 120

6 November 1956 and 25 January 1957, Kingsway Hall

Wolf-Ferrari   Galliera   Columbia 33CX 1545
The Jewels of the Madonna,
Intermezzo

19 November 1956, Kingsway Hall

Hindemith   Hindemith   Columbia 33CX 1676
Horn Concerto   Brain   EMI HLS 7001
                                                EMI RLS 7701*
                                                EMI EH 29 11731
                                                EMI CDC 747 8342

19, 20 & 21 November 1956, Kingsway Hall

Hindemith   Hindemith   Columbia 33CX 1676
Sinfonia Serena

21 November 1956, Kingsway Hall

Hindemith   Hindemith   Columbia 33CX 1512
Nobilissima Visione   EMI EH 29 11731

22 November 1956, Kingsway Hall

Hindemith   Hindemith   Columbia 33CX 1533
Clarinet Concerto   Cahuzac

22, 23 & 24 November 1956, Kingsway Hall

Hindemith   Hindemith   Columbia 33CX 1533
Concert Music for   EMI EH 29 11731
Brass and Strings

24 November 1956, Kingsway Hall

Hindemith   Hindemith   Columbia 33CX 1512
Symphony in B flat   EMI EH 29 11731
for Concert Band

30 November 1956, Abbey Road

Wiren Serenade for Strings; Copland Quiet City	Mackerras	HMV unpublished (recordings incomplete)

10, 11, 12, 13, 14, 15, 17, 18, 19, 20, 21 & 22 December 1956, Kingsway Hall

Strauss Der Rosenkavalier	Karajan Chorus Loughton High School Choir Bancroft's School Choir Schwarzkopf, C.Ludwig Stich-Randall, Welitsch, Meyer, Felbermayer, Kuen, Majkut, Unger, Gedda, Friedrich, Edelmann, Wächter, Bierbach, Pröglhöf	Columbia 33CX 1492/3/4/5 Columbia SAX 2269/70/1/2 EMI SLS 810 EMI EX 29 00453 EMI CDS 749 3548 Excerpts: Columbia 33CX 1777 Columbia SAX 2423

14 December 1956, Kingsway Hall

Smetana Endlich allein.... wie fremd und tot (The Bartered Bride)	Schmidt Schwarzkopf	Columbia SAX 5286 EMI SXDW 3049*
Wagner Was duftet doch der Flieder; unspecified extract, Act 3, probably "O Sachs, mein Freund" (Die Meistersinger von Nürnberg)	Schmidt Schwarzkopf, Edelmann	Columbia unpublished

22 December 1956 and 28 April 1957, Kingsway Hall

Prokofiev Peter and the Wolf (Speech parts added later)	Karajan Ustinov (1) Schneider (2) Rothenberger (3) Hirsch (4)	Columbia 33CX 1559 (1) Columbia SAX 2375 (1) German Columbia C70081 (2) Electrola SHZE 243 (3) French Columbia FCX 30531 (4)

1957

2 January 1957, Walthamstow Town Hall

Mendelssohn Violin Concerto	Boult Rabin	Columbia 33CX 1597

3 January 1957, Walthamstow Town Hall

Ravel Tzigane	Boult Rabin	Columbia 33CX 1597
Wieniawski Violin Concerto No 1	Boult Rabin	Columbia 33CX 1538

4 January 1957, Walthamstow Town Hall

Bruch Scottish Fantasy	Boult Rabin	Columbia 33CX 1538

5 January 1957, Walthamstow Town Hall

Beethoven The Ruins of Athens, Overture & Turkish March; Wolf Italian Serenade	Boult	HMV 7ER 5129

24 January 1957, Kingsway Hall

Zandonai Cavalcata (Giulietta e Romeo)	Galliera	Columbia 33CX 1545
Ravel Daphnis et Chloé, Suite No 2	Galliera	Columbia 33CX 1663 Columbia SAX 2303 EMI CFP 120

25 January 1957, Kingsway Hall

Pick-Mangiagalli Notturno romantico, Waltz; Mascagni Guglielmo Ratcliffe, Intermezzo; Le maschere, Overture	Galliera	Columbia 33CX 1545

28 January 1957, Kingsway Hall

Strauss Don Juan	Galliera	Columbia 33C 1060

28 & 29 January 1957, Kingsway Hall

Wagner Siegfried Idyll	Galliera	Columbia 33C 1060

7, 8, 9, 11, 12, 13 & 14 February 1957, Kingsway Hall

Rossini   Galliera   Columbia 33CX 1507/8/9
Il Barbiere di Siviglia   Chorus   Columbia SAX 2266/7/8
                                Callas, Carturan, Alva,   EMI SLS 853
                                Carlin, Gobbi, Zaccaria,   EMI EX 29 10933
                                Ollendorff   EMI CDS 747 6348
                                                                                Excerpts:
                                                                                Columbia 33CX 1790
                                                                                Columbia SAX 2438

15, 16 & 18 February 1957, Kingsway Hall

Tchaikovsky   Silvestri   HMV ALP 1511
Symphony No 4   HMV ASD 253
                                                                                EMI XLP 30066/SXLP 30066

19 & 20 February 1957, Kingsway Hall

Tchaikovsky   Silvestri   HMV ALP 1495
Symphony No 6   HMV ASD 273
"Pathétique"   EMI XLP 30078/SXLP 30078
                                                                                EMI CFP 40013

21 & 22 February 1957, Kingsway Hall

Tchaikovsky   Silvestri   HMV ALP 1491
Symphony No 5   HMV ASD 261
                                                                                EMI XLP 30065/SXLP 30065

4 March 1957, Kingsway Hall

Shostakovich   Kurtz   HMV ALP 1554
Symphony No 1   HMV ASD 263
                                                                                World Records ST 995
                                                                                EMI CFP 40004

7, 8 & 10 March 1957, Abbey Road

Rachmaninov   Gracis   HMV ALP 1538
Piano Concerto No 4   Michelangeli   HMV ASD 255
                                                                                EMI SXLP 30169

8 March 1957, Abbey Road

Ravel Piano Concerto in G	Gracis Michelangeli	HMV ALP 1538 HMV ASD 255 EMI SXLP 30169
Rossini L'Italiana in Algeri, Overture	Gracis	HMV 7ER 5097

10 March 1957, Abbey Road

Rossini Il Barbiere di Siviglia, Overture	Gracis	HMV 7ER 5097

12 & 13 March 1957, Kingsway Hall

Prokofiev Symphony No 1 "Classical"	Kurtz	HMV ALP 1554 HMV ASD 263 World Records ST 995 EMI SXLP 30266 EMI CFP 40004

14 March 1957, Kingsway Hall

Grieg Symphonic Dance No 4	Fistoulari	HMV ALP 1570
Tchaikovsky Waltz (Swan Lake); Glazunov Concert Waltz	Fistoulari	HMV 7EB 6028/RES 4255

17, 18, 19, 20 & 21 March 1957, Abbey Road

Orff Der Mond	Sawallisch Chorus Childrens' chorus Christ, Kuen, Hotter, Schmitt-Walter, Lagger, Graml, Holloway	Columbia 33CX 1534/5 Excerpts: Columbia 33CX 1811 Columbia SAX 2457

26 March 1957, Kingsway Hall

Walton Johannesburg Festival Overture	Walton	Columbia 33C 1054 EMI HQM 1006 EMI SLS 5246*

26 & 27 March 1957, Kingsway Hall

Brahms Symphony No 3	Klemperer	Columbia 33CX 1536 Columbia SAX 2351 EMI ASD 2707 EMI SLS 804* EMI SXLP 30265

29 March 1957, Kingsway Hall

Brahms   Klemperer   Columbia 33CX 1517
Tragic Overture   Columbia SAX 2362
                                                       EMI ASD 2706
                                                       EMI SLS 804*
                                                       EMI SLS 821*
                                                       EMI SXLP 30238

Brahms   Klemperer   Columbia 33CX 1536
Academic Festival Overture   Columbia SAX 2351
                                                       EMI ASD 2707
                                                       EMI SLS 804*
                                                       EMI SXLP 30255

2, 3 & 5 April and 17 June 1957, Kingsway Hall

Mahler   Kletzki   Columbia 33CX 1541
Symphony No 4   Loose   Columbia SAX 2345
                                                       EMI XLP 30054/SXLP 30054

9 & 11 April 1957, Walthamstow Town Hall

Stravinsky   Kurtz   HMV ALP 1503
Petrushka, Ballet   EMI ENC 111
(1947 version)   EMI XLP 30029

19 & 20 April 1957, Abbey Road

Grieg   Galliera   Columbia 33CX 1531
Piano Concerto   Arrau

20 April 1957 and 19, 20 & 21 June 1958, Abbey Road

Beethoven   Galliera   Columbia 33CX 1616
Piano Concerto No 3   Arrau

26 & 27 April and 1 May 1957, Abbey Road

Beethoven   L.Ludwig   Columbia 33C 1055
Piano Concerto No 4   Gilels   Columbia SBO 2752
                                                       EMI SXLP 30086

28 & 30 April 1957, Abbey Road

Leopold Mozart   Karajan   Columbia 33CX 1559
Toy Symphony   Columbia SAX 2375
(Cassation in G)   EMI SLS 839*
                                                       EMI SXLP 30161

30 April and 1 May 1957, Abbey Road

Beethoven	L.Ludwig	Columbia 33CX 1490
Piano Concerto No 5	Gilels	Columbia SAX 2252
"Emperor"		

2 May 1957, Abbey Road

Kodaly	L.Ludwig	Columbia 33S 1132
Dances of Galanta		

4 May 1957, Abbey Road

Kodaly	L.Ludwig	Columbia 33S 1132
Dances of Marosszek		

5 & 6 May 1957, Walthamstow Town Hall

Tchaikovsky	Kempe	HMV ALP 1566
Symphony No 6		
"Pathétique"		

11, 13 & 14 May 1957, Kingsway Hall

Prokofiev	Schippers	Columbia 33CX 1561
Symphony No 5		

14 May 1957, Kingsway Hall

Wagner	L.Ludwig	Columbia 33CX 1522
Senta's Ballad	Chorus	EMI 1C 187 00786/7*
(Der fliegende Holländer)	Nilsson	
Wagner	L.Ludwig	Columbia 33CX 1522
Liebestod	Nilsson	EMI 1C 187 00786/7*
(Tristan und Isolde)		

15 May 1957, Kingsway Hall

Wagner	L.Ludwig	Columbia 33CX 1522
Einsam in trüben Tagen	Nilsson	EMI 1C 187 00786/7*
(Lohengrin)		

15 & 16 May 1957, Kingsway Hall

Wagner	L.Ludwig	Columbia 33CX 1522
Dich teure Halle	Nilsson	EMI 1C 187 00786/7*
(Tannhäuser)		
Verdi	L.Ludwig	Columbia 33CX 1522
Ritorna vincitor!;	Nilsson	
O patria mia (Aida)		

16 May 1957, Kingsway Hall

Verdi Ecco l'orrido campo... Ma dall' arido stelo (Un Ballo in Maschera)	L.Ludwig Nilsson	Columbia 33CX 1522 EMI 1C 187 00786/7*
Verdi Pace, pace, mio dio (La Forza del Destino)	L.Ludwig Nilsson	Columbia 33CX 1522

24 & 31 May 1957, Walthamstow Town Hall

Schumann Piano Concerto	Galliera Arrau	Columbia 33CX 1531

25 May 1957, Abbey Road

I saw three ships (trad. orch. Mackerras); Franck Panis angelicus; O du fröhliche (trad.)	Mackerras Chorus Schwarzkopf	Columbia 33CX 1482 EMI ASD 3798

25 & 26 May and 30 June 1957, Abbey Road

Silcher Die Lorelei (orch. Mackerras)	Mackerras Schwarzkopf	Columbia unpublished

25 May, 30 June and 1 July 1957, Abbey Road

Gruber Stille Nacht	Mackerras Chorus Schwarzkopf	Columbia 33CX 1482 EMI ASD 3798

26 May 1957, Abbey Road

Humperdinck Weihnachten; Vom Himmel hoch (trad.); In dulci jubilo (trad.); The First Nowell (trad. orch. Mackerras); Easter Alleluia (trad. orch. Mackerras)	Mackerras Chorus Schwarzkopf	Columbia 33CX 1482 EMI ASD 3798
Bach-Gounod Ave Maria (arr. Mackerras)	Mackerras Schwarzkopf	Columbia unpublished

27 & 28 May 1957, Kingsway Hall

Tchaikovsky Schippers Columbia 33CX 1609
Symphony No 4 EMI MFP 2073

29 & 30 May 1957 and 24 & 26 May 1958, Abbey Road

Bach Dart Columbia unpublished
Cantata No 199 Schwarzkopf

30 & 31 May and 2 June 1957, Abbey Road

Bach Dart Columbia unpublished
Cantata No 202 Schwarzkopf

1 June 1957, Abbey Road

Sandmännchen Mackerras Columbia 33CX 1482
(trad. arr. Brahms); Schwarzkopf EMI ASD 3798
Maria auf dem Berge
(trad.);
Gluck
In einem kühlen Grunde

O Tannenbaum Mackerras Columbia unpublished
(trad. arr. Fiske) Schwarzkopf

2 June 1957, Abbey Road

Bach Dart Columbia unpublished
Mein gläubiges Herze Schwarzkopf
(Cantata No 68);
Schafe können sicher
weiden (Cantata No 208)

18 June 1957, Kingsway Hall

Arnold R.Irving HMV CLP 1172
Four Scottish Dances World Records ST 725
 EMI CFP 40308

18 & 19 June 1957, Kingsway Hall

Britten R.Irving HMV CLP 1172
Matinées musicales World Records ST 725
 EMI CFP 40308

19 June 1957, Kingsway Hall

Britten R.Irving HMV CLP 1172
Soirées musicales World Records ST 725
 EMI CFP 40308

26, 27 & 28 June 1957, Kingsway Hall

Tchaikovsky Violin Concerto	Silvestri Ferras	HMV ALP 1543 HMV ASD 278 EMI SXLP 30122

27 & 28 June 1957, Kingsway Hall

Mendelssohn Violin Concerto	Silvestri Ferras	HMV ALP 1543 HMV ASD 278 EMI SXLP 30122

29 June 1957, Kingsway Hall

Liszt Les Préludes	Silvestri	HMV ALP 1648

30 June 1957, Abbey Road

O come all ye faithful (trad.)	Mackerras Chorus Schwarzkopf	Columbia 33CX 1482 EMI ASD 3798

2 July 1957, Kingsway Hall

Sieczynsky Wien, du Stadt meiner Träume; Lehar Einer wird kommen (Der Zarewitsch)	Ackermann Schwarzkopf	Columbia 33CX 1570 Columbia SAX 2283 EMI ASD 2807 EMI CDC 747 2842
Lehar Heut' noch werd' ich Ehefrau (Der Graf von Luxemburg)	Ackermann Chorus Schwarzkopf	Columbia 33CX 1570 Columbia SAX 2283 EMI ASD 2807 EMI CDC 747 2842
Johann Strauss Saffi's Song (Der Zigeunerbaron)	Ackermann Schwarzkopf	Columbia unpublished

2 & 4 July 1957, Abbey Road

Goldmark Violin Concerto	Blech Milstein	Capitol P 8414 EMI XLP 30193/SXLP 30193 Seraphim 60238

3 July 1957, Kingsway Hall

Lehar Hoch, Evoë, Angèle (Der Graf von Luxemburg); Johann Strauss Nun's Chorus and Laura's Song (Casanova, arr. Benatzky)	Ackermann Chorus Schwarzkopf	Columbia 33CX 1570 Columbia SAX 2283 EMI ASD 2807 EMI CDC 747 2842
Zeller Ich bin die Christel von der Post; Schenkt man sich Rosen im Tirol (Der Vogelhändler)	Ackermann Schwarzkopf	Columbia 33CX 1570 Columbia SAX 2283 EMI ASD 2807 EMI CDC 747 2842
Wagner Gar viel und schön (Tannhäuser); Gott grüss' euch, liebe Männer; Mein Herr und Gott (Lohengrin)	Ackermann Edelmann	Columbia 33CX 1568

4 July 1957, Kingsway Hall

Wagner Wotan's Farewell (Die Walküre)	Ackermann Edelmann	Columbia 33CX 1568
Heuberger Im chambre separée (Der Opernball); Suppé Hab' ich nur deine Liebe (Boccaccio)	Ackermann Schwarzkopf	Columbia 33CX 1570 Columbia SAX 2283 EMI ASD 2807 EMI CDC 747 2842
Johann Strauss Seht, o seht (A Night in Venice)	Ackermann Schwarzkopf	Columbia unpublished

4 & 5 July 1957, Kingsway Hall

Lehar Meine Lippen, sie küssen so heiss (Giuditta)	Ackermann Chorus Schwarzkopf	Columbia 33CX 1570 Columbia SAX 2283 EMI ASD 2807 EMI CDC 747 2842

5 July 1957, Kingsway Hall

Zeller Sei nicht bös (Der Obersteiger); Millöcker Ich schenk' mein Herz (Die Dubarry)	Ackermann Schwarzkopf	Columbia 33CX 1570 Columbia SAX 2283 EMI ASD 2807 EMI CDC 747 2842
Millöcker Was ich im Leben beginne (Die Dubarry)	Ackermann Chorus Schwarzkopf	Columbia 33CX 1570 Columbia SAX 2283 EMI ASD 2807 EMI CDC 747 2842
Wagner Das ist Karfreitagszauber (Parsifal); Mögst du, mein Kind (Der fliegende Holländer)	Ackermann Edelmann	Columbia 33CX 1568

16 & 17 July 1957, Kingsway Hall

Strauss Don Juan; Der Rosenkavalier, Suite	Steinberg	Capitol P 8423

25, 26 & 29 July 1957, Kingsway Hall

Falla The Three-Cornered Hat, Ballet Suite	Giulini	Columbia 33CX 1694 Columbia SAX 2341 EMI SXLP 30140 EMI CFP 4512

29 & 30 July 1957, Kingsway Hall

Franck Symphony in D minor	Giulini	Columbia 33CX 1589 EMI XLP 30055/SXLP 30055

2, 3, 4, 5, 6, 7, 9 & 10 September 1957, Kingsway Hall

Strauss Capriccio	Sawallisch Schwarzkopf, C.Ludwig, Moffo, Gedda, Christ, Fleet, Troy, Humphries, Walls, Fyson, Darling, Fischer-Dieskau, Hotter, Wächter, Schmitt-Walter, Hauxvell, Wicks, Winnard, Sawallisch	Columbia 33CX 1600/1/2 World Records OC 230/1/2 EMI 143 5243 EMI CDS 749 0148 Excerpts: World Records OH 233

11 & 12 September 1957, Kingsway Hall

Tchaikovsky The Nutcracker, Suite	Sawallisch	Columbia 33CX 1623 Columbia SAX 2285 EMI CFP 40002

12 September and 12 October 1957 and 28 February 1958, Kingsway Hall

Tchaikovsky	Sawallisch	Columbia 33CX 1623
Swan Lake, Suite		Columbia SAX 2285
		EMI CFP 40002

14 September 1957, Kingsway Hall

Saint-Saens	E.Goossens	HMV ALP 1571
Introduction and	Menuhin	HMV ASD 290
Rondo Capriccioso;		
Havanaise		

14 & 15 September 1957, Abbey Road

Strauss	Rodzinski	HMV ALP 1605
Tod und Verklärung		HMV ASD 270
		World Records STF 723

15 September 1957 and 29 April 1958, Abbey Road

Strauss	Rodzinski	HMV ALP 1605
Dance of the Seven Veils		HMV ASD 270
(Salome)		World Records STF 723

16 & 17 September 1957, Kingsway Hall

Saint-Saens	Giulini	Columbia 33CX 1579
Cello Concerto No 1	Starker	World Records ST 529

17 September 1957, Kingsway Hall

Schumann	Giulini	Columbia 33CX 1579
Cello Concerto	Starker	World Records ST 529

19 September 1957, Abbey Road

Respighi	E.Goossens	HMV ALP 1785
The Fountains of Rome		HMV ASD 366
		EMI SXLP 30068

21 September 1967, Abbey Road

Gluck	Schippers	Columbia 33CX 1596
Divinités du Styx	Farrell	
(Alceste);		
Ponchielli		
Suicidio (La Gioconda);		
Verdi		
Sorta è la notte...		
Ernani, involami (Ernani)		

21 & 25 September 1957, Abbey Road

Weber   Schippers   Columbia 33CX 1596
Ozean, du Ungeheuer   Farrell
(Oberon)

25 September 1957, Abbey Road

Tchaikovsky   Schippers   Columbia 33CX 1596
Adieu forêts   Farrell
(The Maid of Orleans);
Massenet
Il est doux, il est bon
(Hérodoade);
Debussy
Air de Lia
(L'enfant prodigue);
Menotti
To this we've come
(The Consul)

4 & 5 October 1957, Kingsway Hall

Beethoven   Klemperer   Columbia 33CX 1615
Symphony No 2   Columbia SAX 2331
                                                         EMI ASD 2561
                                                         EMI SLS 788*
                                                         EMI ED 29 02521
                                                         EMI CDC 747 1852
                                                         EMI EX 29 03793*

7 & 8 October 1957, Kingsway Hall

Beethoven   Klemperer   Columbia 33CX 1532
Symphony No 6   Columbia SAX 2260
"Pastoral"   EMI ASD 2565
                                                         EMI SLS 788*
                                                         EMI ED 29 02531
                                                         EMI CDC 747 1882
                                                         EMI EX 29 03793*

21 October 1957, Kingsway Hall

Beethoven   Klemperer   Columbia 33CX 1615
Coriolan, Overture   Columbia SAX 2331
                                                         Columbia 33CX 1930
                                                         Columbia SAX 2570
                                                         EMI ASD 2564
                                                         EMI SLS 788*
                                                         EMI SXDW 3032*
                                                         EMI ED 29 02701
                                                         EMI CDC 747 1902
                                                         EMI EX 29 03793*

21 & 22 October 1957, Kingsway Hall

Beethoven Klemperer Columbia 33CX 1702
Symphony No 4 Columbia SAX 2354
 EMI ASD 2563
 EMI SLS 788*
 EMI ED 29 02701
 EMI CDC 747 1852
 EMI EX 29 03793*

25 October 1957, Kingsway Hall

Beethoven Klemperer Columbia 33CX 1575
Egmont, Overture Columbia 33CX 1930
 Columbia SAX 2570
 EMI SLS 788*
 EMI SXDW 3032*
 EMI ASD 2563
 EMI ED 29 02531
 EMI CDC 747 1882
 EMI EX 29 03793*

28 & 29 October 1957, Kingsway Hall

Beethoven Klemperer Columbia 33CX 1554
Symphony No 1 Columbia SAX 2318
 EMI ASD 2560
 EMI SLS 788*
 EMI ED 29 02701
 EMI CDC 747 1842
 EMI EX 29 03793*

29 & 30 October 1957, Kingsway Hall

Beethoven Klemperer Columbia 33CX 1554
Symphony No 8 Columbia SAX 2318
 EMI ASD 2560
 EMI SLS 788*
 EMI ED 29 03281
 EMI CDC 747 1872
 EMI EX 29 03793*

31 October and 21, 22 & 23 November 1957, Kingsway Hall

Beethoven Klemperer Columbia 33CX 1574/5
Symphony No 9 "Choral" Philharmonia Chorus Columbia SAX 2276/7
 Nordmo-Lövberg, C.Ludwig, EMI SLS 788*
 Kmennt, Hotter EMI SLS 790
 EMI SXDW 3051
 EMI ED 29 02721
 EMI CDC 747 1892
 EMI EX 29 03793*

16 November 1957, Abbey Road

Wagner	L.Ludwig	Columbia 33CX 1542
Wie aus der Ferne	Nilsson, Hotter	Columbia SAX 2296
(Der fliegende Holländer)		EMI SXLP 30557

17, 18 & 19 November 1957, Abbey Road

Wagner	L.Ludwig	Columbia 33CX 1542
Die Walküre,	Nilsson, Hotter	Columbia SAX 2296
Act 3 scene 3		EMI SXLP 30557

21 & 25 November 1957, Kingsway Hall

Beethoven	Klemperer	Columbia 33CX 1575
Die Trommel gerühret;	Nilsson	EMI ED 29 02531
Freudvoll und leidvoll;		EMI CDC 747 1882
Klärchens Tod (Egmont)		EMI EX 29 03793*

23 & 24 November and 19 & 20 December 1957, Abbey Road

Mozart	Kurtz	HMV ALP 1676
Flute Concerto No 1	Schaffer	EMI SXLP 30150

25 November 1957, Kingsway Hall

Beethoven	Klemperer	Columbia 33CX 1615
Prometheus, Overture		Columbia SAX 2331
		Columbia 33CX 1930
		Columbia SAX 2570
		EMI ASD 2561
		EMI SLS 788*
		EMI SXDW 3032*
		EMI ED 29 13411

19 & 20 December 1957, Abbey Road

Mozart	Kurtz	HMV ALP 1676
Flute Concerto No 2;	Schaffer	EMI SXLP 30150
Andante K315		

21 December 1957, Abbey Road, and 25 April 1958, Kingsway Hall

Stravinsky	Kurtz	HMV 7ER 5122
Suites for Small Orchestra,		EMI HQM 1026
Nos 1 and 2		

ROYAL FESTIVAL HALL
(General Manager: T. E. Bean)

PHILHARMONIA CONCERT SOCIETY LTD.

Artistic Director:
WALTER LEGGE

presents

PHILHARMONIA ORCHESTRA

Leader: HUGH BEAN

Herbert von Karajan

J. S. BACH: Brandenburg Concerto No. 2 in F major
HUGH BEAN (*Violin*) **SIDNEY SUTCLIFFE** (*Oboe*)
GARETH MORRIS (*Flute*) **HAROLD JACKSON** (*Trumpet*)

BRAHMS: Variations on Corale St. Antonii, Op. 56a

INTERVAL

PROKOFIEV: Symphony No. 5 in B flat major, Op. 100

*Sunday, January 12th, 1958
at 8 p.m.*

Management: IBBS & TILLETT LTD., 124 WIGMORE STREET, W.1

Programme One Shilling

Harpsichord by Thomas Goff

Cover photograph by Fritz Eschen, Berlin

ROYAL FESTIVAL HALL
GENERAL MANAGER: T. E. BEAN

PHILHARMONIA CONCERT SOCIETY LTD

ARTISTIC DIRECTOR:
WALTER LEGGE

PHILHARMONIA
ORCHESTRA
LEADER: HUGH BEAN

ANDRÉ CLUYTENS
CHRISTA LUDWIG

WEBER: Overture, Der Freischütz

MAHLER: Lieder eines fahrenden Gesellen

INTERVAL

BERLIOZ: Symphonie Fantastique

Wednesday, 22nd October, 1958
at 8 p.m.

Programme One Shilling

1958

3 & 4 January 1958, Kingsway Hall

Nussio	H.Krips	Columbia 33SX 1157
Folclore d'Engadine		Columbia SCX 3269

4 & 6 January 1958, Kingsway Hall

Schönherr	H.Krips	Columbia 33SX 1157
Austrian Peasant Dances		Columbia SCX 3269

6 January 1958, Kingsway Hall

Ziehrer   H.Krips   Columbia 33SX 1167
Wiener Bürger;   Columbia SAX 3279
Gungl   EMI XLP 30027/SXLP 30027
Amorettentänze;   EMI CFP 40213
Ivanovici
Donauwellen, Waltzes

7 January 1958, Kingsway Hall

Ziehrer   H.Krips   Columbia 33SX 1167
Weaner Madln;   Columbia SAX 3279
Lanner   EMI XLP 30027/SXLP 30027
Die Schönbrunner;   EMI CFP 40213
Lehar
Gold und Silber, Waltzes

8 January 1958, Kingsway Hall

Verdi	Mackerras	EMI XLP 30019/SXLP 30019
I Vespri Siciliani,		
Ballet Music		

9 January 1958, Kingsway Hall

Weber   Karajan   Columbia 33CX 1571
Invitation to the Dance   Columbia SAX 2302
(orch. Berlioz)   EMI SLS 5019*

Liszt   Karajan   Columbia 33CX 1571
Hungarian Rhapsody No 2   Columbia SAX 2302
                                                 EMI SLS 5019*
                                                 EMI SXDW 3048*

Berlioz   Karajan   Columbia 33CX 1548
Le carnaval romain,   EMI SLS 5019*
Overture   EMI SXLP 30450

9 & 18 January 1958, Kingsway Hall

Berlioz   Karajan   Columbia 33CX 1571
Hungarian March   Columbia SAX 2302
(La Damnation de Faust)   EMI SLS 5019*

10 & 13 January 1958, Kingsway Hall

Respighi   Karajan   Columbia 33CX 1548
The Pines of Rome   EMI SLS 5019*
                                                                                                                         EMI SXLP 30450

13, 14, 15 & 18 January 1958, Kingsway Hall

Offenbach   Karajan   Columbia 33CX 1588
Gaîté Parisienne,   Columbia SAX 2274
Ballet Music   World Records ST 1084
(arr. Rosenthal)   EMI SLS 5019*
                                                                                                                         EMI SXLP 30224

14 & 15 January 1958, Kingsway Hall

Bizet   Karajan   Columbia 33CX 1608
L'Arlésienne,   Columbia SAX 2289
Suite No 1   World Records ST 1044
                                                                                                                         EMI SLS 5019*
                                                                                                                         EMI EMX 2028

Bizet   Karajan   Columbia 33CX 1608
L'Arlésienne,   Columbia SAX 2289
Suite No 2   World Records ST 1044
                                                                                               EMI SLS 5019* (Nos 2 & 4)
                                                                                              EMI EMX 2028

16 January 1958, Kingsway Hall

Bizet   Karajan   Columbia 33CX 1608
Carmen, Suite No 1   Columbia SAX 2289
                                                                              World Records ST 1044
                                                                                   EMI SLS 839*
                                                                                   EMI SXDW 3048*
                                                                                 EMI EMX 2028

Sibelius   Karajan   Columbia 33CX 1571
Valse triste   Columbia SAX 2302
                                                                                  EMI SLS 5019*

17 January 1958, Kingsway Hall

Tchaikovsky 1812, Overture	Karajan	Columbia 33CX 1571 Columbia SAX 2302 EMI SLS 839* EMI SXDW 3048*
Liszt Les Préludes	Karajan	Columbia 33CX 1548 EMI SLS 5019* EMI SXLP 30450

18 January 1958, Kingsway Hall

Rossini Passo a tre and Coro tirolese (Guillaume Tell)	Karajan	Columbia 33CX 1588 Columbia SAX 2274 World Records ST 1084
Gounod Faust, Ballet Music	Karajan	Columbia 33CX 1588 Columbia SAX 2274 World Records ST 1084 EMI SLS 839* EMI SXLP 30224
Strauss Der Rosenkavalier, Suite No 1	Karajan	Columbia unpublished
Josef Strauss Sphärenklänge, Waltz	Karajan	Columbia unpublished

4 & 5 February 1958, Kingsway Hall

Hindemith Mathis der Maler, Symphony	Silvestri	HMV ALP 1597

6 February 1958, Kingsway Hall

Bartok Divertimento for Strings	Silvestri	HMV ALP 1597

8 February 1958, Kingsway Hall

Liszt Tasso	Silvestri	HMV ALP 1648

21 & 24 February 1958, Kingsway Hall

Dvorak Symphony No 9 "From the New World"	Sawallisch	Columbia 33CX 1677 Columbia SAX 2322 EMI CFP 104

22 & 23 February and 4 March 1958, Abbey Road

Strauss Le bourgeois gentilhomme, Suite	Sawallisch	Columbia 33CX 1647

24 February 1958, Kingsway Hall

Dvorak Carnival, Overture	Sawallisch	Columbia 33CX 1677 Columbia SAX 2322 EMI CFP 104
Weber Oberon, Overture	Sawallisch	Columbia 33CX 1652 Columbia SAX 2343 EMI XLP 30038/SXLP 30038

25 February 1958, Kingsway Hall

Weber Euryanthe, Overture	Sawallisch	Columbia 33CX 1652 Columbia SAX 2343 EMI XLP 30038/SXLP 30038

25 & 28 February 1958, Kingsway Hall

Weber Der Freischütz, Overture	Sawallisch	Columbia 33CX 1652 Columbia SAX 2343 EMI XLP 30038/SXLP 30038

26 February 1958, Kingsway Hall

Wagner Siegfried's Rhine Journey and Funeral Music (Götterdämmerung)	Sawallisch	Columbia 33CX 1655

28 February and 1 March 1958, Abbey Road

Mozart Piano Concerto No 21	Sawallisch A.Fischer	Columbia 33CX 1630 EMI SXLP 30124

1 March 1958, Abbey Road

Verdi E strano....Sempre libera (La Traviata)	M.Wolf-Ferrari Scotto	Columbia 33CX 1638 EMI ASD 4022 EMI 101 7411

1, 2 & 6 March 1958, Abbey Road

Donizetti Mad Scene (Lucia di Lammermoor)	M.Wolf-Ferrari Scotto	Columbia 33CX 1638 EMI ASD 4022 EMI 101 7411

1, 2 & 10 March 1958, Abbey Road

Mozart	Sawallisch	Columbia 33CX 1630
Piano Concerto No 22	A.Fischer	EMI SXLP 30124

2 March 1958, Abbey Road

Bellini	M.Wolf-Ferrari	Columbia 33CX 1638
Qui la voce; Vien diletto	Scotto	EMI ASD 4022
(I Puritani)		EMI 101 7411

2 & 6 March 1958, Abbey Road

Rossini	M.Wolf-Ferrari	Columbia 33CX 1638
Una voce poco fà	Scotto	EMI ASD 4022
(Il Barbiere di Siviglia)		EMI 101 7411

6 March 1958, Abbey Road

Puccini	M.Wolf-Ferrari	Columbia 33CX 1638
Signore, ascolta;	Scotto	EMI ASD 4022
Tu che di gel sei cinta		EMI 101 7411
(Turandot);		
O mio babbino caro		
(Gianni Schicchi);		
Boito		
L'altra notte		
(Mefistofele)		
Berlioz	Collingwood	HMV HLP 23
Adieu, fière cité;	Gorr	
Je vais mourir		
(Les Troyens);		
Spontini		
Sur cet autel sacre		
(La Vestale)		

7 March 1958, Abbey Road

Strauss	Rodzinski	HMV ALP 1605
Dance Suite after		HMV ASD 270
Couperin		World Records STF 723

7 & 8 March 1958, Abbey Road

Brahms	Boult	HMV ALP 1704
Piano Concerto No 2	Kentner	HMV ASD 268
		EMI MFP 2053

10, 11 & 12 March 1958, Kingsway Hall

Tchaikovsky	Kurtz	HMV ALP 1609
The Nutcracker, excerpts	Chorus	HMV ASD 289
		EMI SLS 859*

12 & 14 March and 25 April 1958, Kingsway Hall and 30 April 1958, Abbey Road

Tchaikovsky	Kurtz	HMV ALP 1644
Swan Lake, excerpts	Menuhin	HMV ASD 271
		EMI SLS 859*
		EMI CFP 40296

22 April 1958, Kingsway Hall

Wagner	Susskind	Columbia 33CX 1651
Dich, teure Halle	Nordmo-Lövberg	Columbia SAX 2353
(Tannhäuser);		
Einsam in trüben Tagen		
(Lohengrin)		

22 & 23 April 1958, Kingsway Hall

Wagner	Susskind	Columbia 33CX 1651
Euch Lüften, die mein	Nordmo-Lövberg	Columbia SAX 2353
Klagen (Lohengrin)		

23 April 1958, Kingsway Hall

Wagner	Susskind	Columbia 33CX 1651
Allmächtige Jungfrau	Nordmo-Lövberg	Columbia SAX 2353
(Tannhäuser);		
Du bist der Lenz		
(Die Walküre)		

24 April 1958, Kingsway Hall

Verdi	W.Braithwaite	Columbia 33CX 1651
Willow Song & Ave Maria	Nordmo-Lövberg	Columbia SAX 2353
(Otello)	Sinclair	
Verdi	W.Braithwaite	Columbia 33CX 1651
Tu che la vanità	Nordmo-Lövberg	Columbia SAX 2353
(Don Carlo)		
Verdi	W.Braithwaite	Columbia SEL 1670/ESL 6280
Pace, pace, mio Dio	Nordmo-Lövberg	
(La Forza del Destino);		
Ritorna vincitor (Aida)		

30 April 1958, Abbey Road

Mendelssohn	Kurtz	HMV ALP 1669
Violin Concerto	Menuhin	HMV ASD 334
		EMI SLS 5106*
		EMI CDM 769 0032

1, 2 & 3 May and 7 October 1958, Abbey Road

Beethoven Piano Concerto No 1	Galliera Arrau	Columbia 33CX 1625

2 & 3 May and 7 October 1958, Abbey Road

Beethoven Piano Concerto No 2	Galliera Arrau	Columbia 33CX 1696 Columbia SAX 2346 World Records ST 568

10 May 1958, Abbey Road

Beethoven Triple Concerto	Sargent Oborin, D.Oistrakh, Knushevitzky	Columbia 33C 1062 Columbia SBO 2753 EMI SXLP 20081 EMI EMX 2035

12 May 1958, Abbey Road

Beethoven Ah perfido !	Wallberg Nilsson	Columbia 33CX 1629 Columbia SAX 2284 EMI 1C 187 00786/7* Seraphim 60353

13 May 1958, Abbey Road

Weber Ozean, du Ungeheuer (Oberon)	Wallberg Nilsson	Columbia 33CX 1629 Columbia SAX 2284 EMI 1C 187 00786/7* Seraphim 60353
Weber Wie nahte mir der Schlummer...Leise, leise (Der Freischütz)	Wallberg Nilsson	Columbia 33CX 1629 Columbia SAX 2284 Seraphim 60353

13 & 14 May 1958, Abbey Road

Beethoven Abscheulicher ! (Fidelio)	Wallberg Nilsson	Columbia 33CX 1629 Columbia SAX 2284 EMI 1C 187 00786/7* Seraphim 60353

14 May 1958, Abbey Road

Mozart Or sai che l'onore (Don Giovanni)	Wallberg Nilsson	Columbia 33CX 1629 Columbia SAX 2284 EMI 1C 187 00786/7* Seraphim 60353

14, 19 & 20 May 1958, Abbey Road

Prokofiev Violin Concerto No 2	Galliera D.Oistrakh	Columbia 33CX 1660 Columbia SAX 2304 EMI SLS 5004*

17 May 1958, Abbey Road

Mozart Deh vieni; Non so più; Voi che sapete (Le Nozze di Figaro); Vedrai carino; Batti, batti (Don Giovanni)	Galliera Moffo	Columbia 33C 1063 Columbia SBO 2754

17 & 18 May 1958, Abbey Road

Mozart Una donna a quindici anni (Così fan tutte)	Galliera Moffo	Columbia 33C 1063 Columbia SBO 2754
Mozart L'amerò, saro costante (Il rè pastore)	Galliera Moffo	Columbia 33C 1061

18 May 1958, Abbey Road

Mozart Ach ich fühl's (Die Zauberflöte); Alleluja (Exsultate, jubilate); Et incarnatus est (Mass in C minor)	Galliera Moffo	Columbia 33C 1061
Mozart In uomini, in soldati (Così fan tutte); Venite inginocchiatevi (Le Nozze di Figaro)	Galliera Moffo	Columbia 33C 1063 Columbia SBO 2754

18 & 19 May 1958. Abbey Road

Mozart Misera, dove son ?	Galliera Moffo	Columbia 33C 1061

19 May 1958, Abbey Road

Mozart Ach, ich liebte (Die Entführung aus dem Serail)	Galliera Moffo	Columbia 33C 1061

20 May 1958, Abbey Road

Rossini　　　　　　　　　　Leinsdorf　　　　　　　　　　Capitol P 8465/SP 8465
L'Italiana in Algeri;
Weber
Oberon, Overtures

20 & 27 May 1958, Abbey Road

Kodaly　　　　　　　　　　Leinsdorf　　　　　　　　　　Capitol P 8508/SP 8508
Hary Janos, Suite

21 May 1958, Abbey Road

Mozart　　　　　　　　　　Leinsdorf　　　　　　　　　　Capitol P 8465/SP 8465
Le Nozze di Figaro,
Overture

21, 22 & 23 May 1958, Abbey Road

Brahms　　　　　　　　　　Leinsdorf　　　　　　　　　　Capitol P 8483
Haydn Variations
(St Antoni Chorale)

21, 22 & 27 May 1958, Abbey Road

Prokofiev　　　　　　　　　Leinsdorf　　　　　　　　　　Capitol P 8508/SP 8508
Lieutenant Kije, Suite

22 May 1958, Abbey Road

Mozart　　　　　　　　　　D.Oistrakh, cond. & sol.　　　Columbia 33CX 1660
Violin Concerto No 3　　　　　　　　　　　　　　　　　　Columbia SAX 2304
　　　　　　　　　　　　　　　　　　　　　　　　　　　　EMI SXLP 30086

23 & 24 May 1958, Abbey Road

Brahms　　　　　　　　　　Leinsdorf　　　　　　　　　　Capitol P 8483
Symphony No 3

24 May 1958, Abbey Road

Beethoven　　　　　　　　　Leinsdorf　　　　　　　　　　Capitol P 8465/SP 8465
Leonore No 3, Overture

Bach　　　　　　　　　　　Dart　　　　　　　　　　　　Columbia unpublished
Meinem Hirten bleib' ich　　Schwarzkopf
treu (Cantata No 92);
Schafe können sicher
weiden (Cantata No 208)

25 May 1958, Abbey Road

Wagner Lohengrin, Act 2 scene 2 (beginning with Euch Lüften, die mein Klagen)	Wallberg Schwarzkopf, C.Ludwig	Columbia 33CX 1658 Columbia SAX 2300 EMI SXDW 3049*

27 May 1958, Abbey Road

Wagner Die Meistersinger von Nürnberg, Overture; Verdi La Forza del Destino, Overture	Leinsdorf	Capitol P 8465/SP 8465

29 & 30 May 1958, Kingsway Hall

Haydn Cello Concerto in D; Boccherini Cello Concerto in B flat (arr. Grützmacher)	Giulini Starker	Columbia 33CX 1665

31 May 1958, Abbey Road

Franck Psyché et Eros	Giulini	Columbia 33CX 1589 EMI XLP 30055/SXLP 30055
Verdi La Traviata, Act 1 Prelude	Giulini	Columbia 33CX 1726 Columbia SAX 2377 EMI XLP 30094/SXLP 30094

31 May and 2 June 1958, Abbey Road

Verdi La Traviata, Act 3 Prelude	Giulini	Columbia 33CX 1726 Columbia SAX 2377 EMI XLP 30094/SXLP 30094

1 June 1958, Abbey Road

Verdi I Vespri Siciliani; La Forza del Destino, Overtures	Giulini	Columbia 33CX 1726 Columbia SAX 2377 EMI XLP 30094/SXLP 30094

2 June 1958, Abbey Road

Schumann Manfred, Overture	Giulini	Columbia 33CX 1662

3 & 4 June 1958, Kingsway Hall

Schumann Symphony No 3 "Rhenish" (orch. Mahler)	Giulini	Columbia 33CX 1662

16 June 1958, Abbey Road

Beethoven Piano Concerto No 3	Susskind Firkusny	Capitol P 8468/SP 8468 EMI MFP 2040

19, 20 & 22 June 1958, Abbey Road

Beethoven Piano Concerto No 3	Galliera Arrau	Columbia 33CX 1616

21 & 22 June 1958, Abbey Road

Beethoven Piano Concerto No 5 "Emperor"	Galliera Arrau	Columbia 33CX 1653 Columbia SAX 2297 World Records ST 645

1 July 1958, Abbey Road

Tchaikovsky Valse des fleurs (The Nutcracker); Allegro moderato (Symphony No 5);	Mackerras	Columbia SED 5564/ESD 7253
Tchaikovsky Waltz (Swan Lake); Waltz (Eugene Onegin)	Mackerras	Columbia SED 5566/ESD 7258
Tchaikovsky Waltz (The Sleeping Beauty)	Mackerras	Columbia unpublished

4 & 5 July 1958, Kingsway Hall

Grieg Piano Concerto; Liszt Piano Concerto No 2	Vandernoot Cziffra	HMV ALP 1678 HMV ASD 301

7 July & 26 September 1958, Kingsway Hall

Falla El amor brujo	Vandernoot Dominguez	HMV ALP 1727 HMV ASD 297

7 July 1958, Abbey Road

Verdi
Il Trovatore,
Ballet Music
    Mackerras
    EMI XLP 30019/SXLP 30019

10 July 1958, Kingsway Hall

Tchaikovsky
'Twill soon be midnight
(The Queen of Spades);
Tatiana's Letter Scene
(Eugene Onegin);
Smetana
Our dream of love
(The Bartered Bride);
Do I live ? (Dalibor);
Dvorak
Gods of the lake (Rusalka)
    Susskind
    Hammond
    HMV ALP 1680
    HMV ASD 302
    World Records ST 933
    EMI SXLP 30205

Dvorak
Oft will he linger
(Rusalka)
    Susskind
    Hammond
    HMV 7ER 5118

11 July 1958, Kingsway Hall

Puccini
Sola, perduta abbandonata
(Manon Lescaut)
    Susskind
    Hammond
    HMV ALP 1680
    HMV ASD 302
    World Records ST 933
    EMI SXLP 30205
    EMI RLS 29 00143*

Puccini
Entrance of Butterfly
(Madama Butterfly);
Mascagni
Easter Hymn
(Cavalleria Rusticana)
    Susskind
    Chorus
    Hammond
    HMV ALP 1680
    HMV ASD 302
    World Records ST 933
    EMI SXLP 30205

Giordano
La mamma morta
(Andrea Chenier);
Puccini
In questa reggia (Turandot)
    Susskind
    Hammond
    HMV ALP 1680
    HMV ASD 302
    World Records ST 933
    EMI SXLP 30205

25 July 1958, Kingsway Hall

Bruch
Violin Concerto No 1
    Susskind
    Ferras
    HMV ALP 1746
    HMV ASD 314
    EMI CFP 107

26 July 1958, Kingsway Hall

Lalo
Symphonie Espagnole
    Susskind
    Ferras
    HMV ALP 1746
    HMV ASD 314
    EMI CFP 107

28 July 1958, Kingsway Hall

Weber Ruler of the spirits; Jubel; Preciosa, Overtures	Sawallisch	Columbia 33CX 1652 Columbia SAX 2343 EMI XLP 30038/SXLP 30038

29 July 1958, Kingsway Hall

Weber Abu Hassan, Overture	Sawallisch	Columbia 33CX 1652 Columbia SAX 2343 EMI XLP 30038/SXLP 30038
Wagner Die Meistersinger von Nürnberg; Tannhäuser, Overtures	Sawallisch	Columbia 33CX 1655

29 August 1958, Kingsway Hall

Brahms Haydn Variations (St Antoni Chorale)	Kletzki	HMV ALP 1696

29 & 30 August 1958, Kingsway Hall

Wagner Siegfried Idyll	Kletzki	HMV ALP 1696

30 August and 3 September 1958, Kingsway Hall

Rimsky-Korsakov Tsar Saltan, Suite	Kletzki	HMV ALP 1679 HMV ASD 343 EMI CFP 40083

30 August and 4 September 1958, Kingsway Hall

Wagner Träume (Wesendonk Lieder) arranged for violin and orchestra	Kletzki Bean	HMV ALP 1696

1 & 2 September 1958, Kingsway Hall

Rimsky-Korsakov Scheherazade	Matacic	Columbia 33CX 1636 EMI MFP 2013 EMI SIT 60042

3 September 1958, Kingsway Hall

Glinka Jota Aragonesa	Kletzki	HMV ALP 1679 HMV ASD 343 EMI CFP 40083

3 & 4 September 1958, Kingsway Hall

Tchaikovsky Capriccio italien	Kletzki	HMV ALP 1679 HMV ASD 343 EMI CFP 40083 EMI CFP 40341

4 September 1958, Kingsway Hall

Tchaikovsky Andante cantabile (arr. Schmid)	Kletzki	HMV ALP 1679 HMV ASD 343 EMI CFP 40083
Mussorgsky Night on Bare Mountain (orch. Rimsky-Korsakov)	Matacic	Columbia 33CX 1654 Columbia SAX 2327 EMI XLP 30070/SXLP 30070

5 September 1958, Kingsway Hall

Rimsky-Korsakov Russian Easter Festival, Overture; Borodin Prince Igor, Suite (Overture, Polovtsian March & Polovtsian Dances, orch. Rimsky-Korsakov & Glazunov)	Matacic	Columbia 33CX 1654 Columbia SAX 2327 EMI XLP 30070/SXLP 30070

11, 12, 13, 14 & 15 September 1958, Musikvereinssaal, Vienna

Beethoven Missa Solemnis	Karajan Vienna Singverein Schwarzkopf, C.Ludwig, Gedda, Zaccaria	Columbia 33CX 1634/5 World Records ST 914/5 EMI SLS 5198

16 & 17 September 1958, Musikvereinssaal, Vienna

Mozart Symphony No 38 "Prague"	Karajan	Columbia 33CX 1703 Columbia SAX 2356 World Records ST 1032

19, 21 & 24 September 1958, Abbey Road

Verdi Nel dì della vittoria.... Vieni ! t'affretta !; La luce langue; Una macchia è qui tuttora ! (Macbeth)	Rescigno Callas	Columbia 33CX 1628 Columbia SAX 2293 World Records ST 633 EMI ASD 3817 EMI 2C 165 54178-88* EMI CDC 747 7302

20 September 1958, Abbey Road

Bizet Flower Song (Carmen)	Rescigno Fernandi	Columbia ESL 6281/SEL 1672
Donizetti Fra poco (Lucia di Lammermoor)	Rescigno Fernandi	Columbia unpublished
Flotow M'appari (Martha)	Rescigno Fernandi	Columbia ESL 6281/SEL 1672
Verdi O don fatale (Don Carlo)	Rescigno Callas	Columbia unpublished

20, 21 & 24 September 1958, Abbey Road

Verdi   Rescigno   Columbia 33CX 1628
Tu che la vanità   Callas   Columbia SAX 2293
(Don Carlo)   World Records ST 633
                                                                        EMI ASD 3817
                                                                        EMI 2C 165 54178-88*
                                                                        EMI CDC 747 7302

20 & 24 September 1958, Abbey Road

Verdi   Rescigno   Columbia 33CX 1628
Ben io t'invenni....   Callas   Columbia SAX 2293
Anch'io dischiuso un   World Records ST 633
giorno (Nabucco)   EMI ASD 3817
                                                                        EMI 2C 165 54178-88*
                                                                        EMI CDC 747 7302

21 September 1958, Abbey Road

Verdi   Rescigno   Columbia 33CX 1628
Sorta è la notte....   Callas   Columbia SAX 2293
Ernani, Ernani involami   World Records ST 633
(Ernani)   EMI ASD 3817
                                                                        EMI 2C 165 54178-88*
                                                                        EMI CDC 747 7302

22 September 1958, Abbey Road

Mascagni Addio (Cavalleria Rusticana)	Rescigno Fernandi	Columbia ESL 6293/SEL 1691
Boito Dai campi (Mefistofele)	Rescigno Fernandi	Columbia unpublished

22, 23 & 26 September 1958, Abbey Road

Verdi Celeste Aida (Aida)	Rescigno Fernandi	Columbia unpublished

22 & 23 September 1958, Abbey Road

Verdi La donna è mobile (Rigoletto)	Rescigno Fernandi	Columbia ESL 6293/SEL 1691
Puccini Recondita armonia (Tosca)	Rescigno Fernandi	Columbia ESL 6281/SEL 1672

22, 23 & 24 September 1958, Abbey Road

Verdi Questa o quella (Rigoletto)	Rescigno Fernandi	Columbia unpublished

23 September 1958, Abbey Road

Rossini L'Italiana in Algeri, Overture	Rescigno	Columbia unpublished
Puccini E lucevan le stelle (Tosca);	Rescigno Fernandi	Columbia ESL 6281/SEL 1672
Puccini Donna non vidi mai (Manon Lescaut)	Rescigno Fernandi	Columbia unpublished

23, 24 & 26 September 1958, Abbey Road

Ponchielli Cielo e mar (La Gioconda)	Rescigno Fernandi	Columbia unpublished

24 September 1958, Abbey Road

Giordano Amor ti vieta (Fedora)	Rescigno Fernandi	Columbia ESL 6293/SEL 1691
Meyerbeer O Paradiso (L'Africaine)	Rescigno Fernandi	Columbia unpublished

24 & 25 September 1958, Abbey Road

Donizetti Piangete voi ?.... Al dolce guidami castel natio (Anna Bolena)	Rescigno Philharmonia Chorus Callas Sinclair, Lanigan, Rouleau, Robertson	Columbia 33CX 1645 Columbia SAX 2320 World Records ST 591 EMI ASD 3801 EMI 2C 165 54178-88* EMI CDC 747 2832

25 September 1958, Abbey Road

Thomas A vos jeux....Partagez- vous mes fleurs.... Et maintenant écoutez ma chanson (Hamlet); Bellini Oh! s'io potessi.... Col sorriso d'innocenza (Il Pirata)	Rescigno Callas	Columbia 33CX 1645 Columbia SAX 2320 World Records ST 591 EMI ASD 3801 EMI 2C 165 54178-88* EMI CDC 747 2832

29 & 30 September 1958 and 4 April 1959, Kingsway Hall

Tchaikovsky Piano Concerto No 1	Vandernoot Cziffra	HMV ALP 1718 HMV ASD 315 EMI CFP 107

18 October 1958, Abbey Road

Mahler Lieder eines fahrenden Gesellen	Boult C.Ludwig	Columbia 33CX 1671 Columbia SAX 2321 World Records ST 703 EMI SXLP 143 6521
Wagner Im Treibhaus (Wesendonk Lieder)	Boult C.Ludwig	Columbia unpublished

19 October 1958, Abbey Road

Mahler Kindertotenlieder	Vandernoot C.Ludwig	Columbia 33CX 1671 Columbia SAX 2321 World Records ST 703 EMI SXLP 143 6521

24 October 1958, Kingsway Hall

Verdi La Forza del Destino, Overture; Aida, Prelude; La Traviata, Acts 1 & 3 Preludes	Galliera	Columbia unpublished

4 & 5 November 1958, Kingsway Hall

Berlioz Symphonie Fantastique	Cluytens	Columbia 33CX 1673 EMI CFP 168

5 & 18 November 1958, Kingsway Hall

Ravel La valse	Cluytens	Columbia 33CX 1699 Columbia SAX 2355

12 November 1958, Kingsway Hall

Meyerbeer Les patineurs, Ballet (arr. Lambert); Ponchielli Dance of the Hours (La Gioconda)	Mackerras	Columbia 33SX 1207 Columbia SCX 3291 EMI ESD 7115

18 November 1958, Kingsway Hall

Rimsky-Korsakov Capriccio espagnol	Cluytens	Columbia 33CX 1699 Columbia SAX 2355 EMI XLP 20106/SXLP 20106

19 November 1958, Kingsway Hall

Borodin In the Steppes of Central Asia; Mussorgsky Night on Bare Mountain (orch. Rimsky-Korsakov)	Cluytens	Columbia 33CX 1699 Columbia SAX 2355 EMI XLP 20106/SXLP 20106

20 November 1958, Kingsway Hall

Tchaikovsky Romeo and Juliet, Fantasy Overture	Wallberg	Columbia 33CX 1674

20 & 21 November 1958, Kingsway Hall

Tchaikovsky Francesca da Rimini	Wallberg	Columbia 33CX 1674

21 November 1958, Kingsway Hall

Wagner Lohengrin, Preludes to Acts 1 and 3	Wallberg	Columbia unpublished
Tchaikovsky Marche slave	Wallberg	Columbia 33CX 1674

24 November 1958, Kingsway Hall

Ravel Rapsodie espagnole; Chabrier España	Vandernoot	HMV ALP 1727 HMV ASD 297

11 December 1958, Abbey Road

Verdi O tu Palermo (I Vespri Siciliani); Borodin Galitzky's aria (Prince Igor); Tchaikovsky Gremin's aria (Eugene Onegin)	Fistoulari Ladysz	Columbia 33CX 1678

11 & 13 December 1958, Abbey Road

Verdi Ella giammai m'amò (Don Carlo)	Fistoulari Ladysz	Columbia 33CX 1678

12 December 1958, Abbey Road

Verdi Il lacerato spirito (Simone Boccanegra); Tchaikovsky What is in store ? (Iolanta)	Fistoulari Ladysz	Columbia 33CX 1678

12 & 13 December 1958, Abbey Road

Verdi Vieni, o levita (Nabucco)	Fistoulari Ladysz	Columbia 33CX 1678

13 December 1958, Abbey Road

Borodin Igor's aria (Prince Igor)	Fistoulari Ladysz	Columbia 33CX 1678
Meyerbeer Nonnes qui reposez (Robert le Diable)	Fistoulari Ladysz	Columbia unpublished

ROYAL FESTIVAL HALL
GENERAL MANAGER: T. E. BEAN, C.B.E.

PHILHARMONIA CONCERT SOCIETY LTD
Artistic Director: WALTER LEGGE

PHILHARMONIA
ORCHESTRA
Leader: HUGH BEAN

CARLO MARIA GIULINI

June 7   7.30 p.m.   TCHAIKOVSKY Symphony No. 6 in B minor, Pathétique
CHOPIN Piano Concerto No. 2 in F minor
STRAVINSKY Suite, The Firebird (1919 Revision)

CLARA HASKIL

June 11   8 p.m.   ROSSINI Overture, L'Italiana in Algeri
FRANCK Symphonic Variations
WAGNER Vorspiel und Liebestod, Tristan und Isolde
LISZT Hungarian Fantasy
MOUSSORGSKY-RAVEL Pictures at an Exhibition

GYORGY CZIFFRA

Tickets 21/-, 15/-, 10/6, 7/6, 5/-
from Hall (WAT 3191) and usual agents

1959

1 & 2 January 1959, Kingsway Hall

Tchaikovsky Swan Lake, Ballet Suite	Karajan	Columbia SAX 2306 EMI SLS 839* EMI SXLP 30200 Longanesi Periodici CGL 16 EMI EMX 41 22067-1

2 & 3 January 1959, Kingsway Hall

Tchaikovsky The Sleeping Beauty, Ballet Suite	Karajan	Columbia SAX 2306 EMI SLS 839* EMI SXLP 30200 Longanesi Periodici CGL 16 EMI EMX 41 22067-1

3 January 1959, Kingsway Hall

Mascagni L'Amico Fritz, Intermezzo; Verdi La Traviata, Act 3 Prelude; Puccini Manon Lescaut, Intermezzo	Karajan	Columbia SAX 2294 EMI SLS 5019*
Leoncavallo I Pagliacci, Intermezzo	Karajan	Columbia SAX 2294 EMI SLS 5019* EMI SXDW 3048*

5 January 1959, Kingsway Hall

Kodaly Hary Janos, Intermezzo; Mascagni Cavalleria Rusticana, Intermezzo	Karajan	Columbia unpublished
Granados Goyescas, Intermezzo; Mussorgsky Khovantschina, Act 4 Entr'acte (arr. Rimsky-Korsakov); Schmidt Notre Dame, Intermezzo	Karajan	Columbia SAX 2294 EMI SLS 5019*

5 & 6 January 1959, Kingsway Hall

Berlioz Royal Hunt and Storm (Les Troyens)	Karajan Chorus	Columbia SAX 2294 EMI SLS 5019*
Offenbach Les Contes d'Hoffmann, Barcarolle	Karajan	Columbia SAX 2294 EMI SLS 839*
Sibelius Finlandia	Karajan	Columbia 33CX 1750 Columbia SAX 2392 EMI SLS 5019*

7 January 1959, Kingsway Hall

Weinberger	E.Goossens	HMV ALP 1785
Polka and Fugue		HMV ASD 366
(Schwanda the Bagpiper);		EMI CFP 40204
Smetana		
Polka, Furiant and		
Dance of the Comedians		
(The Bartered Bride);		
Glinka		
Jota Aragonesa		

8 January and 5 March 1959, Kingsway Hall

Franck	Silvestri	HMV ALP 1831
Symphony in D minor		HMV ASD 408
		EMI CFP 40090

10, 12 & 13 January and 17 February 1959, Abbey Road

Stravinsky	Markevitch	HMV ALP 1745
Le sacre du printemps		HMV ASD 313
		EMI CFP 129

2, 3, 4 & 5 February 1959, Kingsway Hall

Walton	Walton	Columbia 33CX 1679
Belshazzar's Feast	Philharmonia Chorus	Columbia SAX 2319
	Bell	EMI SXLP 30236
		EMI SLS 5246*

6 February 1959, Kingsway Hall

Grieg	Sargent	HMV 7ER 5161
Lyric Suite		

6 & 16 February 1959, Kingsway Hall

Walton	Walton	Columbia 33CX 1679
Partita		Columbia SAX 2319
		EMI SXLP 30236
		EMI SLS 5246*

13 & 14 February 1959, Abbey Road

Mozart	Boult	Columbia 33CX 1686
Piano Concerto No 23	A.Fischer	Columbia SAX 2335
		EMI SXLP 30148

14 & 15 February 1959, Abbey Road

Mozart	Boult	Columbia 33CX 1686
Piano Concerto No 20	A.Fischer	Columbia SAX 2335
		EMI SXLP 30148

17 February 1959, Abbey Road

Tchaikovsky Romeo and Juliet, Fantasy Overture	Markevitch	Columbia 33CX 1691 Columbia SAX 2339

17 & 18 February 1959, Abbey Road

Tchaikovsky The Nutcracker, Ballet Suite	Markevitch	Columbia 33CX 1691 Columbia SAX 2339

22 & 26 February 1959, Abbey Road

Brahms Violin Concerto	Kondrashin Kogan	Columbia 33CX 1692 Columbia SAX 2307 EMI XLP 30063/SXLP 30063

25 & 27 February 1959, Abbey Road

Lalo Symphonie espagnole	Kondrashin Kogan	Columbia 33CX 1683 Columbia SAX 2329 World Records ST 562 EMI CFP 40040

27 February 1959, Abbey Road

Tchaikovsky Sérénade mélancolique	Kondrashin Kogan	Columbia 33CX 1683 Columbia SAX 2329 World Records ST 562 EMI CFP 40040

27 February 1959, Kingsway Hall

Verdi Nabucco; Giovanna d'Arco, Overtures; Aida, Act 1 Prelude	Serafin	Columbia 33CX 1684 Columbia SAX 2324 EMI 1C 137 290087

3 March and 1 June 1959, St Augustine's, Kilburn

Elgar Enigma Variations	Sargent	EMI XLP 20007/SXLP 20007

5 March 1959, Kingsway Hall

Weber Der Freischütz, Overture	Silvestri	HMV unpublished

16, 17, 18, 19, 20 & 21 March 1959, Kingsway Hall

Donizetti Lucia di Lammermoor	Serafin Philharmonia Chorus Callas, Elkins, Tagliavini, Cappuccilli, Ladysz, Del Ferro, Casellato	Columbia 33CX 1723/4 Columbia SAX 2316/7 EMI SLS 5056 EMI EX 29 08763 EMI CDS 747 4408

31 March 1959, Kingsway Hall

Humperdinck Hansel and Gretel; Mendelssohn A Midsummer Night's Dream, Overtures	Silvestri	HMV ALP 1749 HMV ASD 338
Rimsky-Korsakov May Night, Overture	Silvestri	HMV ALP 1749 HMV ASD 338 EMI XLP 30078/SXLP 30078 EMI CFP 40013
Borodin Prince Igor, Overture (orch. Rimsky-Korsakov)	Silvestri	HMV ALP 1749 HMV ASD 338 EMI XLP 30065/SXLP 30065
Glinka Russlan and Ludmilla, Overture	Silvestri	HMV ALP 1749 HMV ASD 338 EMI XLP 30066/SXLP 30066

1 April 1959, Kingsway Hall

Prokofiev Lieutenant Kije, excerpts	Fistoulari	HMV 7ER 5145

7 April 1959, Abbey Road

Schumann Carnaval, Ballet (orch. various)	R.Irving	HMV CLP 1296 HMV CSD 1271 World Records ST 964

10 April 1959, Abbey Road

Chopin Les Sylphides, Ballet (orch. Douglas)	R.Irving	HMV CLP 1296 HMV CSD 1271 World Records ST 964

14 April 1959, Abbey Road

Saint-Saens Carnival of the Animals	Kurtz H.Menuhin, Simon	HMV ALP 1278 HMV ASD 299 EMI ESD 7114

22 & 23 April 1959, Kingsway Hall

Prokofiev	Kurtz	HMV ALP 1728
Peter and the Wolf	Flanders	HMV ASD 299
		EMI ESD 7114

Verdi	Rescigno	Columbia 33CX 5286
Emilia, te ne prego....	Schwarzkopf, Elkins	Columbia SAX 5286
piangea cantando.....		EMI SXDW 3049*
Ave Maria (Otello)		

22, 23, 24 & 25 April 1959, Kingsway Hall

Tchaikovsky	Kurtz	HMV ALP 1790
The Sleeping Beauty,	Menuhin	HMV ASD 371
excerpts		EMI SLS 859*

23 & 24 April 1959, Kingsway Hall

Puccini	Rescigno	Columbia unpublished
Donde lieta uscì	Schwarzkopf	
(La Bohème)		

24 April 1959, Kingsway Hall

Puccini	Rescigno	Columbia 33CX 5286
O mio babbino caro	Schwarzkopf	Columbia SAX 5286
(Gianni Schicchi);		EMI SXDW 3049*
Si, mi chiamano Mimi		
(La Bohème)		

24 & 25 April 1959, Kingsway Hall

Puccini	Rescigno	Columbia unpublished
Signore, ascolta (Turandot)	Schwarzkopf	

25 April 1959, Kingsway Hall

Puccini	Rescigno	Columbia unpublished
Tu che di gel sei cinta	Schwarzkopf	
(Turandot);		
Verdi		
Addio del passato		
(La Traviata)		

15 & 16 May 1959, Abbey Road

Rossini	Galliera	Columbia unpublished
Semiramide, Overture		

15 & 17 May 1959, Abbey Road and 28 May 1959, Kingsway Hall

Rossini La scala di seta, Overture	Galliera	Columbia unpublished

16 May 1959, Abbey Road

Rossini L'Italiana in Algeri, Overture	Galliera	Columbia unpublished

16 & 17 May 1959, Abbey Road

Rossini William Tell, Overture	Galliera	Columbia unpublished

21 May 1959, Kingsway Hall

Mozart Serenade No 13 "Eine kleine Nachtmusik"	Colin Davis	EMI XLP 20019/SXLP 20019
Mozart Minuet (Divertimento No 17)	Colin Davis	EMI XLP 20019/SXLP 20019

21 & 22 May 1959, Kingsway Hall

Mozart Serenade No 6 "Serenata notturna"	Colin Davis	EMI XLP 20019/SXLP 20019
Mozart Minuet and Rondo (Serenade No 7 "Haffner")	Colin Davis	EMI unpublished

22 May 1959, Kingsway Hall

Mozart Minuet in C K409; Three German Dances K605	Colin Davis	EMI XLP 20019/SXLP 20019

23 & 24 May 1959, Abbey Road

Mozart Piano Concerto No 24	Blech Kentner	EMI XLP 20035/SXLP 20035

25 May 1959, Kingsway Hall

Chopin Les Sylphides, Ballet Suite (arr.Douglas)	Mackerras	Columbia 33SX 1207 Columbia SCX 3291
Brahms Hungarian Dances Nos 5 and 6	Mackerras	Columbia 33SX 1389 Columbia SCX 3427

26 May 1959, Kingsway Hall

Verdi I Vespri Siciliani, Overture	Galliera	Columbia unpublished

26 & 27 May 1959, Kingsway Hall

Verdi Luisa Miller, Overture	Galliera	Columbia unpublished

27 May 1959, Kingsway Hall

Verdi Nabucco, Overture	Galliera	Columbia unpublished

28 May 1959, Kingsway Hall

Rossini La gazza ladra, Overture	Galliera	Columbia unpublished
Dukas L'apprenti sorcier	Galliera	Columbia 33CX 1776 Columbia SAX 2419 World Records ST 582

28 & 29 May 1959, 27 May and 27 June 1960, Kingsway Hall

Rossini-Respighi La boutique fantasque, Ballet Music	Galliera	Columbia 33CX 1776 Columbia SAX 2419 World Records ST 582

1 June 1959, Watford Town Hall

Franck Symphony in D minor	Boult	Reader's Digest RDM 6/RDS 6

2, 3 & 4 June 1959, Kingsway Hall

Tchaikovsky Symphony No 6 "Pathétique"	Giulini	Columbia 33CX 1716 Columbia SAX 2368 World Records ST 634 EMI SXLP 30208

4 June 1959, Kingsway Hall

Ravel Alborada del gracioso	Giulini	Columbia 33CX 1694 Columbia SAX 2341 EMI SXLP 30198 EMI EMX 41 20761

5 June 1959, St Augustine's, Kilburn

Vaughan Williams Fantasia on a theme by Thomas Tallis	Sargent	EMI XLP 20007/SXLP 20007

6 June 1959, St Augustine's, Kilburn

Elgar Serenade in E minor	Sargent	EMI SXLP 30126

8, 9 & 10 June 1959, Kingsway Hall

Ravel Daphnis et Chloé, Suite No 2	Giulini	Columbia 33CX 1694 Columbia SAX 2341 EMI SXLP 30198 EMI EMX 41 20761

9 June 1959, Kingsway Hall

Rossini L'Italiana in Algeri, Overture	Giulini	Columbia 33CX 1726 Columbia SAX 2377 EMI XLP 30094/SXLP 30094 EMI CFP 40379

9 & 10 June 1959, Kingsway Hall

Rossini Il Barbiere di Siviglia, Overture	Giulini	Columbia 33CX 1726 Columbia SAX 2377 EMI XLP 30094/SXLP 30094 EMI CFP 40379

25, 26, 27, 29 & 30 June and 1 & 2 July 1959, Kingsway Hall

Johann Strauss Die Fledermaus	Ackermann Philharmonia Chorus Scheyrer, Lipp, C.Ludwig, Martini, Terkal, Dermota, Berry, Wächter, Majkut, Kunz, Liewehr	Columbia 33CX 1688/9 Columbia SAX 2335/7 EMI 1C 147 01652/3 EMI CFPD 4702 Excerpts: EMI XLP 20091/SXLP 20091

27 June 1959, Kingsway Hall

Cherubini Medea, Overture; Wolf-Ferrari Susanna's Secret & The Jewels of the Madonna, Overture	Rescigno	Columbia unpublished

2 July 1959, Kingsway Hall

Offenbach Orpheus in the Underworld, Overture	Ackermann	Columbia unpublished

4 July 1959, Abbey Road

Chabrier Joyeuse marche; Tchaikovsky Marche slave	Kurtz	HMV ALP 1798 HMV ASD 376

5 July 1959, Abbey Road

Prokofiev March (The Love of Three Oranges); Meyerbeer March (Le Prophète); Rimsky-Korsakov March (Le Coq d'Or); Sousa Stars and Stripes Forever, March	Kurtz	HMV ALP 1798 HMV ASD 376
Berlioz Trojan March (Les Troyens)	Kurtz	HMV unpublished

5 & 7 July 1959, Abbey Road

Johann Strauss father Radetzky March	Kurtz	HMV ALP 1798 HMV ASD 376

7 July 1959, Abbey Road

Berlioz Hungarian March (La Damnation de Faust); Verdi Grand March (Aida)	Kurtz	HMV ALP 1798 HMV ASD 376

14, 15 & 16 September 1959, Abbey Road

Rachmaninov				Susskind				Capitol P 8524/SP 8524
Piano Concerto No 3			Pennario

16, 17, 18, 19, 21, 22, 23, 24, 25 & 27 September and 21 November 1959, Kingsway Hall

Mozart					Giulini					Columbia 33CX 1732/3/4/5
Le Nozze di Figaro			Philharmonia Chorus			Columbia SAX 2381/2/3/4
					Schwarzkopf, Moffo, Gatta,		EMI SLS 5152
					Cossotto, Fusco, Ercolani,		Excerpts:
					Taddei, Wächter, Vinco,			Columbia 33CX 1934
					Cappuccilli				Columbia SAX 2573
										EMI SXLP 30303

1 & 2 October 1959, Abbey Road

Mendelssohn				Barzin					Capitol P 8518/SP 8518
Violin Concerto				Milstein				EMI SXLP 30245
										EMI CFP 40374

2 October 1959, Abbey Road

Bruch					Barzin					Capitol P 8518/SP 8518
Violin Concerto No 1			Milstein				EMI SXLP 30245
										EMI CFP 40374

2, 3 & 4 October 1959, Abbey Road

Mozart					Klemperer				Columbia unpublished
Don Giovanni				Philharmonia Chorus			(recording incomplete)
					Schwarzkopf, Sutherland,
					Sciutti, Alva, Wächter,
					Taddei, Cappuccilli, Frick

7, 8, 9, 10, 11, 12, 13, 14 & 15 October and 23 & 24 November 1959, Abbey Road

Mozart					Giulini					Columbia 33CX 1717/18/19/20
Don Giovanni				Philharmonia Chorus			Columbia SAX 2369/70/71/72
					Schwarzkopf, Sutherland,		EMI SLS 5083
					Sciutti, Alva, Wächter,			EMI CDS 747 2608
					Taddei, Cappuccilli, Frick		Excerpts:
										Columbia 33CX 1918
										Columbia SAX 2559
										EMI SXLP 30300

22, 23 & 24 October 1959, Abbey Road

Beethoven				Klemperer				Columbia 33CX 1721
Symphony No 5								Columbia SAX 2373
										EMI ASD 2564
										EMI SLS 788*
										EMI ED 29 02521
										EMI CDC 747 1872
										EMI EX 29 03793*

23, 24, 25 & 27 October 1959, Abbey Road

Mahler Das Lied von der Erde	Kletzki Fischer-Dieskau, Dickie	HMV ALP 1773/4 HMV ASD 351/2 EMI SXLP 30165 EMI EMX 41 20731

27 October 1959, Abbey Road

Mahler Adagietto (Symphony No 5)	Kletzki	HMV ALP 1774 HMV ASD 352

28 October 1959, Abbey Road

Beethoven Die Weihe des Hauses, Overture	Klemperer	Columbia 33CX 1702 Columbia SAX 2354 Columbia 33CX 1930 Columbia SAX 2570 EMI ASD 2566 EMI SLS 788* EMI SXDW 3032* EMI ED 29 02531 EMI CDC 747 1902 EMI EX 29 03793*
Beethoven King Stephen, Overture	Klemperer	Columbia 33CX 1721 Columbia SAX 2373 Columbia 33CX 1930 Columbia SAX 2570 EMI SLS 788* EMI SLS 790* EMI SXDW 3032* EMI SXDW 3051* EMI ED 29 04011

29 October and 11, 12 & 13 November 1959, Abbey Road

Beethoven Symphony No 3 "Eroica"	Klemperer	Columbia 33CX 1710 Columbia SAX 2364 EMI ASD 2562 EMI SLS 788* EMI SXLP 30310 EMI ED 29 02711 EMI CDC 747 1862 EMI EX 29 03793*

21 & 24 November 1959, Kingsway Hall

Rossini La scala di seta, Overture	Giulini	Columbia 33CX 1726 Columbia SAX 2377 EMI XLP 30094/SXLP 30094 EMI CFP 40379

2 & 4 December 1959, Abbey Road

Verdi   Colin Davis   Columbia 33CX 1728
Ah! fors' è lui....   Moffo   Columbia SAX 2376
Sempre libera
(La Traviata)

2, 4 & 6 December 1959, Abbey Road

Verdi   Colin Davis   Columbia 33CX 1728
Caro nome (Rigoletto)   Moffo   Columbia SAX 2376

4 & 6 December 1959, Abbey Road

Donizetti   Colin Davis   Columbia 33CX 1728
Mad Scene   Moffo   Columbia SAX 2376
(Lucia di Lammermoor)

6 December 1959, Abbey Road

Rossini   Colin Davis   Columbia 33CX 1728
Una voce poco fà   Moffo   Columbia SAX 2376
(Il Barbiere di Siviglia);
Bellini
Ah! Non credea mirarti
(La Sonnambula);
Qui la voce (I Puritani)

PHILHARMONI

(Founder and Artistic D

VIENNA MUSIC FESTIVAL 1960

Sunday, May 29, at 7.30
OTTO KLEMPERER
Beethoven:
Overture, Die Weihe des Hauses
Symphony No. 2
Symphony No. 3 (Eroica)

Monday, May 30, at 7.30
CARLO MARIA GIULINI,
ELISABETH SCHWARZKOPF
Mozart: Symphony No. 39 in E flat
Richard Strauss: Vier letzte Lieder
Wagner: Vorspiel und Liebestod
(Tristan und Isolde)
Stravinsky: Firebird Suite (1919)

Tuesday, May 31, at 7.30
OTTO KLEMPERER
Beethoven:
Overture, Egmont
Symphony No. 4
Symphony No. 5

Thursday, June 2, at 7.30
OTTO KLEMPERER
Beethoven:
Overture, Prometheus
Symphony No. 6
Symphony No. 7

Friday, June 3, at 7.30
HEINZ WALLBERG,
WOLFGANG SCHNEIDERHAN
Schoenberg: Verklärte Nacht
Brahms: Violin Concerto
Ravel: Bolero

Saturday, June 4, at 7.30
OTTO KLEMPERER,
HENRYK SZERYNG
Beethoven:
Overture, Coriolan
Violin Concerto
Symphony No. 8

Tuesday, June 7, at 7.30
OTTO KLEMPERER,
WILMA LIPP, URSULA BOESE,
FRITZ WUNDERLICH, FRANZ CRASS
Beethoven:
Symphony No. 1
Symphony No. 9

Thursday, June 9, at 7.30
CARLO MARIA GIULINI,
LEONTYNE PRICE,
FIORENZA COSSOTTO,
LUIGI OTTOLINI, IVO VINCO
Verdi: Missa da Requiem

A ORCHESTRA

rector: WALTER LEGGE)

EDINBURGH INTERNATIONAL FESTIVAL 1960

Sunday, August 21, at 8
CARLO MARIA GIULINI,
JOAN SUTHERLAND,
FIORENZA COSSOTTO,
LUIGI OTTOLINI, IVO VINCO
Verdi: Missa da Requiem

Monday, August 22, at 8
WOLFGANG SAWALLISCH,
GIOCONDA DE VITO
Reznicek: Donna Diana Overture
Brahms: Violin Concerto
Dvořák: Symphony No. 4

Wednesday, August 24, at 8
CARLO MARIA GIULINI,
CLAUDIO ARRAU
Mozart: Symphony No. 39 in E flat
Mozart: Piano Concerto No. 20 in D minor
Brahms: Symphony No. 1

Thursday, August 25, at 8
WOLFGANG SAWALLISCH,
URSULA BOESE
Brahms: St Anthony Variations
Mahler: Aus des Knaben Wunderhorn
Beethoven: Symphony No. 7

LUCERNE INTERNATIONAL MUSIC FESTIVAL 1960

Thursday, September 1, at 8
OTTO KLEMPERER,
CHRISTA LUDWIG, ERNST HÄFLIGER
Bach: Brandenburg Concerto No. 1
Mahler: Das Lied von der Erde

Saturday, September 3, at 7.30
CARLO MARIA GIULINI,
ANNIE FISCHER
Rossini: Overture, Italian Girl in Algiers
Dvořák: Symphony No. 4
Schumann: Piano Concerto in A minor
Wagner: Vorspiel und Liebestod
(Tristan und Isolde)

Monday, September 5, at 8
OTTO KLEMPERER,
RUDOLF FIRKUSNY
Beethoven:
Overture, Coriolan
Piano Concerto No. 5
Symphony No. 3 (Eroica)

Wednesday, September 7, at 8
GEORGE SZELL,
DIETRICH FISCHER-DIESKAU
Berlioz: Overture, Benvenuto Cellini
Mahler: Kindertotenlieder
Schubert: Symphony No. 7 in C

1960

14 January 1960, Kingsway Hall

Johann Strauss	H.Krips	Columbia 33SX 1277
Emperor Waltz;		Columbia SCX 3346
Tritsch-Tratsch Polka;		EMI XLP 30056/SXLP 30056
Der Zigeunerbaron, Overture		EMI SXLP 30173

14 & 15 January 1960, Kingsway Hall

Johann Strauss	H.Krips	Columbia 33SX 1277
Thunder and Lightning,		Columbia SCX 3346
Polka; Quadrille on themes		EMI XLP 30056/SXLP 30056
from Verdi's Un Ballo in		EMI SXLP 30173
Maschera		

15 January 1960, Kingsway Hall

Johann Strauss	H.Krips	Columbia 33SX 1277
Perpetuum mobile;		Columbia SCX 3346
Artist's Life, Waltz;		EMI XLP 30056/SXLP 30056
Die Fledermaus, Overture		EMI SXLP 30173

18 & 19 January 1960, Abbey Road

Haydn	Klemperer	Columbia 33CX 1748
Symphony No 101 "Clock"		Columbia SAX 2395

19, 20 & 21 January 1960, Abbey Road

Haydn	Klemperer	Columbia 33CX 1748
Symphony No 98		Columbia SAX 2395

22, 25 & 27 January 1960, Abbey Road

Mendelssohn	Klemperer	Columbia 33CX 1736
Symphony No 3 "Scotch"		Columbia SAX 2342
		EMI ED 29 05791
		Toshiba CC33-3264

28 & 29 January and 16 February 1960, Abbey Road

Mendelssohn	Klemperer	Columbia 33CX 1746
A Midsummer Night's Dream,	Philharmonia Chorus	Columbia SAX 2393
Overture and	Harper, Baker	EMI SXLP 30196
Incidental Music		EMI CDC 747 2302

15 February 1960, Abbey Road

Mendelssohn	Klemperer	Columbia 33CX 1736
The Hebrides, Overture		Columbia SAX 2342

15, 17, 18 & 19 February 1960, Abbey Road

Mendelssohn Symphony No 4 "Italian"	Klemperer	Columbia 33CX 1751 Columbia SAX 2398 EMI SXLP 30178 EMI ED 29 05791 Toshiba CC33-3264

23 & 24 February 1960, Abbey Road

Wagner Tannhäuser, Overture	Klemperer	Columbia 33CX 1697 Columbia SAX 2347 EMI ASD 2695 EMI SLS 5075* EMI SXLP 30436 EMI CDC 747 2542

24 & 25 February 1960, Abbey Road

Wagner Der fliegende Holländer, Overture	Klemperer	Columbia 33CX 1697 Columbia SAX 2347 EMI ASD 2695 EMI SLS 5075* EMI SXLP 30436 EMI CDC 747 2542

25 February 1960, Abbey Road, and 3 March 1960, Kingsway Hall

Wagner Lohengrin, Act 1 Prelude	Klemperer	Columbia 33CX 1697 Columbia SAX 2347 EMI ASD 2695 EMI SLS 5075* EMI SXLP 30435 EMI CDC 747 2542

25 February 1960, Kingsway Hall

Tchaikovsky Swan Lake Waltz; Sleeping Beauty Waltz; Berlioz Waltz (Symphonie Fantastique); Gounod Waltz (Faust); Tchaikovsky Waltz (Serenade for Strings)	H.Krips	Columbia 33SX 1300 Columbia SCX 3362

27 February 1960, Abbey Road

Wagner Klemperer Columbia 33CX 1698
Lohengrin, Act 3 Prelude Columbia SAX 2348
 EMI ASD 2696
 EMI SLS 5075*
 EMI SXLP 30525
 EMI CDC 747 2542

Wagner Klemperer Columbia 33CX 1698
Siegfried's Funeral March Columbia SAX 2348
(Götterdämmerung) EMI ASD 2696
 EMI SLS 5075*
 EMI SXLP 30525
 EMI CDC 747 2552

29 February 1960, Kingsway Hall

Chabrier H.Krips Columbia 33SX 1300
Fête polonaise; Columbia SCX 3362
Délibes
Waltz (Naila);
Tchaikovsky
Nutcracker Waltz

Tchaikovsky H.Krips Columbia unpublished
Waltz (Eugene Onegin)

1, 2 & 3 March 1960, Kingsway Hall

Wagner Klemperer Columbia 33CX 1698
Tristan und Isolde, Columbia SAX 2348
Prelude and Liebestod EMI ASD 2696
 EMI SLS 5075*
 EMI SXLP 30525
 EMI CDC 747 2542

2 March 1960, Kingsway Hall

Wagner Klemperer Columbia 33CX 1698
Die Meistersinger von Columbia SAX 2348
Nürnberg, Overture EMI ASD 2696
 EMI SLS 5075*
 EMI SXLP 30525
 EMI CDC 747 2552

2 & 3 March 1960, Kingsway Hall

Wagner Klemperer Columbia 33CX 1697
Rienzi, Overture Columbia SAX 2347
 EMI ASD 2695
 EMI SLS 5075*
 EMI SXLP 30436
 EMI CDC 747 2542

3 March 1960, Kingsway Hall

Wagner Tannhäuser, Act 3 Prelude	Klemperer	Columbia 33CX 1820 Columbia SAX 2464 EMI ASD 2697 EMI SLS 5075* EMI SXLP 30528

5 March 1960, Kingsway Hall

Strauss Dance of the Seven Veils (Salome)	Klemperer	Columbia 33CX 1715 Columbia SAX 2367 EMI SXLP 30298

8 March 1960, Kingsway Hall

Wagner Dance of the Apprentices & Entry of the Masters (Die Meistersinger von Nürnberg)	Klemperer	Columbia 33CX 1698 Columbia SAX 2348 EMI ASD 2696 EMI SLS 5075* EMI SXLP 30525 EMI CDC 747 2552

8 & 9 March 1960, Kingsway Hall

Strauss Till Eulenspiegels lustige Streiche	Klemperer	Columbia 33CX 1715 Columbia SAX 2367 EMI SXLP 30298 EMI ED 29 06161

9 & 10 March 1960, Kingsway Hall

Strauss Don Juan	Klemperer	Columbia 33CX 1715 Columbia SAX 2367 EMI SXLP 30298 EMI ED 29 06161

10 March 1960, Kingsway Hall

Wagner Ride of the Valkyries (Die Walküre)	Klemperer	Columbia 33CX 1820 Columbia SAX 2464 EMI ASD 2697 EMI SLS 5075* EMI SXLP 30528 EMI CDC 747 2552

26 March 1960, Abbey Road

Rossini Karajan Columbia 33CX 1729
La gazza ladra, Overture   Columbia SAX 2378
   EMI SLS 5019*
   EMI SXLP 30203

Rossini Karajan Columbia 33CX 1729
Semiramide, Overture   Columbia SAX 2378
   EMI SXLP 30203

26 & 27 March 1960, Abbey Road

Rossini Karajan Columbia 33CX 1729
La scala di seta,   Columbia SAX 2378
Overture   EMI SXLP 30203

Rossini Karajan Columbia 33CX 1729
William Tell, Overture   Columbia SAX 2378
   EMI SLS 839*
   EMI SXLP 30203

28 & 29 March 1960, Abbey Road

Sibelius Karajan Columbia 33CX 1730
Symphony No 2   Columbia SAX 2379
   EMI SXLP 30414

29 & 30 March 1960, Abbey Road

Rossini Karajan Columbia 33CX 1729
L'Italiana in Algeri,   Columbia SAX 2378
Overture   EMI SXLP 30203

Rossini Karajan Columbia 33CX 1729
Il Barbiere di Siviglia,   Columbia SAX 2378
Overture   EMI SLS 5019*
   EMI SXDW 3048*
   EMI SXLP 30203

11 & 12 April 1960, Abbey Road

Tchaikovsky Kletzki EMI XLP 20027/SXLP 20027
Symphony No 6 "Pathétique"   EMI CFP 40220
   EMI CFP 41 44521

12, 13 & 14 April 1960, Abbey Road

Rimsky-Korsakov Kletzki EMI XLP 20026/SXLP 20026
Scheherazade   EMI CFP 40341

18 & 19 April 1960, Abbey Road

Tchaikovsky Piano Concerto No 1	Galliera Arrau	Columbia 33CX 1731 Columbia SAX 2380 World Records ST 581

19 April 1960, Abbey Road

Weber Konzertstück	Galliera Arrau	Columbia 33CX 1731 Columbia SAX 2380 World Records ST 581 EMI RLS 7712*

20 & 21 April 1960, Abbey Road

Chopin Piano Concerto No 1	Kletzki Pollini	HMV ALP 1794 HMV ASD 370 EMI SXLP 30160 EMI CDM 769 0042

21 & 22 April 1960, Abbey Road

Brahms Piano Concerto No 1	Giulini Arrau	Columbia 33CX 1739 Columbia SAX 2387 EMI CFP 40028

4, 5 & 6 May 1960, Abbey Road

Schumann Symphony No 4	Klemperer	Columbia 33CX 1751 Columbia SAX 2398 EMI SXLP 30178 EMI 1C 197 52497/8/9*
Weber Der Freischütz; Oberon, Overtures	Klemperer	Columbia 33CX 1770 Columbia SAX 2417

4, 5 & 6 May 1960, Kingsway Hall

Stravinsky Symphony in Three Movements	Silvestri	HMV ALP 1819 HMV ASD 401

11 & 12 May 1960, Kingsway Hall

Mozart Horn Concerto No 1; Horn Concerto No 2	Klemperer Civil	Columbia 33CX 1760 Columbia SAX 2406 EMI SXLP 30207 EMI CFP 41 44881

13 May 1960, Abbey Road

Wieniawski Violin Concerto No 2	E.Goossens Rabin	Capitol P 8534/SP 8534 EMI 1C 037 82112

14 May 1960, Abbey Road

Paganini Violin Concerto No 1	E.Goossens Rabin	Capitol P 8534/SP 8534 EMI 1C 037 82112

16 May 1960, Royal Festival Hall (live recording)

Chopin Piano Concerto No 2	Giulini Rubinstein	Replica RPL 2469

18 & 19 May 1960, Kingsway Hall

Mozart Horn Concerto No 3; Horn Concerto No 4	Klemperer Civil	Columbia 33CX 1760 Columbia SAX 2406 EMI SXLP 30207 EMI CFP 41 44881

22, 23 & 24 May 1960 and 10 May 1962, Abbey Road

Schumann Piano Concerto	Klemperer A.Fischer	Columbia 33CX 1842 Columbia SAX 2485 EMI 1C 137 52497/8/3*

24 May 1960 and 10 May 1962, Abbey Road

Liszt Piano Concerto No 1	Klemperer A.Fischer	Columbia 33CX 1842 Columbia SAX 2485

23 & 24 May 1960, Abbey Road

Saint-Saens Carnaval des animaux; Poulenc Concerto for two pianos	Dervaux Whittemore, Lowe	Capitol P 8537/SP 8537

29 May 1960, Musikvereinssaal, Vienna (live recording)

Beethoven Symphony No 3 "Eroica"	Klemperer	Fonit Cetra CDE 1007

31 May 1960, Musikvereinssaal, Vienna (live recording)

Beethoven Egmont, Overture	Klemperer	Fonit Cetra CDE 1008

2 June 1960, Musikvereinssaal, Vienna (live recording)

Beethoven Symphony No 7	Klemperer	Fonit Cetra CDE 1008

4 June 1960, Musikvereinssaal, Vienna (live recording)

Beethoven Coriolan, Overture	Klemperer	Fonit Cetra CDE 1008

13 & 14 June 1960, Abbey Road

Liszt Piano Concerto No 1	Silvestri François	EMI XLP 20028/SXLP 20028 EMI CFP 40057

14 & 17 June 1960, Kingsway Hall

Stravinsky Le chant du rossignol	Silvestri	HMV ALP 1819 HMV ASD 401 EMI CFP 40328

15 June 1960, Abbey Road

Liszt Piano Concerto No 2	Silvestri François	EMI XLP 20028/SXLP 20028 EMI CFP 40057

23 & 24 June 1960, Abbey Road

Brahms Violin Concerto	Fistoulari Milstein	Capitol P 8560/SP 8560 EMI 18 00191

29 & 30 June 1960, Abbey Road

Délibes Sylvia, Ballet Suite; Coppélia, Ballet Suite	R.Irving Menuhin	HMV ALP 1869 HMV ASD 439 EMI CFP 124

13, 14 & 15 July 1960, Watford Town Hall, and 14 & 15 November 1961, Kingsway Hall

Rossini Bel raggio lusinghier (Semiramide)	Tonini Callas	EMI EL 749 4281 EMI CDC 749 4281

15 July 1960, Watford Town Hall

Rossini D'amore al dolce impero (Armida); Verdi Arrigo! ah parli a un core (I Vespri Siciliani)	Tonini Callas	Columbia unpublished

20, 21, 22 & 23 July 1960, Abbey Road

Beethoven Piano Concerto No 5 "Emperor"	Kertesz Richter-Haaser	Columbia 33CX 1775 Columbia SAX 2422

22 & 23 July 1960, Abbey Road

Beethoven Piano Concerto No 4	Kertesz Richter-Haaser	Columbia 33CX 1757 Columbia SAX 2403 EMI CFP 155

12 September 1960, Kingsway Hall

Strauss Leinsdorf Capitol P 8548/SP 8548
Till Eulenspiegels
lustige Streiche

13 September 1960, Kingsway Hall

Ravel Leinsdorf Capitol P 8545/SP 8545
Piano Concerto Browning
for the Left Hand

13, 15 & 16 September 1960, Kingsway Hall

Prokofiev Leinsdorf Capitol P 8545/SP 8545
Piano Concerto No 3 Browning

14, 15 & 16 September 1960, Kingsway Hall

Strauss Leinsdorf Capitol P 8548/SP 8548
Die Frau ohne Schatten,
Interludes
(arr. Leinsdorf)

15 & 16 September 1960, Kingsway Hall

Strauss Leinsdorf Capitol P 8548/SP 8548
Dance of the Seven Veils
(Salome)

17 September 1960, Kingsway Hall

Strauss Leinsdorf Capitol unpublished
Der Rosenkavalier, Suite

20, 21 & 23 September 1960, Kingsway Hall

Sibelius Karajan Columbia 33CX 1750
Symphony No 5 Columbia SAX 2392
  EMI SXLP 30430

21 September 1960, Kingsway Hall

Verdi Karajan Columbia 33CX 1774
Aida, Act 2 Ballet Music Columbia SAX 2421

Suppé Karajan Columbia 33CX 1758
Light Cavalry, Overture Columbia SAX 2404
  World Records ST 838
  EMI SLS 839*
  EMI CFP 40368

21 & 23 September 1960, Kingsway Hall

Waldteufel Les patineurs, Waltz	Karajan	Columbia 33CX 1758 Columbia SAX 2404 World Records ST 838 EMI SLS 839* EMI SXLP 30224 EMI SXDW 3048* EMI CFP 40368

22 September 1960, Kingsway Hall

Borodin Dance of the Polovtsian Maidens; Polovtsian Dances (Prince Igor)	Karajan	Columbia 33CX 1774 Columbia SAX 2421 EMI SLS 5019* EMI SXDW 3048* EMI SXLP 30445

22 & 23 September 1960, Kingsway Hall

Ponchielli Dance of the Hours (La Gioconda)	Karajan	Columbia 33CX 1774 Columbia SAX 2421 EMI SLS 5019*
Wagner Venusberg Music (Tannhäuser)	Karajan	Columbia 33CX 1774 Columbia SAX 2421

23 September 1960, Kingsway Hall

Mussorgsky Dance of the Persian Slaves (Khovantschina, arr. Rimsky-Korsakov)	Karajan	Columbia 33CX 1774 Columbia SAX 2421 EMI SLS 839* EMI SXLP 30200 EMI SXLP 30445 EMI EMX 41 2607-1
Chabrier Joyeuse marche; Weinberger Polka (Schwanda the Bagpiper)	Karajan	Columbia 33CX 1758 Columbia SAX 2404 World Records ST 838 EMI SLS 5019* EMI CFP 40368
Offenbach Orpheus in the Underworld, Overture	Karajan	Columbia 33CX 1758 Columbia SAX 2404 World Records ST 838 EMI SLS 839* EMI CFP 40368

23 & 24 September 1960, Kingsway Hall

Chabrier España	Karajan	Columbia 33CX 1758 Columbia SAX 2404 World Records ST 838 EMI SLS 839* EMI SXDW 3048* EMI CFP 40368

24 September 1960, Kingsway Hall

Johann Strauss father Radetzky March	Karajan	Columbia 33CX 1758 Columbia SAX 2404 World Records ST 838 EMI SXDW 3048* EMI CFP 40368
Johann Strauss Tritsch-Tratsch Polka; Thunder and Lightning, Polka	Karajan	Columbia 33CX 1758 Columbia SAX 2404 World Records ST 838 EMI CFP 40368

27 September 1960, Kingsway Hall

Humperdinck Hänsel und Gretel, Overture	Klemperer	Columbia 33CX 1770 Columbia SAX 2417

27 & 29 September 1960, Kingsway Hall

Humperdinck Dream Pantomime (Hänsel und Gretel)	Klemperer	Columbia 33CX 1770 Columbia SAX 2417

28 September 1960, Kingsway Hall

Weber Euryanthe, Overture	Klemperer	Columbia 33CX 1770 Columbia SAX 2417
Cherubini Anacréon, Overture	Klemperer	Columbia unpublished

29 September 1960, Kingsway Hall

Gluck Iphigenia in Aulis, Overture (arr. Wagner)	Klemperer	Columbia 33CX 1770 Columbia SAX 2417
Mozart Die Entführung aus dem Serail, Overture	Klemperer	Columbia 33CX 1786 Columbia SAX 2436 Columbia 33CX 1948 Columbia SAX 2587 EMI SLS 5048* EMI EX 29 04823*

30 September and 1, 3, 4, 5, 6, 7, 8, 9, 10 & 11 October 1960, Abbey Road

Bach Brandenburg Concertos Nos 1, 2, 3, 4, 5 & 6	Klemperer	Columbia 33CX 1763/4 Columbia SAX 2408/9

22 & 23 October 1960, Abbey Road

Mozart Symphony No 35 "Haffner"	Klemperer	Columbia 33CX 1786 Columbia SAX 2436 EMI SLS 5048* EMI EX 29 04823*

23 October 1960, Abbey Road

Mozart Symphony No 31 "Paris"	Klemperer	Columbia unpublished (recording incomplete)

25 October, 19 November and 3 December 1960, Kingsway Hall

Beethoven Symphony No 7	Klemperer	Columbia 33CX 1869 Columbia SAX 2415 EMI ASD 2566 EMI SLS 788* EMI ED 29 03281 EMI CDC 747 1842 EMI EX 29 03793*

28 October 1960, Kingsway Hall

Dvorak Slavonic Dances Nos 1, 3 and 10	Mackerras	Columbia 33SX 1389 Columbia SCX 3247

30 October 1960, Abbey Road

Bartok Rumanian Dances; Smetana Polka (The Bartered Bride)	Mackerras	Columbia 33SX 1389 Columbia SCX 3247

31 October 1960, Abbey Road

Dvorak Slavonic Dance No 2; Smetana Furiant (The Bartered Bride); Enesco Rumanian Rhapsody No 1	Mackerras	Columbia 33SX 1389 Columbia SCX 3247

1, 2, 3, 4 & 5 November 1960, Kingsway Hall

Bruckner Symphony No 7	Klemperer	Columbia 33CX 1808/9 Columbia SAX 2454/5 EMI ED 29 0041

5 November 1960 and 25 April and 25 October 1961, Kingsway Hall

Wagner Siegfried Idyll	Klemperer	Columbia 33CX 1809 Columbia SAX 2455

16, 17, 18 & 19 November 1960, Kingsway Hall

Schubert Symphony No 9	Klemperer	Columbia 33CX 1754 Columbia SAX 2397 EMI ED 29 04261

20 November 1960 and 24 February 1964, Abbey Road

Beethoven Violin Romance No 2	Pritchard Menuhin	HMV ALP 2070 HMV ASD 618 EMI SXLP 30249 EMI CFP 40365

20 November and 16 December 1960, and 24 February 1964, Abbey Road

Beethoven Violin Romance No 1	Pritchard Menuhin	HMV ALP 2070 HMV ASD 618 EMI SXLP 30249 EMI CFP 40365

21 November 1960, Abbey Road, 25 & 26 November 1960, 3 & 4 January, 14 & 15 April, 4 & 12 May and 28 November 1961, Kingsway Hall

Bach St Matthew Passion	Klemperer Philharmonia Choir Hampstead Parish Church Choir Schwarzkopf, C.Ludwig, Baker, Watts, Pears, Gedda, Fischer-Dieskau, Berry, Brown, Carol Case, Kraus, G.Evans	Columbia 33CX 1799-1803 Columbia SAX 2446-2450 EMI SLS 827* Excerpts: Columbia 33CX 1881 Columbia SAX 2525

22 November and 15 December 1960, Abbey Road

Chausson Poème	Pritchard Menuhin	HMV ALP 2070 HMV ASD 618

27 November 1960 and 24 February 1964, Abbey Road

Paganini Di tanti palpiti	Pritchard Menuhin	HMV unpublished

28 November 1960, Kingsway Hall

Mendelssohn Symphony No 4 "Italian"	Wallberg	EMI XLP 20037/SXLP 20037 EMI MFP 57020

29 November 1960, Kingsway Hall

Mendelssohn Overture, Nocturne and Scherzo (A Midsummer Night's Dream)	Wallberg	EMI XLP 20037/SXLP 20037 EMI MFP 57020

29 & 30 November and 2 December 1960, Kingsway Hall

Bizet Wallberg EMI XLP 20044/SXLP 20044
L'Arlésienne,
Suites Nos 1 and 2

2 December 1960, Kingsway Hall

Bizet Wallberg EMI XLP 20044/SXLP 20044
Carmen, Suite No 1

PHILHARMONIA CONCERT SOCIETY LTD
Artistic Director: WALTER LEGGE

ROYAL FESTIVAL HALL

MOZART
DIE ZAUBERFLÖTE

(Concert Performances)

Monday, May 1, 1961, at 7.30 p.m.
and
Wednesday, May 3, 1961, at 7.30 p.m.

Cast includes:

AGNES GIEBEL	NICOLAI GEDDA
WALTER BERRY	WALTER KREPPEL
INGEBORG HALLSTEIN	JOHN DOBSON
GERDA SCHEYRER	FRANZ CRASS
HILDE KONETZNI	HEATHER HARPER
URSULA BOESE	JEANNETTE SINCLAIR
LISA OTTO	MAUREEN GUY

PHILHARMONIA ORCHESTRA

OTTO KLEMPERER

1961

2 January, 21, 23 & 25 March, 26 April and 4, 5, 6 & 8 May 1961, Kingsway Hall

Brahms	Klemperer	Columbia 33CX 1781/2
Ein deutsches Requiem	Philharmonia Chorus	Columbia SAX 2430/1
	Schwarzkopf	EMI SLS 821
	Fischer-Dieskau	EMI CDC 747 2382

13 January 1961, Abbey Road

Franck	Vandernoot	HMV unpublished
Symphonic Variations	Cziffra	

13 & 14 January 1961, Abbey Road

Liszt	Vandernoot	HMV ALP 2082
Piano Concerto No 1	Cziffra	HMV ASD 629

14 January 1961, Abbey Road

Stravinsky	Vandernoot	HMV ALP 1956
Pulcinella, Suite		HMV ASD 507
		World Records ST 644

16 & 17 January 1961, Kingsway Hall

Brahms	Giulini	Columbia 33CX 1773
Symphony No 1		Columbia SAX 2420
		EMI SLS 5241*

17, 18, 19, 24 & 27 January 1961, Kingsway Hall

Dvorak	Giulini	Columbia 33CX 1759
Symphony No 9		Columbia SAX 2405
"From the New World"		EMI SXLP 30163

19 January 1961, Kingsway Hall

Dvorak	Giulini	Columbia 33CX 1759
Carnival, Overture		Columbia SAX 2405
		EMI SXLP 30163

25 & 26 January 1961, Kingsway Hall

Brahms	Giulini	Columbia 33CX 1778
Haydn Variations		Columbia SAX 2424
(St Antoni Chorale)		EMI SXLP 30278
		EMI SLS 5241*

27 January 1961, Kingsway Hall

Schubert Symphony No 8 "Unfinished"	Giulini	Columbia 33CX 1778 Columbia SAX 2424 EMI SXLP 30278

1 & 2 April 1961, Abbey Road

Mozart Piano Concerto No 17	Kertesz Richter-Haaser	Columbia 33CX 1780 Columbia SAX 2426 World Records ST 1072/ST 718 EMI CFP 40310

2 & 3 April 1961, Abbey Road

Mozart Piano Concerto No 26 "Coronation"	Kertesz Richter-Haaser	Columbia 33CX 1780 Columbia SAX 2426 World Records ST 1072/ST 718 EMI CFP 40310

6, 7, 8, 10 & 25 April 1961, Kingsway Hall

Mahler Symphony No 4	Klemperer Schwarzkopf	Columbia 33CX 1793 Columbia SAX 2441 EMI ASD 2799

14 & 16 April 1961, Abbey Road

Mascagni L'Amico Fritz, Intermezzo	Serafin	HMV ALP 1898 HMV ASD 466 EMI CFP 110

15 April 1961, Abbey Road

Rossini La Cenerentola; Wolf-Ferrari Susanna's Secret, Overtures	Serafin	HMV ALP 1898 HMV ASD 466 EMI CFP 110

15 & 16 April 1961, Abbey Road

Donizetti Don Pasquale, Overture	Serafin	HMV ALP 1898 HMV ASD 466 EMI CFP 110

16 April 1961, Abbey Road

Bellini Norma; Donizetti Linda di Chamonix, Overtures	Serafin	HMV ALP 1898 HMV ASD 466 EMI CFP 110

17 & 20 April 1961, Abbey Road

Johann Strauss   Mackerras   HMV CLP 1722
Graduation Ball,   HMV CSD 1533
Ballet Suite

22 April 1961, Abbey Road

Gounod   Kurtz   HMV ALP 1962
Faust, Ballet Music   HMV ASD 513
                         World Records ST 623

23 & 25 April 1961, Abbey Road

Glinka   Kurtz   HMV ALP 1962
A Life for the Tsar   HMV ASD 513
(rev. Rimsky-Korsakov   World Records ST 623
and Glazunov)

27, 28, 29 & 30 April 1961, Abbey Road

Kabalevsky   Kurtz   HMV ALP 1981
The Comedians,   HMV ASD 532
Ballet Suite   EMI HQM 1026

Rimsky-Korsakov   Kurtz   HMV ALP 1981
Le Coq d'Or, Suite   HMV ASD 532
                         EMI XLP 30076/SXLP 30076

Khatchaturian   Kurtz   HMV ALP 2033
Waltz and Galop   HMV ASD 582
(Masquerade)

Bach   Kurtz   EMI XLP 20058/SXLP 20058
Ach Gott vom Himmel sieh'
darein, Chorale Prelude

28 & 29 April and 10 July 1961, Abbey Road

Stravinsky   Vandernoot   HMV ALP 1956
Le baiser de la fée,   HMV ASD 507
Suite

8 & 9 May 1961, Abbey Road

Offenbach   Mackerras   HMV CLP 1722
Gaité Parisienne, Suite   HMV CSD 1533

9 May 1961, Abbey Road

Johann Strauss   Mackerras   HMV unpublished
Perpetuum mobile;
Tritsch-Tratsch Polka;
Thunder and Lightning,
Polka

9 May 1961, Kingsway Hall

Bach   Klemperer   Columbia unpublished
Harpsichord Concerto   Malcolm
in D minor BWV 1052

11 May 1961, Abbey Road

Grieg   Weldon   Columbia 33SX 1378
Sigurd Jorsalfar, Suite   Columbia SCX 3416
                                                       EMI CFP 40225

Brahms   Weldon   Columbia unpublished
Hungarian Dance No 3

23 & 24 May 1961, Abbey Road

Grieg   Weldon   Columbia 33SX 1378
Holberg Suite;   Columbia SCX 3416
Two Elegiac Melodies;   EMI CFP 40225
Two Norwegian Melodies
(Cowkeeper's Tune and
Country Dance)

23, 25 & 26 May 1961, Abbey Road

Coleridge-Taylor   Sargent   HMV ALP 1899
Hiawatha's Wedding Feast   Royal Choral Society HMV ASD 467
                                  R.Lewis   EMI ESD 7161

29 & 30 May 1961, Abbey Road

Adam   R.Irving   HMV CLP 1598
Giselle, Ballet   HMV CSD 1465
(abridged)   EMI CFP 41 45051

30 May 1961, Abbey Road

Glinka   Weldon   Columbia 33SX 1436
Russlan and Ludmilla,   Columbia SCX 3446
Overture;
Smetana
Dance of the Comedians
(The Bartered Bride);

Grainger   Weldon   Columbia 33SX 1436
Mock Morris;   Columbia SCX 3446
Delius   EMI CFP 4510
La Calinda (Koanga)

31 May 1961, Abbey Road

Prokofiev
March (The Love of
Three Oranges);
Holst
Jupiter (The Planets);
Falla
Dance (El amor brujo);
Mozart
Le Nozze di Figaro,
Overture;
Bach
Air (Suite No 3)   Weldon   Columbia 33SX 1436
     Columbia SCX 3446

Vaughan Williams   Weldon   Columbia 33SX 1436
Greensleeves   Columbia SCX 3446
     EMI CFP 4510

Mendelssohn   Weldon   Columbia 33SX 1570
Scherzo (A Midsummer   Columbia SCX 3499
Night's Dream)

20 & 21 June 1961, Kingsway Hall

Shostakovich   R.Irving   Capitol P 8576/SP 8576
The Age of Gold,
Ballet Suite;
Bartok
The Miraculous Mandarin,
Ballet Suite

23, 24 & 26 June 1961, Kingsway Hall

Beethoven   Leinsdorf   Columbia SAX 2508
Violin Concerto   Milstein   Columbia 33CX 1863
     World Records ST 597

1 July 1961, Kingsway Hall

Puccini   Ferraris   HMV ALP 1978
Recondita armonia (Tosca);   Corelli   HMV ASD 529
Ponchielli
Cielo e mar (La Gioconda);
Giordano
Un di all' azzurro spazie
(Andrea Chenier)

1 & 13 July 1961, Kingsway Hall

Puccini   Ferraris   HMV unpublished
Ch' ella mi creda   Corelli
(La Fanciulla del West)

3 July 1961, Kingsway Hall

Puccini	Ferraris	HMV ALP 1978
Donna non vidi mai	Corelli	HMV ASD 529
(Manon Lescaut);		
Donizetti		
Una vergine, un angel di Dio		
(La Favorita)		

3 & 13 July 1961, Kingsway Hall

Puccini	Ferraris	HMV ALP 1978
Nessun dorma (Turandot);	Corelli	HMV ASD 529
E lucevan le stelle		
(Tosca)		

5 July 1961, Kingsway Hall

Meyerbeer	Ferraris	HMV ALP 1978
Plus blanche que la	Corelli	HMV ASD 529
blance ermine		
(Les Huguenots);		
Bellini		
A te o cara (I Puritani)		

5 & 13 July 1961, Kingsway Hall

Cilea	Ferraris	HMV ALP 1978
L'anima ho stanca	Corelli	HMV ASD 529
(Adriana Lecouvreur)		

16 & 17 October 1961 and 10 April 1964, Kingsway Hall

Falla	Giulini	Columbia 33CX 5265
El amor brujo	De los Angeles	Columbia SAX 5265
		EMI SXLP 30140
		EMI CFP 4512

18, 19 & 20 October 1961, Kingsway Hall

Tchaikovsky	Klemperer	Columbia 33CX 1812
Symphony No 6		Columbia SAX 2458
"Pathétique"		EMI SLS 5003*
		EMI EM 29 02823*

20 October 1961, Kingsway Hall

Johann Strauss	Klemperer	Columbia 33CX 1814
Emperor Waltz;		Columbia SAX 2460
Wiener Blut, Waltz		EMI SXLP 30226

23 October and 13 November 1961, Kingsway Hall

Strauss	Klemperer	Columbia 33CX 1789
Tod und Verklärung		Columbia SAX 2437
		EMI ED 29 06161

24 October 1961, Kingsway Hall

Wagner　　　　　　　　Klemperer　　　　　　　Columbia 33CX 1820
Entry of the Gods into　　　　　　　　　　　　Columbia SAX 2464
Valhalla (Das Rheingold)　　　　　　　　　　　EMI ASD 2697*
　　　　　　　　　　　　　　　　　　　　　　EMI SLS 5075*
　　　　　　　　　　　　　　　　　　　　　　EMI SXLP 30528
　　　　　　　　　　　　　　　　　　　　　　EMI CDC 747 2552

24 October and 13 November 1961, Kingsway Hall

Wagner　　　　　　　　Klemperer　　　　　　　Columbia 33CX 1820
Forest Murmurs　　　　　　　　　　　　　　　Columbia SAX 2464
(Siegfried)　　　　　　　　　　　　　　　　EMI ASD 2697
　　　　　　　　　　　　　　　　　　　　　　EMI SLS 5075*
　　　　　　　　　　　　　　　　　　　　　　EMI SXLP 30528
　　　　　　　　　　　　　　　　　　　　　　EMI CDC 747 2552

30 October 1961, Kingsway Hall

Klemperer　　　　　　　Klemperer　　　　　　　Columbia 33CX 1814
Merry Waltz & One Step　　　　　　　　　　　Columbia SAX 2460
(Das Ziel)　　　　　　　　　　　　　　　　　EMI SXLP 30226
　　　　　　　　　　　　　　　　　　　　　　EMI ED 29 03321

30 October and 2 December 1961, Kingsway Hall

Johann Strauss　　　　　Klemperer　　　　　　　Columbia 33CX 1814
Die Fledermaus, Overture　　　　　　　　　　Columbia SAX 2460
　　　　　　　　　　　　　　　　　　　　　　EMI SXLP 30226

31 October and 2 December 1961, Kingsway Hall

Weill　　　　　　　　　Klemperer　　　　　　　Columbia 33CX 1814
Kleine Dreigroschenmusik　　　　　　　　　　Columbia SAX 2460
　　　　　　　　　　　　　　　　　　　　　　EMI SXLP 30226
　　　　　　　　　　　　　　　　　　　　　　EMI ED 29 03321

3 & 4 November 1961, Kingsway Hall

Strauss　　　　　　　　Klemperer　　　　　　　Columbia 33CX 1789
Metamorphosen　　　　　　　　　　　　　　　Columbia SAX 2437

13 & 14 November 1961, Kingsway Hall

Rossini Selve opaca (William Tell)	Tonini Callas	EMI EL 749 4281 EMI CDC 747 4281

13 & 14 November 1961 and 13 April 1962, Kingsway Hall

Rossini Nacqui all' affano.... Non più mesta (La Cenerentola)	Tonini Callas	EMI EL 749 4281 EMI CDC 749 4281

14 November 1961, Kingsway Hall

Donizetti Quel guardo il cavaliere... So anch'io la virtù magica (Don Pasquale)	Tonini Callas	Columbia unpublished
Wagner Parsifal, Act 1 Prelude	Klemperer	Columbia 33CX 1820 Columbia SAX 2464 EMI ASD 2697 EMI SLS 5075* EMI SXLP 30528 EMI CDC 747 2552

14 & 15 November 1961, Kingsway Hall

Rossini Bel raggio lusinghier (Semiramide)	Tonini Callas	Columbia unpublished

15 November 1961, Kingsway Hall

Donizetti Com' è bello quale incanto (Lucrezia Borgia)	Tonini Callas	Columbia unpublished

16 November 1961, Kingsway Hall

Bellini Sorgete, è in me dover... Lo sognai ferito esangue (Il Pirata)	Tonini Callas Sinclair, Young	EMI ASD 2791 EMI 2C 165 54178-88* EMI CDC 747 2832

22 November 1961, Kingsway Hall

Wagner Siegfried's Rhine Journey (Götterdämmerung)	Klemperer	Columbia 33CX 1820 Columbia SAX 2464 EMI ASD 2697 EMI SLS 5075* EMI SXLP 30528 EMI CDC 747 2552

22, 23 & 24 November 1961 and 15 & 24 March 1962, Kingsway Hall

Mahler	Klemperer	Columbia 33CX 1929/30
Symphony No 2	Philharmonia Chorus	Columbia SAX 2473/4
"Resurrection"	Schwarzkopf	EMI SLS 806
	Rössl-Majdan	

4, 5, 6, 7, 8 & 9 December 1961, Kingsway Hall

Bach	Klemperer	Columbia unpublished
Mass in B minor	Philharmonia Chorus	(choruses only recorded)

ROYAL FESTIVAL HALL
General Manager: T. E. Bean, C.B.E.

PHILHARMONIA CONCERT SOCIETY Ltd

ARTISTIC DIRECTOR:
WALTER LEGGE

PHILHARMONIA ORCHESTRA

LEADER: HUGH BEAN

OTTO KLEMPERER
NATHAN MILSTEIN

BEETHOVEN	Overture, Leonore No. 3
TCHAIKOVSKY	Violin Concerto in D
MOZART	Serenata Notturna, K. 239
MOZART	Symphony No. 40 in G minor

Sunday, May 20, 1962, at 7.30 p.m.

Programme One Shilling and Sixpence

1962

17 & 18 January and 18 & 19 April 1962, Kingsway Hall

Dvorak	Giulini	Columbia 33CX 1815
Symphony No 8		Columbia SAX 2461
		World Records ST 590

18 & 19 January 1962, Kingsway Hall

Dvorak	Giulini	Columbia 33CX 1815
Scherzo capriccioso		Columbia SAX 2461
		World Records ST 590

29 & 30 January 1962, Abbey Road

Rachmaninov	Pritchard	HMV ALP 1923
Piano Concerto No 2	Ogdon	HMV ASD 492
		EMI SXLP 30552

3, 6, 7, 8, 9, 10, 12, 13, 14 & 17 February 1962, Kingsway Hall

Beethoven	Klemperer	Columbia 33CX 1804/5/6
Fidelio	Philharmonia Chorus	Columbia SAX 2451/2/3
	C.Ludwig, Hallstein,	EMI SLS 5006
	Vickers, Berry, Crass,	Excerpts:
	Frick, Unger, Wehofschitz,	Columbia 33CX 1907
	Wolansky	Columbia SAX 2547
		EMI SXLP 30307

27 February 1962, Royal Festival Hall (live recording)

Weber	Prêtre	Opera Dubs OD 101/2*
Ocean, thou mighty monster	Callas	Melodram MEL 674*
(Oberon);		
Verdi		
La luce langue (Macbeth)*;		
Rossini		
Nacqui all' affano		
(La Cenerentola);		
Massenet		
Pleurez mes yeux (Le Cid);		
Donizetti		
Mad Scene and Finale		
(Anna Bolena)	*incomplete	

6 & 7 March 1962, Kingsway Hall

Mozart	Klemperer	Columbia 33CX 1843
Symphony No 41 "Jupiter"		Columbia SAX 2486
		EMI SLS 5048*
		EMI EX 29 04823*
		EMI CDC 747 8522

8 & 28 March 1962, Kingsway Hall

Mozart	Klemperer	Columbia 33CX 1843
Symphony No 40		Columbia SAX 2486
		EMI SLS 5003*
		EMI SLS 5048*
		EMI EX 29 04823*
		EMI CDC 747 8522

10 March 1962, Abbey Road

Rimsky-Korsakov Le Coq d'Or, Suite	Kurtz	HMV ALP 1985 HMV ASD 533 EMI XLP 30076/SXLP 30076

21, 22 & 23 March 1962, Kingsway Hall

Brahms Alto Rhapsody	Klemperer Philharmonia Chorus C.Ludwig	Columbia 33CX 1817 Columbia SAX 2452 EMI ASD 2391 EMI SLS 821* EMI SXLP 27 00001
Wagner Wesendonk Lieder	Klemperer C.Ludwig	Columbia 33CX 1817 Columbia SAX 2452 EMI ASD 2391 EMI SXLP 27 00001
Wagner Isoldes Liebestod (Tristan und Isolde)	Klemperer C.Ludwig	Columbia 33CX 1817 Columbia SAX 2452 EMI SXLP 27 00001

26, 27 & 28 March 1962, Kingsway Hall

Mozart Symphony No 38 "Prague"; Symphony No 39	Klemperer	Columbia 33CX 1824 Columbia SAX 2468 EMI SLS 5048* EMI EX 29 04823*

27 March 1962, Dominion Cinema, Southall

Verdi Aida, excerpts	Downes J. McCarthy Chorus Shuard, Craig	HMV unpublished (test recording only)

28 & 30 March and 16 May 1962, Kingsway Hall

Stravinsky Symphony in Three Movements	Klemperer	Columbia 33CX 1949 Columbia SAX 2588

9, 10 & 11 April 1962, Kingsway Hall

Tchaikovsky Romeo and Juliet, Fantasy Overture	Giulini	Columbia 33CX 1840 Columbia SAX 2483
Tchaikovsky Francesca da Rimini	Giulini	Columbia 33CX 1840 Columbia SAX 2483 EMI SXLP 30509

9 & 13 April 1962, Kingsway Hall

Verdi O don fatale (Don Carlo); Weber Ocean, thou mighty monster (Oberon)	Tonini Callas	Columbia unpublished

10 & 14 April 1962, Kingsway Hall

Rossini Gibson World Records unpublished
William Tell;
Il Barbiere di Siviglia,
Overtures;
Verdi
La Traviata, Acts 1
and 3 Preludes

11, 12, 13 & 19 April 1962, Kingsway Hall

Debussy Giulini Columbia 33CX 1818
La Mer Columbia SAX 2463
 EMI SXLP 30146

14, 18, 19, 25 & 26 April 1962, Kingsway Hall

Debussy Giulini Columbia 33CX 1818
Trois Nocturnes Philharmonia Choir Columbia SAX 2463
 EMI SXLP 30146

21 & 22 April 1962, Abbey Road

Brahms Giulini Columbia 33CX 1822
Piano Concerto No 2 Arrau Columbia SAX 2466
 EMI CFP 40034

25 & 27 April 1962, Kingsway Hall

Verdi Tonini Columbia unpublished
Addio del passato Schwarzkopf
(La Traviata);
Puccini
Tu che di gel sei cinta;
Signore, ascolta
(Turandot);
Donde lieta uscì
(La Bohème);
Rossini
Selve opaca (William Tell)

26 April 1962, Kingsway Hall

Tchaikovsky Giulini Columbia unpublished
Symphony No 5   (recording incomplete)

6 & 10 May 1962, Abbey Road

Bliss Sargent HMV ALP 1948
Piano Concerto Barnard HMV ASD 499
 EMI SLS 5080*

8 & 9 May 1962, Kingsway Hall

Vaughan Williams Barbirolli HMV ALP 1957
Symphony No 5 HMV ASD 508
 EMI ASD 2698

9 May and 27 August 1962, Kingsway Hall

Elgar	Barbirolli	HMV ALP 1998
Enigma Variations		HMV ASD 548
		EMI SLS 5030*
		EMI ESD 7169

19, 25 & 28 June 1962, Kingsway Hall

Strauss	Maazel	Columbia 33CX 1823
Till Eulenspiegels		Columbia SAX 2467
lustige Streiche		World Records ST 935
		EMI SXLP 30133

20 & 25 June 1962, Kingsway Hall

Debussy	Maazel	Columbia 33CX 1841
Prélude à l'après-midi		Columbia SAX 2484
d'un faune		World Records ST 830
		EMI SXLP 30233
		EMI EMX 2008

22 & 23 June 1962, Kingsway Hall

Brahms	Kletzki	HMV ALP 1999
Double Concerto	Ferras, Tortelier	HMV ASD 549
		World Records ST 699
		EMI SLS 27 00013*

23, 26, 27 & 28 June and 23 August 1962, Kingsway Hall

Strauss	Maazel	Columbia 33CX 1823
Also sprach Zarathustra		Columbia SAX 2467
		World Records ST 935
		EMI SXLP 30133

28 & 29 June and 23 August 1962, Kingsway Hall

Mussorgsky	Maazel	Columbia 33CX 1841
Pictures from an		Columbia SAX 2484
Exhibition (orch. Ravel)		World Records ST 830
		EMI SXLP 30233
		EMI EMX 2008

2, 3, 4, 5, 6, 7, 9 & 12 July 1962, Kingsway Hall

Lehar	Matacic	EMI AN 101-2/SAN 101-2
The Merry Widow	Philharmonia Chorus	EMI SLS 823
	Schwarzkopf, Steffek,	EMI CDS 747 1788
	Gedda, Wächter, Knapp,	Excerpts:
	Wood, McNab, Parker,	EMI ALP 2252/ASD 2252
	Willett, Murray, Phillips,	
	Equiluz, Strohbauer,	
	Böheim	

4 July 1962, Kingsway Hall

Verdi   Gibson   World Records unpublished
La Forza del Destino;
Rossini
La gazza ladra, Overtures

27 August 1962, Kingsway Hall

Elgar   Barbirolli   HMV ALP 1998
Cockaigne, Overture   HMV ASD 548
                                                   EMI SLS 5030*
                                                   EMI ESD 7169

28 & 29 August 1962, Kingsway Hall

Elgar   Barbirolli   HMV ALP 1989
Symphony No 1   HMV ASD 540
                                                   EMI ASD 2748
                                                   EMI SLS 5030*
                                                   EMI SXLP 30268
                                                   EMI EMX 41 20841

28 & 29 August 1962 and 14, 15 & 16 July 1966, Kingsway Hall

Elgar   Barbirolli   EMI ALP 2292/ASD 2292
Pomp and Circumstance,   EMI SLS 5030*
Marches Nos.   EMI SXLP 30456
1, 2, 3, 4 and 5

10, 11, 12, 13, 14, 15, 17 & 18 September 1962, Kingsway Hall

Mozart   Böhm   EMI AN 103-6/SAN 103-6
Così fan tutte   Philharmonia Chorus   EMI SLS 5028
                             Schwarzkopf, C.Ludwig,   Excerpts:
                             Steffek, Kraus, Taddei,   EMI ALP 2265/ASD 2265
                             Berry   EMI SXLP 30457

2, 4 & 9 October 1962, Kingsway Hall

Britten   Giulini   Columbia 33CX 1915
Variations and Fugue   Columbia SAX 2555
on a theme of Purcell   EMI SXLP 30240
(Young Person's Guide to
the Orchestra)

9 October 1962, Kingsway Hall

Britten   Giulini   Columbia 33CX 1915
Four Sea Interludes   Columbia SAX 2555
(Peter Grimes)   EMI SXLP 30240

10 & 11 October 1962, Kingsway Hall

Brahms Symphony No 2	Giulini	Columbia 33CX 1855 Columbia SAX 2498 EMI SLS 5241*

12 October 1962, Kingsway Hall

Brahms Tragic Overture	Giulini	Columbia 33CX 1872 Columbia SAX 2516 EMI SLS 5241*

12 October and 9 & 12 November 1962, Kingsway Hall

Brahms Symphony No 3	Giulini	Columbia 33CX 1872 Columbia SAX 2516 EMI SLS 5241*

16 October 1962, Abbey Road

Coleridge-Taylor Petite Suite de Concert	Weldon	HMV PES 5285 EMI SXLP 30123 EMI CFP 4510 EMI ESD 7161
Vaughan Williams Folks Songs from Somerset, March	Weldon	HMV CLP 1645 HMV CSD 1495 World Records ST 927

17 & 18 October 1962, Abbey Road

Prokofiev Violin Concerto No 1	Giulini Milstein	Columbia 33CX 5275/SAX 5275 EMI SXLP 30235

18 October 1962, Abbey Road

Mozart Violin Concerto No 3	Giulini Milstein	Columbia unpublished

22 & 23 October 1962, Kingsway Hall

Berlioz Harold In Italy	Colin Davis Menuhin	HMV ALP 1986 HMV ASD 537 EMI SXLP 30314

29, 30 & 31 October 1962, Abbey Road

Coates Covent Garden (London Suite) Oxford Street (London Again); Harty The Fair Day (Irish Symphony); Arnold Scottish Dance No 1; Walton Orb and Sceptre, March; Grainger Londonderry Air	Weldon	HMV CLP 1645 HMV CSD 1495 World Records ST 927
Traditional songs: Devonshire cream and cider; In summertime on Bredon; David of the white rock; Blow the wind southerly; An Eriskay love lilt	Weldon Harvey	HMV CLP 1645 HMV CSD 1495 World Records ST 927

27 & 28 November 1962 and 21 & 22 March 1963, Kingsway Hall

Shostakovich Symphony No 12 "The Year 1917"	Prêtre	HMV ALP 2009 HMV ASD 559 EMI CFP 141

10, 11, 12 & 13 December 1962, Kingsway Hall

Verdi Four Sacred Pieces	Giulini Philharmonia Chorus Baker	EMI AN 120/SAN 120 EMI SXLP 30508 EMI CDS 747 2578

13 December 1962, Kingsway Hall

Rossini William Tell, Overture	Giulini	Columbia 33CX 1919 Columbia SAX 2560 EMI SXLP 30143 EMI CFP 40379

14 December 1962, Kingsway Hall

Rossini Semiramide, Overture	Giulini	Columbia 33CX 1919 Columbia SAX 2560 EMI SXLP 30143 EMI CFP 40379

17 & 18 December 1962, Abbey Road

Tchaikovsky Piano Concerto No 1	Barbirolli Ogdon	HMV ALP 1991 HMV ASD 542 EMI SXLP 30552

ROYAL FESTIVAL HALL
General Manager: T. E. Bean, C.B.E.

PHILHARMONIA CONCERT SOCIETY Ltd

ARTISTIC DIRECTOR:
WALTER LEGGE

PHILHARMONIA ORCHESTRA

PRINCIPAL CONDUCTOR: OTTO KLEMPERER

SCHUBERT: Symphony No. 8 in B minor (Unfinished) D.759
RACHMANINOV: Piano Concerto No. 2 in C minor, Op. 18

JOHN OGDON

BEETHOVEN: Symphony No. 5 in C minor, Op. 67

LORIN MAAZEL

Monday, April 22, 1963, at 8 p.m.

Programme One Shilling and Sixpence

1963

16, 17, 18, 19 & 21 January 1963, Kingsway Hall

Tchaikovsky Klemperer Columbia 33CX 1854
Symphony No 5 Columbia SAX 2497
 EMI EM 29 02823*

23, 24 & 25 January and 2 February 1963, Kingsway Hall

Tchaikovsky Klemperer Columbia 33CX 1851
Symphony No 4 Columbia SAX 2494
 EMI EM 29 02823*

4 & 6 February 1963, Kingsway Hall

Schubert Klemperer Columbia 33CX 1870
Symphony No 8 Columbia SAX 2514
"Unfinished" EMI SLS 5003*
 EMI ED 29 04601

18 & 19 February and 14 & 18 May 1963 and 20 March 1964, Kingsway Hall

Stravinsky Klemperer Columbia 33CX 1949
Pulcinella, Suite Columbia SAX 2588

21 & 22 March 1963, Kingsway Hall

Shostakovich Prêtre HMV ALP 2009
Festival Overture HMV ASD 559
 EMI CFP 141

11 April 1963, Kingsway Hall

Dvorak Weldon Columbia 33SX 1570
Carnival, Overture; Columbia SCX 3499
Mendelssohn
Scherzo (A Midsummer
Night's Dream);
Verdi
La Traviata, Act 1 Prelude;
Smetana
Polka (The Bartered Bride);
Tchaikovsky
Waltz (Serenade for Strings)

20 April 1963, Abbey Road

Beethoven Giulini Columbia 33CX 1903
Piano Concerto No 3 Richter-Haaser Columbia SAX 2543
 Toshiba EAC 30064

22, 23 & 24 April 1963, Kingsway Hall

Verdi Ella giammai m'amo (Don Carlo); Uldino, non hai veduto... Mentre gonfiarsi l'anima (Attila); Borodin How goes it, Prince ? (Prince Igor); Gluck O toi, l'objet le plus aimable (Iphigénie en Aulide)	Semkow Christoff	HMV ALP 2025 HMV ASD 574

23, 24, 25 & 26 April and 17 & 18 September 1963, Kingsway Hall

Berlioz Symphonie fantastique	Klemperer	Columbia 33CX 1898 Columbia SAX 2537 EMI SLS 5003* EMI EMX 2030

13, 15 & 16 May 1963, Kingsway Hall

Schubert Symphony No 5	Klemperer	Columbia 33CX 1870 Columbia SAX 2514 EMI ED 29 04601

18 & 21 May 1963, Kingsway Hall

Wagner Entry of the Guests (Tannhäuser)	Weldon	Columbia unpublished
Tchaikovsky 1812, Overture	Weldon Royal Marines Band	Columbia 33SX 1570 Columbia SCX 3499

29 May and 1 June 1963, Abbey Road

Stravinsky The Firebird, Suite (1919 version)	J.Krips	HMV ALP 2112 HMV ASD 654 EMI CFP 40328
Strauss Der Rosenkavalier, Suite	J.Krips	HMV ALP 2112 HMV ASD 654

31 May 1963, Royal Festival Hall (live recording)

Rossini Bel raggio lusinghier (Semiramide)	Prêtre Callas	Legendary Records LR 111

1 June 1963, Abbey Road

Brahms Haydn Variations (St Antoni Chorale)	J.Krips	HMV ALP 2023 HMV ASD 573

1 & 3 June 1963, Abbey Road

Saint-Saens	Fistoulari	Angel 36005
Violin Concerto No 3	Milstein	EMI SXLP 30159
		Angel RL 32056

1, 3 & 6 June 1963, Abbey Road

Chausson	Fistoulari	Angel 36005
Poème	Milstein	EMI SXLP 30159
		Angel RL 32056

4, 6 & 10 June 1963 and 3, 4 & 9 June 1964, Abbey Road

Mozart	Milstein, cond. & sol.	Columbia 33CX 5254/SAX 5254
Violin Concerto No 4		

4, 6 & 10 June 1963 and 10 & 11 June 1964, Abbey Road

Mozart	Milstein, cond. & sol.	Columbia 33CX 5254/SAX 5254
Violin Concerto No 5		

10, 11 & 12 June 1963, Abbey Road

Prokofiev	Kletzki	HMV ALP 2029
Symphony No 5		HMV ASD 578
		EMI CFP 200

16 June 1963, Abbey Road

Strauss	Dohnanyi	World Records ST 459
Burleske	Wayenberg	

19 June 1963, Abbey Road

Rachmaninov	Dohnanyi	World Records ST 459
Rhapsody on a theme	Wayenberg	
of Paganini		

18 & 19 June 1963, Kingsway Hall

Bloch	Kletzki	HMV ALP 2035
Violin Concerto	Menuhin	HMV ASD 584
		EMI SXLP 30177
		EMI EX 29 08643*

20 June and 29 July 1963, Kingsway Hall

Grieg	Fistoulari	EMI XLP 20058/SXLP 20058
Holberg Suite		

20 & 21 June and 10 July 1963, Kingsway Hall

Saint-Saens Danse macabre; Tchaikovsky Romeo and Juliet, Fantasy Overture	Gamba	HMV CLP 1848 HMV CSD 1592

22 June 1963, Abbey Road

Brahms Tragic Overture; Academic Festival Overture	J.Krips	HMV ALP 2023 HMV ASD 573

24, 25 & 28 June 1963, Abbey Road

Prokofiev Romeo and Juliet, Ballet Suite	Kurtz	HMV CLP 1831 HMV CSD 1585 World Records ST 684

25, 26 & 27 June 1963, Abbey Road

Mozart Flute and Harp Concerto	Menuhin Schaffer, Costello	HMV ALP 2026 HMV ASD 575 World Records ST 937
Telemann Flute Suite in A minor	Menuhin Schaffer	HMV ALP 2026 HMV ASD 575 World Records ST 937

26 & 29 June and 1 & 3 July 1963, Abbey Road

Rimsky-Korsakov Tsar Saltan, Suite; Dubinushka	Kurtz	HMV ALP 2033 HMV ASD 582 EMI XLP 30076/SXLP 30076
Rimsky-Korsakov The Snow Maiden, Suite	Kurtz	HMV ALP 2033 HMV ASD 582

27, 28 & 29 June and 1, 2 & 3 July 1963, Abbey Road

Prokofiev Piano Concerto No 3; Piano Concerto No 5	Rowicki François	Columbia 33CX 1889 Columbia SAX 2533

10 July 1963, Kingsway Hall

Rimsky-Korsakov Capriccio espagnol	Gamba	HMV CLP 1848 HMV CSD 1592

29 July 1963, Kingsway Hall

Tchaikovsky Andante cantabile	Fistoulari	EMI XLP 20058/SXLP 20058

<u>16, 17, 18, 19, 20, 21, 22, 23, 24, 25, 26 & 27 September 1963 and 7 April 1964, Kingsway Hall</u>

Verdi Requiem Mass	Giulini Philharmonia Chorus Schwarzkopf, C.Ludwig, Gedda, Ghiaurov	EMI AN 133-4/SAN 133-4 EMI SLS 909 EMI CDS 747 2578

<u>18, 19, 20, 24, 25 & 26 September 1963, Kingsway Hall</u>

Bruckner Symphony No 4 "Romantic"	Klemperer	Columbia 33CX 1928 Columbia SAX 2569 EMI SXLP 30167

<u>15 October 1963, Abbey Road</u>

Walton Henry V, Suite	Walton	Columbia 33CX 1883 Columbia SAX 2527 World Records ST 656 EMI SXLP 30139 EMI SLS 5246*
Walton Funeral March (Hamlet)	Walton	Columbia 33CX 1883 Columbia SAX 2527 World Records ST 656 EMI SXLP 30139

<u>15 & 16 October 1963, Abbey Road</u>

Walton Richard III, Prelude and Suite	Walton	Columbia 33CX 1883 Columbia SAX 2527 World Records ST 656 EMI SXLP 30139 EMI SLS 5246*(Prelude only)

<u>16 October 1963, Abbey Road</u>

Walton Spitfire Prelude & Fugue	Walton	EMI SXLP 30139 EMI SLS 5246*

<u>16, 17 & 18 October 1963, Abbey Road</u>

Mozart Symphony No 31 "Paris"	Klemperer	Columbia 33CX 1906 Columbia SAX 2546 EMI SLS 5048* EMI EX 29 04823*

<u>18 & 19 October 1963, Abbey Road</u>

Mozart Symphony No 34	Klemperer	Columbia 33CX 1906 Columbia SAX 2546 EMI SLS 5048* EMI EX 29 04823*

28, 29 & 30 October and 2 December 1963, Kingsway Hall

Falla	Frühbeck de Burgos	HMV ALP 2059
The Three-Cornered Hat	De los Angeles	HMV ASD 608
		EMI SXLP 30187

30 & 31 October and 1 & 2 November 1963, Kingsway Hall

Dvorak	Klemperer	Columbia 33CX 1914
Symphony No 9		Columbia SAX 2554
"From the New World"		EMI SLS 5003*

4, 5, 6 & 7 November 1963, Kingsway Hall

Beethoven	Klemperer	Columbia 33CX 1902
Leonore No 3, Overture		Columbia SAX 2542
		EMI ASD 2568
		EMI SLS 790*
		EMI SLS 788*
		EMI SXDW 3032*
		EMI SXDW 3051*
		EMI ED 29 04011
		EMI CDC 747 1902

Beethoven	Klemperer	Columbia 33CX 1902
Leonore No 2, Overture		Columbia SAX 2542
		EMI ASD 2561
		EMI SLS 788*
		EMI SXDW 3032*
		EMI ED 29 04011
		EMI CDC 747 1902

Beethoven	Klemperer	Columbia 33CX 1902
Leonore No 1, Overture		Columbia SAX 2542
		EMI ASD 2565
		EMI SLS 788*
		EMI SXDW 3032*
		EMI ED 29 04011
		EMI CDC 747 1902

7 & 8 November 1963, Kingsway Hall

Schubert	Klemperer	Columbia unpublished
Symphony No 4 "Tragic"		(recording incomplete)

8 November 1963 and 10 & 11 February 1964, Kingsway Hall

Schumann	Klemperer	Columbia unpublished
Symphony No 1 "Spring"		

29 November 1963, Abbey Road

Rossini	Erede	HMV ALP 2057
Sois immobile	Gobbi	HMV ASD 606
(William Tell);		EMI HQS 143 6721
Donizetti		
Come paride		
(L'elisir d'Amore);		
Giordano		
La donna russa (Fedora)		

30 November 1963, Abbey Road

Cilea	Erede	HMV ALP 2057
Ecco il monologo	Gobbi	HMV ASD 606
(Adriana Lecouvreur)		EMI HQS 143 6721

Verdi	Erede	HMV ALP 2057
Plebe! Patrizi!	Gobbi	HMV ASD 606
(Simone Boccanegra)		EMI HQS 143 6721
		EMI HLM 7018

1 December 1963, Abbey Road

Verdi	Erede	HMV ALP 2057
Quand' ero paggio	Gobbi	HMV ASD 606
(Falstaff)		EMI HQS 143 6721

Credo in un dio crudel	Erede	HMV ALP 2057
(Otello)	Gobbi	HMV ASD 606
		EMI HQS 143 6721
		EMI HLM 7018

21 & 22 December 1963, Abbey Road

Rachmaninov	Pritchard	HMV unpublished
Rhapsody on a theme	Ogdon	
of Paganini		

22 December 1963, Abbey Road

Liszt-Busoni	Pritchard	HMV ALP 2051
Rapsodie espagnole;	Ogdon	HMV ASD 600
Liszt		World Records ST 697
Hungarian Fantasia		

23 & 24 December 1963, Abbey Road

Tippett	Colin Davis	HMV ALP 2073
Piano Concerto	Ogdon	HMV ASD 621
		EMI SLS 5080*
		EMI EX 29 02283*

1964

On 10 March 1964 Walter Legge released a statement to the press announcing that he was suspending the activities of the Philharmonia Orchestra for an indefinite period. It would fulfil its present commitments, which included the completion of a number of recording sessions for EMI.

The reasons for the suspension are too involved to discuss here, but Legge's own resignation from EMI in 1963 is relevant. For a number of years there had been a rationalisation of EMI's recording programme by the International Classical Repertoire Committee, and Legge was no longer able to work in his own inimitably independent and expensive way. From about mid-1959 recording work had begun to fall off as the repertoire was re-recorded in stereo, and EMI was looking for a new contract with the Philharmonia which offered fewer sessions and which did not pay the same high royalties on record sales. This meant that the orchestra would have to look to concerts as a more significant proportion of their work and income, but to do so meant competing for subsidy in the open market. Legge was not prepared to compete on someone else's terms, nor was he prepared to compromise on standards in order to make the orchestra pay. He therefore chose to suspend the Philharmonia.

The players themselves immediately re-formed as a self-governing body. In a very short time they had secured the name "New Philharmonia" as an operating title, and obtained recording work with EMI and Decca. Other companies soon offered them work; the orchestra was no longer under exclusive contract to EMI.

Walter Legge eventually sold his shares in Philharmonia to EMI, and EMI thus acquired the royalties that continued to be paid on sales of records made by the pre-1964 Philharmonia Orchestra. In 1972 EMI signed away the use of the name "Philharmonia" to an orchestra in Philadelphia, but only five years later the New Philharmonia sought back and won an agreement to use the title again.

1964

14 & 15 February 1964, Abbey Roau

Liszt	Vandernoot	HMV ALP 2082
Totentanz;	Cziffra	HMV ASD 629
Hungarian Fantasy		

16 February 1964, Abbey Road

Debussy	Vandernoot	HMV unpublished
Petite Suite		

17, 18 & 19 February 1964, Kingsway Hall

Mahler	Klemperer	EMI ASD 2391
Wo die schönen Trompeten	C.Ludwig	EMI SXLP 27 00001
blasen; Das irdische Leben		
(Des Knaben Wunderhorn);		
Ich bin der Welt abhanden		
gekommen; Um Mitternacht;		
Ich atmet' einen linden		
Duft (Rückert-Lieder)		

19, 20, 21 & 22 February and 7 & 8 November 1964*, Kingsway Hall, and 6, 7, 8 & 9 July 1966, Abbey Road

Mahler	Klemperer	EMI AN 179/SAN 179
Das Lied von der Erde	C.Ludwig, Wunderlich	EMI EL 29 04401
		EMI CDC 747 2312

(* sessions on 7 & 8 November 1964 were the last recording sessions of the original Philharmonia Orchestra. From July 1964, the orchestra was being engaged and recorded under the title New Philharmonia Orchestra.)

24 & 25 February, 9, 10, 11, 12, 13, 14, 16, 17, 18, 19 March, 20, 21 & 22 July, 28 & 29 September, 1, 2, 8 & 9 October and 2 & 3 November 1964, Kingsway Hall

Handel	Klemperer	EMI AN 146-8/SAN 146-8
Messiah	Philharmonia Chorus	EMI SLS 915
	Schwarzkopf, Hoffman,	Excerpts:
	Boese*, Baker*, Gedda,	EMI ALP 2288/ASD 2288
	Pears*, Hines	

(*these artists took part in the earlier sessions, but are not heard in the published recording)

24, 25, 26 & 31 March, 1, 2, 3, 4, 6, 7, 8 & 10 April 1964, Kingsway Hall

Mozart	Klemperer	EMI AN 137-9/SAN 137-9
Die Zauberflöte	Philharmonia Chorus	EMI SLS 912
	Janowitz, Popp, Schwarzkopf,	Excerpts:
	C.Ludwig, Höffgen, Pütz,	EMI ALP 2314/ASD 2314
	Giebel, Reynolds, Veasey,	EMI ESD 100 3261
	Gedda, Unger, Liebl,	
	Berry, Frick, Crass	

1, 2 & 3 April 1964, Kingsway Hall

Rossini La gazza ladra, Overture	Giulini	Columbia 33CX 1919 Columbia SAX 2560 EMI SXLP 30143 EMI CFP 40379
Rossini La Cenerentola; Tancredi, Overtures	Giulini	Columbia 33CX 1919 Columbia SAX 2560 EMI SXLP 30143

1 & 2 June 1964, Abbey Road

Beethoven Violin Romances Nos 1 & 2	Milstein, cond. & sol.	Seraphim 60238

3, 4 & 9 June 1964, Abbey Road

Mozart Violin Concerto No 3	Milstein, cond. & sol.	Columbia unpublished

22, 23 & 24 July 1964, Kingsway Hall

Tchaikovsky Symphony No 5	Prêtre	HMV ALP 2089 HMV ASD 636

10, 11, 14, 16 & 18 September 1964, Kingsway Hall

Verdi O ben s'addice (Giovanna d'Arco); D'amor sull' ali rosee (Il Trovatore); Ma dall' arido stelo; Morro, ma prima in grazia (Un Ballo in maschera); O don fatale; Tu che la vanità (Don Carlo); Puccini Che il bel sogno (La Rondine); In questa reggia (Turandot); Ponchielli Suicidio (La Gioconda); Cilea Esser madre e un inferno (L'Arlesiana); Mascagni Voi lo sapete (Cavalleria Rusticana)	De Fabritiis Tebaldi	Decca LXT 6152/SXL 6152
Bellini Qui la voce (I Puritani)	De Fabritiis Tebaldi	Decca unpublished

12, 13, 14, 15 & 16 October 1964, Abbey Road

Haydn Symphony No 88	Klemperer	Columbia 33CX 1931 Columbia SAX 2571
Haydn Symphony No 104 "London"	Klemperer	Columbia 33CX 1931 Columbia SAX 2571 EMI ED 29 03571

29 & 30 October 1964, Abbey Road

Mozart Così fan tutte, Overture	Klemperer	Columbia 33CX 1948 Columbia SAX 2587 EMI SLS 5048* EMI EX 29 04823*

29 & 30 October and 4 November 1964, Abbey Road

Mozart Serenade No 13 "Eine kleine Nachtmusik"	Klemperer	Columbia 33CX 5252 Columbia SAX 5252 EMI EX 29 04823*

29 & 30 October and 9 & 14 November 1964, Abbey Road

Mozart Don Giovanni; Le Nozze di Figaro; La Clemenza di Tito, Overtures	Klemperer	Columbia 33CX 1948 Columbia SAX 2587 EMI SLS 5048* EMI EX 29 04823*

6, 10, 11, 12, 16. 17, 18 & 19 November 1964, Kingsway Hall

Bruckner Symphony No 6	Klemperer	Columbia 33CX 1943 Columbia SAX 2582 EMI SXLP 30448

9 & 14 November 1964, Abbey Road

Mozart Masonic Funeral Music	Klemperer	Columbia 33CX 1948 Columbia SAX 2587 EMI EX 29 04823* EMI SLS 5048* EMI EX 29 04823*
Mozart Idomeneo, Overture	Klemperer	Columbia unpublished

4 December 1964 and 2 June 1965, Wembley Town Hall

Holbrooke Poem No 4 "Ulalume"	Brooke	Unpublished

17 & 18 December 1964, Kingsway Hall

Britten Sinfonia da Requiem	Britten	Decca LXT 6175/SXL 6175 Decca SXL 6641 Decca 417 312-1

Royal Festival Hall
(General Manager: John Denison, C.B.E.)
Tuesday, June 21, 1966, at 8

MENDELSSOHN   Symphony No. 4

BRUCKNER   Symphony No. 4

SAWALLISCH   New Philharmonia Orchestra
Leader: Hugh Bean

*In association with the Arts Council
and the Greater London Council*

Programme Two Shillings

1965

5, 6 & 24 February 1965, Kingsway Hall

Bartok Violin Concerto No 2	Dorati Menuhin	EMI ALP 2281/ASD 2281 EMI SXLP 30533
Bartok Violin Concerto No 1	Dorati Menuhin	EMI ASD 2323 EMI SXLP 30533

18 & 26 March 1965, Abbey Road

I could have danced all night; Get me to the church on time; Someone to watch over me; The man I love (My Fair Lady)	Philips unpublished

27 March 1965, Denham Studios

Barsukov Piano Concerto in E flat	Boult Barsukov	Pathé DTX 344/ASTX 344 Everest SDBR 3167

10, 27, 28 & 31 May 1965, Kingsway Hall

Christmas carols (arr. Gamley): Joy to the world; It came upon the midnight; O Holy night; O Divine redeemer; What child is this ?; Adeste fideles; Twelve days of Christmas; Good King Wenceslas; Hark the herald angels; Virgin's slumber song; Ave Maria; The holly and the ivy; Angels we have heard; Deck the halls	Bonynge Ambrosian Singers Sutherland	Decca LXT 6193/SXL 6193

17 & 18 May 1965 and 22 August 1966, Kingsway Hall

Falla Love the Magician; Granados Goyescas, Intermezzo; Ravel Alborada del gracioso; Pavane pour une infante défunte	Frühbeck de Burgos Mistral	Decca SXL 6287 Decca JB 50

24 & 25 May 1965, Kingsway Hall

Mussorgsky   Black   Decca PFS 4084
Pictures from an
exhibition, extracts;
Khatchaturian
Sabre Dance (Gayaneh);
Posford-Maschwitz
At the Balalaika

Tchaikovsky   Black   Decca PFS 4084
Trepak (The Nutcracker);   Chorus
Five traditional songs
arr. Black:
Meadowland; Two Guitars;
Under Moscow skies; Dark eyes;
Song of the Volga Boatmen

Gershwin   Black   Decca PFS 4098
An American in Paris
(recording published under the name of "London Festival Orchestra")

4, 5, 6 & 7 June 1965, Abbey Road

Prokofiev   Frühbeck de Burgos   Columbia 33CX 5275
Violin Concerto No 2   Milstein   Columbia SAX 5275
                                                                                     EMI SXLP 30255

12, 13, 14, 15 & 16 June 1965, Abbey Road

Orff   Frühbeck de Burgos   EMI AN 162/SAN 162
Carmina Burana   New Philharmonia Chorus   EMI ESD 7177
                                   Popp, Unger, Noble,
                                   Wolansky

10 & 11 September 1965, Kingsway Hall

Debussy   Stokowski   Decca PFS 4095
La cathédrale engloutie   Decca SDD 455
(arr. Stokowski)   <u>Japanese Decca K30Y 1546</u>

Tchaikovsky   Stokowski   Decca PFS 4083
The Sleeping Beauty,
Ballet Suite

15 September 1965, Kingsway Hall

Tchaikovsky   Stokowski   Decca PFS 4083
Swan Lake, Ballet Suite

Mussorgsky   Stokowski   Decca PFS 4095
Pictures from an   Decca SDD 455
exhibition (arr.Stokowski)   Decca VIV 25
                                                                                     <u>Japanese Decca K30Y 1546</u>

20, 21 & 23 September 1965, Abbey Road

Mozart Symphony No 29; Symphony No 33	Klemperer	Columbia 33CX 5256 Columbia SAX 5256 EMI SLS 5048* EMI EX 29 04823*

25 & 26 September and 19, 20, 21 & 22 October 1965, Abbey Road

Haydn Symphony No 102	Klemperer	Columbia 33CX 5266/SAX 5266

30 September and 1, 4, 6, 7, 8, 11, 12 & 13 October 1965, Kingsway Hall

Beethoven Missa Solemnis	Klemperer New Philharmonia Chorus Söderström, Höffgen, Kmennt, Talvela	EMI AN 165-6/SAN 165-6 EMI SLS 922

14, 18 & 21 October 1965, Abbey Road

Bartok Piano Concerto No 1	Sargent Ogdon	HMV ASD 2347 EMI SXLP 30514

21 & 22 October 1965, Abbey Road

Bartok Piano Concerto No 3	Sargent Ogdon	HMV ASD 2347 EMI SXLP 30514

18, 19, 20, 21 & 22 October and 1 November 1965, Kingsway Hall

Mozart Symphony No 40; Symphony No 41 "Jupiter"	Giulini	Decca LXT 6225/SXL 6225 Decca JB 8 Decca 417 727-2

19, 20, 21 & 22 October 1965, Abbey Road

Haydn Symphony No 100 "Military"	Klemperer	Columbia 33CX 5266/SAX 5266 EMI ED 29 03571

21, 22, 23, 25 & 27 October 1965, Abbey Road

Schumann Symphony No 1 "Spring"; Manfred, Overture	Klemperer	Columbia 33CX 5269/SAX 5269 EMI 1C 197 52497/8/9*

5 November 1965, Kingsway Hall

Britten	Gerhardt	RCA GL 25006
Variations and Fugue		(originally published by
on a theme of Purcell		Reader's Digest)
(Young Person's Guide to		
the Orchestra)		
Binge		
Elizabethan Serenade;		
Elgar		
Nimrod (Enigma Variations);		
Chanson de matin;		
Walton		
Touch her soft lips (Henry V);		
Toye		
The Haunted Ballroom;		
Arnold		
Four Scottish Dances		

11 December 1965, Kingsway Hall

Offenbach	Münch	Decca LK 4767/PFS 4096
Gaité Parisienne, Ballet		Decca VIV 60

28 December 1965, Westminster Abbey

Music from the 900th	Guest	HMV ALP 2264/ASD 2264
Anniversary Service in	Westminster Abbey Choir	
Westminster Abbey:		
Bliss		
Ceremonial Prelude;		
Vaughan Williams		
O be joyful (Psalm 100);		
Elgar		
Spirit of the Lord		
(The Apostles);		
Britten		
Festival Te Deum;		
Walton		
Crown Imperial		
(Coronation March);		
God save the Queen (arr.Elgar);		
Hymns: Now thank we all		
our God; It came upon		
the midnight clear		

28, 29 & 30 December 1965, Kingsway Hall

Elgar	Boult	HMV ALP 2259/ASD 2259
Violin Concerto	Menuhin	EMI SXLP 29 00001

1966

11 & 13 January 1966, Watford Town Hall

Liszt Piano Concerto No 1; Chopin Piano Concerto No 2	Pritchard Rosen	CBS 61094

13 January 1966, Watford Town Hall

Mendelssohn Wedding March and Nocturne	Pritchard	CBS unpublished

21, 22, 24 & 25 January 1966, Kingsway Hall

Beethoven Violin Concerto	Klemperer Menuhin	HMV ALP 2285/ASD 2285 EMI EG 29 02741 EMI CDM 769 0012

10, 11, 12, 14 & 15 February 1966, Abbey Road

Franck Symphony in D minor	Klemperer	Columbia 33CX 5276/SAX 5276 EMI SLS 5003*

23 February and 20 June 1966, Abbey Road

Bellini Son geloso del zefiro errante (La Sonnambula)	Downes Freni, Gedda	EMI ASD 2473

10, 11, 14 & 16 March and 12, 18, 19 & 20 July 1966, Kingsway Hall

Songs from operetta and musical comedy by Romberg (The Student Prince & The Desert Song); Rodgers (The Boys from Syracuse); Kern (Music in the air & Show Boat); Friml (Rose Marie); Herbert (The only girl); Fraser-Simson (Maid of the mountains); German (Tom Jones); Offenbach (La Périchole); Massenet (Chérubin); Zeller (Der Vogelhändler); Millöcker (The Dubarry); Fall (Die geschiedene Frau, Die spanische Nachtigall, Die Dollarprinzessin, Madame Pompadour & Der liebe Augustin); Lehar (Eva, Die lustige Witwe & Paganini); Oscar Straus (Waltz Dream, Chocolate Soldier); Heuberger (Der Opernball); Johann Strauss (Casanova); Kreisler (The King steps out); Posford (Balalaika)	Bonynge Sutherland	Decca SET 349/350

18 & 19 April 1966, Watford Town Hall

Mozart
Violin Concerto No 5;
Violin Concerto No 7

Gibson
Szeryng

Philips SAL 3588
Philips 6747 376*

26, 27, 28 & 29 April 1966, Abbey Road

Beethoven
Piano Concerto No 5
"Emperor"

Leitner
Gelber

EMI SXLP 20104
EMI EMX 41 20141

26, 27, 28 & 29 April and 11 & 12 November 1966, Abbey Road

Beethoven
Piano Concerto No 3

Leitner
Gelber

EMI SXLP 20107

8 May 1966, Royal Festival Hall (live recording)

Mozart
Requiem Mass

Giulini
New Philharmonia Chorus
Lorengar, Veasey,
R.Lewis, Shirley-Quirk

Hunt Productions CD 527*

14, 16, 17, 20 & 24 May 1966, Abbey Road

Mozart
Piano Concerto No 24;
Piano Concerto No 27

Kurtz
A.Fischer

Columbia SAX 5287

15 May 1966, Royal Festival Hall (live recording)

Beethoven
Missa Solemnis

Giulini
New Philharmonia Chorus
Lorengar, Veasey,
R.Lewis, Borg

Hunt Productions CD 527*

17 & 18 May 1966, Abbey Road

Ravel
Rapsodie espagnole;
Pavane pour une
infante défunte

Giulini

Columbia 33CX 5265/SAX 5265
EMI EMX 41 20761

6, 8, 10 & 11 June 1966, Abbey Road

Glazunov
Violin Concerto;
Dvorak
Violin Concerto

Frühbeck de Burgos
Milstein

EMI ASD 2365

11 June 1966, West Hampstead Studios

Vivaldi	Stokowski	Decca PFS 4124
The Four Seasons	Bean	Decca VIV 3

12 & 13 June 1966, Abbey Road

Prokofiev	Frühbeck de. Burgos	EMI ASD 2315
Symphony No 1 "Classical"		EMI ESD 7019

15, 17, 18, 19, 22, 23, 24, 25, 27, 28, 29 & 30 June and 3 & 4 July 1966, Abbey Road

Mozart	Klemperer	EMI AN 172-5/SAN 172-5
Don Giovanni	New Philharmonia Chorus	EMI SLS 923
	Watson, Freni, C.Ludwig,	EMI SLS 143 4623
	Gedda, Ghiaurov, Crass,	Excerpts: EMI ASD 2508
	Berry, Montarsolo	

20 June 1966, Abbey Road

Donizetti	Downes	EMI ASD 2473
Tornami a dir;	Freni, Gedda	
Cerchero lontana terra		
(Don Pasquale);		
Verrano a te		
(Lucia di Lammermoor);		
Bellini		
Prendi l'anel ti dono		
(La Sonnambula)		
Bellini	Downes	EMI unpublished
Fra poco (La Sonnambula)	Freni, Gedda	

22 & 24 June 1966, Walthamstow Town Hall

Mendelssohn	Sawallisch	Philips AXS 4004*
Symphony No 4 "Italian";		Philips SAL 3727
Symphony No 5		Philips 6707 005*
"Reformation"		Philips 412 008-1

3, 4 & 5 July 1966, Wembley Town Hall

Beethoven	Galliera	Philips SAL 3616
Violin Concerto	Grumiaux	Philips 420 348-2

5 July 1966, Abbey Road

Donizetti	Downes	EMI unpublished
So' anchio la virtù	Freni	
(Don Pasquale)		

10 July 1966, Abbey Road

Reger
An die Hoffnung

Mackerras
C. Ludwig

EMI unpublished

14, 15 & 16 July 1966, Kingsway Hall

Elgar
Froissart, Overture

Barbirolli

HMV ALP 2292/ASD 2292
EMI SLS 5030*
EMI SXLP 30456

Elgar
Elegy for strings;
Sospiri

HMV ALP 2292/ASD 2292
EMI SLS 5030*
EMI SXLP 30456
EMI CDC 747 537-2

18, 19 & 20 July 1966, Kingsway Hall

Bax
Symphony No 6

Del Mar

Lyrita RCS 35/SCRS 35

21 & 22 July 1966, Kingsway Hall

Holst
The Planets

Boult
Ambrosian Singers

HMV ALP 2301/ASD 2301
EMI ESD 7135

16, 17, 18, 19, 20 & 21 August 1966, Watford Town Hall

Tchaikovsky
Suites Nos 1, 2, 3 & 4

Dorati

Philips SBAL 22
Philips 6768 035

6 September 1966, Abbey Road

Carter
Variations for Orchestra

Prausnitz

CBS 72717

12 September 1966, Kingsway Hall

Tchaikovsky
Symphony No 5

Stokowski

Decca LK 4882/PFS 4129
Decca SDD 493
Japanese Decca K30Y 1541

28 & 29 September 1966, Kingsway Hall

Bartok
Viola Concerto

Dorati
Menuhin

EMI ASD 2323

18, 19, 21 & 22 October 1966, Kingsway Hall

Walton
Symphony No 1

Sargent

HMV ALP 2299/ASD 2299
EMI SXLP 30138

403

9, 10, 11 & 12 November 1966, Abbey Road

Stravinsky Le sacre du printemps	Frühbeck de Burgos	EMI ASD 2315

16 & 17 November 1966, Kingsway Hall

Stravinsky Fireworks	Frühbeck de Burgos	EMI TWO 239 EMI CFP 40348
Ravel Bolero	Frühbeck de Burgos	EMI ESD 7019

16, 17 & 18 November 1966, Kingsway Hall

Brahms Nänie; Wolf Morgenhymnus; Van Nuffel In convertendo; Mozart Ave verum corpus; Beethoven Die Ehre Gottes; Bruckner Motets: Locus iste; Os justi; Ave Maria; Virga Jesse; Christus factus est	Pitz New Philharmonia Chorus	EMI ASD 2325

18 & 19 November 1966, Abbey Road

Beethoven Piano Concerto No 4	Frühbeck de Burgos Bishop-Kovacevich	World Records ST 961

8 & 9 December 1966, Kingsway Hall

Dvorak Symphony No 9 "From the New World"	Dorati	Decca LK 4880/PFS 4128 Decca JB 37

19, 20 & 21 December 1966, Barking Town Hall

Debussy La Mer; Jeux; Prélude à l'après-midi d'un faune	Boulez	CBS 72533 CBS 60143 CBS MYK 42546

RAFAEL KUBELIK

MAHLER

Symphony No. 2
(Resurrection)

Elsie Morison

Norma Procter

New Philharmonia Chorus
Chorus Master Wilhelm Pitz

New Philharmonia Orchestra
Leader Carlos Villa

ROYAL ALBERT HALL
Manager F. J. Mundy

Sunday 10 December 1967 at 7.30
Programme Two Shillings

1967

4 & 5 January 1967, Kingsway Hall

Bizet L'Arlésienne, Suite, Carmen, Suite	Münch	Decca PFS 4127
Respighi The Fountains of Rome; The Pines of Rome	Münch	Decca PFS 4131

15, 16, 17, 18, 21, 22, 23 & 24 February 1967, Kingsway Hall

Mahler Symphony No 9	Klemperer	Columbia SAX 5281/2 EMI SXDW 3021

15, 17, 20 & 25 February 1967, Kingsway Hall

Verdi Tu che in seno (La Forza del Destino); La donna e mobile (Rigoletto); Ah la paterna mano (Macbeth); Quando le sere (Luisa Miller); Come rugiada al cespite (Ernani); Puccini Che gelida manina (La Bohème); Gounod Ah lève-toi soleil (Roméo et Juliette); Massenet Ah tout est bien (Le Cid); Catalani Neh verde niaggio (Loreley)	Ferraris Corelli	EMI unpublished

27 February and 1 March 1967, Abbey Road

Vaughan Williams Symphony No 6	Boult	EMI ASD 2329 EMI SLS 822* EMI ASD 2847 EMI SLS 154 7083* EMI ED 29 04081 EMI CDC 747 2152
Vaughan Williams The Lark Ascending	Boult Bean	EMI ASD 2329 EMI ASD 2847 EMI SLS 822*

9, 10, 11, 14 & 15 March 1967, Kingsway Hall

Bruckner Symphony No 5	Klemperer	Columbia SAX 5288/9
Mozart Serenade No 12	Klemperer	Columbia SAX 5290 EMI SXDW 3050* EMI CFP 41 4448

17 & 18 March 1967, Abbey Road

Mozart Piano Concerto No 25	Klemperer Barenboim	Columbia SAX 5290

29 & 30 March 1967, Kingsway Hall

Dohnanyi Variations on a Nursery Song	Dohnanyi Wild	Reader's Digest (USA RD 4062) Quintessence PMC 7054

30 & 31 March 1967, Kingsway Hall

Beethoven Violin Concerto	Horenstein Gruenberg	Reader's Digest (USA RD 4060) Chandos CBR 1024

30 & 31 March 1967, Abbey Road

Stravinsky Petrushka, Ballet	Klemperer	Columbia unpublished

1 & 2 April 1967, Watford Town Hall

Mahler Das klagende Lied	Morris Ambrosian Singers Zylis-Gara, Reynolds, Kaposy	Delysé ECB 3187/DS 6087 Decca SDD 327 Nimbus NI 5085

5, 6, 7, 10 & 11 April 1967, Wembley Town Hall

Haydn Violin Concerto in G; Schubert Rondo in A; Mozart Adagio K261; Rondo K373	Leppard Grumiaux	Philips SAL 3660
Handel Il Pastor Fido, Overture	Leppard	Philips SAL 3674

24 April 1967, Salle Pleyel, Paris (live recording)

Mahler Symphony No 9	Klemperer	Columbia unpublished (private recording by Pathé)

16, 20 & 21 May 1967, Abbey Road

Rachmaninov Piano Concerto No 2; Rhapsody on a theme of Paganini	Atzmon Anievas	EMI ASD 2361 EMI SLS 855*

17, 19 & 20 May 1967, Kingsway Hall

Mozart Requiem	Frühbeck de Burgos New Philharmonia Chorus Mathis, Bumbry, Shirley, Rintzler	EMI SAN 193 EMI CFP 4399

24 & 25 May 1967, Abbey Road

Ravel Daphnis et Chloé, Ballet	Frühbeck de Burgos	EMI ASD 2355

6, 7 & 9 June 1967, Wembley Town Hall

Tchaikovsky Francesca da Rimini; Hamlet, Fantasy Overture	Markevitch	Philips USA 900 234 Philips CPC 0047 (cassette only)

10 June 1967, Kingsway Hall

Schoenberg Chamber Symphony No 2	Prausnitz	EMI ASD 2349

14, 15, 16, 21, 22 & 23 June 1967, Walthamstow Town Hall

Mendelssohn Symphony No 1; Symphony No 2 "Hymn of Praise"	Sawallisch New Philharmonia Chorus Donath, Hansmann, Kmennt	Philips AXS 4004* Philips 6707 005* Philips 6700 023
Mendelssohn Symphony No 3 "Scotch"; Ruy Blas, Overture	Sawallisch	Philips AXS 4004* Philips SAL 3739 Philips 6707 005*

20, 21 & 23 July 1967, Abbey Road

Bartok Piano Concerto No 1; Piano Concerto No 3	Boulez Barenboim	EMI ASD 2476 EMI EG 29 08461

17, 18 & 19 August 1967, Kingsway Hall

Mahler Symphony No 6	Barbirolli	EMI SLS 778 EMI CFP 41 44243

17, 18 & 19 August and 25 September 1967, Kingsway Hall

Schoenberg Pelleas und Melisande	Barbirolli	EMI ASD 2459

20, 21 & 22 August 1967, Abbey Road

Brahms Piano Concerto No 1	Barbirolli Barenboim	EMI ASD 2353 EMI SXLP 30283 EMI EMX 41 2085-1

22 August 1967, Abbey Road

Strauss Metamorphosen	Barbirolli	EMI SLS 778*

22 & 23 August 1967, Abbey Road

Berlioz Les nuits d'été	Barbirolli Baker	EMI ASD 2444 EMI SLS 5013*

24, 25, 26, 27, 28, 29, 30 & 31 August and 1, 2, 3, 4, 5, 6, 7 & 8 September 1967, Walthamstow Town Hall

Mozart Così fan tutte	Leinsdorf Ambrosian Opera Chorus L.Price, Troyanos, Raskin, Shirley, Milnes, Flagello	RCA SER 5575/6/7/8

27 & 28 August 1967, Abbey Road

Brahms Piano Concerto No 2	Barbirolli Barenboim	EMI ASD 2413 EMI EMX 2110
Schumann Piano Concerto	Barbirolli Barenboim	EMI unpublished

9 & 10 September 1967, Walthamstow Town Hall, and 9, 10 & 11 November 1967, Wembley Town Hall

Sibelius Symphony No 5; Night Ride and Sunrise	Prêtre	RCA SB 6775

18 September 1967, Abbey Road

Dallapiccola Piccola musica notturna; Busoni Reigen; Berceuse	Prausnitz	Argo ZRG 757

4, 5, 10, 11, 14 & 28 October and 3 & 4 November 1967, Abbey Road

Beethoven Piano Concerto No 1	Klemperer Barenboim	EMI SLS 941* EMI ASD 2616 EMI SLS 5180*
Beethoven Piano Concerto No 2	Klemperer Barenboim	EMI SLS 941* EMI ASD 2608 EMI SLS 5180*
Beethoven Piano Concerto No 3	Klemperer Barenboim	EMI SLS 941* EMI ASD 2579 EMI SLS 5180*
Beethoven Piano Concerto No 4	Klemperer Barenboim	EMI SLS 941* EMI ASD 2550 EMI SLS 5180*
Beethoven Piano Concerto No 5 "Emperor"	Klemperer Barenboim	EMI SLS 941* EMI ASD 2500 EMI SLS 5180*
Beethoven Choral Fantasia	Klemperer John Alldis Choir Barenboim	EMI SLS 941* EMI ASD 2608 EMI SLS 5180*

7, 8, 13, 16 & 20 October 1967, Bishopsgate Institute

Ives Symphony No 1; Symphony No 2; Symphony No 3 "Camp Meeting"; Symphony No 4; Scene No 1 "Halloween"	Farberman Ambrosian Singers	Vanguard VSL 11039/40/41

16, 17 & 18 October 1967, Wembley Town Hall

Verdi I Vespri Siciliani; La Forza del Destino; Giovanna D'Arco; Luisa Miller, Overtures; Macbeth; Aida, Preludes; La Traviata, Acts 1 & 3 Preludes	Markevitch	Philips SFM 23023 Philips 6580 073

18, 20, 23, 24, 25, 26, 30 & 31 October and 6, 7, 9 & 10 November 1967, Kingsway Hall

Bach Mass in B minor	Klemperer BBC Chorus Giebel, Baker, Gedda, Prey, Crass	EMI SLS 930

22 October 1967, Olympic Studios

Christmas music (no details available)	Alwyn	CBS unpublished

1 & 2 November 1967, Kingsway Hall

Albeniz   Frühbeck de Burgos   Decca SXL 6355
Suite española (arr. Burgos)

29 November 1967, Kingsway Hall

Elgar   Bliss   Reader's Digest
Cockaigne, Overture;   RDM 2322/RDS 2322
Bliss
Things to come
(No 7, Incidental music)

Arne   Bliss   Reader's Digest
Rule Britannia;   Royal Choral Society   RDM 2322/RDS 2322
Parry   Bainbridge
Jerusalem

5 December 1967, Walthamstow Town Hall

Vaughan Williams   Bliss   Reader's Digest
Greensleeves;   RDM 2322/RDS 2322
Borodin
Nocturne;
Handel
Arrival of the Queen of Sheba;
Rossini
Il Viaggio a Rheims, Overture;
Holst
Marching Song

5 & 6 December 1967, Wembley Town Hall

Pergolesi   Leppard   Philips SAL 3674
L'Olimpiade;
Handel
Il pastor fido;
Grétry
Le jugement de Midas;
Rameau
Pygmalion;
Bononcini
Polifemo;
Sacchini
Oedipe à Colone;
Méhul
La chasse du jeune Henri,
Overtures;
Scarlatti
Sinfonia in B flat

20 December 1967, Trinity College Chapel, Cambridge

Fauré	Willcocks	EMI ASD 2358
Requiem	King's College Choir	
	Chilcott, Carol Case	
Fauré	Willcocks	EMI ASD 2358
Pavane pour une	King's College Choir	
infante défunte		

27 & 28 December 1967, Kingsway Hall

Ravel	Barbirolli	EMI ASD 2444
Shéhérazade	Baker	EMI SLS 5013*

LEOPOLD STOKOWSKI

WAGNER
Overture, Rienzi

SKRYABIN
Le Poème de l'Extase

BERLIOZ
Symphonie Fantastique

New Philharmonia Orchestra
Leader Carlos Villa

ROYAL FESTIVAL HALL
General Manager John Denison CBE
Tuesday 18 June 1968 at 8
Programme Two Shillings

1968

<u>8, 9, 10 & 11 January 1968, Walthamstow Town Hall</u>

Tchaikovsky 1812, Overture	Buketoff Ambrosian Singers RAF Central Band	RCA SB 6763 RCA LSB 4081
Rachmaninov Three Russian Folksongs	Buketoff Ambrosian Singers	RCA SB 6763 RCA LSB 4081
Rachmaninov Spring Cantata	Buketoff Ambrosian Singers Shaw	RCA SB 6763 RCA LSB 4081

<u>18, 19 & 20 January 1968, Abbey Road, and 22 & 23 April 1968, Kingsway Hall</u>

Beethoven Symphony No 6 "Pastoral"	Giulini	EMI ASD 2535

<u>22 & 23 January and 12 February 1968, Abbey Road</u>

Vaughan Williams Symphony No 4	Boult	EMI ASD 2375 EMI SLS 822* EMI SLS 154 7083* EMI ED 29 04171 EMI CDC 747 2152

<u>14, 15 & 16 February 1968, Kingsway Hall</u>

Vaughan Williams Symphony No 3	Boult M.Price	EMI ASD 2393 EMI SLS 822* EMI SLS 154 7083* EMI CDC 747 2142
Vaughan Williams In the Fen Country	Boult	EMI ASD 2393 EMI SLS 822* EMI ASD 2847
Vaughan Williams Norfolk Rhapsody No 1	Boult	EMI ASD 2375 EMI SLS 822* EMI ASD 2847 EMI ED 29 04171

<u>17, 18, 19, 21, 22, 23, 24 & 28 February and 8, 9, 10, 11, 13 & 14 March 1968, Abbey Road</u>

Wagner Der fliegende Holländer	Klemperer BBC Chorus Silja, Burmeister, Kozub, Adam, Talvela, Unger	EMI SLS 934

<u>20, 21 & 22 February 1968, Wembley Town Hall</u>

Tchaikovsky Symphony No 2 "Little Russian"	Abbado	DG 139 381 DG 2542 113

28 & 29 February 1968, Kingsway Hall

Mendelssohn A Midsummer Night's Dream, Incidental Music	Frühbeck de Burgos Ambrosian Singers Van Bork, Hodgson	Decca SXL 6405 Decca JB 72

6, 7, 8, 15 & 16 March 1968, Kingsway Hall

Respighi The Fountains of Rome; The Pines of Rome	Frühbeck de Burgos	EMI TWO 239 EMI CFP 40348
Stravinsky Circus Polka	Frühbeck de Burgos	EMI TWO 239 EMI ESD 7019 EMI CFP 40348
Chabrier España	Frühbeck de Burgos	EMI ESD 7019
Turina Rapsodia sinfonica; Espla La pajara; Turina La Oracion	Frühbeck de Burgos	EMI unpublished

17 & 18 March 1968, Abbey Road

Weber Clarinet Concerto No 1; Clarinet Concertino; Rossini Theme and Variations	Frühbeck de Burgos De Peyer	EMI ASD 2455 EMI CFP 41 45021

20 & 21 March 1968, Wembley Town Hall

J.C.Bach Tomistocle, Overture; Symphony in G minor op 6 no 6; Two Symphonies in B flat op 9 no 1 & op 18 no 2	Leppard	Philips SAL 3685

22 March and 11 October 1968, Abbey Road

Klemperer Symphony No 2; J'accuse	Klemperer	EMI unpublished

5, 6 & 7 April 1968, Abbey Road

Strauss
Don Quixote

Klemperer
Du Pré

EMI unpublished
(recording incomplete)

8 April 1968, Abbey Road

Strauss
Don Quixote

Barenboim
Du Pré

EMI unpublished
(recording incomplete)

8 April and 11 May 1968, Abbey Road

Schumann
Cello Concerto

Barenboim
Du Pré

EMI ASD 2498
EMI SLS 895*
EMI 1C 037 01943

18, 19 & 20 April 1968, Kingsway Hall

Respighi
The Fountains of Rome;
Roman Festivals

Freccia

Reader's Digest (USA RD 4068)

22 & 23 April and 12 July 1968, Kingsway Hall

Brahms
Symphony No 4

Giulini

EMI SLS 5241*

29 & 30 April 1968, Kingsway Hall

Tchaikovsky
Symphony No 5

Horenstein

Reader's Digest RDS 9384
RCA GL 25007

8, 10 & 11 May 1968, All Saints, Tooting

Bach
Magnificat in D

Barenboim
New Philharmonia Chorus
Popp, Baker,
Tear, Hemsley

EMI ASD 2533

9 May 1968, Abbey Road

Rossini
William Tell,
Ballet Music;
Gounod
Faust, Ballet Music

Mackerras

EMI TWO 275

Berg
Sieben frühe Lieder

Mackerras
C.Ludwig

EMI unpublished
(recording incomplete)

1 & 2 June 1968, Walthamstow Town Hall

Barber Knoxville, Summer of 1915; Two scenes from Antony and Cleopatra (Give me some music; Give me my robe, put on my crown)	Schippers L.Price	RCA SB 6799

3, 4, 5 & 7 June 1968, Walthamstow Town Hall

Mozart Ch' io mi scordi di te; Porgi amor; Deh vieni, non tardar (Le Nozze di Figaro); Se il padre (Idomeneo); Ach, ich fühl's (Die Zauberflöte); L'amero saro costante (Il re pastore)	Adler L.Price	RCA SB 6813

10, 12, 14 & 17 June 1968, Walthamstow Town Hall

Handel See the raging flames arise (Joshua); Rossini Resta immobile (William Tell); Wagner O du mein holder Abendstern (Tannhäuser); Thomas O vin, dissipe la tristesse (Hamlet); Offenbach Scintille diamant (Les contes d'Hoffmann); Tchaikovsky Yeletzky's aria (The Queen of Spades); Puccini Nulla, silenzio (Il Tabarro); Levy Too weak to kill the man I hate (Mourning becomes Elektra)	Guadagno Milnes	RCA SER 5584
Verdi Tregua e cogl' Unni (Attila)	Guadagno Ambrosian Singers Milnes, Mitchinson	RCA SER 5584
Verdi Morir ! Tremenda cosa (La Forza del Destino)	Guadagano Milnes, Fyson	RCA SER 5584

19 & 20 June 1968, Kingsway Hall

Berlioz Symphonie fantastique	Stokowski	Decca PFS 4160
Wagner Rienzi, Overture	Stokowski	Decca unpublished

20, 21 & 24 June 1968, Kingsway Hall

Brahms Rinaldo	Abbado Ambrosian Singers King	Decca SXL 6386
Brahms Song of Destiny	Abbado Ambrosian Singers	Decca SXL 6386

1, 2, 3, 6, 8 & 9 July 1968, Kingsway Hall

Mendelssohn Elijah	Frühbeck de Burgos New Philharmonia Chorus Wandsworth School Boys'Choir G.Jones, Baker, Woolf Gedda, Fischer-Dieskau	EMI SLS 935

12, 13, 14, 16, 17, 18, 19, 20, 21, 23 & 30 August and 30 October 1968 Walthamstow Town Hall, and 2 November 1968, Abbey Road

Verdi Otello	Barbirolli Ambrosian Opera Chorus G.Jones, Di Stasio, McCracken, Fischer-Dieskau, Di Palma, Giacomotti, Andreolli, Monreale, Thomas	EMI SLS 940 EMI EX 29 01373

16, 17, 18, 19, 21, 22 & 23 September 1968, Abbey Road

Bach Brandenburg Concertos Nos. 1, 2, 3, 4, 5 & 6	Littaur	EMI SXLP 20110/1

18, 19, 20, 24, 25, 26, 27 & 28 September 1968, Kingsway Hall

Mahler Symphony No 7	Klemperer	EMI 781 EMI SLS 781 EMI CFPD 41 44423

24 September 1968, Abbey Road

Saint-Saens Cello Concerto No 1	Barenboim Du Pré	EMI ASD 2498 EMI SLS 895* EMI 1C 037 01943

3, 5, 6 & 7 October 1968, Abbey Road

Schumann Symphony No 2	Klemperer	EMI ASD 2454 EMI 1C 197 52497/8/3*
Schumann Genoveva, Overture	Klemperer	EMI ASD 2454

9 & 11 October 1968, Abbey Road

Walton Viola Concerto	Walton Menuhin	EMI ASD 2542

12, 13 & 14 October 1968, Abbey Road

Beethoven Symphony No 7; Rameau Gavotte with Variations (arr. Klemperer)	Klemperer	EMI ASD 2537

13, 14 & 15 October 1968, Walthamstow Town Hall

Grieg Four Symphonic Dances; Four Norwegian Dances	Gould	RCA LSC 3158 RCA LSB 4019

18 October 1968, Salle Pleyel, Paris (live recording)

Rameau Gavotte with Variations (arr. Klemperer); Mozart Symphony No 38 "Prague"; Beethoven Symphony No 7	Klemperer	EMI unpublished (Private recording by Pathé)

2 November 1968, Abbey Road

Corelli Oboe Concerto	Barbirolli Rothwell	EMI ASD 2496

18, 19, 20, 21 & 22 November 1968, Kingsway Hall

Stravinsky The Firebird, Ballet (* also includes rehearsal sequences)	Ansermet	Decca SET 468/468A* Decca 414 141-1 Decca 414 141-2

2 & 3 December 1968, Olympic Studios

Kupfermann Libretto for Orchestra	Farberman	GMP SRS 12025
Lessard Sinfonietta Concertante;	Farberman	GMP SRS 12026
Farberman Medea, Suite		GMP unpublished

3, 4, 5 & 6 December 1968, Abbey Road

Beethoven Symphony No 5	Boulez	CBS 72862
Beethoven Meeres stille, glückliche Fahrt	Boulez John Alldis Choir	CBS 72862
Boulez Livres	Boulez	CBS 73213
Debussy Trois Nocturnes	Boulez John Alldis Choir	CBS 72785
Debussy Clarinet Rhapsody	Boulez De Peyer	CBS 72785

30 & 31 December 1968 and 11 January 1969, Kingsway Hall

Wagner Die Meistersinger von Nürnberg; Der fliegende Holländer, Overtures; Tristan und Isolde, Prelude and Liebestod	Paita	Decca PFS 4158 Lodia LOCD 770

RAFAEL FRÜHBECK DE BURGOS

and

THE NEW PHILHARMONIA ORCHESTRA

record for Decca

watch for details of new recordings

The New Philharmonia Orchestra has already appeared on Decca records accompanying Renata Tebaldi in her new recital record ⓢSXL 6152 ⓜLXT 6152

stereo or mono records

Buy RECORDS MAGAZINE—
6d monthly from your newsagent or record dealer
The Decca Record Company Limited
Decca House   Albert Embankment   London   SE1

1969

4 January 1969, All Saints, Tooting

Bruckner Te Deum	Barenboim New Philharmonia Chorus Pashley, Finnilä, Tear, Garrard	EMI ASD 2533

14 & 15 January 1969, Wembley Town Hall

J.C.Bach Catone; Rameau Les Paladins; Zais; Mozart La finta giardiniera; Scarlatti Il giardino di rose; Cimarosa I traci amanti, Overtures; Boyce Cambridge Installation Ode; Locatelli Introduttione teatrale	Leppard	Philips SAL 3760 Philips 412 406-1

23, 24 & 25 January 1969, Kingsway Hall

Vaughan Williams Five Tudor Portraits	Willcocks Bach Choir Bainbridge, Carol Case	EMI ASD 2489 EMI SLS 5082* EMI ED 29 12531 EMI CDC 747 0232

5, 6, 7 & 8 February 1969, Abbey Road

Schumann Symphony No 3 "Rhenish"	Klemperer	EMI ASD 2547 EMI 1C 197 52497/8/9*
Schumann Faust, Overture	Klemperer	EMI ASD 2547

15, 18, 19 & 20 February 1969, Kingsway Hall

Wagner Dich teure Halle (Tannhäuser); Einsam in trüben Tagen (Lohengrin); Liebestod (Tristan und Isolde); Bizet Habañera (Carmen); Saint-Saens Amour, viens aider ma faiblesse; Mon coeur s'ouvre à ta voix (Samson et Dalila); Massenet Adieu, notre petite table; N'est-ce plus ma main (Manon)	Guadagno Tebaldi	Decca SET 439/440*

22, 26 & 27 February and 1 March 1969, Kingsway Hall

Verdi
Ritorna vincitor (Aida);
Puccini
Quando m'en vo (La Bohème);
Rossini
La regata veneziana
(arr. Gamley);
Lara
Granada;
Ponce
Estrellita
Tosti
A vucchella
Cardillo
Catari, catari
De Curtis
Non ti scordar di me
Rodgers
If I loved you (Carousel)

Bonynge
Tebaldi

Decca SET 439/440*

26 February and 3, 5 & 6 March 1969, Kingsway Hall

Auber
Marco Spada; Lestocq;
Adam
Giralda; La poupée;
Lecocq
La fille de Mme. Angot;
Thomas
Mignon;
Planquette
Les cloches de Corneville;
Boieldieu
Le calipne de Bagdad,
Overtures

Bonynge

Decca SXL 6422

10 March 1969, Abbey Road

Klemperer
Symphony No 4

Klemperer

EMI unpublished

10 March 1969, Abbey Road, and 31 October and 3 November 1969, All Saints, Tooting

Klemperer
Symphony No 2

Klemperer

EMI ASD 2575
EMI ED 29 03321

15 & 16 March 1969, Abbey Road

Chopin Piano Concerto No 2;
Andante spianato and
Grande Polonaise

Gibson
Orozco

EMI unpublished

1 & 2 April 1969, Abbey Road

Délibes
Coppélia, excerpts;
Sylvia, excerpts;
Rossini
William Tell, Ballet music;
Gounod
Faust, Ballet music

Mackerras

EMI TWO 275

1, 2, 3, 8, 9, 11, 12, 14, 15, 24 & 25 April 1969, Kingsway Hall

Meyerbeer Les Huguenots	Bonynge Ambrosian Opera Chorus Sutherland, Tourangeau, Arroyo, Vrenios, Ghiuselev, Bacquier, Cossa, Wakefield, J.Ward, Noble, Thomas, Gibbs, Grant, Coster	Decca SET 460/1/2/3

17 & 18 April 1969, Kingsway Hall

Granados La maya y el ruiseñor (Goyescas)	Frühbeck de Burgos De los Angeles	EMI unpublished
Villa-Lobos Bachianas Brasilieras Nos 5 and 7	Frühbeck de Burgos De los Angeles, M.Price	EMI unpublished

23 April 1969, Kingsway Hall

Wagner Rienzi, Overture; Lohengrin, Acts 1 & 3 Preludes	Hurst	Decca PFS 4205
Wagner Wotan's Farewell (Die Walküre)	Hurst Ward	Decca PFS 4205

29 April 1969, Abbey Road

Debussy Printemps	Boulez	CBS 72785

14 & 15 May 1969, Barking Town Hall

Nielsen Symphony No 5; Saga-Drom	Horenstein	Unicorn RHS 300

28 & 29 May 1969, Abbey Road

Beethoven Egmont, Overture	Giulini	EMI ASD 2535
Weber Der Freischütz, Overture	Giulini	EMI unpublished

9, 12 & 13 June 1969, Walthamstow Town Hall

Beethoven Concerto in D (Violin Concerto in the version for piano and orchestra)	Ozawa P.Serkin	RCA LSB 4008

11 & 13 June 1969, Walthamstow Town Hall

Mozart
Symphony No 35 "Haffner";
Symphony No 28

Ozawa

RCA VICS 1630

17 & 18 June 1969, Walthamstow Town Hall

Schmitt
La Tragédie de Salomé;
Duparc
Léonore;
Chausson
Viviane

De Almeida

RCA SB 6834

16, 17, 18 & 19 July 1969, Watford Town Hall

Mahler
Symphony No 5

Barbirolli

EMI SLS 785

Mahler
Blicke mir nicht in die Lieder; Ich atmet' einen linden Duft; Um Mitternacht; Liebst du um Schönheit; Ich bin der Welt abhanden gekommen (Rückert-Lieder)

Barbirolli
Baker

EMI SLS 785*
EMI SLS 5013*
EMI ASD 4409
EMI CDC 747 7932

Tchaikovsky
Romeo and Juliet, Fantasy Overture

Barbirolli

EMI unpublished
(recording incomplete)

21, 22, 23, 24 & 25 July 1969, Walthamstow Town Hall

Rossini
Serbami ognor; Alle più calde immagini (Semiramide);
Donizetti
Dio, che mi vedi;
Sul suo capo aggravi un Dio (Anna Bolena);
Bellini
Mira, o Norma (Norma);
Puccini
Flower Duet (Madama Butterfly);
Ponchielli
E un anatema !; L'amo come il fulgor del creato (La Gioconda)

Guadagno
Caballé, Verrett

RCA SER 5590

Offenbach
Belle nuit (Les Contes d'Hoffmann);
Verdi
Silenzio ! Aida verso noi s'avanza (Aida)

Guadagno
Ambrosian Opera Chorus
Caballé, Verrett

RCA SER 5590

18 August 1969, Walthamstow Town Hall

Auber	De Almeida	RCA VICS 1678
Le cheval de bronze;		
Thomas		
Mignon, Overtures		

18, 21, 22, 25, 26, 27 & 30 August 1969 and 25 January 1970, Watford Town Hall

Verdi	Barbirolli	EMI SLS 950
Requiem Mass	New Philharmonia Chorus	EMI CFP 41 44283
	Caballé, Cossotto,	
	Vickers, R.Raimondi	

19, 20, 21, 22, 23, 24, 25, 26, 27 & 30 August 1969, Walthamstow Town Hall

Verdi	Mehta	RCA SER 5586/7/8
Il Trovatore	Ambrosian Opera Chorus	RCA RD 86194
	L.Price, Cossotto,	
	Domingo, Milnes, Giaotti,	
	Bainbridge, Davies,	
	Riley, Taylor	

30 August 1969, Walthamstow Town Hall

Gounod	De Almeida	RCA VICS 1678
Faust, Ballet Music;		
Hérold		
Zampa, Overture		

30 August 1969 and 25 June 1970, Walthamstow Town Hall

Offenbach	De Almeida	RCA VICS 1678
Orpheus in the Underworld,		
Overture		

16, 17, 18 & 19 September and 6, 17 & 18 October 1969, Abbey Road

Bach	Klemperer	EMI SLS 808
Orchestral Suites		
Nos 1, 2, 3 and 4		

29 September 1969, West Hampstead Studios

Operatic arias	Gardelli	Decca unpublished
(unspecified)	Aragall	

1 October 1969, Abbey Road

Tchaikovsky	Barbirolli	EMI ASD 2738
Francesca da Rimini		

2, 3 & 4 October 1969, West Hampstead Studios

Rossini William Tell, Il Signor Bruschino, La scala di seta, Il Barbiere di Siviglia, La gazza ladra, L'assiedo di Corinto, Overtures	Gardelli	Decca SDD 392 Decca VIV 52

6, 17 & 18 October 1969, Abbey Road

Beethoven Overture, Adagio and Finale (Die Geschöpfe des Prometheus)	Klemperer	EMI SXDW 3032* EMI ED 29 04011 EMI CDC 747 1882

21, 22, 23, 24, 28, 30 & 31 October 1969, All Saints, Tooting

Wagner Die Walküre, Act 1	Klemperer Dernesch, Cochran, Sotin	EMI SLS 968

25, 26 & 27 October 1969, Watford Town Hall

Cherubini Symphony in D; Weber Symphony No 1	Böttcher	Philips 6500 154 Philips 412 374-1

10, 11 & 12 November 1969, Barking Town Hall

Mozart Violin Concerto No 3	Gibson Szeryng	Philips 6500 036 Philips 6707 011* Philips 6747 376*
Mozart Sinfonia Concertante K364	Gibson Szeryng, Giuranna	Philips 6707 011* Philips 6747 376*

1970

4 January 1970, Walthamstow Town Hall

Mozart Violin Concertone K190	Gibson Szeryng	Philips 6707 011* Philips 6747 376*

5, 6 & 7 January 1970, Barking Town Hall

Mozart Violin Concerto No 1; Rondo in C	Gibson Szeryng	Philips 6500 035 Philips 6707 011* Philips 6747 376*
Mozart Violin Concerto No 2; Violin Concerto No 4; Rondo Concertante in B flat	Gibson Szeryng	Philips 6707 011* Philips 6747 376*
Mozart Adagio in E	Gibson Szeryng	Philips 6500 036 Philips 6707 011* Philips 6747 376*

8, 10, 11, 12, 13, 15, 16, 19, 20, 21, 22, 25, 26, 29, 30 & 31 January 1970, Abbey Road

Mozart Le Nozze di Figaro	Klemperer John Alldis Choir Söderstrom, Grist Berganza, Burmeister, M.Price, Cahill, Kanawa, G.Evans, Bacquier, Hollweg Brokmeier, Langdon, Grant	EMI SLS 955

4 & 5 February 1970, Wembley Town Hall

Mozart Dies Bildnis ist bezaubernd schön (Die Zauberflöte); Wenn der Freude Tränen fliessen; O wie ängstlich, o wie traurig (Die Entführung aus dem Serail); Nelle guerre (La finta semplice); Rase, Schicksal, wüte immer (Zaide)	Galliera Hollweg	Philips 6500 042
Mozart Perle di gioia (Ascanio in Alba)	Galliera Hollweg	Philips unpublished

6, 7, 18, 19, 20 & 21 February 1970, Kingsway Hall

Bruckner Symphony No 9	Klemperer	EMI ASD 2719

9 & 10 February 1970, Abbey Road

Haydn Symphony No 95	Klemperer	EMI ASD 2818

12, 14 & 15 February 1970, Wembley Town Hall

Mozart Die Maurerfreude; Dir, Seele des Weltalls, Cantatas	De Waart Ambrosian Singers Hollweg	Philips 6500 020 Philips 6747 389*
Mozart Laut verkünde unsre Freude, Cantata	De Waart Ambrosian Singers Hollweg, Partridge, Dean	Philips 6500 020 Philips 6747 389*

14 February 1970, Abbey Road

Klemperer Symphony No 3	Klemperer	EMI unpublished

18, 19, 20 & 21 February 1970, Kingsway Hall

Howells Hymnus Paradisi	Willcocks Bach Choir King's College Choir Harper, Tear	EMI ASD 2600 EMI ESD 102 0661

12, 13 & 16 June 1970, Watford Town Hall

Gounod Voici la vaste plaine (Mireille); Massenet Ah! me voilà seule (Thaïs)	Giovaninetti Caballé	DG 2530 073
Gounod Il était un roi de Thulé... Ah! Je ris de me voir si belle (Faust); Je veux vivre dans le rêve (Roméo et Juliette); Meyerbeer O beau pays de Touraine (Les Huguenots); Charpentier Depuis le jour (Louise); Bizet Je dis que rien ne m'épouvante (Carmen)	Giovaninetti Caballé	DG 2530 073 DG 415 446-1

15 June 1970, Kingsway Hall

Stravinsky Petrushka, Ballet	Leinsdorf	Decca PFS 4207

14, 15, 16, 17, 18, 21, 23, 24, 25, 27, 28 & 29 July 1970, All Saints, Tooting

Massenet Manon	Rudel Ambrosian Opera Chorus Sills, Kern, Gedda, Bacquier, Souzay, Raynaud, T'Hezan, Castel, Fyson, Trempont	EMI SLS 800

1, 2, 3, 4 & 5 September 1970, Wembley Town Hall

Bach Concerto for Violin & Oboe	De Waart Grumiaux, Holliger	Philips 6500 119
Bach Double Violin Concerto	De Waart Grumiaux, Toyoda	Philips 6500 119
Vivaldi Violin Concerto op 3 no 6	De Waart Grumiaux	Philips 6500 119

7 & 8 September 1970, Watford Town Hall

Mahler Symphony No 1	Morris	Pye TPLS 13037 Pye GSGC 2045

10 & 11 September 1970, Wembley Town Hall

Beethoven Triple Concerto	Inbal Arrau, Szeryng, Starker	Philips 6500 129

11, 12 & 13 September 1970, Wembley Town Hall

Schumann Symphony No 1 "Spring"; Symphony No 4	Inbal	Philips 6500 134

15, 16 & 17 September 1970, Kingsway Hall

Beethoven Violin Concerto	Boult Suk	EMI ASD 2667 EMI CFP 4409
Beethoven Coriolan, Overture	Boult	EMI ASD 2667 EMI CFP 4409

15, 16, 17 & 18 September 1970, All Saints, Tooting

Beethoven Mass in C	Giulini New Philharmonia Chorus Ameling, Baker, Altmeyer, Rintzler	EMI ASD 2661

12, 13 & 14 October 1970, Wembley Town Hall

Beethoven Violin Romances Nos 1 & 2; Wieniawski Romance (Concerto No 2); Svendsen Romance; Berlioz Rêverie et caprice; Wieniawski Légende; Tchaikovsky Sérénade mélancolique	De Waart Grumiaux	Philips 6580 047

24, 26 & 27 October 1970, Wandsworth School and All Saints, Tooting

Wagner Wotan's Farewell and Magic Fire Music (Die Walküre)	Klemperer Bailey	EMI SLS 968*

28 & 29 October 1970, Abbey Road

Rachmaninov Piano Concerto No 2	G.Cziffra jun. Cziffra	EMI TWO 360

29 & 30 October and 2, 3, 4, 10, 11 & 14 November 1970, Kingsway Hall

Bruckner Symphony No 8	Klemperer	EMI SLS 872

19, 20 & 21 December 1970, Wembley Town Hall

Strauss Oboe Concerto	De Waart Holliger	Philips 6500 174
Mozart Oboe Concerto	De Waart Holliger	Philips 6500 174 Philips 6527 190

29, 30 & 31 December 1970, Watford Town Hall

Beethoven Piano Concerto No 2; Piano Concerto No 4	Galliera Haebler	Philips 6527 028

1971

2 & 4 January 1971, Kingsway Hall

Donizetti Com' è gentil (Don Pasquale)	Magiera Ambrosian Singers Pavarotti	Decca SXL 6498
Boito Ogni mortal mister... Giunto sul passo estremo (Mefistofele); Ponchielli Cielo e mar (La Gioconda); Puccini Che gelida manina (La Bohème); Pietri Io conosco un giardino (Maristella)	Magiera Pavarotti	Decca SXL 6498

25, 27, 28, 29 & 30 January and 3, 4, 6, 8, 9, 10, 12, 13, 15 & 18 February 1971, Kingsway Hall

Mozart Così fan tutte	Klemperer John Alldis Choir M.Price, Minton, Popp, Alva, G.Evans, Sotin	EMI SLS 961 Excerpts: EMI 1C 037 02368

29 & 31 January 1971, Bishopsgate Institute

Mozart Clarinet Concerto; Nielsen Clarinet Concerto	Leppard McCaw	Unicorn UNS 239

7 March 1971, Wembley Town Hall

J.C.Bach Bassoon Concerto	Cohen Brooke	Blenheim SLCW 1013

20, 22, 24, 27, 28 & 31 March and 1 April 1971, Wembley Town Hall

Boccherini Symphonies op 12: Nos 1, 2, 3, 4, 5 & 6	Leppard	Philips 6703 034

29 & 30 March 1971, Barking Town Hall

Strauss Tod und Verklärung; Tchaikovsky Francesca da Rimini	Maazel	Decca PFS 4227

1, 2, 7 & 8 April 1971, Kingsway Hall

Franck arr. Gamley Panis angelicus; Schubert arr. Gamley Ave Maria; Traditional arr. Gamley Adeste fideles	Guadagno Ambrosian Singers Tebaldi	Decca SXL 6524
Adam arr. Gamley O Holy Night; Traditional arr. Gamley Tu scendi dalla stelli; Schubert arr. Melichar Mille cherubini in coro; Brahms arr. Gamley Wiegenlied; Bach-Gounod arr. Gamley Ave Maria; Gounod arr. Gamley O divine redeemer	Guadagno Tebaldi	Decca SXL 6524

28 & 29 April 1971, Walthamstow Town Hall

Vorisek Symphony in D; Martinu Symphony No 6	Bialoguski	Unicorn RHS 309

7, 9 & 10 June 1971, All Saints, Tooting

Bruckner Mass in E minor	Barenboim New Philharmonia Chorus Harper, Reynolds, Tear, Rintzler	EMI ASD 2836

9, 10 & 11 June 1971, Wembley Town Hall

Schumann Symphony No 2; Overture, Scherzo & Finale	Inbal	Philips 6580 269

24 & 25 June 1971, Abbey Road

Ravel La Valse; Bolero; Pavane pour une infante défunte; Alborada del gracioso	Maazel	EMI TWO 409 EMI EMX 2007

27, 28, 29 & 30 June 1971, Watford Town Hall

Schumann Symphony No 3 "Rhenish"	Inbal	Philips 6570 152

28, 29 & 30 June and 1 & 2 July 1971, Walthamstow Town Hall

Puccini	Leinsdorf	RCA SER 5619
Il Tabarro	John Alldis Choir	
	Dominguez, Gale,	
	Domingo, Milnes, De Palma,	
	El Hage, Langridge, Rogers	

6, 7, 8, 9, 11, 12, 13, 14 & 15 July 1971, Walthamstow Town Hall, and 29 December 1971, Abbey Road

Puccini	Bartoletti	EMI SLS 962
Manon Lescaut	Ambrosian Opera Chorus	EMI EX 29 11753
	Caballé, Domingo,	EMI CDS 747 4988
	Sardinero, Mangin, Tear,	
	Van Allan, Wallis, Lloyd,	
	Dickerson, Partridge, Howell	

19 July 1971, Abbey Road

Mendelssohn	Downes	RCA LSB 4080
Violin Concerto	Eto	

20, 21, 22, 24 & 25 July 1971, Walthamstow Town Hall

Puccini	Downes	RCA SER 5674
Si, mi chiamano Mimì;	L.Price	
Donde lieta uscì;		
Quando m' en vo		
(La Bohème);		
Addio, mio dolce amor (Edgar);		
Ore dolci e divine		
(La Rondine);		
Vissi d'arte (Tosca);		
In quelle trine morbide;		
Sola, perduta abbandonata		
(Manon Lescaut);		
Se come voi piccina io fossi		
(Le Villi):		
Un bel dì (Madama Butterfly);		
Laggiù nel soledad		
(La Fanciulla del West)		

21 & 22 July 1971, Abbey Road

Tchaikovsky	Downes	RCA LSB 4080
Violin Concerto	Eto	

23 & 24 July 1971, Abbey Road

Beethoven	Lovett	Japanese RCA RVC 2258
Violin Romance No 2;	Eto	
Saint-Saens		
Introduction and		
Rondo capriccioso;		
Sarasate		
Zigeunerweisen		

31 July and 2 August 1971, Watford Town Hall

Sessions Rhapsody; Symphony No 8	Prausnitz	Argo ZRG 702

26 & 27 August 1971, All Hallows, Gospel Oak

Rimsky-Korsakov Scheherazade	Maazel	Lion unpublished

27 & 28 August 1971, All Hallows, Gospel Oak

Prokofiev Peter and the Wolf; Britten Variations and Fugue on a theme of Purcell (Young Person's Guide to the Orchestra)	Leppard R.Baker	EMI CFP 185

7, 8 & 10 September 1971, Walthamstow Town Hall

Brahms Violin Concerto	Colin Davis Grumiaux	Philips 6500 299 Philips 6527 197

12 & 13 September 1971, Abbey Road

Rachmaninov Piano Concerto No 1; Piano Concerto No 4	Frühbeck de Burgos Anievas	EMI SLS 855*

18 & 19 September 1971, Abbey Road

Haydn Symphony No 92 "Oxford"	Klemperer	EMI ASD 2818

20 & 21 September 1971, Abbey Road

Mozart Wind Serenade No 11	Klemperer	EMI SXDW 3050*

4 & 5 October 1971, Walthamstow Town Hall

Khachaturian Piano Concerto; Liszt Hungarian Fantasia	Ozawa Entremont	CBS 72981

26 & 28 October 1971, Walthamstow Town Hall

Prokofiev   Maazel   Decca PFS 4255
Piano Concerto No 3 Margalit

Mussorgsky   Maazel   Decca PFS 4255
Pictures from an exhibition
(orch. Ravel)

8 & 9 December 1971, Abbey Road

Dohnanyi   Pritchard   Pye TPLS 13052
Piano Concerto No 1 Vazsonyi   Pye Virtuoso PVCD 8398

21, 22 & 23 December 1971, Abbey Road

Grieg   Berglund   EMI ASD 2802
Piano Concerto;   Ogdon
Schumann
Piano Concerto

1972

In many ways 1972 was a critical year for the (New) Philharmonia. The orchestra faced severe financial losses and badly needed a new young principal conductor. Otto Klemperer was nearly eighty-eight and fast nearing the end of his concert and recording career. He retired from the concert platform in January 1972, and later in the year from his remaining recording commitments with the New Philharmonia. Lorin Maazel had been appointed Associate Principal Conductor in November 1970, but was not given the power he wanted and resigned in March 1972.

EMI was negotiating with the New Philharmonia and London Philharmonic Orchestras over the possibility of a merger to form a "super" orchestra that would record and give concerts. These talks broke down in November 1972, when the Council of the New Philharmonia pulled out of the negotiations.

Two things saved the orchestra at this point: a wealthy City banker, Ian Stoutzker, offered to buy the orchestra outright, or at least to offer guarantees of financial support; and in December Riccardo Muti made his début with the orchestra and was offered the post of Principal Conductor early in 1973.

1972

<u>4 & 5 January 1972, Barking Town Hall</u>

Maxwell Davies Fantasia No 2	Groves	Argo ZRG 712

<u>9 March 1972, Kingsway Hall</u>

Chopin Piano Concerto No 1	Maazel Margalit	Decca PFS 4311

<u>26 & 27 March 1972, Barking Town Hall</u>

Schubert Symphony No 9	Guschlbauer	Erato STU 70720

<u>31 May and 1 June 1972, Abbey Road</u>

Copland El Salon Mexico; Latin American Sketches	Copland	CBS 73451
Copland The Red Pony, Ballet music	Copland	CBS unpublished
Copland New England Countryside; Of Mice and Men; Our Town, Film music	Copland	CBS 61672

<u>20, 21, 22, 23 & 24 June 1972, Walthamstow Town Hall</u>

Mascagni Intanto amici (Cavalleria Rusticana); Gounod Salut, demeure (Faust); Ah! leve-toi soleil (Roméo et Juliette); Verdi Questa o quella (Rigoletto); O tu che in seno (La Forza del Destino); Di, tu se fedele (Un Ballo in Maschera); Cilea L'anima ho stanca (Adriana Lecouvreur); Puccini Non piangere, Liu (Turandot); Una parola sola (Fanciulla); Avete torto (Gianni Schicchi); Bizet Je crois entendre (Les Pêcheurs de Perles)	Santi Domingo	RCA ARL1 0048

29 July 1972, Walthamstow Town Hall

Bernstein　　　　　　　　　Dods　　　　　　　　　　　RCA LRL2 7531
Simple Song (Mass);　　　　Milnes　　　　　　　　　　RCA GL 89792
Maria (West Side Story)

31 July and 1, 2, 3, 4, 5, 7, 8, 9 & 11 August 1972, Walthamstow Town Hall

Puccini　　　　　　　　　　Mehta　　　　　　　　　　　RCA ARL2 0105
Tosca　　　　　　　　　　　John Alldis Choir　　　　　RCA RD 80105
　　　　　　　　　　　　　L.Price, Domingo, Milnes,
　　　　　　　　　　　　　Grant, Egerton, Pearl,
　　　　　　　　　　　　　Gibbs, Rippon, Plishka

3, 4 & 5 August 1972, Abbey Road

Tchaikovsky　　　　　　　　Kamu　　　　　　　　　　　EMI CFP 40349
Violin Concerto　　　　　　Hölscher

Tchaikovsky　　　　　　　　Kamu　　　　　　　　　　　Electrola SHZE 369
Valse Scherzo　　　　　　　Hölscher

10, 14, 19 & 21 August 1972, Kingsway Hall

Dvorak　　　　　　　　　　　Bonynge　　　　　　　　　　Decca SXL 6619
Songs my mother taught me;　Sutherland
Mendelssohn
Auf Flügeln des Gesanges;
Del Riego
Homing;
Massenet
Si les fleurs avaient des yeux;
Gounod
Quand je chante;
Nelson
Mary of Argyll;
Délibes
Le rossignol
La Forge
I came with a song;
Juncker
I was dreaming;
Hahn
Si mes vers avaient des ailes;
Massenet
Crépuscule
Abt
Der Kukkuk;
Grieg
Solveig's Song (Peer Gynt);
Worth
Midsummer;
Liszt
Quand je dors;
Délibes
Les filles de Cadiz

14, 15, 16, 18, 19 & 21 August 1972, Walthamstow Town Hall

Boito Giunto sul passo (Mefistofele); Verdi Ella mi fu rapita (Rigoletto); Lunga da lei (La Traviata); Bizet Flower Song (Carmen); Giordano Come un bel dì (Andrea Chenier)	Milnes Domingo	RCA ARL1 0122
Gounod O sainte médaille (Faust); Bizet Toreador's Song (Carmen); Mascagni Il cavallo scalpita (Cavalleria Rusticana); Massenet Vision fugitive (Hérodiade)	Domingo Milnes	RCA ARL1 0122
Verdi Perfidi ! (Macbeth); Eri tu (Un Ballo in Maschera)	Domingo Milnes	RCA unpublished

15, 18, 22, 25 & 26 August 1972 and 21 May 1973, Kingsway Hall

Délibes Sylvia, Ballet	Bonynge	Decca SXL 6635/6 Decca 414 257-1

6 September 1972, Kingsway Hall

Tchaikovsky Sérénade mélancolique	Kamu Hölscher	Electrola SHZE 369

12 September 1972, Abbey Road

Bennett Elegy for Caroline Lamb	Dods Mark	EMI CSD 3728

26, 27, 28 & 29 September 1972, Walthamstow Town Hall

Mendelssohn Violin Concerto; Violin Concerto in D minor	Krenz Grumiaux	Philips 6500 465

11, 12, 13, 14, 15 & 16 October 1972, Abbey Road

Tchaikovsky	Maazel	EMI SLS 865*
Piano Concerto No 1;	Gilels	EMI ASD 3067
Piano Concerto No 3		EMI EMX 2001

Tchaikovsky	Maazel	EMI SLS 865*
Piano Concerto No 2	Gilels	
(arr. Siloti)		

18 & 22 October and 13 November 1972, Walthamstow Town Hall

Mahler	Morris	Philips 6700 067
Symphony No 10 (ed. Cooke)		

3, 4, 5, 6, 8 & 10 November 1972, Abbey Road

Brahms	Downes	Japanese RCA RVC 2270
Violin Concerto	Eto	

Bruch	Downes	Japanese RCA
Violin Concerto No 1;	Eto	(catalogue no. not known)
Lalo		
Symphonie espagnole		

25 November 1972, Abbey Road

Shostakovich	M.Shostakovich	EMI ASD 2936
Violin Concerto No 1	D.Oistrakh	EMI ASD 4046

1973

17 & 18 January 1973, Kingsway Hall

Beethoven Symphony No 7; Egmont, Overture	Stokowski	Decca PFS 4342
Rimsky-Korsakov Capriccio espagnol	Stokowski	Decca PFS 4333

23 January 1973, Barking Town Hall

Beethoven Piano Concerto No 5 "Emperor"	Segal Firkusny	Decca PFS 4291 Castle CCD 105

2 & 3 February 1973, Abbey Road

Rachmaninov Piano Concerto No 3	Ceccato Anievas	EMI SLS 855*

13 & 15 February 1973, All Saints, Tooting

Mozart Mass in C minor	Leppard John Alldis Choir Cotrubas, Kanawa, Krenn, Sotin	EMI ASD 2959 EMI EG 29 03041

23, 24, 26 & 27 February 1973, Abbey Road

Schubert Symphony No 5; Symphony No 8 "Unfinished"	Fischer-Dieskau	EMI ASD 2942

27 & 28 February 1973, Barking Town Hall

Prokofiev Violin Concerto No 2; Paganini Violin Concerto No 1	Devos Hasson	EMI CFP 40052

30 March 1973, Hornsey Town Hall

Brahms Double Concerto	Masur R.Ricci, G.Ricci	Turnabout TV 34593

7, 10 & 12 May 1973, Kingsway Hall

Massenet Thérese	Bonynge Linden Singers Tourangeau, Davies, Quilico, Taylor, Caley, Opie	Decca SET 572

21 May 1973, Kingsway Hall

Puccini E lucevan le stelle (Tosca)	Bonynge Pavarotti	Decca unpublished
Flotow M'appari (Martha)	Bonynge Pavarotti	Decca SXL 6649

22 & 24 May and 4 & 6 June 1973, Kingsway Hall

Handel Bonynge Decca SXL 6629
Verdi prati (Alcina); Tebaldi
Ombra mai fu (Xerxes);
Gluck
Divinités du Styx (Alceste);
O del mio dolce ardor
(Elena e Paride);
Pergolesi
Stizzoso, mio stizzoso
(La serva padrona);
Martini arr. Gamley
Plaisir d'amour;
Eight arias arr. Gamley:
Sarti
Lungi dal caro bene;
Bononcini
Deh piu a me non v'ascondete;
Scarlatti
Le violette;
Paisiello
Nel cor piu non mi sento;
Chi vuol la zingarella;
Pergolesi
Tre giorni son che Nina;
Vivaldi
Piango gemo sospiro

2 & 4 July 1973, Walthamstow Town Hall

Dvorak Symphony No 9 "From the New World"	Stokowski	RCA ARL2 0334*

6 & 7 July 1973, Walthamstow Town Hall

Strauss Vier letzte Lieder	Leinsdorf L.Price	RCA ARL1 0333

9, 10 & 11 July 1973, Walthamstow Town Hall

Strauss Empress' Awakening Scene (Die Frau ohne Schatten)	Leinsdorf Ambrosian Opera Chorus L.Price	RCA ARL1 0333
Strauss Da geht er hin (Der Rosenkavalier); Freihild's aria (Guntram)	Leinsdorf L.Price	RCA ARL1 0333

30 July 1973, All Hallows, Gospel Oak

Mussorgsky Pictures from an exhibition (orch. Ravel);	Mackerras	Vanguard VSD 71188 Vanguard CD 25023
Mussorgsky Khovantschina, Act 4 Prelude (orch.Rimsky-Korsakov)	Mackerras	Vanguard VSD 71188

31 July and 1, 2, 3, 6, 7, 8, 9 & 10 August 1973, Watford Town Hall

Bellini Norma	Levine John Alldis Choir Sills, Verrett, Di Giuseppe, Plishka, Wallis, Tear	ABC Dunhill ATS 20017

11, 12, 13 & 14 August 1973, Walthamstow Town Hall

Halévy La Juive	De Almeida Ambrosian Opera Chorus Arroyo, Moffo, Tucker, Giaiotti, Sabate, Fyson	RCA ARL1 0447

13, 14 & 15 August 1973, Kingsway Hall

Moeran Symphony in G minor	Boult	Lyrita SRCS 70
Delius Marche caprice	Boult	Lyrita SRCS 71

15, 16, 17, 18, 19, 20, 21, 22, 23, 24 & 26 August 1973, Walthamstow Town Hall

Verdi I Vespri Siciliani	Levine John Alldis Choir Arroyo, Ewing, Domingo, Milnes, R.Raimondi, Goeke, Collins, Sharpe, Morris, Van Allan, Byers	RCA ARL4 0370

17, 24, 25 & 28 September 1973, St Giles, Cripplegate

Kabalevsky Symphony No 2; Miaskovsky Symphony No 21	Measham	Unicorn RHS 346
Nitzsche St Giles Cripplegate	Measham	Unicorn unpublished

18 & 19 September 1973, Walthamstow Town Hall

Howells Elegy; Merry Eye; Music for a Prince	Boult	Lyrita SRCS 69
Vaughan Williams March (The Wasps)	Boult	Lyrita SRCS 71

20, 21, 22 & 23 September 1973, Brent (Wembley) Town Hall

Bruch Violin Concerto No 1; Scottish Fantasy	Wallberg Grumiaux	Philips 6500 780

24, 27, 28 & 29 September 1973, All Saints, Tooting

Cherubini Requiem in D minor	Muti Ambrosian Singers	EMI ASD 3073

8 November 1973, Fairfield Halls, Croydon

Beethoven Symphony No 6 "Pastoral"	Guschlbauer	Erato STU 70839

17, 18 & 20 December 1973, Abbey Road

Rachmaninov Five Etudes-Tableaux (orch. Respighi); Tchaikovsky The Voyevode, Symphonic Ballad	Krasnapolsky	EMI ASD 3013

1974

4 & 5 January 1974, Walthamstow Town Hall

Elgar Falstaff; Enigma Variations	A.Davis	Lyrita SRCS 77
Elgar Pomp and Circumstance, March No 5	A.Davis	Lyrita SRCS 99

8 & 9 January 1974, Kingsway Hall

Banks Horn Concerto; Searle Aubade	Del Mar Tuckwell	Argo ZRG 726

23 & 24 January 1974, Abbey Road

Schmidt Variations on a Hussar's Song	Bauer	EMI CSD 3759 EMI ED 29 11721
Arriaga Symphony in D minor	Bauer	EMI CSD 3769

11 & 13 February 1974, Walthamstow Town Hall

Beethoven Symphony No 9 "Choral"	Ozawa Ambrosian Singers Napier, Reynolds, Brilioth, Ridderbusch	Philips 6747 119 Philips 416 884-2

17, 20 & 21 June 1974, Walthamstow Town Hall

Brahms Symphony No 4; Academic Festival Overture	Stokowski	RCA ARL1 0719

2, 3, 4, 5, 6, 7, 8, 9 & 11 July 1974, Walthamstow Town Hall

Verdi Aida	Muti Covent Garden Chorus Caballé, Cossotto, Casas, Domingo, Cappuccilli, Ghiaurov, Roni, Martinucci	EMI SLS 977 EMI CDS 747 2718

4, 8, 9, 10, 11, 12 & 13 July 1974, Abbey Road

Vaughan Williams Sir John in Love	Davies John Alldis Choir Eathorne, Palmer, Watts, Bainbridge, Herincx, Lloyd, Jenkins, Tear, R.Jones, Dickerson, Johnston, J.Noble, Winfield, Rowlinson, Van Allan, English, Richard, Wheatley, Varcoe, Ethridge	EMI SLS 980

14, 15, 16, 18 & 19 July 1974, Walthamstow Town Hall

Bizet O Dieu Brahma ! (Les pêcheurs de perles)	Maag Ambrosian Opera Chorus Moffo, Mitchinson	RCA ARD1 0844
Meyerbeer Robert, toi que j'aime (Robert le Diable)	Maag Moffo, Jenkins	RCA ARD1 0844
Donizetti Chacun le sait, chacun le dit (La fille du régiment); Thomas Mad Scene (Hamlet)	Maag Ambrosian Opera Chorus Moffo	RCA ARD1 0844
Berlioz D'amour l'ardente flamme (La Damnation de Faust); Massenet Il est doux, il est bon (Hérodiade); Air des lettres (Werther); Charpentier Depuis le jour (Louise); Gounod Je veux vivre dans ce rêve (Roméo et Juliette)	Maag Moffo	RCA ARD1 0844

26, 28, 30 & 31 July and 1, 2, 3, 5 & 6 August 1974, Walthamstow Town Hall

Massenet Thaïs	Rudel Ambrosian Opera Chorus Moffo, Bainbridge, Clark, Bacquier, Carreras, Diaz, Butler, Fyson, Cash	RCA ARL3 0842

<u>5, 6, 8, 10 & 13 August 1974, Walthamstow Town Hall</u>

Verdi Perfidi!...Pietà, rispetto amore...mal per me (Macbeth)	Santi Ambrosian Opera Chorus Milnes, Clark, Jenkins	RCA ARL1 0851
Verdi Ferma ed ascolta...Sacra la scalta e d'un consorte (Luisa Miller)	Santi Milnes, Hudson	RCA ARL1 0851
Saint-Saens Donc le pape est hostile... Qui donc commande (Henry VIII)	Santi Milnes, Brecknock	RCA ARL1 0851
Verdi Alzati!...Eri tu (Un Ballo in Maschera); Massenet Aux troupes du Sultan... Promesse de mon amour (Le roi de Lahore); Grétry O Richard! O mon roi! (Richard Coeur de Lion); Weber Wo berg' ich mich ? (Euryanthe)	Santi Milnes	RCA ARL1 0851

<u>7, 8 & 9 August 1974, Abbey Road</u>

Liszt Piano Concerto No 1; Piano Concerto No 2	Atzmon Ohlsson	EMI ASD 3159
Mendelssohn Son and Stranger, Overture	Atzmon	EMI ESD 7003

<u>9 & 11 August 1974, Abbey Road</u>

Mendelssohn Ruy Blas; Athalie; Calm Sea and Prosperous Voyage; The Hebrides, Overtures	Atzmon	EMI ESD 7003

<u>14, 15 & 16 August 1974, Brent Town Hall</u>

Tchaikovsky Violin Concerto; Saint-Saens Introduction and Rondo Capriccioso	Leinsdorf Fodor	RCA ARL1 0781
Paganini Violin Concerto No 1	Leinsdorf Fodor	RCA ARL1 1565
Beethoven Violin Romance No 2	Leinsdorf Fodor	RCA unpublished

16, 17, 19, 20, 21, 22, 23 & 24 August 1974, Brent Town Hall

Verdi   Gardelli   Philips 6703 064
I Masnadieri   Ambrosian Opera Chorus
                          Caballé, Bergonzi,
                          R.Raimondi, Cappuccilli,
                          Sandor, Mazzieri, Elvin

8 & 9 September 1974, Kingsway Hall

Rachmaninov   A.Davis   Decca PFS 4327
Piano Concerto No 2   Vered

28 & 30 September, 1, 11, 13 & 14 October and 3, 4 & 5 December 1974, Brent Town Hall

Verdi   Santi   Philips 6747 193
Ciel pietoso (Oberto);   Bergonzi
Pietoso al lungo pianto
(Un giorno di regno);
Come poteva un angelo
(I Lombardi);
Come rugiada al cespite (Ernani);
Non maledirmi, o prode
(I Due Foscari);
Sotto una quercia (Giovanna d'Arco);
Cara patria; Che non avrebbe
il misero (Attila);
Ah la paterna mia (Macbeth);
Al mio stanco cadavere
(Il Corsaro);
La pia materna mano
(La Battaglia di Legnano);
Quando le sere al placido
(Luisa Miller);
Questa o quella; Parmi veder;
La donna è mobile (Rigoletto);
Sotto il sol (Aroldo);
Deh miei bollenti spiriti
(La Traviata);
Sento avvampar nel l'anima
(Simone Boccanegra);
Giorno di pianto (Vespri Siciliani);
Ma se m'è forza perderti
(Un Ballo in Maschera);
Oh tu che in seno agli angeli
(La Forza del Destino);
Io la vidi e al suo sorriso
(Don Carlo);
Celeste Aida (Aida);
Dio! Mi potevi scagliar;
Niun mi tema (Otello);
Dal labbro il canto estasiato
vola (Falstaff)

Verdi   Santi   Philips 6747 193
Irne lungi (Alzira);   Ambrosian Singers
Ah sì ben mio...Di quella Bergonzi
pira (Il Trovatore);
Di' tu se fedele
(Un Ballo in Maschera)

16 October 1974, Brent Town Hall

Tchaikovsky Santi Philips unpublished
Francesca da Rimini (test recording only)

22 & 23 October 1974, Walthamstow Town Hall

Tchaikovsky Del Mar Contour 2870 419
Romeo and Juliet,
Fantasy Overture;
1812, Overture;
Marche slave

GLC ROYAL FESTIVAL HALL
Waterloo Room
London SE1 8XX

Saturday 4 May 1985
at 7 pm

Vintage PHILHARMONIA Recordings
1945-1960

A lecture recital,
with recorded illustrations,
by
JOHN HUNT
Chairman,
Wilhelm Furtwängler Society UK

Organised jointly by the Elisabeth
Schwarzkopf/Walter Legge Society and the
Wilhelm Furtwängler Society UK, to
commemorate the Philharmonia
Orchestras's fortieth birthday and the work
of its founder and artistic director,
Walter Legge

———◆———

Tickets
(including an interval glass of wine):
Members of both societies £2.00,
available from Miss P. Hancox, 11 Heron
Court, 72 Honor Oak Road, London SE23
(please enclose sae)
Non-members £3.50,
available from 2 April from RFH Box
Office, telephone 928-3191, credit cards 928-8800

1975

<u>11 & 12 February 1975, Kingsway Hall</u>

Tchaikovsky Symphony No 1 "Winter Daydreams"	Muti	EMI ASD 3213 EMI SLS 154 5303 <u>EMI CDC 747 8662</u>

<u>17, 18, 19 & 20 March 1975, Kingsway Hall</u>

Hoddinott Sinfonietta; Night Music	Atherton	Argo ZRG 824
Hoddinott Dives and Lazarus	Atherton Welsh National Opera Chorale Allen	Argo ZRG 824
Hoddinott Viola Concerto	Atherton Erdelyi	Argo ZRG 824

<u>18 May and 18, 21, 24, 27 & 31 July 1975, Kingsway Hall</u>

Elgar The Dream of Gerontius	Boult London Philharmonic Choir John Alldis Choir Watts, Gedda, Lloyd	EMI SLS 987 <u>EMI CDS 747 2088</u>

<u>19 & 20 May 1975, Abbey Road</u>

Rachmaninov Rhapsody on a theme of Paganini; Dohnanyi Variations on a Nursery Song	Koizumi Ortiz	EMI ASD 3197

<u>16, 17, 18, 19, 20, 23, 25 & 26 June 1975, Abbey Road</u>

Bellini I Capuleti e i Montecchi	Patanè John Alldis Choir Sills, Baker, Gedda, Lloyd, Herincx	EMI SLS 986

<u>28, 29 & 30 June and 2, 3, 4, 5, 8 & 10 July 1975, Watford Town Hall</u>

Verdi Un Ballo in maschera	Muti Covent Garden Chorus Arroyo, Cossotto, Grist, Domingo, Cappuccilli, Giorgetti, Howell, Collins, Van Allan	EMI SLS 984 EMI EX 29 07103

<u>17, 18, 19, 20, 21, 22 & 23 August 1975, Brent Town Hall</u>

Verdi Il Corsaro	Gardelli Ambrosian Opera Chorus Caballé, Norman, Carreras, Mastromei, Grant, J.Noble, Oliver	Philips 6700 098 <u>Philips 416 398-2</u>

<u>18, 19, 21 & 22 August 1975, Walthamstow Town Hall</u>

Film Themes: The bad and the beautiful; Forever Amber; Laura	Raksin	RCA unpublished

<u>24, 26 & 27 August 1975, Walthamstow Town Hall</u>

Paganini Violin Concerto No 1; Mendelssohn Violin Concerto	Maag Fodor	RCA ARL1 1565

<u>28 & 31 August 1975, Walthamstow Town Hall</u>

Moeran Rhapsody No 3	N.Braithwaite McCabe	Lyrita SRCS 91
Berkeley Piano Concerto	N.Braithwaite Wilde	Lyrita SRCS 91
Leigh Agincourt	N.Braithwaite	Lyrita SRCS 95
Leigh Jolly Roger, Overture	N.Braithwaite	Lyrita SRCS 99

<u>28, 29 & 30 August 1975, Walthamstow Town Hall</u>

Finzi Clarinet Concerto	Handley Denman	Lyrita SRCS 92
Finzi Grand Fantasia and Toccata	Handley	Lyrita SRCS 92
Finzi Eclogue	Handley Katin	Lyrita SRCS 92
Finzi Let us garlands bring Two Milton Sonnets; Farewell to arms;	Handley Partridge, J.Noble, Carol Case	Lyrita SRCS 93

<u>28, 29 & 30 August 1975, Walthamstow Town Hall, and 4 & 10 November 1976, Kingsway Hall</u>

Finzi In terra pax	Handley John Alldis Choir Manning, J.Noble	Lyrita SRCS 93

1, 2 & 3 September 1975, Brent Town Hall

Tchaikovsky Violin Concerto	Krenz Grumiaux	Philips 6500 086
Tchaikovsky Sérénade mélancolique	Krenz Grumiaux	Philips unpublished

1 & 2 October 1975, Kingsway Hall

Mendelssohn Symphony No 3 "Scotch"; Calm Sea and Prosperous Voyage, Overture	Muti	EMI ASD 3184

22 October 1975, Abbey Road

Walker Variations; Kupfermann Atto; Still Afro-American Symphony (third movement); Lombarde Rock n' Roll Rhapsody	Freeman	Orion unpublished

3 November 1975, Henry Wood Hall

Fauré Sicilienne (Masques et bergamasques); Milhaud Symphony No 1; Debussy Clair de lune; Honegger Pastorale d'été; Ravel Pavane pour une infante défunte; Delius On hearing the first cuckoo; Summer night on the river; Ibert Escales (2nd movement)	Jackson	Prelude PRS 2512

17 November 1975, Walthamstow Town Hall

Revueltas Sensemaya; Redes; Caminos; Itinerarios; Janitzio	Mata	RCA RL 12320
Revueltas El Ranacuajo; Homenaje; Cuauhnahuac; Danza geometrica	Mata	RCA unpublished

25 & 26 November 1975, Henry Wood Hall

Saint-Saens Violin Concerto No 3; Introduction and Rondo Capriccioso; Havanaise	Handley Amoyal	Erato STU 70985

28 & 29 November 1975, Kingsway Hall

Xenakis Antikthon; Aroura; Synaphai	Howarth	Decca HEAD 13

15 & 16 December 1975, Abbey Road

Franck Symphony in D minor; Fauré Pelleas et Mélisande, Suite	A.Davis	CBS 76526
Wagner Tannhäuser, Overture	A.Davis	CBS unpublished

1976

<u>19, 21, 22, 23 & 24 January, 29 & 31 March and 1 April 1976, Abbey Road</u>

Charpentier Louise	Prêtre Ambrosian Opera Chorus Cotrubas, Berbié, Domingo, Bacquier, Sénéchal, Guitton	CBS 79302 <u>Japanese CBS 73DC 318/19/20</u>

<u>27 & 28 January 1976, Kingsway Hall</u>

Mozart Symphony No 25; Symphony No 29	Muti	EMI ASD 3326
Mozart Divertimento K136	Muti	EMI unpublished

<u>29 January 1976, Kingsway Hall</u>

Verdi Attila, Overture	Muti	EMI ASD 3366

<u>29 January 1976, Kingsway Hall, and 19 & 21 November 1976, Abbey Road</u>

Verdi Nabucco, Overture	Muti	EMI ASD 3366

<u>29 January 1976, Kingsway Hall, and 12 January 1977, Abbey Road</u>

Verdi I Vespri Sicilani; Luisa Miller, Overtures	Muti	EMI ASD 3366

<u>2, 3, 5 & 6 February 1976, Abbey Road</u>

Mathias Worlde's Joie	Willcocks Bach Choir Choristers of St George's Chapel Windsor J.Price, Bowen, Rippon	EMI ASD 3301

<u>24 February 1976, Henry Wood Hall</u>

Mozart Deh vieni non tardar (Le Nozze di Figaro); Ach ich fühl's (Die Zauberflöte); Ach ich liebte (Die Entführung aus dem Serail); Donizetti So anchio la virtu magica (Don Pasquale)	Pritchard Cotrubas	CBS 76521

27 & 28 February 1976, Abbey Road

Bruch Violin Concerto No 2; Scottish Fantasy	Lopez-Cobos Perlman	EMI ASD 3310

17 & 18 March 1976, St Giles Cripplegate

Brahms Piano Concerto No 1	Masur Woodward	RCA LRL1 5132

4 April 1976, Kingsway Hall

Rubbra Symphony No 2	Handley	Lyrita SRCS 96

9 & 10 April 1976, Abbey Road

Grieg Peer Gynt, Suites Nos 1 and 2; Songs: Fra Monte Picino; The Swan; I Love You; Songs arr. A.Davis: The Way of the World; The Princess	A.Davis Söderström	CBS 76527 CBS 40132*
Grieg Elegaic Melody ; Wagner Venusberg Music (Tannhäuser)	A.Davis	CBS unpublished

13 & 14 April 1976, Kingsway Hall

Sibelius Finlandia; Valse triste; The Swan of Tuonela; Karelia, Suite	Kord	Decca PFS 4378 Decca SPA 549

2 & 3 May 1976, Abbey Road

Dvorak Symphony No 9 "From the New World"	Muti	EMI ASD 3285 EMI EG 29 02751

5, 6 & 7 May 1976, Henry Wood Hall

Saint-Saens Cello Concerto; Fauré Elégie	Mackerras Schiff	DG 2530 793

18, 19, 20, 21, 23, 25, 27, 29 & 30 June 1976, Abbey Road

Massenet Thaïs	Maazel John Alldis Choir Sills, Gedda, Milnes, Van Allan, Ettridge, Murray, Burrowes, Connors, Keane	EMI SLS 993

5, 7, 8, 9, 13, 14, 15, 16, 18, 19, 20 & 21 July 1976, Abbey Road

Verdi Macbeth	Muti Ambrosian Opera Chorus Cossotto, Carreras, Milnes, R.Raimondi, Borgato, Fyson, Bernardi, Del Bosco, J.Noble, Taylor	EMI SLS 992 EMI EX 29 03853 EMI CDS 747 9548

7, 8, 15 & 16 July 1976, Henry Wood Hall

Puccini Suor Angelica	Maazel Ambrosian Opera Chorus Desborough School Choir Scotto, Horne, Cotrubas, Payne, Knight, Howard, Cryer, Cable, Bainbridge, Minty, Jennings, D.Jones, Connors, Gunson, Brown, Murray, MacGregor	CBS 76570 CBS 79312*

23 July 1976, Abbey Road

Mendelssohn Symphony No 4 "Italian"	Muti	EMI ASD 3365

10 August 1976, Palacio de Belas Artes, Mexico City

Chavez Piano Concerto	Mata Rodriguez	RCA ARL1-3341
Chavez Chaconne	Mata	RCA ARL1-3341

17, 18, 19, 20, 22, 23 & 24 August 1976, Watford Town Hall

Donizetti Lucia di Lammermoor	Lopez-Cobos Ambrosian Opera Chorus Caballé, Carreras, Ramey, Sardiniero, Ahnsjö, Belli, Murray	Philips 6703 080

25 August 1976, Kingsway Hall

Rubbra Festival Overture	Handley	Lyrita SRCS 96
Bush Yorick Overture	Handley	Lyrita SRCS 95

31 August and 1 September 1976, Walthamstow Town Hall

Dvorak Symphony No 9 "From the New World"	Handley	Enigma VAR 1018 ASV ABM 759
Borodin Prince Igor, Overture	Handley	Enigma unpublished

9 & 10 September 1976, Abbey Road

Schumann Symphony No 4	Muti	EMI ASD 3365 EMI SLS 5199* EMI CFP 4393

11 & 15 September 1976, Abbey Road

Prokofiev Piano Concerto No 1; Chopin Variations on Mozart's La ci darem la mano	Freeman Syme	Orion ORS 76221
Tchaikovsky Elegy in G	Freeman	Orion ORS 76221

13 September 1976, Abbey Road

Villa-Lobos Momoprecoce	Ashkenazy Ortiz	EMI ASD 3429

22 & 24 October 1976, Abbey Road

Copland Symphony No 3	Copland	CBS 61869

22 & 23 October and 24 & 25 November 1976, Kingsway Hall

Vivaldi Magnificat	Muti New Philharmonia Chorus Berganza, Valentini-Terrani	EMI ASD 3418 EMI CDC 747 9902

22 & 23 October and 24 & 25 November 1976, Kingsway Hall, and 28 & 29 June 1977, Abbey Road

Vivaldi Gloria	Muti New Philharmonia Chorus Berganza, Valentini-Terrani	EMI ASD 3418 EMI CDC 747 9902

4 & 10 November 1976, Kingsway Hall

Hadley The trees so high	Handley	Lyrita SRCS 103

9 November 1976, Kingsway Hall

Coates Summer Days, Suite; The Merrymakers, Overture; March (The Three Elizabeths)	Boult	Lyrita SRCS 107

9 November 1976, Henry Wood Hall

Puccini Tu che gi gel sei cinta (Turandot); Folle amore (La Rondine); Si mi chiamano Mimi (La Bohème)	Pritchard Cotrubas	CBS 76521
Puccini Donde lieta usci (La Bohème)	Pritchard Cotrubas	CBS unpublished

19 & 21 November 1976, Abbey Road

Tchaikovsky Romeo and Juliet, Fantasy Overture	Muti	EMI ASD 3488 EMI 154 5303* EMI EG 29 10671 EMI CDC 747 8572

19 & 21 November 1976 and 12 January 1977, Abbey Road

Verdi La Battaglia di Legnano, Overture	Muti	EMI ASD 3366

29 & 30 November and 1, 2 & 3 December 1976, All Saints, Tooting

Brahms Ein deutsches Requiem	Maazel Ambrosian Singers Cotrubas, Prey	CBS 79211
Brahms Alto Rhapsody	Maazel Ambrosian Singers Minton	CBS 79211*

4 December 1976, Henry Wood Hall

Verdi Pace, pace, mio dio (La Forza del Destino); Caro nome (Rigoletto)	Pritchard Cotrubas	CBS 76521

6 December 1976, Kingsway Hall

Coates In the Country; Evening in Town; The Three Bears, Fantasy	Boult	Lyrita SRCS 107

<u>7 & 9 December 1976, Barking Town Hall</u>

Hoddinott Piano Concerto No 3	Schönzeler Woodward	RCA RL 25082
Hoddinott Landscapes; Sinfonietta No 2	Schönzeler	RCA RL 25082

1977

New Philharmonia Orchestra

Information

New Philharmonia Orchestra Limited
Registered Office: 12 de Walden Court
85 New Cavendish Street London W1M 7RA
Telephone: 01-580 9961
Cables: Newphil London W1

One of the worst-kept secrets in the music world is that the New Philharmonia Orchestra is shortly to revert to its old title of Philharmonia Orchestra. We are delighted to be able to confirm that we have now resolved all the contractual problems and that all appearances of the orchestra on or after September 1st 1977 should be billed as "Philharmonia Orchestra" - i.e. omitting the prefix "New".

All recordings made on or after the 17th February 1977 which will be released on or after the 1st September 1977 should also be billed as "Philharmonia Orchestra".

1977

12 January 1977, Abbey Road

Verdi Giovanna d'Arco; La Forza del Destino, Overtures	Muti	EMI ASD 3366

13 & 20 January 1977, All Saints, Tooting

Duruflé Requiem; Danse lente	A.Davis Ambrosian Singers Desborough School Choir Kanawa, Nimsgern	CBS 76633

1 February 1977, Abbey Road

Villa-Lobos Bachianas Brazilieras No 3	Ashkenazy Ortiz	EMI ASD 3429

4 & 7 February 1977, Kingsway Hall

Tchaikovsky Violin Concerto	Ashkenazy Belkin	Decca SXL 6854

7 & 8 February 1977, Kings College Chapel, Cambridge

Elgar Coronation Ode; Parry I was glad	Ledger Kings College Choir Kneller Hall Band Lott, Hodgson, Martin, Roberts	EMI ASD 3345

15 & 16 March 1977, Walthamstow Town Hall

Tchaikovsky Violin Concerto	Fistoulari Wanawi	Trio PA 1149
Bruch Violin Concerto No 1	Fistoulari Wanawi	Japanese RCA (catalogue number not available)

23 & 24 March and 1, 5 & 6 April 1977, Abbey Road

Saint-Saens Violin Concertos Nos 1, 2, & 3; Violin Concerto No 4 (Morceau de concert); Violin Romances in C & D flat; Le déluge, Prelude; Havanise; Introduction and Rondo Capriccioso; Caprice andalous; Caprice (orch. Ysaÿe)	Dervaux Hoelscher	EMI SLS 5103
Saint-Saens La muse et la poète	Dervaux Hoelscher, Kirshbaum	EMI SLS 5103*

28 March 1977, Abbey Road

Tchaikovsky Symphony No 2 "Little Russian"	Muti	EMI ASD 3488 EMI 154 5303* EMI CDC 747 8672

5, 6 & 14 April 1977, Watford Town Hall

Mathias Clarinet Concerto	Atherton De Peyer	Decca ZRG 882
Mathias Laudi	Atherton G.Evans	Decca ZRG 882
Mathias Elegy for a Prince; Vistas	Atherton	Decca ZRG 882

13 & 14 April 1977, Kingsway Hall

Tchaikovsky Valse-Scherzo	Ashkenazy Belkin	Decca SXL 6854
Tchaikovsky Manfred Symphony	Ashkenazy	Decca SXL 6853

16, 18, 19 & 22 April 1977, Kingsway Hall

Italian arias arr. Faris: Tosti L'alba separa dalla luce l'ombra; L'ultima canzone; Beethoven In questa tomba oscura; Bellini Vaga luna che inargenti; Caldara Alma del core; Ciampi attr. Pergolesi Tre giorni son che Nina; Donizetti Il barcaiuolo; Giordani Caro mio ben; Gluck Che farò senza Euridice (Orfeo ed Euridice); Leoncavallo Mattinata; Rossini La promessa	Gamba Pavarotti	Decca SXL 7013 Decca 414 454-2

27 & 28 April and 16 May 1977, All Saints, Tooting

Puccini Vissi d'arte (Tosca); Si mi chiamano Mimi (La Bohème); Un bel dì (Madama Butterfly); Boito L'altra notte (Mefistofele); Verdi Pace pace mio Dio; Madre pietosa vergine (La Forza del Destino)	Guadagno Lorange	Musicart unpublished
Puccini Viene la sera (Madama Butterfly); O dolci mani (Tosca); O soave fanciulla (La Bohème); Verdi Io vengo a domandar (Don Carlo)	Guadagno Lorange, Aragall	Musicart unpublished

9 June 1977, St Jude on the Hill

Kreisler Liebesfreud; Liebesleid; Caprice viennois; Recitative and Scherzo- Caprice; Syncopation; Schön Rosmarin; Tambourin chinois; Violin Concerto in C (after Vivaldi); Granados arr. Kreisler Danse espagnole; Albeniz arr. Kreisler: Tango Falla arr. Kreisler Spanish Dance (La vida breve)	Howarth Gruenberg	Decca PFS 4423

25, 26, 28 & 30 May 1977, Henry Wood Hall

Puccini Il Tabarro	Maazel Ambrosian Opera Chorus Scotto, Domingo, Wixell, Knight, Kenny, Sénéchal, Wicks, Treleaven, Jeffes	CBS 75641 CBS 79312*

13 & 14 June 1977, Abbey Road

Ketèlby In a Persian Market; In a Monastery Garden; In a Chinese Temple Garden	Lanchbery Ambrosian Singers	EMI ASD 3542 EMI CDC 747 8062
Ketèlby In the Mystic Land of Egypt	Lanchbery Ambrosian Singers V.Midgley	EMI ASD 3542 EMI CDC 747 8062
Ketèlby Sanctuary of the Heart	Lanchbery Temperley	EMI ASD 3542 EMI CDC 747 8062

13 & 14 June 1977, Abbey Road (contd.)

Chal Romano (Gypsy Lad); The Clock and the Dresden Figures; Bells Across the Meadow; In the Moonlight	Lanchbery	EMI ASD 3542 EMI CDC 747 8062

20, 21, 22, 23, 27 & 29 June and 2, 4, 5 & 8 July 1977, All Saints, Tooting

Thomas Mignon	De Almeida Ambrosian Opera Chorus Horne, Welting, Vanzo, Von Stade, Zaccaria, Battedou, Hudson, Meloni	CBS 79401 Japanese CBS 82DC 309/10/11

24 & 25 June and 21 July 1977, Abbey Road

Tchaikovsky Symphony No 3 "Polish"	Muti	EMI ASD 3449 EMI 154 5303* EMI CDC 747 8682

4, 5, 7, 8 & 9 July 1977, Henry Wood Hall

Donizetti Ugo Conte di Parigi	Francis Geoffrey Mitchell Choir J.Price, Harrhy, Kenny, Arthur, Jones, Du Plessis	Opera Rara OR 1

7, 9, 11, 12, 14 & 15 July 1977, Walthamstow Town Hall

Mozart D'Oreste, d'Ajace ! (Idomeneo); Berlioz D'amour l'ardente flamme (La Damnation de Faust); Wagner Dich teure Halle (Tannhäuser); Verdi La luce langue (Macbeth); Johann Strauss Klänge der Heimat (Die Fledermaus); Dvorak Song to the Moon (Rusalka); Cilea Poveri fiori (Adriana Lecouvreur); Korngold Glück, das mir verblieb (Die tote Stadt); Menotti While I waste these precious hours (Amelia goes to the Ball)	Santi L.Price	RCA ARL1 2529
Puccini In questa reggia (Turandot)	Santi Ambrosian Opera Chorus L.Price, Barioni	RCA ARL1 2529
Mascagni Voi lo sapete (Cavalleria Rusticana)	Santi L.Price, Bainbridge	RCA ARL1 2529

10, 11, 14, 16, 19, 20 & 21 July 1977 and 5, 6, 7 & 8 February 1978, Kingsway Hall

Verdi	Muti	EMI SLS 5132
Nabucco	Ambrosian Opera Chorus	EMI EX 29 07833
	Scotto, Obraztsova,	EMI CDS 747 4838
	Luchetti, Manuguerra,	
	Ghiaurov, Lloyd,	
	Collins, Edwards	

18 & 20 July 1977, All Saints, Tooting

Fauré	A.Davis	CBS 76734
Requiem	Ambrosian Singers	
	Popp, Nimsgern	
Fauré	A.Davis	CBS 76734
Pavane		

21, 22 & 24 July 1977, Kingsway Hall

Cilea	Patanè	EMI ASD 3459
Acerba voluttà	Obraztsova	
(Adriana Lecouvreur);		
Mascagni		
Voi lo sapete		
(Cavalleria Rusticana);		
Saint-Saens		
Printemps qui commence;		
Mon coeur s'ouvre à ta voix		
(Samson et Dalila);		
Bizet	Patanè	EMI ASD 3459
Séguidille (Carmen)	Obraztsova, Pogson	

25, 26 & 27 July 1977, Kingsway Hall, and 19 & 20 September 1977, Abbey Road

Prokofiev	Muti	EMI SLS 5110
Ivan the Terrible	Ambrosian Singers	
	Arkhipova, Mokrenko,	
	Morgunov	

8 & 11 August 1977, Abbey Road

Arnold	Dilkes	EMI ASD 3487
Flute Concerto No 2;	Solum	
Concerto for flute		
and strings		
Arnold	Dilkes	EMI ASD 3487
Sinfoniettas Nos 1 and 2		

10, 11, 13 & 16 August 1977, All Saints, Tooting

Puccini	Guadagno	Musicart unpublished
Tosca	(details of soloists cannot	
	be traced for this, presumably	
	abortive, recording)	

11, 12, 13, 14, 15 & 16 August 1977, Abbey Road

Cilea Adriana Lecouvreur	Levine Ambrosian Opera Chorus Scotto, Obraztsova, Domingo, Milnes, Luccardi, Watson, Murray, Andreolli, Crook, Hudson	CBS 79310 Japanese CBS 64DC 321/2

17 August 1977, Abbey Road

Verdi Il Trovatore, Act 2 scene 2, beginning (Stride la vampa!... Condotta ell' era in ceppi al suo destin tremendo)	Stapleton Ambrosian Opera Chorus Obraztsova, Luys	EMI ASD 3459
Verdi O don fatale (Don Carlo)	Stapleton Obraztsova	EMI ASD 3459

30 & 31 August 1977, Kingsway Hall

Brahms Piano Concerto No 2	Fistoulari Vered	Decca PFS 4428

19 & 20 September 1977, Abbey Road

Beethoven Piano Concerto No 3	Muti Richter	EMI ASD 3543 EMI CDM 769 0132

3 & 7 October 1977, Abbey Road

Glazunov The Seasons, Ballet; Concert Waltzes Nos 1 and 2	Svetlanov	EMI ASD 3601 EMI EG 29 02961 EMI CDC 747 8472

19, 20, 21 & 24 October 1977, Abbey Road

Schumann Symphony No 3 "Rhenish"	Muti	EMI ASD 3696 EMI SLS 5199* EMI CFP 4395
Schumann Symphony No 2	Muti	EMI ASD 3648 EMI SLS 5199* EMI CFP 4395

14, 15, 16 & 17 November 1977, Kingsway Hall

Haydn The Creation	Frühbeck de Burgos Philharmonia Chorus Donath, Tear, Van Dam	EMI SLS 5125 EMI CFPD 41 44443

1978

21, 22, 24 & 25 January 1978, Henry Wood Hall

Clementi rev. Spada Symphony No 1; Symphony No 2; Symphony No 3 "Great National Symphony"; Symphony No 4	Scimone	Erato STU 71174
Rossini L'Italiana in Algeri; Semiramide, Overtures	Scimone	Erato STU 71178

17, 18, 19 & 20 February and 25 & 27 June 1978, Kingsway Hall

Verdi Requiem Mass	Muti Ambrosian Singers Scotto, Baltsa, Luchetti, Nesterenko	EMI SLS 5185

23 & 24 February, 7, 15 & 16 March, 11, 12, 13, 19 & 22 May, 6, 7 & 24 June, 1, 9, 14, 16 & 18 July and 24, 25 & 26 October 1978, CBS Studios

Khasho Symphony No 8 "The Chian Rhapsody (Scio)"; Symphony No 9 "The Chian Rhapsody (Scio Liberata)"; Symphony No 10 "The Wandering Aegean Sailor"	Khasho	Argenti unpublished (private recordings)

26, 27 & 28 February and 1, 3 & 4 March 1978, All Saints, Tooting

Wagner Die Meistersinger von Nürnberg; Rienzi; Tannhäuser; Der fliegende Holländer, Overtures	Maazel	CBS 76883 Japanese CBS 35DC 45

26, 27 & 28 February, 1, 3 & 4 March and 1, 4, 5 & 12 June 1978, All Saints, Tooting

Puccini Madama Butterfly	Maazel Ambrosian Opera Chorus Scotto, Knight, Murray, Domingo, Wixell, Summers, Andreolli, King, Keyte, Byers	CBS 79313 Japanese CBS 64DC 326/7

13 & 14 March 1978, All Saints, Tooting

Rachmaninov Symphony No 2	Tung	Enigma K53568 ASV ACM 2016
Strauss Don Juan	Tung	Enigma unpublished

20, 21, 22, 25 & 26 April 1978, Henry Wood Hall

Dvorak Symphony No 9 "From the New World"; Mussorgsky Pictures at an exhibition (orch. Macal); Night on Bare Mountain (orch. Rimsky-Korsakov)	Macal	Sofrason unpublished

24 April 1978 and 10 January 1979, Kingsway Hall

Sibelius Violin Concerto	Ashkenazy Belkin	Decca SXL 6953

27 & 28 May 1978, All Saints, Tooting

Rossini Edipo e Colono, Incidental music	Scimone Ambrosian Singers Ghiuselev	Fonit Cetra ITL 70054

5 & 6 June 1978, Kingsway Hall

Mozart Piano Concerto No 20; Piano Concerto No 24	Frühbeck de Burgos Devetzi	EMI unpublished

8 June 1978, Walthamstow Town Hall

Mendelssohn Violin Concerto	Fistoulari Wanawi	Japanese RCA (catalogue number not available)

14, 16, 18, 21, 23 & 24 June 1978, All Saints, Tooting

Massenet Cendrillon	Rudel Ambrosian Opera Chorus Von Stade, Welting, Berbié, Cahill, Bainbridge, Gedda, Bastin, Meloni, Crook, Noble, Du Plessis	CBS 79323 <u>Japanese CBS 64DC 316/7</u>

20 & 21 June 1978, Kingsway Hall

Mozart Piano Concerto No 19	Ashkenazy, cond. & sol.	Decca SXL 6947 <u>Decca 414 4332</u>
Mozart Piano Concerto No 22	Ashkenazy, cond. & sol.	Decca SXL 6982

26 & 27 June 1978, Brent Town Hall

Tchaikovsky   Ashkenazy   Gale GMFD 179 007
Romeo and Juliet,
Fantasy Overture;
Capriccio italien; Elegy in G

1 & 2 July 1978, Kingsway Hall

Tchaikovsky   Muti   EMI ASD 3717
Symphony No 5   EMI 154 5303*
                                                        EMI CDC 747 8592

8, 9 & 10 July 1978, Kingsway Hall

Rossini   Muti   EMI ASD 3903
Semiramide, Overture   EMI EG 29 02781
                                                        EMI CDM 747 1182

Schumann   Muti   EMI SLS 5199*
Die Braut von Messina,   EMI CFP 4395
Overture

Schumann   Muti   EMI ASD 3648
Hermann und Dorothea,   EMI SLS 5199*
Overture   EMI CFP 4394

8, 9 & 10 July 1978, Kingsway Hall, and 5 & 6 April 1979, Abbey Road

Rossini   Muti   EMI ASD 3903
La scala di seta;   EMI EG 29 02781
William Tell, Overtures   EMI CDC 747 1182

11 July 1978 and 11 & 16 July 1980, Kingsway Hall

Verdi   Muti   EMI ASD 4015
I Vespri Siciliani,
Ballet music

17 & 18 July 1978, Walthamstow Town Hall

Bennett   Willcocks   Decca ZRG 907
Spells   Bach Choir
                               Manning

21 & 22 July 1978, Walthamstow Town Hall

Lloyd   Downes   Lyrita SRCS 113
Symphony No 8

7 & 8 August 1978, Kingsway Hall

Tchaikovsky   Ashkenazy   Decca SXL 6919
Symphony No 4

10 & 11 August 1978, Kingsway Hall

Maxwell Davies Symphony	Rattle	Decca HEAD 21

12, 13, 14, 16, 17, 18, 19, 20 & 23 August 1978, Abbey Road

Verdi Rigoletto	Rudel Ambrosian Opera Chorus Sills, Dunn, Murray, Burgess, Kraus, Milnes, Ramey, O'Neill, King, Rawnsley, Smith, Watt	EMI SLS 5193

14 & 15 August 1978, Henry Wood Hall

Hopkins The Music Man	Hopkins	Unicorn RHS 360

15 August 1978, Kingsway Hall

Bennett Aubade	Atherton	Decca ZRG 907

5 September 1978, CBS Studios

Handel Berenice, Overture	Boulez	CBS 76834

16 & 17 September 1978, Kingsway Hall

Mozart Requiem	Giulini Philharmonia Chorus Donath, C.Ludwig, Tear, Lloyd	EMI ASD 3723

18 & 19 September 1978, St John's, Smith Square

Britten Les Illuminations	Giulini Tear	DG 2531 199

21, 22, 23, 24, 25, 27, 29 & 30 September 1978, Brent Town Hall

Rossini Otello	Lopez-Cobos Ambrosian Opera Chorus Von Stade, Carreras, Condo, Pastine, Fisichella, Ramey, K.Lewis, Leoz	Philips 6769 023 <u>Excerpts:</u> Philips 9500 716

30 September and 2 October 1978, Abbey Road

Schumann Symphony No 1 "Spring"	Muti	EMI ASD 3781 EMI SLS 5199* EMI CFP 4393

16 October 1978, Kingsway Hall

Sibelius Two Serious Melodies; Serenade No 2	Ashkenazy Belkin	Decca SXL 6953

16 October 1978 and 10 January 1979, Kingsway Hall

Sibelius Serenade No 1	Ashkenazy Belkin	Decca SXL 6953

18, 22 & 23 October 1978, Kingsway Hall

Rodrigo Fantasia para un gentilhombre; Concierto pastoral	Mata Galway	RCA RL 25193 RCA GL 85446

28, 29 & 31 October 1978, Abbey Road

Saint-Saens Romance; Popp Scherzo fantastique; Doppler L'oiseau des bois; Kimmer Divertissement; Fürstenau Rondo brillant	Dilkes Solum	EMI ASD 3744

Philharmonia Orchestra

Leader: Carl Pini

Greater London Council
Royal Festival Hall
Director: George Mann OBE

Tchaikovsky Cycle 1979
Riccardo Muti

Gidon Kremer

Andrei Gavrilov

This Tchaikovsky Cycle is dedicated
by the Philharmonia Orchestra and
Riccardo Muti, to the memory of

Walter Legge

These concerts are given with financial
assistance from the London Orchestral
Concert Board representing the
Arts Council of Great Britain and the
Greater London Council

Programme 50p

1979

<u>2, 3, 4 & 5 January 1979, Abbey Road</u>

Dvorak Symphony No 8; Carnival, Overture	A.Davis	CBS 76893

<u>2, 3, 4 & 5 January and 10 & 11 December 1979, Abbey Road</u>

Dvorak Symphony No 9 "From the New World"	A.Davis	CBS 76817

<u>10, 14 & 15 January 1979, Henry Wood Hall</u>

Donizetti Ne m'oubliez pas	Judd Geoffrey Mitchell Choir Elkins, Oliver, Du Plessis	Opera Rara OR 4
Donizetti All' afflitto e dolce il pianto (Roberto Devereux)	Judd Elkins	Opera Rara unpublished

<u>18, 19 & 21 January 1979, Abbey Road</u>

Mendelssohn Symphony No 5 "Reformation"	Muti	EMI ASD 3781
Tchaikovsky Symphony No 4	Muti	EMI ASD 3816 EMI 154 5303* EMI EG 29 10671 EMI CDC 747 8602

<u>22 & 28 January 1979, Kingsway Hall</u>

Bantock Overture to a Greek Tragedy	N.Braithwaite	Lyrita SRCS 123
Balfe Galop (The Bohemian Girl)	N.Braithwaite	Lyrita SRCS 99

<u>23, 24, 25 & 26 January 1979, Kingsway Hall</u>

Alwyn Miss Julie	Tausky Gomez, Mitchinson, D.Jones, Luxon	Lyrita SRCS 121/2

<u>9 & 10 February 1979, Henry Wood Hall</u>

Schumann Piano Concerto; Schubert-Liszt Wanderer Fantasy	Sanderling Rogoff	Unicorn RHS 367

22 & 23 February 1979, Walthamstow Town Hall

Brahms   Sanderling   RCA RL 25231
Violin Concerto   Mordkovich   RCA GL 71072

2, 3, 4 & 30 March 1979, Abbey Road

Orff   Muti   EMI ASD 3900
Carmina Burana   Philharmonia Chorus   EMI CDC 747 1002
                                Southend Boys Choir
                                Auger, Van Kesteren,
                                Summers

12 & 13 March 1979, Kingsway Hall

Donizetti   De Almeida   Philips 9500 073
Ballet music from
L'Assiedo di Calais,
La Favorita, Les Martyrs
and Dom Sebastian

13 & 15 March 1979, All Saints, Tooting

Berlioz   Tung   Enigma K53593
Symphonie fantastique   ASV ABM 754

5 & 6 April 1979, Abbey Road

Mozart   Muti   EMI ASD 143 5281
Piano Concerto No 22   Richter   EMI CDM 769 0132

Mozart   Muti   EMI unpublished
Piano Concerto No 15   Richter

7, 8, 9, 10 & 12 April 1979, Watford Town Hall

Rodrigo   Navarro   DG 2531 208
Concierto di Aranjuez;   Yepes, Monden   DG 415 349-2
Concierto madrigal

25, 26 & 27 April 1979, Kingsway Hall

Lloyd   Downes   Lyrita SRCS 124
Symphony No 5

1 May 1979, Henry Wood Hall

Grieg   Macal   Forlane UM 3536
Piano Concerto;   Clidat
Franck
Symphonic Variations

16 & 17 May 1979, Kingsway Hall

Mozart Piano Concerto No 16	Ashkenazy, cond. & sol.	Decca SXL 7010 Decca 411 612-2
Mozart Piano Concerto No 24	Ashkenazy, cond. & sol.	Decca SXL 6947 Decca 414 433-2 Decca 417 726-2

17 & 18 May 1979 and 17, 18 & 24 March 1980, Kingsway Hall

Tchaikovsky Symphony No 6 "Pathétique"	Ashkenazy	Decca SXL 6941 Decca 411 615-2

30 & 31 May and 1, 2 and 4 June 1979, Kingsway Hall

Leoncavallo I Pagliacci	Muti Ambrosian Opera Chorus Scotto, Nurmela, Carreras, Benelli, Allen	EMI SLS 5187* EMI EX 29 08113*

18, 21, 22, 23, 24, 29 & 30 June and 1 & 4 July 1979, Kingsway Hall

Bellini I Puritani	Muti Ambrosian Opera Chorus Caballé, Hamari, Kraus, Manuguerra, Ferrin, Elenkov, O'Neill	EMI SLS 5201

27 June 1979, Abbey Road

Canteloube Chants d'Auvergne	De Almeida Von Stade	CBS unpublished (recording incomplete)

4 & 5 July 1979, Abbey Road

Tchaikovsky Piano Concerto No 1	Muti Gavrilov	EMI ASD 3818 EMI EG 29 03271

12, 13 & 14 July 1979, Kingsway Hall

Saint-Saens Piano Concerto No 1	Dutoit Rogé	Decca D244D3*
Saint-Saens Piano Concerto No 4	Dutoit Rogé	Decca D244D3* Decca SXL 7008

18, 19 & 21 July 1979, Abbey Road

Dvorak Symphony No 7	A.Davis	CBS 79342
Dvorak Symphony No 3	A.Davis	CBS awaiting release

18, 19 & 21 July and 10 & 11 December 1979, Abbey Road

Dvorak Symphony No 6	A.Davis	CBS 36708

1 & 2 August 1979, Henry Wood Hall

Stanford Clarinet Concerto	Francis King	Hyperion A 6601 Hyperion CDA 66001

1, 2, 4, 5 & 8 August 1979, Walthamstow Town Hall

Handel Where'er you walk (Semele); Weber Ozean, du Ungeheuer (Oberon); Verdi Caro nome (Rigoletto); Wagner Liebestod (Tristan und Isolde); Leoncavallo Ballatella (I Pagliacci); Britten Soliloquy and Prayer (Gloriana)	H.Lewis L.Price	RCA ARL1 3522
Bellini Casta Diva (Norma)	H.Lewis Ambrosian Opera Chorus L.Price, Martinovich	RCA ARL1 3522

3, 4, 5, 6 & 7 August 1979, Watford Town Hall

Mascagni Cavalleria Rusticana	Muti Ambrosian Opera Chorus Southend Boys' Choir Caballé, Hamari, Varnay, Carreras, Manuguerra,	EMI SLS 5187* EMI EX 29 08113*

9 September 1979, Abbey Road

Grieg Piano Concerto	Ashkenazy Ortiz	EMI ASD 3960

10, 11, 24 & 26 September and 3, 4 & 5 October 1979, All Saints, Tooting

Meyerbeer Dinorah	Judd Geoffrey Mitchell Choir Cook, D.Jones, Hill Smith, Oliver, Du Plessis, Earle, Caley	Opera Rara OR 5

17 & 18 September 1979, Abbey Road

Schubert Symphony No 9 "Great"	Muti	EMI unpublished

3 & 4 October 1979, Walthamstow Town Hall

Blake	Del Mar	Decca ZRG 922
Violin Concerto	Brown	

9 & 10 October 1979, Henry Wood Hall

Paer Giusti, ah sostenete (Achille); Winter Mi lasci, o madre amata (Il Ratto di Proserpina); Zingarelli Anima mia, deh credi (Ines de Castro); Mayr Rendi il consorte amato (L'Amor Coniugale); Weigl Dopo il fremente nembo (Ginerva di Scozia); Puccitta Un palpito mi sento (La Caccia di Enrico IV); Mosca Ai capricci della sorte (L'Italiana in Algeri)	Parry Harrhy, D.Jones, Hill Smith, Caley, Smythe	Opera Rara ORH 101*
Mayr Elisa, Overture	Parry	Opera Rara ORH 101*
Paganini Aria from Le Rivali Generose	Parry D.Jones	Opera Rara unpublished
Mayr Per pieta, deh non lasciarmi (Ginerva di Scozia)	Parry D.Jones, Hill Smith	Opera Rara ORH 102*

22 October 1979, Abbey Road

Franck Symphonic Variations; Les Djinns	Ashkenazy Ortiz	EMI ASD 3960

10 & 11 November 1979, Kingsway Hall

Sibelius Symphony No 2	Ashkenazy	Decca SXDL 7513 Decca 410 206-2 Decca 421 069-2*

14, 15 & 16 November 1979, Abbey Road

Tchaikovsky   Muti   EMI ASD 3901
Symphony No 6 "Pathétique"   EMI 154 5303*
                                                             EMI EG 29 04991
                                                             EMI CDC 747 8592

Rossini   Muti   EMI ASD 3903
Il Viaggio a Reims,   EMI EG 29 02781
L'Assiedo di Corinto,   EMI CDC 747 1182
Overtures

18 & 19 November 1979, Abbey Road

Schubert   Guschlbauer   Erato STU 71322
Rosamunde,   Ambrosian Singers
Incidental Music   Neubauer

28 & 29 November 1979, Henry Wood Hall

Finzi   Francis   Hyperion A 6601
Clarinet Concerto   King   Hyperion CDA 66001

17 & 18 December 1979, Abbey Road

Sibelius   Dutoit   Erato STU 71324
Violin Concerto   Amoyal   Erato ECD 88109

Sibelius   Dutoit   Erato STU 71324
Two Humoresques   Amoyal

1980

3 & 7 January 1980, Abbey Road

Tchaikovsky Waltz (The Sleeping Beauty)	Siegel	K-Tel ONE 1292 K-Tel STAR 2008 K-Tel RTL 2084 K-Tel RTL 2075
Tchaikovsky Waltz (Eugene Onegin)	Siegel	K-Tel RTL 2084
Tchaikovsky Romeo and Juliet, Fantasy Overture	Scholz	K-Tel ONE 1291 K-Tel STAR 2008 K-Tel RTL 2075
Wagner Tannhäuser; Nicolai The Merry Wives of Windsor, Overtures	Scholz	K-Tel STAR 2008
Tchaikovsky Waltz (Serenade for Strings)	Scholz	K-Tel RTL 2084
Rossini William Tell; Glinka Russlan and Ludmilla, Overtures	Scholz	K-Tel unpublished

17, 18 & 24 March 1980, Kingsway Hall

Sibelius Symphony No 4	Ashkenazy	Decca SXDL 7517 Decca 400 056-2 Decca 421 069-2*
Sibelius Finlandia	Ashkenazy	Decca SXDL 7517 Decca 400 056-2
Sibelius Luonnotar	Ashkenazy Söderström	Decca SXDL 7517 Decca 400 056-2

20 & 21 March 1980, Kingsway Hall

Mozart Piano Concerto No 23; Piano Concerto No 27	Ashkenazy, cond. & sol.	Decca SXDL 7530 Decca 400 087-2
Mozart Concert Rondo K382	Ashkenazy, cond. & sol.	Decca SXL 6982

27 March 1980, Henry Wood Hall

Rossini L'Assiedo di Corinto; Otello; Maometto Secondo, Overtures	Scimone	Erato STU 71178

27 March 1980, Henry Wood Hall (contd.)

Rossini Torvaldo e Dorlinska, Overture	Scimone	Erato unpublished

1 April 1980, Kingsway Hall

Rubbra Symphony No 6	Del Mar	Lyrita SRCS 127

8 & 9 April 1980, Brent Town Hall

Lalo Cello Concerto; Caplet Epiphanie	Dutoit Lodéon	Erato STU 71368
Tchaikovsky Swan Lake, Ballet Suite	Dutoit	Erato unpublished

30 May and 1 June 1980, Abbey Road

Tchaikovsky Suite No 2; Suite No 4 "Mozartiana"	Tilson Thomas	CBS 36702

12 & 14 June 1980, Kingsway Hall

Saint-Saens Phaeton; Danse macabre; La jeunesse d'Hercule; Le rouet d'Omphale; Marche héroique	Dutoit	Decca SXL 6975

30 June 1980, Henry Wood Hall

Cimarosa Tremante, confusa (Artemisia); Generali Sorgera la nuova aurora (Pamela Nubile); Lavigna Come potro resistere ? (Hoango); Gnecco Ed un tal patto solo (La prima prova dell' opera Gli Orazi e Curiazi)	Parry Christie, Harrhy, D.Jones, Dugdale, Mercer, Oliver, Goldthorpe, Opie, Earle	Opera Rara ORH 101*
Mayr Il pesciolin guizzando (Le finte rivali); Dove salvarmi ? (Adelasia ed Alermo)	Parry Montague, Christie, Harrhy, Dugdale, Doghan	Opera Rara ORH 102*

5, 6, 7, 8, 9, 10, 11, 12, 13, 14, 15 & 16 July 1980, Kingsway Hall

Verdi	Muti	EMI SLS 5240
La Traviata	Ambrosian Opera Chorus	EMI CDS 747 0598
	Scotto, Walker, Buchan,	EMI CDS 747 5388
	Kraus, Bruson, Newman,	
	Van Allan, Kennedy, Keyte,	
	Mariategui, Cosotti	

11 & 16 July 1980, Kingsway Hall

Verdi	Muti	EMI ASD 3979
Choruses from	Ambrosian Opera Chorus	EMI CDC 747 2742
Il Trovatore; I Lombardi		

17 & 18 July 1980, Kingsway Hall

Cherubini	Muti	EMI ASD 4071
Requiem Mass in C minor	Ambrosian Singers	
Rossini	Muti	EMI ASD 3903
Il Barbiere di Siviglia,		EMI EG 29 02781
Overture		EMI CDC 747 1182

29, 30 & 31 July and 1, 2 & 11 August 1980, Kingsway Hall

Puccini	Levine	EMI SLS 5213
Tosca	Ambrosian Opera Chorus	
	Scotto, Domingo, Bruson,	
	Capecchi, Cheek, Velis,	
	Hudson, Perlman, Martinez	

3, 4, 7 & 9 August 1980, Abbey Road

Wolf-Ferrari	Pritchard	CBS 36733
Il Segreto di Susanna	Scotto, Bruson	

12 & 13 August 1980, Walthamstow Town Hall

Bartok	Rattle	Decca ZRG 936
Violin Concerto No 2	Brown	

3 & 4 September 1980, Abbey Road

Dvorak	A.Davis	CBS 37272
Symphony No 5		

8 September 1980, Kingsway Hall

Rubbra	Del Mar	Lyrita SRCS 127
Symphony No 8		

14, 15 & 16 September 1980, Abbey Road

Beethoven	Giulini	EMI ASD 4059
Violin Concerto	Perlman	EMI CDC 747 0022

20 October 1980, Kingsway Hall

Mozart	Ashkenazy, cond. & sol.	Decca SXDL 7556
Piano Concerto No 12		Decca 410 214-2

28 October 1980, Kingsway Hall

Sibelius	Ashkenazy	Decca SXDL 7541
Symphony No 5		Decca 410 016-2
		Decca 421 069-2*

4 & 5 November 1980, Brent Town Hall

Hoddinott	Groves	Unicorn RHD 401
Nocturnes and Cadenzas	Welsh	
Hoddinott	Groves	Unicorn RHD 401
Sinfonia Fidei	Chorus	
	Gomez, Burrows	
Hoddinott	Groves	Unicorn RHD 401
Jack Straw, Overture		

19 & 20 November 1980, Abbey Road

Stravinsky	Tilson Thomas	CBS 37271
Petrushka;		CBS MK 37271
Scherzo à la russe		

24 & 25 November 1980, Abbey Road

Poulenc	Prêtre	EMI ASD 4067
Les biches, Ballet;	Ambrosian Singers	EMI EMX 2107
Pastourelle; Bucolique;		
Matelote provençale		

10 & 11 December 1980, Henry Wood Hall

Dvorak	A.Davis	CBS awaiting release
Symphony No 1		

29 & 30 December 1980, Kingsway Hall

Holst	Rattle	EMI ASD 4047
The Planets	Ambrosian Singers	EMI EMX 2106

1981

4, 5, 6 & 7 January 1981, Walthamstow Town Hall

Beethoven Symphony No 1	Sanderling	EMI SLS 5239* EMI ASD 4151
Beethoven Symphony No 4	Sanderling	EMI SLS 5239* EMI ASD 4153 EMI EG 29 12891
Beethoven Symphony No 5	Sanderling	EMI SLS 5239* EMI ASD 4136 EMI EG 29 12891
Beethoven Coriolan, Overture	Sanderling	EMI SLS 5239* EMI ASD 4136

8, 9, 10, 12, 13, 14, 15, 16 & 17 January 1981, Abbey Road

Beethoven Symphony No 2	Sanderling	EMI SLS 5239* EMI ASD 4151
Beethoven Symphony No 3 "Eroica"	Sanderling	EMI SLS 5239* EMI ASD 4152 EMI EG 29 12881
Beethoven Symphony No 6 "Pastoral"	Sanderling	EMI SLS 5239* EMI ASD 4154
Beethoven Symphony No 7	Sanderling	EMI SLS 5239* EMI ASD 4155
Beethoven Symphony No 8	Sanderling	EMI SLS 5239* EMI SLS 5244*

17 January 1981, Abbey Road and 4 & 6 February 1981, Kingsway Hall

Beethoven Symphony No 9 "Choral"	Sanderling Philharmonia Chorus Armstrong, Finnie, Tear, Tomlinson	EMI SLS 5239* EMI SLS 5244

21 & 22 January 1981, Kingsway Hall

Mozart Mass in C minor	Muti Philharmonia Chorus	EMI unpublished (recording incomplete)

4 & 6 February 1981, Kingsway Hall

Beethoven Fidelio, Overture	Sanderling	EMI SLS 5239* EMI ASD 4152 EMI EG 29 12881
Beethoven Egmont, Overture	Sanderling	EMI SLS 5239* EMI ASD 4153
Beethoven Prometheus, Overture	Sanderling	EMI SLS 5239* EMI ASD 4155

18 & 19 February 1981, Walthamstow Town Hall

Offenbach La vie parisienne; Barbe-bleue; La périchole; Orfée aux enfers; La Belle Hélène; La Grande Duchesse de Gerolstein; La fille du tambour-major, Overtures	Marriner	Philips 6514 098 Philips 411 476-2

24, 25 & 27 March 1981, Kingsway Hall

Beethoven Symphony No 5; Leonore No 3, Overture	Ashkenazy	Decca SXDL 7540 Decca 400 060-2
Sibelius En Saga	Ashkenazy	Decca SXDL 7541 Decca 410 016-2

28 March 1981, Kingsway Hall

Mozart Piano Concerto No 13	Ashkenazy, cond. & sol.	Decca SXDL 7556 Decca 410 214-2

14 & 16 April 1981, Brent Town Hall

Tchaikovsky Violin Concerto	Dutoit Amoyal	Erato STU 71452 Erato ECD 88109
Tchaikovsky Sérénade mélancolique; Valse-Scherzo	Dutoit Amoyal	Erato STU 71452

18 April 1981, Brent Town Hall

Tchaikovsky Piano Concerto No 1	Dutoit Devoyon	Erato STU 71451

27 & 28 April 1981, Abbey Road

Tchaikovsky Violin Concerto	Ozawa Spivakov	EMI ASD 4173
Tchaikovsky Capriccio italien	Ozawa	EMI ASD 4173

11 May 1981, Watford Town Hall

Knussen Symphony No 3	Tilson Thomas	Unicorn RHD 400

12 & 13 June 1981, Abbey Road

Franck Symphonic Variations; Fauré Ballade; D'Indy Symphonie cévennole	Dutoit Entremont	CBS 37269

25, 27, 28, 29 & 30 June and 6 July 1981, Kingsway Hall, and 30 November 1981, Abbey Road

Gluck Orfeo ed Euridice	Muti Ambrosian Opera Chorus Baltsa, Marshall, Gruberova	EMI SLS 5255

3 & 10 July 1981, Kingsway Hall

Tchaikovsky Manfred Symphony	Muti	EMI ASD 4169 EMI SLS 154 5303* EMI CDC 747 4122

14 & 15 July 1981, Walthamstow Town Hall

Lloyd Symphony No 4	Downes	Lyrita SRCS 129

6, 7, 8, 9, 11, 12, 13, 14, 15 & 16 August 1981, Watford Town Hall

Rossini Mosè in Egitto	Scimone Ambrosian Opera Chorus Anderson, Gal, Browne, R.Raimondi, Palacio, Fisichella, K.Lewis, Nimsgern	Philips 6769 081

14, 15, 16 & 17 August 1981, Abbey Road

Gershwin An American in Paris; Rhapsody No 2; Catfish Row; Cuban Overture; Prokofiev Overture op 42	Tilson Thomas	CBS unpublished

24 & 25 August 1981, Watford Town Hall

Rossini Stabat mater	Giulini Philharmonia Chorus Ricciarelli, Gonsalez, Valentini-Terrani, R.Raimondi	DG 2532 046 DG 410 034-2

9 & 10 October 1981, Abbey Road

Sibelius Symphony No 5; Night Ride and Sunrise	Rattle	EMI ASD 4168 EMI CDC 747 0062

23 & 25 October 1981, All Saints, Tooting

Grieg Symphonic Dances;	Leppard	Philips 6514 203
Grieg Elegaic Melodies	Leppard	Philips unpublished
Grieg Variations on an Old Norwegian Romance	Leppard	Philips 6514 203 Philips 420 081-2

2 & 3 November 1981, Abbey Road

Walton Symphony No 1	Haitink	EMI ASD 4091

25 & 26 November 1981, Abbey Road

Mozart Violin Concerto No 2; Violin Concerto No 4	Muti Mutter	EMI ASD 4185 EMI CDC 747 0112

18, 19, 29 & 30 December 1981, Abbey Road

Dvorak Symphony No 2; Scherzo capriccioso	A.Davis	CBS awaiting release
Elgar Enigma Variations; Pomp and Circumstance, Marches Nos 2, 3, 4 and 5	A.Davis	CBS 37755

1982

9 & 10 February 1982, Kingsway Hall

Beethoven Symphony No 6 "Pastoral"	Ashkenazy	Decca SXDL 7578 Decca 410 003-2

12 February 1982, Kingsway Hall

Mozart Piano Concerto No 25	Ashkenazy, cond. & sol.	Decca 411 810-1 Decca 411 810-2

1, 2, 3 & 12 March and 19 & 20 April 1982, Abbey Road

Tchaikovsky The Nutcracker	Lanchbery	EMI SLS 5273* EMI SLS 5270

24 & 25 March 1982, Kingsway Hall

Sibelius Symphony No 7	Ashkenazy	Decca SXDL 7580 Decca 411 935-2 Decca 421 069-2*
Sibelius Tapiola	Ashkenazy	Decca SXDL 7580 Decca 411 935-2

19 & 20 April and 12, 16, 17, 18, 19 & 20 May 1982, Abbey Road

Tchaikovsky Swan Lake	Lanchbery	EMI SLS 5273* EMI SLS 5271

4 & 5 May 1982, Abbey Road

Debussy La Mer	Tilson Thomas	CBS 37832 CBS MK 37832
Debussy Trois Nocturnes	Tilson Thomas Ambrosian Singers	CBS 37832 CBS MK 37832

24 & 25 May 1982, St John's, Smith Square

Sibelius The Swan of Tuonela; Finlandia; Tapiola; Lemminkainen's Return; Valse triste	Berglund	EMI ASD 4186 EMI CDC 747 4842

26 & 27 May 1982, Henry Wood Hall

Rachmaninov Piano Concerto No 2; Rhapsody on a theme of Paganini	Levi Tirimo	EMI CFP 4383

28 & 30 May and 1 June 1982, Abbey Road

Beethoven Piano Concerto No 5 "Emperor"	Sawallisch Egorov	EMI ASD 143 4331

6 June 1982, Henry Wood Hall

Paer
Se sentissi qual fiamma
vorace (Agnese di Fitzhenry);
Mosca
Se non avete in seno
(Le sposi in cimento);
Nicolini
Gelida mano io sento
(Trajano in Dacia);
Pavesi
Minacci, ah parti indegno
(Elisabetta d'Inghilterra);
Fioravanti
Con pazienza sopportiamo
(I virtuosi ambulanti)

Parry
Geoffrey Mitchell Choir
Dugdale, Korman, Mercer,
Hill Smith, Harrhy,
Montague, John, Leggate,
Du Plessis, Smythe, Earle

Opera Rara ORH 101*

8 June 1982, Rosslyn Hill Chapel

Hall Lewis
Osservaccioni II

Hall Lewis

Private recording
(unpublished)

25 & 26 June 1982, Kingsway Hall

Schumann
Violin Concerto;
Sibelius
Violin Concerto

Muti
Kremer

EMI ASD 143 5191
EMI CDC 747 1102

28, 29 & 30 June and 8, 9, 10 & 11 July 1982, Kingsway Hall

Donizetti
Don Pasquale

Muti
Ambrosian Opera Chorus
Freni, Winbergh, Nucci,
Bruscantini, Fabbris

EMI SLS 143 4363

2 July 1982, Kingsway Hall

Mozart
Symphony No 24

Muti

EMI ASD 143 5281

12, 13, 14, 15, 16, 21 & 22 July 1982, Abbey Road

Tchaikovsky
The Sleeping Beauty

Lanchbery

EMI SLS 5273*
EMI SLS 5272

15 & 16 August 1982, Abbey Road

Dvorak
Symphony No 4

A.Davis

CBS awaiting release

21 August 1982, Henry Wood Hall

Paer
Se sentissi qual fiamma vorace (Agnese di Fitzhenry);
Nicolini
Parmi sentir nell' anima (I baccanali di Roma);
Winter
Sommo Dio, che in sen mi vidi (Zaira);
Paer
Ah Sofia ! (Sargino);
Una soave calma (Sofonisba);
Portogallo
Son regina (La Semiramide);
Righini
Un cenno mi chiedi ? (Gerusalemme Liberata);
Paisiello
Del mio gentil sebeto (Il passaggio di Monte San Bernardo)

Parry
Geoffrey Mitchell Choir
Harrhy, Kenny, Montague, Korman, Mercer, K.Lewis, Leggate, Du Plessis, Smythe, John

Opera Rara ORH 101*

Garcia
Unspecified duet (Il Califfo di Bagdad)

Parry
Soloists unidentified

Opera Rara unpublished

26 September 1982, Kingsway Hall

Mozart
Piano Concerto No 15

Ashkenazy, cond. & sol.

Decca SXL 7010
Decca 411 612-2

28 September 1982, Kingsway Hall

Dvorak
Cello Concerto;
Bruch
Kol Nidrei

Ashkenazy
Harrell

Decca SXDL 7608
Decca 410 144-2

30 September 1982, Kingsway Hall

Mussorgsky
Pictures at an exhibition

Ashkenazy

Decca 410 121-1
Decca 410 121-2

18 & 19 October 1982, Walthamstow Town Hall

Delius
Cello Concerto;
Holst
Invocation;
Vaughan Williams
Fantasia on Sussex Folk Tunes

Handley
Lloyd Webber

RCA RS 9010
RCA RD 70800

26, 27 & 28 October 1982, Abbey Road

Mendelssohn　　　　　　　　Tilson Thomas　　　　　　CBS 39007
Violin Concerto;　　　　　Lin　　　　　　　　　　　　CBS MK 39007
Saint-Saens
Violin Concerto No 3

17 & 18 November 1982, Kingsway Hall

Janacek　　　　　　　　　　Rattle　　　　　　　　　　EMI ASD 143 5221
Sinfonietta; Taras Bulba　　　　　　　　　　　　　　EMI CDC 747 0482

26 & 27 November 1982, Kingsway Hall

Sullivan-Mackerras　　　　Mackerras　　　　　　　　Decca SXDL 7619
Pineapple Poll, Ballet;
Sullivan
Di Ballo, Overture

1983

23 & 24 January 1983, Abbey Road

Dvorak Slavonic Dances op 46	A.Davis	CBS awaiting release

9 & 10 February 1983, Kingsway Hall

Mozart Piano Concerto No 20	Ashkenazy, cond. & sol.	Decca 414 337-1 Decca 414 337-2
Beethoven Egmont, Overture	Ashkenazy	Decca 411 941-1 Decca 411 941-2
Borodin Polovtsian Dances (Prince Igor)	Ashkenazy	Decca 410 121-1 Decca 410 121-2
Borodin Prince Igor, Overture	Ashkenazy	Decca unpublished

6 & 7 March 1983, Abbey Road

Rodrigo Concierto di Aranjuez; Fantasia para un gentilhombre	Frémaux Williams	CBS 37848 CBS MK 37848

10 & 11 March 1983, All Saints, Tooting

Puccini Messa di Gloria	Scimone Ambrosian Singers Carreras, Prey	Erato NUM 75090

16 & 17 March 1983, Kingsway Hall

Mendelssohn A Midsummer Night's Dream, Incidental Music	Marriner Ambrosian Singers Augér, Murray	Philips 411 106-1 Philips 411 106-2

24 March 1983, St Barnabas, Woodside Park

Moreno-Buendia Suite Concertante	Dutoit Robles	Decca 411 738-1

20 & 21 April 1983, Walthamstow Town Hall

Elgar Symphony No 1	Haitink	EMI ASD 107 7941
Elgar Pomp and Circumstance, March No 5	Haitink	EMI unpublished

11 May 1983, Kingsway Hall

Sibelius   Ashkenazy   Decca 414 267-1
Symphony No 3   Decca 414 267-2
                                                       Decca 421 069-2*

24 & 25 June 1983, Kingsway Hall

Schubert   Sinopoli   DG 410 862-1
Symphony No 8 "Unfinished"   DG 410 862-2
Mendelssohn
Symphony No 4 "Italian"

27 June 1983, Henry Wood Hall

Hall Lewis   Hall Lewis   Private recording
Moto for string orchestra   (unpublished)

29 & 30 June 1983, Walthamstow Town Hall

Strauss   Prêtre   RCA RL 70071
Also sprach Zarathustra   RCA RD 70071

6, 7 & 12 July 1983, Abbey Road

Vivaldi   Wilbrandt   Philips 412 321-1
The Four Seasons   Warren-Green   Philips 412 321-2

12 & 13 July 1983, Walthamstow Town Hall

Gershwin   Marriner   Philips 411 123-1
Rhapsody in Blue;   Dichter   Philips 411 123-2
Addinsell
Warsaw Concerto;
Litolff
Scherzo;
Chopin
Fantasia on Polish themes;
Weber
Polacca brillante

2 & 3 August 1983, Kingsway Hall

Brahms   Sawallisch   RCA RD 70072
Violin Concerto   Ughi

9, 10 & 11 August and 5 & 6 September 1983, CTS Studios

Carl Davis   Carl Davis   CTS CDL 1464
The Far Pavilions

15, 16, 17 & 18 August 1983, St John's, Smith Square

Fauré Ballade; Fantasie; Ravel Piano Concerto in G	A.Davis Varsano	CRD PAD 173

16 & 17 August 1983, St Barnabas, Woodside Park

Rodrigo Concierto di Aranjuez (transcribed by the composer for harp and orchestra)	Dutoit Robles	Decca 411 738-1

23, 24 & 25 August 1983, St John's, Smith Square

Wagner Starke Scheite (Götterdämmerung); Dich teure Halle; Allmächtige Jungfrau (Tannhäuser); Einsam in trüben Tagen (Lohengrin); Liebestod (Tristan und Isolde)	Joo Marton	Sefel SEFD 5024 Sefel SEFCD 5024
Strauss Salome, Closing scene; Elektra, Monologue; Guntram, Act 2 scene 3; Die Aegyptische Helena, Act 2 scene 1	Joo Marton	Sefel unpublished

27, 28 & 30 August 1983, St John's, Smith Square

Strauss Der Rosenkavalier, Suite; Die Frau ohne Schatten, Symphonic Fantasy	Joo	Sefel SEFD 5028 Sefel SEFCD 5028
Strauss Ein Heldenleben	Joo	Sefel SEFD 5027 Sefel SEFCD 5027

30 & 31 August 1983, St John's, Smith Square

Mendelssohn A Midsummer Night's Dream	Joo King's College Chapel Choir	Sefel SEFD 5025 Sefel SEFCD 5025

25 & 26 October 1983, Kingsway Hall

Beethoven Symphony No 7; Coriolan, Overture	Ashkenazy	Decca 411 941-1 Decca 411 941-2

29 October 1983, Kingsway Hall

Mozart Piano Concerto No 26	Ashkenazy, cond. & sol.	Decca 411 810-1 Decca 411 810-2

13 December 1983, Henry Wood Hall

Mayr Ov' è la bella vergine ? (Alfredo il Grande); Ah se morir potessi (Elena); Se fiero, Ippolito (Fedra); Sempre uniti insiem saremo (Cora); Dov' è la destra ? (La Rosa Bianca e la Rosa Rossa)	Parry Montague, Moreno, Walker, Kenny, Leggate, John, Smythe, Doghan	Opera Rara ORH 102*

14, 15, 16, 19, 20, 21, 22 & 23 December 1983, Kingsway Hall

Rossini Maometto Secondo	Scimone Ambrosian Opera Chorus Anderson, Zimmermann, Ramey, Palacio, Dale	Philips 412 148-1 Philips 412 148-2

19 & 20 December 1983, All Saints, Tooting

Haydn Horn Concertos Nos 1 and 2	Warren-Green Thompson	Nimbus NIM 2141 Nimbus NIM 5010
Haydn Trumpet Concerto	Warren-Green Wallace	Nimbus NIM 2141 Nimbus NIM 5010

28, 29 & 30 December 1983 and 3, 4 & 5 January 1984, Kingsway Hall

Puccini Manon Lescaut	Sinopoli Covent Garden Chorus Freni, Fassbaender, Domingo, Bruson, Rydl, Gambill, Macpherson, Fryatt, Thomas, Curtis, Tomlinson	DG 413 893-1 DG 413 893-2

1984

17 & 18 January 1984, All Saints, Tooting

Respighi	Simon	Chandos ABRD 1098
Church Windows;		Chandos CHAN 8371
Brazilian Impressions		

17 & 18 January and 1 & 2 August 1984, All Saints Tooting

Various composers	Simon	Chandos ABRD 1119
L'Eventail de Jeanne		Chandos CHAN 8356

22 & 23 March 1984, Abbey Road

Elgar	Haitink	EMI EL 27 01471
Symphony No 2		EMI CDC 747 2992

8, 9 & 10 May 1984, Abbey Road

Brahms	Pesek	Midas unpublished
Symphony No 2;		
Symphony No 3		

16 June 1984, Walthamstow Town Hall

Sibelius	Ashkenazy	Decca 414 267-1
Symphony No 6		Decca 414 267-2
		Decca 421 069-2*

19 June 1984, Walthamstow Town Hall

Mozart	Ashkenazy, cond. & sol.	Decca 414 337-1
Piano Concerto No 18		Decca 414 337-2

27 June 1984, All Saints, Tooting

Hall Lewis	Hall Lewis	Private recording
Atto for string orchestra		(unpublished)

3, 4, 5 & 8 July 1984, Abbey Road

Cherubini	Muti	EMI EL 27 02831
Coronation Mass;	Philharmonia Chorus	
Marche réligieuse		

8, 9 & 10 July 1984, Abbey Road

Haydn Trumpet Concerto; Bach Brandenburg Concerto No 2; Torelli Trumpet Concerto in D; Telemann Trumpet Concerto in D	Muti André	EMI EL 27 02691 EMI CDC 747 3112

1 & 2 August 1984, All Saints, Tooting

Various composers Les Maries de la Tour Eiffel	Simon	Chandos ABRD 1119 Chandos CHAN 8356

3 & 4 October 1984, All Saints, Tooting

Tchaikovsky Symphony No 5; Borodin Polovtsian Dances (Prince Igor)	Joo	Sefel unpublished

5 & 6 October 1984, All Saints, Tooting

Paganini Violin Concerto No 2	Joo Fodor	Sefel unpublished
Tchaikovsky Marche slave; 1812, Overture; Glinka Russlan and Ludmilla, Overture	Joo	Sefel unpublished

8 October 1984, All Saints, Tooting

Elgar Cello Concerto; Saint-Saens Cello Concerto	Joo Rolston	Sefel unpublished
Mendelssohn Violin Concerto	Joo Warren-Green	Sefel unpublished

29 October 1984, Walthamstow Town Hall

Sibelius Symphony No 1	Ashkenazy	Decca 414 534-1 Decca 414 534-2 Decca 421 069-2*

2 November 1984, Walthamstow Town Hall

Mozart Piano Concerto No 9	Ashkenazy, cond. & sol.	Decca 414 543-1 Decca 414 543-2

27, 28 & 29 December 1984, All Saints, Tooting

Albinoni Trumpet Sonata in C; Trumpet Sonata in D; Torelli Concerto for 4 Trumpets; Monteverdi Toccata for 6 Trumpets; Alberti Sinfonia for 4 Trumpets; Vivaldi Concerto for 2 Trumpets; Bononcini Concerto for 2 Trumpets; Francheschini Concerto for 2 Trumpets; Purcell Trumpet Sonata in D	Warren-Green Wallace, Miller	Nimbus NIM 5017
Leopold Mozart Horn Concerto in D; Vivaldi Concerto for 2 Horns; Haydn Concerto for 2 Horns; Rosetti Horn Concerto in D minor	Warren-Green Thompson, Watkins	Nimbus NIM 5018

31 December 1984 and 22 January 1985, All Saints, Tooting

Respighi Belkis, Queen of Sheba; Metamorphoses	Simon	Chandos ABRD 1142 Chandos CHAN 8405

Philharmonia Orchestra

Patron: HRH The Prince of Wales
KG, KT, PC, GCB

President: Vincent Meyer

Principal Conductor:
Giuseppe Sinopoli

Principal Guest Conductor:
Esa-Pekka Salonen

Composer in Residence:
Oliver Knussen

Leaders:
Christopher Warren-Green & Peter Thomas

Wednesday
13 November 1985
at 7.30

This concert, promoted by Philharmonia Limited, is given with financial assistance from the London Orchestral Concert Board representing the Arts Council of Great Britain and the Greater London Council

Esa Pekka-Salonen

Sibelius: Symphonic Fantasy, Pohjola's Daughter

Mendelssohn: Symphony No. 4 (Italian)

Dmitri Alexeev

Brahms: Piano Concerto No. 1

Sponsored by Nissan UK Limited

Greater London Council
Royal Festival Hall
Programme 80p

25, 26, 28 & 29 January 1985, All Saints, Tooting

Mahler Symphony No 5	Sinopoli	DG 415 476-1 DG 415 476-2
Mahler Frühlingsmorgen; Um schlimme Kinder artig zu machen; Selbstgefühl; Nicht wiedersehen; Ablösung im Sommer; Zu Strassburg auf der Schanz (Lieder und Gesänge aus der Jugendzeit)	Sinopoli Weikl	DG 415 476-1 DG 415 959-2

8 February 1985, St Barnabas, Woodside Park

Sibelius Karelia Suite	Ashkenazy	Decca 414 534-1 Decca 414 534-2

9 February 1985, St Barnabas, Woodside Park

Mozart Piano Concerto No 8	Ashkenazy, cond. & sol.	Decca 414 543-1 Decca 414 543-2

19 & 20 February 1985, Abbey Road

Mozart Piano Concerto No 17; Piano Concerto No 20	Sawallisch Egorov	EMI EL 27 03621

27, 28, 30 & 31 March 1985, CTS Studios

Christmas songs; Have yourself a merry little Christmas; Angels from the realms of glory; La virgen lava panales; O Holy Night; Winter Wonderland; The most wonderful birthday of all; White Christmas; Silent Night; Mary's boy child; Twelve days of Christmas; The little drummer boy; Silver bells	Carl Davis Kanawa	CTS PROLP 12

3 & 4 April 1985, Abbey Road

Shostakovich Symphony No 10	Rattle	EMI EL 27 03151 EMI CDC 747 3522

25, 26, 27 & 30 May 1985, Abbey Road

Tchaikovsky The Nutcracker	Tilson Thomas Ambrosian Singers	CBS 42173 CBS M2K 3/248

28 & 29 May 1985, Walthamstow Town Hall

Beethoven Piano Concerto No 1; Piano Concerto No 2	Sinopoli Argerich	DG 415 682-1 DG 415 682-2

9 & 12 June 1985, Walthamstow Town Hall

Jolivet Trumpet Concerto No 2; Tomasi Trumpet Concerto	Salonen Marsalis	CBS 42096 CBS MK 42096
Jolivet Concertino for Trumpet, Piano and Strings	Salonen Marsalis, Sheppard	CBS 42096 CBS MK 42096

19 June 1985, Henry Wood Hall

Hall Lewis Destini	Hall Lewis	Private recording (unpublished)

3, 4, 5 & 6 September 1985, Watford Town Hall

Mahler Symphony No 2 "Resurrection"	Sinopoli Philharmonia Chorus Plowright, Fassbaender	DG 415 959-1 DG 415 959-2
Mahler Lieder eines fahrenden Gesellen	Sinopoli Fassbaender	DG 415 959-1 DG 415 959-2

9, 10 & 11 September 1985, Abbey Road

Puccini In questa reggia; Tu che di gel sei cinta (Turandot); Senza mamma (Suor Angelica); O mio babbino caro (Gianni Schicchi); Un bel dì; Che tua madre; Tu, tu, piccolo iddio (Madama Butterfly); Se come voi piccina (Le Villi); Si mi chiamano Mimì; Quando m'en vo; Donde lieta uscì (La Bohème); Vissi d'arte (Tosca); In quelle trine morbide; Sola, perduta (Manon Lescaut)	Guadagno Dimitrova	EMI EL 27 03871

9, 10 & 11 September 1985, Olympic Studios

Calandrelli	Stratta	GRP 91024
Concerto for Jazz Clarinet;	Daniels	GRP D 9533
Bach		
Siciliana;		
Daniels		
Circle Dance;		
Zito		
Aja's Theme & Divertimento;		
C.P.E.Bach/Calandrelli		
Solfegietto Metamorphosis		

12, 13, 14, 18, 19, 20 & 21 September 1985 and 9 January, 24 February and 3 June 1986, Watford Town Hall

Verdi	Sinopoli	DG 419 203-1
La Forza del Destino	Ambrosian Opera Chorus	DG 419 203-2
	Plowright, Baltsa, Carreras,	
	Rigby, Bruson, Burchuladze,	
	Pons, Tomlinson, Van Allan,	
	Curtis, Salomaa	

8 & 9 October 1985, All Saints, Tooting

Dvorak	Warren-Green	Chandos ABRD 1172
Serenade for Strings;		Chandos CHAN 8459
Wind Serenade		

22 & 25 October 1985, Walthamstow Town Hall

Rimsky-Korsakov	Ashkenazy	Decca 417 301-1
Scheherazade;		Decca 417 301-2
Tsar Sultan, Suite		

10, 11, 12 & 14 November 1985, Abbey Road

Messiaen	Salonen	CBS 42126
Turangalîla Symphony	Crossley, Murail	CBS M2K 42271

13 December 1985, Henry Wood Hall

Morlacchi	Parry	Opera Rara awaiting release
Buona sera	Hill Smith, Moreno, Best,	
(Il Barbiere di Siviglia);	Bickley, Bromley, John,	
Generali	Smythe	
Giusto ciel, correte, andate		
(Adelina);		
Donizetti		
Ah, qual colpo !		
(Pietro il Grande)		

Philharmonia Orchestra

APRES L'APRES-MIDI

SIMON RATTLE
conducts

Thursday 8 May at 7.30
Royal Festival Hall
MARIA EWING
Debussy: Prélude à l'après-midi d'un faune
Ravel: Shéhérazade Boulez: Rituel
Ravel: Trois Poèmes de Stéphane Mallarmé
Debussy: Iberia

Sunday 11 May at 7.30
Royal Festival Hall
ANN MURRAY
Ravel: L'Éventail de Jeanne
Satie: Parade Duparc: Songs with Orchestra
Debussy: Le Martyre de Saint-Sébastien —
Symphonic Fragments
Koechlin: Les Bandar-Log Ravel: La Valse

Thursday 15 May at 7.30
Royal Festival Hall
KATIA and MARIELLE LABÈQUE
ELISE ROSS DINAH HARRIS MARY KING
AMERAL GUNSON ALEXANDER OLIVER
HENRY HERFORD RAIMOND HERINCX
ST. CLEMENT DANES SCHOOL CHOIR
PHILHARMONIA CHORUS
Ravel: Alborada del gracioso Poulenc: Concerto for 2 Pianos
Debussy: Jeux Ravel: L'Enfant et les Sortilèges

Saturday 17 May at 7.45
Queen Elizabeth Hall
PETER DONOHOE
Debussy: La Boîte à joujoux
Messiaen: Oiseaux Exotiques
Boulez: Eclat Ravel: Ma Mère l'Oye

Monday 19 May at 7.30
Royal Festival Hall
ELISABETH SÖDERSTRÖM
PHILHARMONIA CHORUS
Poulenc: La Voix Humaine
Messiaen: Et Exspecto Resurrectionem Mortuorum
Ravel: Daphnis et Chloé (complete)

Sponsored by

CHANEL

1986

13 & 14 January 1986, All Saints, Tooting

Tchaikovsky Violin Concerto	Simon Shkolnikova	Cala CAMC 1/2 (cassette) Cala CADC 1/2
Beethoven Symphony No 5	Simon	Cala CAMC 1/2 (cassette) Cala CADC 1/2

1 February 1986, Henry Wood Hall

Mayr Caro albergo (Medea in Corinto); Weber Non paventar mia vita ! (Ines de Castro); Manfroce Si tenero ama (Ecuba); Mosca Mentre guardo (Le bestie in uomini); Meyerbeer Di gioja, di pace (Emma di Resburgo)	Parry Geoffrey Mitchell Choir Kenny, Bovino, Montague, Mills, Nicoll, Nilon, Dalton	Opera Rara awaiting release

13 & 14 February 1986, Henry Wood Hall

Penderecki Cello Concerto	Penderecki Rostropovich	Erato awaiting release

12, 13 & 14 March 1986, Watford Town Hall

Fauré Requiem	Giulini Philharmonia Chorus Battle, A.Schmidt	DG 419 243-1 DG 419 243-2
Ravel Pavane pour une infante défunte	Giulini	DG 419 243-1 DG 419 243-2

21 & 22 March 1986, Henry Wood Hall

Sibelius Symphony No 5; Pohjola's Daughter	Salonen	CBS 42366 CBS MK 42356

16 & 17 April 1986, All Saints, Tooting

Wagner Lohengrin, Prelude Act 3	Simon	Cala CAMC 1/2 (cassette) Cala CADC 1/2
Johann Strauss Voices of Spring, Waltz; Thunder & Lightning, Polka; Sibelius The Swan of Tuonela; Mussorgsky Night on Bare Mountain; Barber Adagio for Strings; Ravel Bolero; Elgar Pomp and Circumstance, March No 1	Simon	Cala CAMC 3/4 (cassette) Cala CADC 3/4
Saint-Saens Introduction and Rondo Capriccioso	Simon Chase	Cala CAMC 3/4 (casette) Cala CADC 3/4

30 April and 1 May 1986, Walthamstow Town Hall

Mozart Piano Concerto No 5; Piano Concerto No 14	Ashkenazy, cond. & sol.	Decca awaiting release

23 & 24 June 1986, Watford Town Hall

Hummel Trumpet Concerto in E; Neruda Trumpet Concerto in E flat; F.Weber Variations in F; Diabelli Fanfares for 6 Trumpets; Weber Marcia vivace; Altenburg Concerto in C	Warren-Green Wallace	Nimbus NIM 5065

5 July 1986, St John's, Smith Square

Handel
Sibillar gl' angui
d'Aletto (Rinaldo);
Mozart
Madamina (Don Giovanni);
Rossini
La calumnia
(Il Barbiere di Siviglia);
Deh ti ferma (Semiramide);
Bellini
Vi ravviso (La Sonnambula);
Verdi
Mentre gionfarsi (Attila);
Tu sul labbro (Nabucco);
Boito
Son lo spirito;
Ecco il mondo (Mefistofele);
Montemezzi
Sono stanco
(L'Amore dei Tre Re)

Renzetti
Ambrosian Opera Chorus
Ramey

Philips awaiting release

24 & 25 July 1986, Abbey Road

Rodrigo
Concierto di Aranjuez;
Serenata

Mata
Romero

EMI awaiting release

28 & 29 July 1986, Henry Wood Hall

Strauss
Burleske; Parergon

Del Mar
Hobson

Arabesque Z 6567

1, 2, 3, 4, 5, 7 & 8 August 1986 and 1 May 1987, Walthamstow Town Hall

Halévy
La Juive

De Almeida
Ambrosian Opera Chorus
Varady, Anderson, Carreras,
Furlanetto, Massis,
Schirrer

Philips awaiting release

25, 26 & 27 September 1986, Watford Town Hall

Mahler
Symphony No 6

Sinopoli

DG awaiting release

29 & 30 September 1986, Watford Town Hall

Beethoven
Violin Concerto;

Sinopoli
Mintz

DG awaiting release

29 & 30 September 1986 and 14 April 1987, Watford Town Hall

Beethoven
Violin Romances
Nos 1 and 2

Sinopoli
Mintz

DG awaiting release

28, 29 & 30 October 1986, Walthamstow Town Hall

Mozart
Piano Concerto No 6;
Piano Concerto No 11
  Ashkenazy, cond. & sol.
  Decca awaiting release

10 & 12 November 1986, Abbey Road

Rubbra
Symphony No 3;
Symphony No 4
  Del Mar
  Lyrita awaiting release

19 & 20 November 1986, All Saints, Tooting

Rachmaninov
Symphony No 2
  Janssons
  Chandos awaiting release

24, 25, 27 & 28 November and 2 December 1986, Conway Hall

Donizetti
Emilia di Liverpool
  Parry
Geoffrey Mitchell Choir
Kenny, Mason, Dalton,
Bruscantini, Merritt,
Mills, Thornton-Holmes
  Opera Rara awaiting release

26 November 1986, Walthamstow Town Hall

Rachmaninov
Rhapsody on a theme
of Paganini
  Haitink
Ashkenazy
  Decca awaiting release

12 & 13 December 1986, Abbey Road

Sterndale Bennett
Piano Concerto No 2;
Piano Concerto No 5;
The Naiades, Overture
  N.Braithwaite
Binns
  Lyrita awaiting release

18 & 19 December 1986, All Saints, Tooting

Caldara
Ciro Riconuscito;
Coriolanus, Overtures;
Albinoni
Il nome glorioso, Sinfonia;
Sinfonia in B minor (attrib.);
Scarlatti
Il Giardino di rose, Sinfonia
  Wright
Wallace
  Nimbus awaiting release

Stradella
Trumpet Concerto in D;
Alberti Sonata a due
Corelli Sonata in D
Torelli Concerto in D
Vivaldi Concerto in D
for 2 Trumpets
  Wallace, cond. & sol.
  Nimbus awaiting release

1987

18 March and 11 April 1987, Walthamstow Town Hall

Elgar
Symphony No 2
Sinopoli
DG awaiting release

10 April 1987, Watford Town Hall

Mahler
Adagio (Symphony No 10)
Sinopoli
DG awaiting release

11 & 14 April 1987, Watford Town Hall

Elgar
Enigma Variations
Sinopoli
DG awaiting release

15, 16, 17, 18, 19, 20, 21 & 22 April 1987, Watford Town Hall

Puccini
Madama Butterfly
Sinopoli
Cast includes
Freni, Berganza
(further details
awaiting confirmation)
DG awaiting release

24 & 25 April 1987, Henry Wood Hall

Mozart
Flute Concerto No 1;
Flute Concerto No 2
Varviso
Hall
Awaiting release

20 & 21 May 1987, St Barnabas, Woodside Park

Mozart
Piano Concerto No 1;
Piano Concerto No 2;
Piano Concerto No 3;
Piano Concerto No 4
Ashkenazy, cond. & sol.
Decca awaiting release

29 & 30 May 1987, Abbey Road

Bizet
Carmen, Suites Nos 1 & 2;
Grieg
Peer Gynt, Suite No 1;
Solveig's song (Suite No 2)
Seaman
Cirrus awaiting release

31 May 1987, Conway Hall

Unspecified material	Parry	Opera Rara awaiting release

19 June 1987, Henry Wood Hall

Hall Lewis Concerto for string orchestra	Hall Lewis	Private recording (unpublished)

26 & 27 June 1987, Abbey Road

Wagner Starke Scheite (Götterdämmerung)	D'Avalos A.Evans	ASV awaiting release
Wagner Rhine Journey and Funeral March (Götterdämmerung); Tannhäuser, Overture	D'Avalos	ASV awaiting release

28 & 29 June 1987, Abbey Road

Elgar Pomp and Circumstance, March No 1; Salut d'amour; Ponchielli Dance of the Hours (La Gioconda); Lehar Gold and Silver, Waltz; Suppé Light Cavalry, Overture; Wolf-Ferrari The Jewels of the Madonna, Intermezzo; Waldteufel Les patineurs, Waltz; Mascagni Cavalleria Rusticana, Intermezzo; Borodin In the Steppes of Central Asia; Ivanovici Donauwellen, Waltz; Handel arr. Helmesberger Largo (Xerxes)	A.Davis	Toshiba awaiting release

Recordings scheduled for August 1987

Verdi Operatic arias	Delogu Estes	Philips
Offenbach Overtures and Ballet music	De Almeida	Philips

Appendix A:
The conductors of the Philharmonia Orchestra on record

Index of page numbers

Abbado, Claudio	414, 418
Ackermann, Otto	240, 245, 246, 258, 263, 273, 281, 282, 309, 310, 311, 345, 346
Adler, Peter Herman	417
Almeida, Antonio de	425, 426, 444, 465, 476, 506, 509
Alwyn, Kenneth	410
Ansermet, Ernest	419
Arnold, Malcolm	279
Ashkenazy, Vladimir	459, 462, 463, 469, 470, 472, 476, 477, 478, 480, 483, 485, 488, 490, 492, 493, 494, 495, 496, 497, 500, 502, 505, 507, 508
Atherton, David	452, 463, 471
Atzmon, Moshe	408, 448
Barbirolli, Sir John	378, 379, 380, 403, 408, 409, 412, 418, 425, 426
Barenboim, Daniel	416, 418, 419, 422, 433
Bartoletti, Bruno	434
Barzin, Leon	347
Bauer, Hans	446
Benitende-Neglia, Tomaso	224
Berglund, Paavo	436, 488
Bernard, Anthony	186, 191, 246
Bernstein, Leonard	154
Bialoguski, Michael	433
Black, Stanley	397
Blech, Harry	296, 309, 343
Bliss, Sir Arthur	254, 257, 259, 411
Boettcher, Wilfried	427
Böhm, Karl	185, 186, 380
Bonynge, Richard	396, 400, 423, 424, 439, 440, 442, 443
Boulez, Pierre	404, 408, 420, 424, 471
Boult, Sir Adrian	153, 201, 238, 302, 322, 334, 339, 344, 396, 399, 403, 406, 414, 430, 444, 445, 452
Braithwaite, Nicholas	453, 474, 507
Braithwaite, Warwick	148, 154, 156, 160, 173, 174, 175, 176, 178, 182, 187, 193, 195, 200, 208, 225, 323
Britten, Benjamin	394
Brooke, Gwydion	394
Buketoff, Igor	414
Cameron, Basil	151, 160, 161, 232
Cantelli, Guido	208, 228, 242, 258, 259, 261, 278, 279, 292
Ceccato, Aldo	442
Cluytens, André	228, 229, 335
Cohen, Raymond	432
Collingwood, Lawrance	160, 164, 178, 180, 195, 235, 271, 272, 322
Copland, Aaron	438, 459

511

Curiel, Glauco	281, 282, 283
Cziffra, György jnr.	431
Dart, Thurston	308, 326
D'Avalos, Francesco	509
Davies, Meredith	447
Davis, Andrew	449, 455, 457, 462, 466, 474, 476, 477, 482, 483, 487, 492, 494, 509
Davis, Carl	493, 500
Davis, Sir Colin	343, 349, 381, 390, 435
Del Mar, Norman	403, 450, 478, 481, 482, 506, 507
Delogù, Gaetono	509
Dervaux, Pierre	358, 462
Devos, Gerard	442
Dilkes, Neville	466, 472
Dobrowen, Issay	153, 154, 155, 161, 162, 163, 172, 173, 184, 185, 192, 193, 196, 197, 204, 205, 230
Dods, Marcus	439, 440
Dohnanyi, Christoph von	386, 407
Domingo, Placido	440
Dorati, Antal	396, 403, 404
Downes, Edward	377, 400, 402, 434, 441, 470, 475, 486
Dutoit, Charles	476, 479, 481, 485, 486, 492, 494
Dykes Bower, John	201, 255
Erede, Alberto	168, 169, 175, 177, 390
Fabritiis, Olivero de	393
Farberman, Harold	410, 419
Ferraris, Franco	370, 371, 406
Fischer, Edwin	194, 228, 234, 257
Fischer-Dieskau, Dietrich	442
Fistoulari, Anatole	190, 195, 196, 197, 200, 202, 206, 209, 217, 219, 223, 225, 227, 229, 230, 232, 237, 266, 288, 295, 304, 336, 341, 359, 386, 387, 462, 467, 469
Fitelberg, Gregor	178
Francis, Alun	465, 477, 479
Freccia, Massimo	416
Freeman, Paul	454, 459
Frémaux, Louis	492
Frühbeck de Burgos, Rafael	389, 396, 397, 401, 402, 404, 408, 411, 415, 418, 424, 435, 467, 469
Furtwängler, Wilhelm	173, 194, 200, 221, 238, 245, 261
Galliera, Alceo	153, 155, 156, 160, 162, 163, 164, 165, 173, 190, 197, 198, 232, 233, 239, 240, 246, 247, 248, 270, 271, 272, 273, 274, 279, 288, 290, 291, 293, 295, 299, 300, 302, 303, 305, 307, 324, 325, 328, 334, 342, 343, 344, 357, 402, 428, 431
Gamba, Piero	387, 463
Gardelli, Lamberto	426, 427, 449, 453
Gellhorn, Peter	195, 197
Gennai, Leopoldo	179
Gerhardt, Charles	399
Gibson, Sir Alexander	378, 380, 400, 423, 427, 428
Giovaninetti, Reynaldo	429
Giulini, Carlo Maria	280, 296, 297, 311, 312, 327, 328, 344, 345, 347, 348, 357, 358, 366, 367, 371, 376, 377, 378, 380, 381, 382, 384, 388, 393, 398, 401, 414, 416, 424, 430, 471, 483, 487, 504
Goehr, Walter	218
Goossens, Sir Eugene	250, 287, 295, 312, 339, 358
Gould, Morton	419
Gracis, Ettore	303, 304
Groves, Sir Charles	438, 483

Guadagno, Anton	417, 422, 425, 433, 464, 466, 501
Guest, Douglas	399
Guschlbauer, Theodor	438, 445, 479
Haitink, Bernard	487, 492, 496, 507
Hall Lewis, Robert	489, 493, 501, 509
Handley, Vernon	453, 455, 457, 458, 459, 490
Hindemith, Paul	300
Hollingsworth, John	168
Hopkins, Anthony	471
Horenstein, Jascha	407, 416, 424
Howarth, Elgar	455, 464
Hurst, George	424
Inbal, Eliahu	430, 433
Irving, Ernest	160, 162, 163, 180
Irving, Robert	227, 228, 241, 242, 257, 258, 259, 308, 341, 359, 369, 370
Jackson, William	454
Jacques, Reginald	150
Janssons, Mariss	507
Jellinek, Walter	279
Jones, Geraint	218
Joo, Arpad	494, 497
Judd, James	474, 477
Kamu, Okko	439, 440
Karajan, Herbert von	174, 188, 189, 202, 203, 210, 220, 223, 229, 230, 242, 243, 244, 245, 248, 249, 260, 261, 263, 264, 265, 273, 274, 276, 277, 278, 280, 293, 301, 305, 318, 319, 320, 331, 338, 356, 360, 361, 362
Kempe, Rudolf	281, 282, 292, 293, 306
Kertesz, Istvan	359, 367
Khachaturian, Aram	266
Khasho, Youssef	468
Klemperer, Otto	263, 264, 265, 280, 283, 290, 294, 295, 299, 304, 305, 313, 314, 315, 347, 348, 352, 353, 354, 355, 357, 358, 359, 362, 363, 364, 366, 367, 369, 371, 372, 373, 374, 376, 377, 384, 385, 388, 389, 392, 394, 398, 400, 402, 406, 407, 410, 414, 415, 416, 418, 419, 422, 423, 426, 427, 428, 429, 431, 432, 435
Kletzki, Paul	155, 156, 167, 168, 175, 176, 183, 192, 206, 207, 223, 235, 242, 243, 244, 254, 255, 256, 270, 277, 283, 305, 330, 331, 348, 356, 357, 379, 386
Koizumi, Kazuhiro	452
Kondrashin, Kyril	340
Kord, Kazimierz	457
Krasnapolsky, Yuri	445
Krenz, Jan	440, 454
Krips, Henry	286, 318, 352, 353, 354
Krips, Josef	166, 167, 385, 387
Kubelik, Rafael	178, 179, 187, 188, 193, 202, 206, 207, 217, 225, 226
Kurtz, Efrem	272, 275, 303, 304, 305, 315, 323, 341, 342, 346, 368, 377, 387, 401
Lambert, Constant	148, 149, 150, 152, 154, 155, 182, 191, 196
Lanchbery, John	464, 465, 488, 489
Ledger, Philip	462
Leinsdorf, Erich	292, 326, 327, 360, 370, 409, 429, 434, 443, 448
Leitner, Ferdinand	401
Leppard, Raymond	407, 411, 415, 422, 432, 435, 442, 487
Levi, Yoel	488
Levine, James	444, 467, 482
Lewis, Henry	477
Littaur, David	418

Lopez-Cobos, Jesus	457, 458, 471
Lovett, Leon	434
Ludwig, Leopold	305, 306, 307, 315
Maag, Peter	453
Maazel, Lorin	379, 432, 433, 435, 436, 438, 441, 458, 460, 464, 468
Macal, Zdenek	469, 475
Mackerras, Sir Charles	275, 293, 297, 298, 299, 301, 307, 308, 309, 318, 328, 329, 335, 344, 363, 368, 402, 416, 423, 444, 457, 491
Magiera, Leone	432
Malko, Nicolai	161, 172, 179, 189, 191, 198, 216, 217, 233, 234, 240, 241, 257, 271, 280, 287, 288
Markevitch, Igor	187, 190, 194, 197, 200, 209, 210, 226, 254, 255, 256, 257, 258, 259, 339, 340, 408, 410
Marriner, Sir Neville	485, 492, 493
Martinon, Jean	265
Masur, Kurt	442, 457
Mata, Eduardo	454, 458, 472, 506
Matacic, Lovro von	263, 264, 266, 267, 286, 287, 330, 331, 379
Mathieson, Muir	174, 178, 183, 187
Measham, David	444
Mehta, Zubin	426, 439
Menges, Herbert	234, 264, 265, 273, 274, 279, 287, 291, 295, 296
Menuhin, Sir Yehudi	387
Miles, Maurice	148, 151
Milnes, Sherrill	440
Milstein, Nathan	386, 393
Morris, Wyn	407, 430, 441
Mudie, Michael	183, 201
Munch, Charles	399, 406
Muti, Riccardo	445, 452, 454, 456, 457, 458, 459, 460, 462, 463, 465, 466, 467, 468, 470, 472, 474, 475, 476, 477, 479, 482, 484, 486, 487, 489, 496
Navarro, Garcia	475
Oistrakh, David	326
Ozawa, Seiji	424, 425, 435, 486
Paita, Carlos	420
Parikian, Manoug	257
Parry, David	478, 481, 489, 490, 495, 502, 504, 507, 508
Patane, Franco	155
Patanè, Giuseppe	452, 466
Penderecki, Krzysztof	504
Pesek, Libor	496
Pitz, Wilhelm	404
Prausnitz, Frederick	403, 408, 409, 435
Prêtre, Georges	376, 382, 384, 385, 393, 409, 456, 483, 493
Pritchard, Sir John	222, 226, 227, 228, 254, 266, 267, 364, 376, 390, 400, 436, 456, 460, 482
Raksin, David	453
Rattle, Simon	471, 482, 483, 487, 491, 500
Rawsthorne, Alan	263
Renzetti, Donato	506
Rescigno, Nicola	331, 332, 333, 334, 342, 346
Rieger, Fritz	234
Rignold, Hugo	278
Robertson, James	191, 194, 195, 198, 202
Robinson, Stanford	173, 182, 188, 201
Rodzinski, Artur	312, 322
Rosbaud, Hans	244
Rowicki, Witold	387
Rudel, Julius	430, 469, 471

Salonen, Esa-Pekka	501, 502, 504
Sanderling, Kurt	474, 475, 484, 485
Santi, Nello	438, 448, 449, 450, 465
Sargent, Sir Malcolm	162, 163, 164, 178, 179, 180, 199, 219, 232, 272, 275, 280, 288, 289, 324, 339, 340, 345, 369, 378, 398, 403
Sawallisch, Wolfgang	259, 292, 296, 304, 311, 312, 320, 321, 322, 330, 402, 408, 488, 493, 500
Schippers, Thomas	306, 308, 312, 313, 417
Schmidt, Heinrich	301
Scholz, Alfred	480
Schönzeler, Hans-Hubert	461
Schüchter, Wilhelm	207, 211, 218, 219, 220, 221, 229, 231, 249, 250, 256
Schwarz, Rudolf	217, 230, 231, 235, 239, 240, 241, 256, 275, 276
Scimone, Claudio	468. 469, 480, 486, 492, 495
Seaman, Christopher	508
Sébastian, Georges	203, 204
Segal, Uri	442
Semkow, Jerzy	385
Serafin, Tullio	262, 263, 340, 341, 367
Shostakovich, Maxim	441
Siegel, Lawrence	480
Silvestri, Constantin	303, 307, 320, 339, 340, 341, 357, 359
Simon, Geoffrey	496, 497, 498, 504, 505
Sinopoli, Giuseppe	493, 495, 500, 501, 502, 506, 508
Sivieri, Enrico	238
Stapleton, Robin	467
Steinberg, William	311
Stokowski, Leopòld	202, 397, 402, 403, 418, 442, 443
Stratta, Ettore	502
Susskind, Walter	148, 149, 150, 151, 152, 154, 161, 163, 164, 165, 167, 172, 174, 175, 176, 177, 183, 184, 185, 186, 192, 193, 194, 196, 201, 205, 206, 207, 208, 210, 221, 221, 232, 235, 236, 237, 238, 289, 291, 292, 294, 295, 323, 328, 329, 347
Svetlanov, Yevgeny	467
Tausky, Vilem	152, 216, 219, 474
Tilson Thomas, Michael	481, 483, 486, 487, 488, 491, 501
Tonini, Antonio	359, 373, 377, 378
Toscanini, Arturo	227
Tung, Ling	468, 475
Tzipine, Georges	260
Vandernoot, André	328, 334, 336, 366, 368, 392
Varviso, Silvio	508
Waart, Edo de	429, 430, 431
Wallace, John	507
Wallberg, Heinz	324, 327, 335, 364, 365, 445
Walton, Sir William	149, 154, 155, 195, 208, 237, 273, 304, 339, 388
Warren-Green, Christopher	495, 498, 502, 505
Weigert, Hermann	203, 204
Weldon, George	148, 152, 153, 166, 169, 188, 192, 204, 209, 234, 235, 241, 243, 246, 247, 248, 289, 290, 369, 370, 381, 382, 384, 385
Whitehead, James	152
Wilbrandt, Thomas	493
Willcocks, Sir David	412, 422, 429, 456, 470
Wolf-Ferrari, Manno	321, 322
Wright, Simon	507
Zamboni, Rinaldo	172

Appendix B:
Index of Works recorded by the Philharmonia Orchestra

This listing attempts to summarise the scope of the orchestra's recording work. Page numbers given are those on which the different recordings of a work occur, and will afford comparisons of particular interest in the case of the most popular and most recorded items.

In order to keep the index down to a manageable size, certain simplifications have had to be introduced. All existing extracts from longer works, whether they be overtures, arias, ensembles, suites or the like, are described as "excerpts". By referring to the pages indicated, the reader will quickly be able to identify the excerpts from a particular work.

Following Philharmonia's change of management in 1964, many more compilation LPs were recorded for a large number of labels, containing such material as operetta, musical comedy, Italian popular songs and arias, Christmas carols and so on, and including music of a traditional nature or by anonymous composers. Although as much detail as the orchestra can provide is included in the discography, these items have to a large extent been omitted from this index.

Adam
Giselle
369

Giralda - overture
423

La poupée de Nuremberg
- overture
423

Addinsell
Warsaw Concerto
493

Passionate friends
- film music
183

Albeniz
Iberia
287

Suite espanola
411

Tango
464

Alberti
Trumpet Sinfonia
498

Trumpet Sonata
507

Albinoni
Oboe Concerto op 7 no 6
192

Oboe Concerto op 7 no 3
- excerpt
192

Trumpet Sonatas in C and D
498

Il nome glorioso - Sinfonia
507

Sinfonia in B minor
507

Alfano
Don Juan - excerpt
172

Altenburg
Concerto for trumpets
505

Alwyn
Miss Julie
474

Arne
Rule Britannia
219, 411

Arnold
English Dances
242, 279

Scottish Dances
308, 399

Flute Concertos Nos 1 and 2
466

Sinfoniettas Nos 1 and 2
466

Homage to the Queen
242

Tam O'Shanter - overture
279

Arriaga
Symphony in D minor
446

Auber
Le cheval de bronze
- overture
426

Lestocq - overture
423

Marco Spada - overture
423

La muette de Portici
- excerpt
239

C.P.E. Bach
Solfegietto Metamorphosis
arr. Calandrelli
502

J.C. Bach
Bassoon Concerto
432

Sinfonia in B flat op 9
148, 415

Sinfonia in B flat op 18
415

Sinfonia in G minor op 6
415

Catone - overture
422

Bach
Brandenburg Concertos
- complete
362, 418

Brandenburg Concerto No 2
234, 496

Brandenburg Concerto No 5
228

Keyboard Concerto in D minor
154, 369

2-Keyboard Concerto in C
291

3-Keyboard Concerto in E
194

Oboe Concerto arr. Tovey
185, 221

Oboe and Violin Concerto
430

Violin Concerto in A minor
186, 205, 238, 296

516

Violin Concerto in E
176, 281

2-Violin Concerto in E
152, 246, 281, 430

Siciliana
502

Chorale prelude
Ach Gott vom Himmel sieh'
368

Orchestral Suites
- complete
265, 426

Orchestral Suite No 2
148

Orchestral Suite No 3
- excerpt
370

Cantata No 51
176

Cantata No 51 - excerpt
153

Cantata No 68 - excerpt
197, 308

Cantata No 82
174, 191

Cantata No 92
326

Cantata No 199
308

Cantata No 202
308

Cantata No 208
326

Cantata No 208 - excerpt
308

Magnificat in D
416

Mass in B minor
229, 374, 410

Saint Matthew Passion
364

Saint Matthew Passion
- excerpt
194

Ave Maria arr. Gounod
307, 433

The Wise Virgins
arr. Walton
- excerpt
204, 237

Balakirev

Islamay
266, 287

Russia
266

Thamar
266

Symphony No 1
188

Overture on Russian Themes
267

Balfe

The Bohemian Girl - excerpt
474

Banks

Horn Concerto
446

Bantock

Overture to a Greek Tragedy
474

Barber

Adagio for strings
243, 505

Knoxville, Summer of 1915
417

Souvenirs
272

Antony and Cleopatra
- excerpt
417

Barsukov

Piano Concerto
396

Bartok

Piano Concerto No 1
398, 408

Piano Concerto No 3
398, 408

Viola Concerto
403

Violin Concerto No 1
396

Violin Concerto No 2
245, 396, 482

Concerto for orchestra
210

Dance Suite
254

Divertimento
320

Music for strings,
percussion and celesta
189

Two Portraits
154

Rumanian Dances
149, 363

The Miraculous Mandarin
- suite
370

Bax

Symphony No 6
403

Beethoven

Symphony No 1
249, 314, 484

Symphony No 2
248, 313, 484

Symphony No 3 "Eroica"
229, 280, 348, 358, 484

Symphony No 4
248, 314, 484

Symphony No 5
154, 245, 280, 292, 347,
420, 484, 485, 504

Symphony No 6 "Pastoral"
243, 313, 414, 445, 488

Symphony No 7
190, 210, 280, 292, 358,
363, 418 (2), 442, 484, 494

Symphony No 8
249, 314, 484

Symphony No 9 "Choral"
261, 278, 314, 446, 484

Piano Concerto No 1
179, 270, 295, 324, 410,
501

Piano Concerto No 2
153, 228, 324, 410, 431,
501

Piano Concerto No 3
163, 199, 257, 296, 305,
328 (2), 384, 401, 410, 467

Piano Concerto No 4
153, 203, 228, 257, 274,
279, 305, 359, 404, 410,
431

Piano Concerto No 5
"Emperor"
161, 163, 200, 203, 273,
279, 306, 324, 359, 401,
410, 442, 485

Violin Concerto
188, 238, 370, 400, 402,
407, 430, 483, 506

Violin Concerto arr. for
piano
424

Triple Concerto
324, 430

Violin Romance No 1
186, 194, 238, 283, 364,
393, 431, 506

Violin Romance No 2
175, 194, 238, 283, 364,
393, 431, 434, 448, 506

Fidelio - complete
- complete
375
- excerpts
198, 263, 265, 324, 485

Coriolan - overture
168, 218, 233, 242, 313, 359,
430, 484, 494

Die Weihe des Hauses
- overture
261, 294, 348

Egmont - excerpts
153, 211, 242, 314, 315, 358,
424, 442, 485, 492

King Stephen - overture
348

Die Geschöpfe des Prometheus
- excerpts
234, 315, 427, 485

Die Ruinen von Athen - excerpts
302, 235

Leonore No 1 - overture
265, 389

Leonore No 2 - overture
265, 389

Leonore No 3 - overture
162, 168, 233, 244, 265, 326,
389, 485

Grosse Fuge
290

Choral Fantasy
410

Mass in C
430

Missa Solemnis
331, 398, 401

Meeresstille Cantata
420

Die Ehre Gottes
404

Ah perfido !
236, 263, 324

In questa tomba oscura
463

German Dances Nos 11 and 12
174

Bellini

I Capuleti ed i Montecchi
- complete
452
- excerpt
202

I Puritani
- complete
476
- excerpts
208, 322, 334, 349, 371, 393

Il Pirata - excerpts
334, 373

Norma - excerpts
186, 225, 367, 425, 477

La Sonnambula - excerpts
197, 224, 238, 246, 349,
400, 402, 506

Vaga luna che inargenti
463

Benedict

Carnival of Venice
187

Richard Rodney Bennett

Aubade
471

Spells
470

Elegy for Lady Caroline
Lamb
440

Sterndale Bennett

Piano Concertos Nos 2 and 5
507

The Naiades - overture
507

Berg

Violin Concerto
244

Sieben frühe Lieder
416

Berkeley

Piano Concerto
453

Berlioz

Symphonie fantastique
260, 335, 385, 418, 475

Symphonie fantastique
- excerpt
353

Harold en Italie
381

La Damnation de Faust
- excerpts
193, 209, 238, 249, 255, 298,
318, 346, 447, 465

Les Troyens - excerpts
250, 298, 322, 338, 346

Le carnaval romain -
overture
172, 223, 249, 298, 319

Le corsair - overture
207, 249

Béatrice et Bénédict
- overture
206

Les francs juges - overture
207

Benvenuto Cellini -
overture
207

Rêverie et caprice
155, 431

Les nuits d'été
409

Berners

Nicholas Nickleby
- film music
160

Les sirènes - film music
163

Bernstein

Mass - excerpt
439

West Side Story - excerpt
439

Binge

Elizabethan Serenade
399

Bixio

Roads through the forest;
One night with you
168

Bizet

Agnus Dei
178

L'Arlésienne - excerpts
179, 223, 319, 365, 406

Carmen - excerpts
165, 175, 198, 208, 211,
260, 261, 300, 319, 332,
365, 406, 422, 429, 440,
466, 508

Jeux d'enfants
280

La jolie fille de Perth
- excerpt
271

Les pêcheurs de perles
- excerpts
239, 438, 447

Blake

Violin Concerto
478

Bliss

Piano Concerto
378

Music for strings
254

Miracle in the Gorbals
254

Ceremonial Prelude
399

Phoenix March
152

Welcome to the Queen
257

Things to come - excerpt
411

Bloch

Violin Concerto
386

Boccherini

Cello Concerto in B flat
327

Symphony in C minor
297

Six Symphonies op 12
432

Overture in D
297

Minuet
241

Boieldieu

Le calife de Bagdad
- overture
423

Boito

Mefistofele - excerpts
184, 189, 237, 262, 322,
332, 432, 440, 464, 506

Bononcini

2-Trumpet Concerto
498

Polifemo - Overture
411

Borodin

Symphony No 1
272

Symphony No 2
172, 254, 280

Symphony No 3
280

In the Steppes of Central
Asia
150, 235, 335, 509

Nocturne
180, 295, 411

Prince Igor - excerpts
156. 184, 185, 192, 193,
208, 221, 224, 225, 234,
264, 288, 331, 336, 341,
361, 385, 459, 492, 497

Boulez

Livres
420

Bourgeois

All people that on earth
201

Boyce

Symphonies Nos 2, 4 and 5
- excerpts
279

Cambridge Installation Ode
422

Brahms

Symphony No 1
220, 227, 242, 283, 299,
366

Symphony No 2
207, 227, 274, 299, 378,
381, 496

Symphony No 3
227, 278, 290, 304, 326,
381, 496

Symphony No 4
227, 274, 299, 416, 446

Piano Concerto No 1
160, 225, 234, 357, 409,
457

Piano Concerto No 2
161, 322, 409, 467

Violin Concerto
155, 235, 255, 340, 359,
435, 441, 475, 493

Double Concerto
217, 288, 379, 442

St Antoni Variations
197, 227, 264, 274, 326,
330, 366, 385

Academic Festival Overture
218, 305, 387, 446

Tragic Overture
168, 227, 299, 305, 381,
387

Hungarian Dances - excerpts
176, 207, 344, 369

518

Ein deutsches Requiem
366, 460

Alto Rhapsody
377, 460

Nanie
404

Rinaldo
418

Song of Destiny
418

Wiegenlied
433

Britten

Piano Concerto
287

Sinfonia da Requiem
394

Frank Bridge Variations
248

Variations and Fugue on a
theme of Purcell
226, 380, 399, 435

Matinées musicales
308

Soirées musicales
308

Les Illuminations
471

Gloriana - excerpt
477

Peter Grimes
- Four Sea Interludes
380

Festival Te Deum
399

Bruch

Violin Concerto No 1
178, 232, 295, 329, 347,
440, 445, 462

Violin Concerto No 2
457

Kol Nidrei
490

Scottish Fantasy
302, 445, 457

Ave Maria
236

Bruckner

Symphony No 4 "Romantic"
264, 388

Symphony No 5
407

Symphony No 6
394

Symphony No 7
363

Symphony No 8
131

Symphony No 9
428

Scherzo in D minor
287

Te Deum
422

Mass in E minor
433

Locus iste; Os juste;
Ave Maria; Virga Jesse;
Christus factus est
404

Bull

Shepherds away

Bush

Yorick - overture

Busoni

Berceuse
409

Reigen
409

Tanzwalzer
254

Butterworth

Banks of Green Willow
151

Calandrelli

Jazz Clarinet Concerto

Caldara

Ciro Riconusciuto - overture
507

Coriolanus - overture
507

Canteloube

Songs of the Auvergne
476

Caplet

Epiphanie
481

Cardillo

Catari, catari
194, 423

Carter

Variations for orchestra
403

Catalani

La Wally - excerpts
186, 263, 299, 300

Loreley - excerpt
299

Chabrier

Espana
229, 244, 298, 336, 361,
415

Fête polonaise
226, 298, 354

Marche joyeuse
277, 346, 361

Ballabille
196

Le roi malgré lui
- excerpt
226

Charpentier

Louise
- complete
456
- excerpts
165, 192, 429, 447

Chausson

Poème
155, 364, 386

Viviane
425

Chavez

Piano Concerto
458

Chaconne
458

Cherubini

Symphony in D
427

Marche réligieuse
496

Coronation Mass
496

Requiem in C minor
482

Requiem in D minor
445

Anacréon - overture
362

Medée - excerpt
346

Chopin

Piano Concerto No 1
295, 357, 438

Piano Concerto No 2
156, 235, 358, 400, 423

Andante spianato and
grande polonaise
423

Fantasy on Polish airs
493

Variations on Mozart's
La ci darem la mano
459

Les Sylphides
- complete
341
- excerpts
255, 344

Autumn Leaves
275

Nocturne No 8
275

Omaggio a Bellini;
Inno alla patria
arr. Glinsky
188

Cilea

Adriana Lecouvreur
- complete
467
- excerpts
182, 186, 237, 253, 371,
390, 438, 465, 486

L'Arlesiana - excerpts
168, 239, 393

Cimarosa

I traci amanti - overture
422

Artemisa - excerpt
481

Clarke

Trumpet Voluntary
153, 169

Clementi

Symphonies Nos 1, 2, 3
and 4
468

519

Walford Davies

Solemn Melody
192

Carl Davis

The Far Pavilions
- music for TV series
493

Coates

London Suite - excerpt
382

London Again Suite
- excerpt
382

Merrymakers - overture
460

Summer Days Suite
460

Three Bears Fantasy
460

The Three Elizabeths
- excerpt
460

Evening in Town
460

In the country
460

Coleridge-Taylor

Hiawatha
369

Petite suite de concert
381

Copland

Symphony No 3
459

El salon mexico
438

Quiet city
301

Latin American Sketches
438

New England Countryside
438

The Red Pony
438

Our town - film music
438

Of mice and men
- film music
438

Cuban Dance
298

Corelli

Oboe Concerto
419

Sonata in D
507

Cornelius

Der Barbier von Bagdad
292

D'Albert

Tiefland - excerpt
220

Dallapiccola

Piccola musica notturna
409

Daniels

Circle Dance
502

Debussy

La Mer
197, 244, 261, 377, 404, 488

Trois Nocturnes
197, 377, 488

Trois Nocturnes - excerpts
278

Petite suite
392

Printemps
424

Prélude à l'après-midi
160, 259 (2), 379, 404

Jeux
404

Le martyre de
Saint Sébastian
259

L'enfant prodige
- excerpt
313

Clarinet Rhapsody
420

Clair de lune
454

La cathédrale engloutie
397

Délibes

Sylvia
- complete
257, 440
- excerpts
289, 359

Coppélia - excerpts
359, 423

Les filles de Cadiz
- excerpt
439

Lakmé - excerpts
247, 263

Naila - excerpt
354

Delius

Cello Concerto
490

Piano Concerto
155

Marche caprice
444

Summer night on the river
454

On hearing the first cuckoo
454

Koanga - excerpt
369

Diabelli

Fanfares for 6 Trumpets

Dohnanyi

Piano Concerto No 1
436

Konzertstuck for Cello
294

Ruralia Hungarica Suite
229

Suite for Orchestra
258

Variations on a Nursey Song
227, 232, 407, 452

Donizetti

Anna Bolena - excerpts
334, 376, 425

L'assiedo di Calais
- excerpt
475

Don Sebastiano - excerpt
475

Betley - excerpt
179

Don Pasquale
- complete
489
- excerpts
197, 367, 373, 402, 432

L'Elisir d'Amore
- excerpts
151, 168, 188, 219, 238, 239, 390

Emilia di Liverpool
- complete
507

La Favorita - excerpts
239, 371, 475

La fille du régiment
- excerpt
447

Linda di Chamonix
- excerpts
156, 367

Lucia di Lammermoor
- complete
341, 458
- excerpts
187, 321, 332, 349

Lucrezia Borgia - excerpt
373

Les martyrs - excerpt
475

Ne m'oubliez pas
474

Pietro il Grande - excerpt
502

Roberto Devereux - excerpt
474

Ugo Conte di Parigi
465

Doppler

L'oiseau des bois
472

Dukas

L'apprenti sorcier
226, 258, 344

Duparc

Léonore
425

Duruflé

Requiem
462

Danse lente
462

Dvorak

Symphony No 1
483

Symphony No 2
487

Symphony No 3
476

Symphony No 4
489

Symphony No 5
482

Symphony No 6
477

Symphony No 7
206, 476

Symphony No 8
178, 259, 376, 474

Symphony No 9
"From the New World"
160, 247, 287, 320, 366,
389, 404, 443, 457, 459,
469, 474

Violin Concerto
401

Cello Concerto
179, 275, 294, 490

Carnival Overture
235, 321, 366, 384, 474

Legend No 10
193

Scherzo capriccioso
150, 154, 187, 259, 376,
487

Serenade for strings
502

Wind Serenade
502

Slavonic Dances op 46
240, 492

Slavonic Dances op 72
240

Slavonic Dances - excerpts
363

Biblical Songs - excerpts
182

Songs my mother taught me
439

Symphonic Variations
288

The Peasant a rogue
- overture
150

Rusalka - excerpt
216, 329, 465

The Spectre's Bride
- excerpt
163

Dyson

The Canterbury Pilgrims
- excerpt
163

Easdale

The Red Shoes - film music
183

The Scarlet Pimpernel
- excerpt
187

Elgar

Symphony No 1
380

Symphony No 2
492, 496, 508

Violin Concerto
399

Cello Concerto
497

Enigma Variations
243, 340, 379, 446, 487,
508

Enigma Variations - excerpt
399

The Dream of Gerontius
452

The Apostles - excerpt
399

The Kingdom - excerpt
164

Coronation Ode
462

Sea Pictures
148, 152

Sea Pictures - excerpt
151

Chanson de matin;
Chanson de nuit
180

Cockaigne Overture
247, 380, 411

Elegy for strings
403

Falstaff
446

Froissart Overture
403

God save the Queen (arr.)
399

Pomp and Circumstance
Marches
- complete
380
- excerpts
179, 201, 247, 248, 446,
487, 492, 505, 509

Salut d'amour
509

Serenade in E minor
345

Sospiri
403

Enesco

Rumanian Rhapsody No 1
363

Espla

La pajara
415

Falla

El amor brujo
- complete
328, 371, 396
- excerpt
370

La vida breve - excerpts
173, 464

El sombrero de tre picos
- complete
389
- excerpts
153, 210, 258, 311

Farberman

Medea - suite
419

Fauré

Ballade
486, 494

Elégie
279, 294, 457

Fantaisie
275, 494

Masques et bergamasques
- excerpt
454

Pavane
162, 412, 466

Pelléas et Mélisande
- excerpts
455

Finzi

Clarinet Concerto
453

Eclogue
453

Grand Fantasy and Toccata
453

Farwell to arms
453

In terra pax
453

Let us garlands bring
453

Two Milton sonnets
453

Fioravanti

I virtuosi ambulanti
- excerpt
489

Flotow

Martha - excerpts
239, 332, 443

Franck

Symphony
173, 311, 339, 344, 400,
455

Symphonic Variations
186, 188, 203, 366, 475,
478, 486

Les djinns
477

Les Eolides
165

Psyché et Eros
327

Panis angelicus
433

Francheschini

2-Trumpet Concerto
498

Furstenau

Rondo brillant
472

Garcia

Il califfo di Bagdad
- excerpt
490

Generali

Adelina - excerpt
502

Pamela nubile - excerpt
481

German

Merrie England - excerpts
148, 194

Gershwin

An American in Paris
397, 487

Rhapsody in Blue
493

Catfish Row
487

Cuban Overture
487

Rhapsody No 2
487

Giordano

Andrea Chenier - excerpts
164, 193, 195, 246, 262,
329, 333, 370, 440

Fedora - excerpt
390

Glazunov

Violin Concerto
267, 401

Concert Waltzes
298, 467

Raymonda - ballet
286

Ruses d'amour
198

The Seasons
- complete
467
- excerpts
191, 275

Stenka Razin
288

Les vendredis - excerpt
241

Glière

The Red Poppy - excerpts
179, 298

Glinka

Jota aragonesa
150, 179, 330, 339

Kamarinskaya
270

A Life for the Tsar
- excerpts
218, 224, 368

Russlan and Ludmilla
- excerpts
198, 207, 216, 288, 298,
341, 369, 480, 497

Valse-Fantaisie
179

Gluck

Alceste - excerpts
230, 312, 443

Elena e Paride - excerpt
443

Iphigénie en Aulide
- excerpts
200, 217, 362, 385

Orfeo ed Euridice
- complete
486
- excerpts
151, 176, 198, 463

Gnecco

Gli Orazi e Curazi
- excerpt
481

Goldmark

Violin Concerto
309

Eugene Goossens

Oboe Concerto
175

Gounod

Faust - excerpts
160, 172, 184, 188, 224,
225, 227, 297, 320, 353,
368, 416, 423, 426, 429,
438, 440

Mireille - excerpt
429

La reine de Saba - excerpt
151

Roméo et Juliette
- excerpts
151, 239, 429, 447

Mors et Vita - excerpt
241

Quand je chante
439

O divine redeemer
433

Grainger

Handel in the Strand
182

Londonderry Air
182, 289, 382

Mock Morris
182, 369

Molly on the shore
182

Granados

Goyescas - excerpts
183, 190, 204, 260, 338,
396, 424

Danzas espanoles
229, 464

Grétry

Le jugement de Midas
- overture
411

Richard Coeur de Lion
- excerpt
448

Grieg

Piano Concerto
165, 202, 245, 264, 296,
304, 328, 436, 475, 477

Elegaic Melodies
149, 237, 295, 369, 457,
487

Holberg Suite
230, 237, 369, 386

Norwegian Dances
217, 292, 419

Norwegian Melodies
369

Peer Gynt - excerpts
217, 289, 439, 457, 508

Lyric Suite
241, 339

Old Norwegian Romance
487

Sigurd Jorsalfar Suite
369

Symphonic Dances
205, 304, 419, 487

Eros
172

From Monte Pincio
172, 176, 457

I love thee
457

Last Spring
164

The Princess
457

A Swan
172, 457

Varen
176

Way of the world
457

Gungl

Amorettentanze
318

Hadley

The trees so high
459

Hahn

Si mes vers avaient des ailes
439

Halévy

La Juive
444, 506

Hall Lewis

Destini
501

Moto
493

Osservaccioni II
489

Handel

Organ Concerto op 4 no 2
177, 220

Organ Concerto op 4 no 4
220

Organ Concerto op 7 no 8
221

Organ Concerto op 7 no 16
221

Concerto Grosso op 6 no 4
290

Concerto Grosso op 6 no 5
190

Water Music - excerpts
210, 220

Messiah
- complete
392
- excerpts
148, 150, 151, 201, 230,
234

Zadok the Priest
201

Dank sei dir Herr
178

Acis and Galatea - excerpt
148

Alcina - excerpt
443

Berenice - excerpts
192, 471

Giulio Cesare - excerpts
209, 241

Joshua - excerpts
209, 417

Judas Maccabeus - excerpts
150, 153, 156

Orlando - excerpt
241

Il pastor fido - excerpts
407, 411

Rinaldo - excerpt
506

Solomon - excerpt
411

Samson - excerpts
178, 188, 209

Semele - excerpt
477

Serse - excerpts
178, 192, 443, 509

Harty

Irish Symphony - excerpt
382

Haydn

Symphony No 80
267

Symphony No 88
394

Symphony No 92 "Oxford"
435

Symphony No 94 "Surprise"
297

Symphony No 95
429

Symphony No 98
352

Symphony No 100 "Military"
281, 398

Symphony No 101 "Clock"
352

Symphony No 102
398

Symphony No 194 "London"
154, 292, 394

Cello Concerto in D
202, 327

Violin Concerto in G
407

Violin Concerto in C
161

Horn Concertos Nos 1 and 2
495

2-Horn Concerto
498

Trumpet Concerto
153, 206, 495, 496

Divertimento à 3
495

Serenade
241

Notturno in C
267

Nelson Mass - excerpt
255

The Creation
- complete
467
- excerpts
150, 153

The Seasons - excerpts
151, 163

The spirit's song
152

Hérold

Zampa - overture
233, 270, 426

Heuberger

Der Opernball - excerpt
310

Hindemith

Horn Concerto
264, 300

Clarinet Concerto
300

Symphony in B flat
300

Sinfonia serena
300

Concert music for strings and brass
300

Mathis der Maler
320

Nobilissima Visione
264, 300

Hoddinott

Sinfonietta No 1
452

Sinfonietta No 2
461

Sinfonia Fidei
483

Piano Concerto
461

Viola Concerto
452

Dives and Lazarus
452

Landscapes
461

Night Music
452

Nocturnes and Cadenzas
483

Jack Straw - overture
483

Holbrooke

Poem No 4 "Ulalume"
394

Holst

The Planets
403, 483

The Planets - excerpt
370

Saint Paul's Suite
246, 274

Invocation
490

Marching song
411

Honegger

Piano Concertino
209

Pastorale d'été
454

Hopkins

The Music Man
471

Howells

Elegy
445

Hymnus Paradisi
429

Merry Eye
445

Music for a Prince
445

Hummel

Trumpet Concerto
505

Humperdinck

Hansel und Gretel
- complete
243
- excerpts
166, 209, 341, 362

Ibert

Escales - excerpt
454

Elizabethan Suite
280

D'Indy

Symphonie cévennole
486

Ippolitov-Ivanov

Caucasian Sketches
179, 211, 242

Caucasian Sketches
- excerpts
204, 298

Ivanovici

Donauwellen Waltz
318, 509

Ives

Symphonies Nos 1, 2, 3 and 4
410

Scene No 1 "Halloween"
410

Janacek

Sinfonietta
491

Taras Bulba
491

Jolivet

Trumpet Concerto;
Trumpet Concertino
501

Kabalevsky

Symphony No 2
444

Colas Breugnon - excerpts
249

The Comedians - suite
368

Ketelby

In a Persian Market;
In a Monastery Garden;
Chal Romano;
In the mystic land of Egypt;
Bells across the Meadow;
The Clock and the Dresden
Figures; In the Moonlight;
In a Chinese Temple Garden;
Sanctuary of the Heart
464

Khachaturian

Piano Concerto
435

Violin Concerto
250, 266

In memoriam
266

Gayaneh - excerpts
161, 266, 397

Masquerade - excerpts
266, 368

Knasho

Symphony No 8;
Symphony No 9;
Symphony No 10
468

Kimmer

Divertissement
472

Klemperer

Symphony No 2
415, 423

Symphony No 3
429

Symphony No 4
423

Merry Waltz and One-Step
372

J'accuse
415

Gavotte and Variations
(after Rameau)
418(2)

Knussen

Symphony No 3
486

Kodaly

Dances of Galanta
306

Dances of Marosszek
306

Hary Janos - excerpts
231, 261, 326, 338

Korngold

Die tote Stadt - excerpts
237, 465

Kreisler

Liebesleid; Liebesfreud;
Caprice viennois;
Recitative and
Scherzo-Caprice; Schön
Rosmarin; Syncopation;
Tambourin chinois; Violin
Concerto after Vivaldi
464

Kupfermann

Libretto for orchestra
419

Ato
454

Lalo

Symphonie espagnole
194, 265, 295, 329, 340, 441

Cello Concerto
481

Lambert

Apparitions - ballet
182

Aubade héroique
182

Horoscope - ballet
182

The Rio Grande
182

Lanner

Die Schonbrunner - waltz
318

Lavigna

Hoango - excerpt
481

Lecocq

La fille de Madame Angot
- overture
423

Lehar

Gold and Silver Waltz
318, 509

Giuditta - excerpt
310

Der Graf von Luxemburg
- excerpts
309, 310

Das Land des Lachelns
240

Die lustige Witwe
240, 379

Der Zarewitsch - excerpt
309

Leigh

Agincourt
453

Jolly Roger - overture
453

Leimer

Piano Concerto in C minor;
Piano Concerto for the
left hand
265

Leoncavallo

I Pagliacci
- complete
476
- excerpts
156, 164, 177. 186, 211,
246, 260, 338, 477

Lessard

Sinfonietta Concertante
419

Levy

Mourning becomes Electra
- excerpt
417

Liadov

Baba Yaga
172

Berceuse
163

Kikimora
259

Eight Russian Folksongs
241

Lincke

Glow Worm Idyll - excerpt
275

Lipatti

Piano Concertino
275

Liszt

Piano Concerto No 1
219, 273, 358, 359, 366, 400, 448

Piano Concerto No 2
165, 235, 328, 359, 448

Hungarian Fantasia
175, 273, 390, 392, 435

Hungarian Rhapsody No 1
240

Hungarian Rhapsody No 2
163, 235, 241, 318

Hungarian Rhapsody No 3
240

Hungarian Rhapsody No 6
240

Mazeppa
229

Mephisto Waltz
254

Les Préludes
229, 233, 309, 320

Tasso
320

Totentanz
227, 392

Quand je dors
439

Liszt/Busoni

Rapsodie espagnole
390

Liszt/Schubert

Wanderer Fantasy
474

Litolff

Scherzo
174, 493

Lloyd

Symphony No 4
486

Symphony No 5
475

Symphony No 8
470

Locatelli

Introduttione teatrale
422

Lombarde

Rock 'n Roll Rhapsody
454

Lortzing

Der Waffenschmied - excerpt
240

Der Wildschutz - excerpt
240

Zar und Zimmermann
- excerpt
240

Mahler

Symphony No 1
430

Symphony No 2 "Resurrection"
374, 501

Symphony No 4
305, 367

Symphony No 5
425, 500

Symphony No 5 - excerpt
348

Symphony No 6
408, 506

Symphony No 7
418

Symphony No 9
406, 407

Symphony No 10 (ed. Cooke)
441

Symphony No 10 - Adagio
508

Das Lied von der Erde
348, 392

Das klagende Lied
407

Lieder eines fahrenden
Gesellen
221, 334, 501

Kindertotenlieder
334

Des Knaben Wunderhorn
- excerpts
392

Ruckert-Lieder
392, 425

Lieder und Gesange aus
der Jugendzeit
500

Manfroce

Ecuba - excerpt
504

Marcello

Oboe Concerto
151, 161

Martini

Plaisir d'amour
443

Martinu

Double Concerto
193

Symphony No 6
433

Mascagni

L'Amico Fritz - excerpts
193, 211, 338, 367

Cavalleria Rusticana
- complete
477
- excerpts
150, 177, 201, 209, 211,
261, 329, 332, 338, 393,
438, 440, 465, 466, 477,
509

Guglielmo Ratcliff
- excerpt
302

Le maschere - excerpt
302

Massenet

Cendrillon
469

Le Cid - excerpts
202, 376

Hérodiade - excerpts
193, 201, 313, 440, 447

Manon
- complete
430
- excerpts
169, 183, 184, 202, 206,
236, 238, 239, 247, 422

Le Roi de Lahore - excerpt
448

Thaïs
- complete
447, 458
- excerpts
204, 237, 261, 429

Thérèse
442

Werther - excerpt
239

Crépuscule; Si les fleurs
avaient des yeux
439

Mathias

Clarinet Concerto
463

World's Joie
456

Laudi
463

Elegy for a Prince
463

Vistas
463

Maxwell Davies

Symphony
471

Fantasia No 2
438

Mayr

Adelasia ed Alermo
- excerpt
591

Alfredo il Grande - excerpt
495

L'amor conjugale - excerpt
478

Cora - excerpt
495

Elena - excerpt
495

Elisa - excerpt
478

Fedra - excerpt
495

Le finte rivali - excerpts
478, 481

Medea in Corinto - excerpt
504

La Rosa Bianca e la Rosa
Rossa - excerpt
495

Mazziotti

Ritorno
172

Medtner

Piano Concerto No 1
166

Piano Concerto No 2
162

Piano Concerto No 3
162

Méhul

La chasse du jeune Henri
- overture
411

Mendelssohn

Symphony No 1
408

Symphony No 2
"Hymn of Praise"
408

Symphony No 3 "Scotch"
352, 408, 454

Symphony No 4 "Italian"
208, 278, 353, 364, 402,
458, 493

Symphony No 5 "Reformation"
402, 474

Piano Concerto No 1
178

Violin Concerto
156, 259, 283, 302, 309,
323, 347, 434, 440, 453,
469, 491, 497

Violin Concerto in D minor
238, 440

Capriccio brillant
234

Athalia - excerpt
209, 448

Calm sea and prosperous
voyage - overture
- overture
187, 448, 454

Elijah
- complete
418
- excerpts
151, 183

The Fair Melusine - overture
225

The Hebrides - overture
210, 218, 255, 288, 289,
352, 448

A Midsummer Night's Dream
- complete
255, 352, 415, 492, 494
- excerpts
148, 193, 217, 341, 364,
370, 384, 400

Ruy Blas - overture
256, 288, 408, 448

Son and Stranger - overture
256, 448

Songs without words
- excerpt
241

Auf Flugeln des Gesanges
439

Menotti

The Consul - excerpt
313

Amelia goes to the ball
- excerpt
465

Meyerbeer

L'Africaine - excerpts
219, 333

Dinorah
- complete
477
- excerpts
263, 271

Emma di Resburgo - excerpt
504

Les Huguenots
- complete
424
- excerpts
371, 429

Les patineurs - excerpts
335

Le Prophète - excerpts
204, 346

Robert le Diable - excerpts
336, 447

Miaskovsky

Symphony No 21
444

Cello Concerto
289

Milhaud

Symphony No 1
454

Piano Concerto No 1
209

Cello Concerto
294

Le Carnaval d'Aix
260

Millöcker

Die Dubarry - excerpt
311

Moeran

Symphony in G minor
444

Rhapsody No 3
453

Montemezzi

L'Amore di tre Re
- excerpt
506

Monteverdi

Toccata for 6 Trumpets
498

Moreno-Buendia

Suite Concertante
492

Morlacchi

Il Barbiere di Siviglia
- excerpt
502

Mosca

Le bestie in uomini
- excerpt
504

Le sposi in cimento
- excerpt
489

Leopold Mozart

Horn Concerto
498

Toy Symphony
305

Mozart

Symphony No 24
489

Symphony No 25
295, 456

Symphony No 28
425

Symphony No 29
264, 292, 398, 456

Symphony No 31 "Paris"
363, 388

Symphony No 33
398

Symphony No 34
281, 388

Symphony No 35 "Haffner"
230, 363, 425

Symphony No 36 "Linz"
294

Symphony No 38 "Prague"
294, 331, 377, 419

Symphony No 39
293, 295, 377

Symphony No 40
294, 376, 398

Symphony No 41 "Jupiter"
245, 263, 376, 398

Piano Concertos Nos 1, 2, 3 and 4
508

Piano Concerto No 5
505

Piano Concerto No 6
507

Piano Concerto No 8
500

Piano Concerto No 9
176, 497

Piano Concerto No 11
507

Piano Concerto No 12
256, 257, 483

Piano Concerto No 13
485

Piano Concerto No 14
232, 256, 505

Piano Concerto No 15
245, 475, 490

Piano Concerto No 16
476

Piano Concerto No 17
367, 500

Piano Concerto No 18
496

Piano Concerto No 19
469

Piano Concerto No 20
177, 244, 257, 359, 469, 492, 500

Piano Concerto No 21
234, 321

Piano Concerto No 22
322, 469, 475

Piano Concerto No 23
203, 256, 273, 339, 480

Piano Concerto No 24
177, 245, 273, 343, 401, 469, 476

Piano Concerto No 25
167, 244, 407, 488

Piano Concerto No 26 "Coronation"
367, 495

Piano Concerto No 27
256, 401, 480

2-Piano Concerto
290

Concert Rondo for piano and orchestra
480

Violin Concerto No 1
232, 428

Violin Concerto No 2
428, 487

Violin Concerto No 3
205, 259, 281, 326, 381, 427

Violin Concerto No 4
206, 266, 386, 428, 487

Violin Concerto No 5
205, 254, 296, 386, 401

Violin Concerto No 7
401

Violin Concertone
428

Rondo concertante for violin and orchestra
428

Adagio for violin and orchestra
407, 428

Rondo for violin and orchestra
407, 428

Sinfonia Concertante for violin and viola
427

Sinfonia Concertante for wind
249

Clarinet Concerto
277, 432

Flute Concertos Nos 1 and 2
315, 508

Flute and Harp Concerto
387

Andante for flute and orchestra
315

Horn Concerto No 1
248, 357

Horn Concerto No 2
152, 248, 357

Horn Concerto No 3
248, 358, 393

Horn Concerto No 4
248, 358

Oboe Concerto
431

Adagio and Fugue in C minor
290

Masonic Funeral Music
394

Minuet in C
343

German Dances K605
255, 343

A Musical Joke
279

String Divertimento in F
456

Divertimento No 15
220

Divertimento No 17
- excerpt
343

Serenade No 6 "Serenata notturna"
267, 290, 343

Serenade No 7 "Haffner"
- excerpt
343

Serenade No 11
435

Serenade No 12
407

Serenade No 13
"Eine kleine Nachtmusik"
249, 281, 290, 343, 394

Mass in C minor
442, 484

Mass in C minor - excerpt
167, 324

Requiem
401, 408, 471

Ave verum corpus
255, 278, 404

Exsultate jubilate
150, 176, 227

Exsultate jubilate
- excerpt
325

Ch' io mi scordi di te ?
273, 417

Misera, dove son ?
193, 236, 325

Nehmt meinen Dank
273

Die Maurerfreude;
Dir, Seele des Weltalls;
Laut verkunde unsre Freude
429

Ascanio in Alba - excerpt
428

La Clemenza di Tito
- excerpts
226, 394

Così fan tutte
- complete
260, 380, 409, 432
- excerpts
160, 195, 196, 226, 282,
325, 394

Don Giovanni
- complete
347 (2), 402
- excerpts
166, 193, 206, 218, 222,
224, 226, 277, 324, 325,
394, 506

Die Entfuhrung aus dem
Serail
- excerpts
167, 217, 325, 362, 428,
456

La finta giardiniera
- overture
226

La finta semplice - excerpt
428

Idomeneo - excerpts
167, 202, 226, 282, 394,
417, 465

Le Nozze di Figaro
- complete
347, 428
- excerpts
164, 165, 166, 173, 183,
184, 191, 205, 210, 222,
224, 226, 277, 282, 325,
326, 370, 394, 417, 456

Il re pastore - excerpts
325, 417

Der Schauspieldirektor
- overture
226

Zaide - excerpt
428

Die Zauberflote
- complete
392
- excerpts
166, 174, 195, 222, 225,
282, 325, 417, 428, 456

Mussorgsky

Pictures at an exhibition
280, 379, 397, 436, 444,
469, 490

Pictures at an exhibition
- excerpts
397

Night on Bare Mountain
206, 216, 235, 297, 331,
335, 469, 505

Boris Godunov - excerpts
184, 188, 189, 236

Khovantschina - excerpts
154, 165, 192, 196, 211,
217, 235, 261, 264, 270,
338, 361, 444

The Capture of Kars
- excerpt
236

Sorochintsky Fair
- excerpt
236

Gopak
179, 191, 298

Intermezzo in B minor
236

Scherzo in B flat
236

Song of the flea
197

Neruda

Trumpet Concerto
505

Nicolai

The Merry Wives of Windsor
- overture
206, 218, 270, 276, 289,
480

Nicolini

Trajano in Dacia - excerpt
489

I Baccanali di Roma
- excerpt
490

Nielsen

Symphony No 5
424

Clarinet Concerto
432

Saga Drom
424

Nitzsche

St Giles Cripplegate
444

Van Nuffel

In convertendo
404

Nussio

Folclore d'Engadine
318

Offenbach

Barbe-Bleue - overture
485

La Belle Hélène - overture
485

Les Contes d'Hoffmann
- excerpts
216, 261, 338, 417, 425

La fille du tambour-major
- overture
485

Gaité Parisienne
- excerpts
319, 368, 399

La Grande Duchesse de
Gérolstein - overture
485

Orfée aux enfers - excerpts
209, 276, 346, 361, 426,
485

La Périchole - overture
485

La vie parisienne
- overture
485

Paer

Achille - excerpt
478

Agnese di Fitzhenry
- excerpt
489, 490

Sofonisba - excerpt
490

Paganini

Violin Concerto No 1
266, 358, 448, 453

Violin Concerto No 2
192, 497

Di tanti palpiti
364

Le rivali generosi
- excerpt
478

Paisiello

Il passaggio di Monte
San Bernardo - excerpt
490

Parry

I was glad
462

Jerusalem
219, 411

Pavesi

Elizabetta d'Inghilterra
- excerpt
489

Penderecki

Cello Concerto
504

Pergolesi

L'Olimpiade - overture
411

La serva padrona
- excerpt
443

Pick-Mangiagalli

Notturno romantico
332

Pietri

Maristella - excerpt
432

527

Pizzetti

La Pisanella
272

Planquette

Les cloches de Corneville
- overture
423

Ponce

Estrellita
156, 423

Ponchielli

La Gioconda - excerpts
182, 240, 264, 289, 312,
333, 335, 361, 370, 393,
425, 432, 509

Popp

Scherzo fantastique
472

Portogallo

La Semiramide - excerpt
490

Poulenc

2-Piano Concerto
358

Les biches
483

Bucolique
483

Matelote provencale
483

Pastourelle
483

Prokofiev

Symphony No 1 "Classical"
210, 271, 304, 402

Symphony No 5
306, 386

Symphony No 7
271

Piano Concerto No 1
291, 459

Piano Concerto No 2
265, 325

Piano Concerto No 3
291, 360, 387, 436

Piano Concerto No 5
387

Violin Concerto No 1
381, 442

Violin Concerto No 2
397, 442

Cello Concerto
294

Overture op 42
487

Peter and the Wolf
194, 301, 342, 435

The Gamblers - excerpts
250

Ivan the Terrible
466

Lieutenant Kije - excerpts
326, 341

The Love of Three Oranges
- excerpts
271, 346, 370

Le pas d'acier
257

Romeo and Juliet
- excerpts
387

Puccini

La Bohème - excerpts
183, 192, 198, 208, 262,
283, 342, 423, 432, 434,
460, 464, 501

La Fanciulla del West
- excerpts
151, 160, 282, 370, 434,
438

Gianni Schicchi - excerpts
182, 262, 283, 432, 438,
501

Madama Butterfly
- complete
468
- excerpts
151, 160, 198, 262, 282,
283, 329, 425, 434, 464,
501

Manon Lescaut
- complete
434, 495
- excerpts
164, 260, 262, 329, 333,
338, 371, 434, 501

La Rondine - excerpts
393, 434, 460

Suor Angelica
- complete
458
- excerpts
262, 282, 501

Il Tabarro
- complete
434, 464
- excerpts
177, 417

Tosca
- complete
439, 466, 482
- excerpts
154, 168, 172, 175, 177,
182, 184, 283, 333, 370,
371, 434, 443, 464, 501

Turandot - excerpts
154, 184, 188, 198, 201,
262, 322, 329, 342, 371,
378, 393, 438, 460, 465,
501

Le villi - excerpts
434, 501

Puccitta

La Caccia di Enrico IV
- excerpt
478

Purcell

Dido and Aeneas
- complete
148, 218
- excerpts
176

Chaconne
149

Trumpet Sonata
498

Soul of the world
201

Rachmaninov

Symphony No 2
278, 468, 507

Piano Concerto No 1
180, 257, 435

Piano Concerto No 2
234, 248, 282, 375, 408,
431, 449, 488

Piano Concerto No 3
173, 183, 347, 442

Piano Concerto No 4
303, 435

Paganini Rhapsody
165, 178, 278, 386, 390,
408, 452, 488, 507

Etudes-Tableaux
445

Spring Cantata
414

Three Russian Folksongs
414

Rameau

Les paladins - overture
422

Pygmalion - overture
411

Zais - overture
422

Ravel

Piano Concerto in G
154, 304, 494

Piano Concerto for the
left hand
360

Alborada del gracioso
345, 396, 433

Boléro
243, 404, 433, 505

Daphnis et Chloé - ballet
408

Daphnis et Chloé
- 2nd suite
256, 259, 278, 302, 345

Ma mère l'oye - suite
297

Pavane pour une infante
défunte
228, 396, 401, 433, 454,
504

Rapsodie espagnole
244, 336, 401

Shéherazade
412

Tzigane
281, 302

La valse
335, 433

Rawsthorne

Piano Concerto No 1
291

Symphonic Studies
152

Practical cats
263

Street Corner - overture
152

Reger

An die Hoffnung
403

528

Respighi

Belkis, Queen of Sheba
- suite
498

Brazilian Impressions
198, 272, 496

Church Windows
496

The Fountains of Rome
272, 312, 406, 415, 416

The Pines of Rome
319, 406, 415

Metamorphoses
498

Roman Festivals
416

Reznicek

Donna Diana - overture
277

Revueltas

Sensemaya; Redes;
Caminos; Itinerarios;
Janitzio; El Ranacuajo;
Homenaje; Cuauhnahuac;
Danza geometrica
454

Righini

Gerusalemme liberata
- excerpt
490

Rimsky-Korsakov

Baba Yaga
229

Capriccio espagnol
211, 271, 335, 387, 442

Le coq d'or - excerpts
230, 247, 287, 346, 368, 377

Dubinishka
387

Flight of the bumble bee
179, 298

Invisible City of Kitesh
- excerpt
219

Ivan the Terrible
- overture
288

May Night - overture
206, 341

Piano Concerto
227

The Prophet - excerpt
197

Russian Easter Festival Overture
197, 287, 331

Scheherazade
207, 230, 330, 356, 435, 502

Skaska
150, 229

The Snow Maiden - excerpts
229, 288, 298, 387

Tsar Sultan - excerpts
230, 330, 387, 502

Rodrigo

Concierto de Aranjuez
475, 492, 506

Concierto de Aranjuez
arranged for harp
494

Concierto madrigal
475

Concierto pastoral
472

Fantasia para un
gentilhombre
472, 492

Serenata
506

4 Madrigales amatores
187

Rosas

Sobre las clas
509

Rosetti

Horn Concerto
498

Rossini

Theme and Variations
for clarinet
415

Stabat mater
487

La regata veneziana
423

Armida - excerpt
359

L'Assiedo di Corinto
- overture
427, 479, 480

Il Barbiere di Siviglia
- complete
303, 356
- excerpts
190, 247, 263, 304, 322,
345, 349, 378, 427, 482,
506

La Cenerentola - excerpts
232, 367, 373, 376, 393

Edipo a Colono - excerpt
469

La gazza ladra - overture
190, 228, 344, 356, 380, 393, 427

L'Italiana in Algeri
- excerpts
232, 304, 326, 333, 343,
345, 356, 468

Maometto Secondo
- complete
495
- overture
480

Mosè
486

Otello
- complete
471
- overture
480

La scala di seta - overture
232, 343, 348, 356, 427, 470

Semiramide - excerpts
233, 342, 356, 359, 373,
382, 385, 425, 468, 470

Il signor bruschino
- overture
232, 427

Il viaggio a Reims
- overture
479

Tancredi - overture
393

Tornaldo e Dorlinska
- excerpt
480

William Tell - excerpts
193, 202, 216, 232, 320,
343, 356, 373, 378, 382,
390, 416, 417, 423, 427,
470, 480

Rossini/Respighi
La boutique fantasque
227, 239, 344

Roussel

Symphony No 4
188

Rubbra

Symphony No 2
457

Symphony No 3
507

Symphony No 4
507

Symphony No 6
481

Symphony No 8
482

Festival Overture
458

Rubinstein

Melody in F
275

Sacchini

Oedipe à Colone - overture
411

Saint-Saens

Piano Concerto No 1
476

Piano Concerto No 2
161

Piano Concerto No 4
260, 476

Violin Concerto No 1
462

Violin Concerto No 2
462

Violin Concerto No 3
386, 455, 462, 491

Violin Concerto No 4
462

Cello Concerto
167, 279, 289, 312, 418,
457, 497

Caprice (orch. Ysaye)
462

Caprice andalous
462

Danse macabre
255, 289, 387, 481

Le déluge
462

Havanaise
293, 312, 455, 462

Introduction and
Rondo Capriccioso
312, 434, 448, 455, 462,
505

La jeunesse d'Hercule
481

Marche héroique
481

La muse et le poète
462

Phaeton
481

Romance in C;
Romance in D flat
462

Romance in D (arr. flute)
472

Le rouet d'Omphale
481

Etienne Marcel - excerpt
237

Henry VIII - excerpt
448

Samson et Dalila - excerpts
156, 207, 208, 230, 289,
422, 466

Le carnaval des animaux
254, 341, 358

Le carnaval des animaux
- excerpt
275

Sarasate

Zigeunerweisen
434

Satie

Parade
257

Scarlatti

Sinfonia in B flat
411

Oboe Concerto
161, 185

Oboe Concerto - excerpt
151

Il giardino di rose
- overture
422, 507

O cessate
172

Scarlatti/Tommasini
The Good-Humoured Ladies
258

Schnabel

Rhapsody
192

Schmidt

Variations on a Hussar's
Song
446

Notre Dame - intermezzo
338

Schmitt

La tragédie de Salomé
425

Schoenberg

Chamber Symphony No 2
408

Pelleas und Melisande
409

Schönherr

Austrian Peasant Dances
318

Schubert

Symphony No 4 "Tragic"
389

Symphony No 5
272, 385, 442

Symphony No 8 "Unfinished"
155, 239, 274, 279, 367,
384, 442, 493

Symphony No 9 "Great"
364, 438, 477

Rondo in A
407

Rosamunde - excerpts
223, 479

Ave Maria
433

Schumann

Symphony No 1 "Spring"
389, 398, 430, 472

Symphony No 2
419, 433, 467

Symphony No 3 "Rhenish"
328, 422, 433, 467

Symphony No 4
242, 357, 430, 459

Piano Concerto
174, 230, 245 (2), 296,
307, 358, 409, 436, 474

Cello Concerto
289, 312, 416

Violin Concerto
489

Overture, Scherzo and
Finale
433

Die Braut von Messina
- overture
470

Faust - overture
422

Genoveva - overture
419

Hermann und Dorothea
- overture
470

Manfred - overture
327, 398

Scriabin

Piano Concerto
185

Poème de l'extase
287

Rêverie
287

Searle

Aubade
446

Sessions

Symphony No 8
435

Rhapsody
435

Shostakovich

Symphony No 1
303

Symphony No 10
272, 500

Symphony No 12
"The Year 1917"
382

Piano Concerto No 1
265

Violin Concerto No 1
441

Festival Overture
384

The Age of Gold - suite
272, 370

Sibelius

Symphony No 1
277, 497

Symphony No 2
277, 356, 478

Symphony No 3
277, 493

Symphony No 4
243, 480

Symphony No 5
210, 360, 409, 483, 487,
504

Symphony No 6
276, 496

Symphony No 7
276, 488

Violin Concerto
149, 469, 479, 489

Serenades for violin
and orchestra;
Serious Melodies for
violin and orchestra
472

Humoresques for violin
and orchestra
479

En Saga
175, 277, 485

Finlandia
172, 223, 289, 338, 457,
480, 488

Karelia - suite
457, 500

Lemminkainen's Return
488

Luonnotar
480

Night Ride and Sunrise
409, 487

Pohjola's Daughter
504

The Swan of Tuonela
457, 488, 505

Tapiola
244, 488

Valse triste
176, 255, 319, 457, 488

Sieczynsky

Wien du Stadt meiner
Träume
309

Smetana

Ma Vlast - excerpts
245, 263

The Bartered Bride
- excerpts
160, 195, 206, 217, 243,
301, 329, 339, 363, 369,
384

Dalibor - excerpt
329

The Kiss - excerpt
195

Sousa

Stars and stripes forever
244, 346

El capitan
244

Spontini

La vestale - excerpt
322

Stanford

Clarinet Concerto
477

Still

Afro-American Symphony
- excerpt
454

Stradella

Trumpet Concerto
507

Johann Strauss father

Radetzky March
167, 276, 346, 362

Johann Strauss

Artist's Life Waltz
274, 352

The Blue Danube
276

Casanova - excerpt
310

Emperor Waltz
276, 352, 371

Die Fledermaus
- complete
273, 345
- excerpts
167, 271, 352, 372, 465

Eine Nacht in Venedig
- complete
258
- excerpt
310

Perpetuum mobile
352, 368

Pizzicato Polka
167, 274, 277

Tales from the Vienna Woods
167

Thunder and Lightning Polka
276, 352, 362

Tritsch-Tratsch Polka
276, 352, 362, 368

Voices of Spring
185, 505

Wiener Blut
258

Wiener Blut Waltz
371

Der Zigeunerbaron
- complete
258
- excerpts
276, 309, 352

Quadrille on themes from Verdi's "Un Ballo in Maschera"
352

Johann Strauss/Dorati
Graduation Ball
368

Josef Strauss

Music of the spheres
270, 320

Delirium Waltz
276

Richard Strauss

Burleske
227, 386, 506

Parergon for piano and orchestra
506

Horn Concerto No 1
162, 296

Horn Concerto No 2
165, 296

Oboe Concerto
164

Also sprach Zarathustra
379, 493

Le bourgeois gentilhomme
- suite
321

Dance Suite from Couperin
322

Don Juan
155, 210, 302, 311, 355, 468

Don Quixote
416 (2)

Ein Heldenleben
494

Metamorphosen
372, 409

Till Eulenspiegels lustige Streiche
210, 355, 360, 379

Tod und Verklarung
243, 271, 312, 372, 432

Vier letzte Lieder
194, 246, 443

Die Aegyptische Helena
- excerpt
494

Arabella - excerpts
220, 263

Ariadne auf Naxos
260

Capriccio
- complete
311
- excerpt
246

Elektra
494

Die Frau ohne Schatten
- excerpts
360, 443, 494

Guntram - excerpt
443, 494

Der Rosenkavalier
- complete
301
- excerpts
311, 320, 360, 385, 443, 494

Salome - excerpts
312, 355, 360, 494

Stravinsky

Le chant du rossignol
359

Le baiser de la fée
368

Circus Polka
415

Fireworks
404

Jeu de cartes
220

L'oiseau de feu
- complete
419
- excerpts
155, 156, 297, 385

Petrushka
305, 407, 429, 483

Petrushka - excerpt
256

Pulcinella - suite
366, 384

Le sacre du printemps
209, 339, 404

Scherzo à la russe
483

Suite No 1
315

Suite No 2
315

Suite No 2 - excerpt
255

Symphony in 3 movements
357, 377

Sullivan

Di Ballo - overture
491

Iolanthe; The Mikado; Ruddigore; Yeomen of the Guard - overtures
293

Sullivan/Mackerras
Pineapple Poll
491

Suppé

The Beautiful Galathea
- overture
270, 276

Boccaccio - excerpt
310

Light Cavalry - overture
235, 270, 277, 286, 360, 509

Morning, Noon and Night in Vienna - overture
191, 270, 286

Pique Dame - overture
191, 270, 286

Poet and Peasant - overture
218, 286, 288

Die Irrfahrt ins Gluck
- overture
286

Svendsen

Romance
431

Szymanowski

Violin Concerto No 1
178

Taneyev

Suite de concert
288

Tartini

Concertino (arr. Jacob)
148

Tchaikovsky

Symphony No 1
"Winter Daydreams"
452

Symphony No 2
"Little Russian"
296, 414, 463

Symphony No 3 "Polish"
465

Symphony No 4
154, 234, 243, 303, 308, 384, 470, 474

531

Symphony No 5
156, 220, 303, 378, 384,
393, 403, 416, 470, 497

Symphony No 6 "Pathétique"
161, 228, 274, 303, 306,
344, 356, 371, 476, 479

Manfred Symphony
254, 463, 486

Piano Concerto No 1
148, 185, 248, 334, 357,
382, 441, 476, 485

Piano Concerto No 2
441

Piano Concerto No 3
441

Violin Concerto
194, 293, 309, 434, 439,
448, 454, 462, 485, 486,
504

Sérénade mélancolique
282, 340, 431, 440, 454,
485

Valse-Scherzo for violin
and orchestra
439, 463, 485

Rococo Variations
279, 289

Suite No 1
403

Suite No 2
403, 481

Suite No 3
191, 272, 403

Suite No 4 "Mozartiana"
232, 403, 481

Andante cantabile
(arr. Schmid)
331, 387

Capriccio italien
192, 233, 331, 470, 486

Elegy in G
459, 470

Francesca da Rimini
335, 337, 408, 426, 432,
450

Hamlet
223, 259, 286, 408

Marche slave
180, 211, 335, 346, 450,
497

Romeo and Juliet
208, 223, 271, 335, 340,
377, 387, 425, 450, 460,
470, 480

Russian Dance (orch.Schmid)
275

Serenade for strings
162, 223, 353

Serenade for strings
- excerpt
384, 480

The Tempest
286, 288

The Voyevode
- symphonic ballad
444

1812 Overture
161, 234, 320, 385, 414,
450, 497

Eugene Onegin - excerpts
175, 205, 219, 239, 328,
329, 336, 354, 480

Iolanta - excerpt
336

The Maid of Orleans
- excerpts
195, 207, 313

The Nutcracker
- complete
488, 501
- excerpts
161, 200, 223, 271, 311,
323, 328, 340, 354, 397

The Queen of Spades
- excerpts
195, 216, 329, 417

The Sleeping Beauty
- complete
289, 489
- excerpts
209, 216, 217, 229, 275,
328, 338, 342, 353, 397,
480

Swan Lake
- complete
488
- excerpts
229, 241, 258, 304, 312,
323, 328, 338, 353, 397,
481

Telemann

Trumpet Concerto in D
496

Suite in A minor
for flute and orchestra
387

Thomas

Mignon
- complete
465
- excerpts
168, 423, 426

Hamlet - excerpts
334, 417, 447

Raymond - excerpts
180, 191

Tippett

Concerto for double
string orchestra
218

Piano Concerto
390

Tomasi

Trumpet Concerto
501

Torelli

Trumpet Concerto in D
496

Trumpet Concerto in D
507

Concerto for 4 Trumpets
498

Turina

Danzas fantasticas
229

La oracion
415

Rapsodia sinfonica
186, 415

Saeta
183

Poema No 3
183

Vaughan Williams

Symphony No 3 "Pastoral"
414

Symphony No 4
414

Symphony No 5
378

Symphony No 6
406

Oboe Concerto
221

Hugh the Drover - excerpt
194

Scott of the Antarctic
- film music
180

Sir John in Love
447

The Wasps - excerpt
445

The Loves of Joanna
Godden - film music
162

Fantasia on a theme of
Thomas Tallis
248, 345

Fantasy on Sussex
Folksongs
490

Five Tudor Portraits
422

Flos campi
153

Folksongs from Somerset
- march
381

Fantasia on Greensleeves
370, 411

In the Fen Country
414

The Lark Ascending
406

Norfolk Rhapsody
414

Psalm 100
399

Serenade to Music
201

Verdi

Aida
- complete
446
- complete
160, 166, 187, 200, 201,
205, 216, 233, 238, 264,
281, 282, 306, 323, 332,
334, 340, 346, 360, 377,
410, 423, 425, 449

Alzira - excerpts
299, 449

Aroldo - excerpt
449

Attila - excerpts
385, 417, 449, 456, 506

Un Ballo in Maschera
- complete
452
- excerpts
177, 182, 196, 198, 205,
281, 282, 307, 393, 438,
440, 448, 449

La battaglia di Legnano
- overture
200, 460

Il Corsaro
- complete
453
- excerpt
449

Don Carlo - excerpts
185, 188, 216, 323, 332,
336, 377, 385, 393, 449,
464, 467

I Due Foscari - excerpt
449

Ernani - excerpts
200, 208, 224, 312, 332,
449

Falstaff
- complete
293
- excerpts
282, 390, 449

La Forza del Destino
- complete
502
- excerpts
153, 182, 186, 187, 191,
200, 205, 225, 233, 238,
281, 299, 307, 323, 327,
334, 380, 410, 417, 438,
449, 460, 462, 464

Giovanna d'Arco - excerpts
187, 340, 393, 410, 449,
462

I Lombardi - excerpts
449, 482

Luisa Miller - excerpts
200, 299, 344, 410, 448,
449, 456

Macbeth
- complete
458
- excerpts
187, 331, 376, 410, 440,
448, 449, 465

I Masnadieri
449

Nabucco
- complete
466
- excerpts
224, 225, 233, 299, 332,
336, 340, 344, 456, 506

Oberto - excerpt
449

Otello
- complete
418
- excerpts
191, 193, 205, 216, 247,
323, 342, 390, 449

Rigoletto
- complete
471
- excerpts
156, 167, 185, 196, 219,
230, 246, 271, 333, 349,
438, 440, 449, 460, 477

Simon Boccanegra - excerpts
- excerpts
336, 390, 449

La Traviata
- complete
482
- excerpts
151, 174, 198, 202, 233,
246, 247, 261, 282, 321,
327, 334, 342, 349, 378,
384, 410, 440, 449, 482

Il Trovatore
- complete
426
- excerpts
196, 198, 200, 246, 282,
329, 393, 449, 467, 482

I Vespri Siciliani
- complete
444
- excerpts
218, 224, 233, 263, 318,
327, 336, 344, 359, 410,
449, 456, 470

Four Sacred Pieces
382

Requiem Mass
388, 426, 468

Requiem Mass - excerpt
172

Verdi/Mackerras
The Lady and the Fool
275

Vieuxtemps

Violin Concerto No 4
201

Violin Concerto No 5
266

Villa-Lobos

Bachianas Brasileiras
- excerpts
424, 462

Momoprecoce
459

Vitali

Chaconne (arr. Respighi)
175

Vivaldi

Gloria
459

Magnificat
459

The Four Seasons
280, 402, 493

Oboe Concerto op 8 no 9
185

Violin Concerto
"Il Piacere"
238

Violin Concerto op 3 no 6
430

Concerto for two horns
498

2-Trumpet Concerto
498

2-Trumpet Concerto in D
507

Vorisek

Symphony in D
414

Wagner

Der fliegende Holländer
- complete
433
- excerpts
150, 168, 216, 219, 306,
311, 315, 353, 414, 420,
468

Götterdämmerung - excerpts
173, 203, 204, 221, 321,
354, 373, 494, 509

Lohengrin - excerpts
167, 190, 203, 204, 207,
291, 306, 310, 323, 327,
335, 353, 354, 422, 424,
494, 505

Die Meistersinger von
Nürnberg - excerpts
161, 207, 301, 327, 330,
354, 355, 420, 468

Parsifal - excerpts
203, 204, 311, 373

Das Rheingold - excerpts
179, 372

Rienzi - overture
354, 418, 424, 468

Siegfried - excerpts
203, 372

Tannhauser - excerpts
153, 160, 162, 173, 175,
177, 185, 190, 204, 242,
256, 264, 291, 306, 310,
323, 330, 353, 355, 361,
385, 417, 422, 455, 457,
465, 468, 480, 494, 509

Tristan und Isolde
- complete
221
- excerpts
173, 186, 196, 204, 207,
221, 242, 306, 354, 377,
420, 422, 477, 494

Die Walkure
- Act 1
427
- excerpts
179, 185, 310, 315, 323,
355, 424, 427, 431

Siegfried Idyll
176, 208, 303, 330, 363

Wesendonk Lieder
377

Wesendonk Lieder - excerpts
330, 334

Waldteufel

Estudiantina - waltz
191, 286

Espana - waltz
286

Les grenadiers - waltz
286

Les patineurs - waltz
191, 244, 286, 361, 509

Pomona - waltz
196, 286

Mon rêve - waltz
286

Sur la plage - waltz
196

Walker

Variations
454

Walton

Symphony No 1
208, 403, 487

Violin Concerto
195

Viola Concerto
154, 419

Belshazzar's Feast
339

Crown Imperial
237, 399

Façade - excerpts
196, 273

Hamlet - film music
174

Hamlet - excerpt from
film music
388

Henry V - film music
155

Henry V - excerpts from
film music
149, 388, 399

Johannesburg Festival
Overture
304

Orb and Sceptre
237, 382

Partita for orchestra
339

Portsmouth Point Overture
237

Richard III - excerpt
388

Scapino Overture
208

533

Spitfire Prelude and
Fugue
388

Troilus and Cressida
- excerpts
273

Warlock

Capriol Suite
274

Weber

Symphony No 1
427

Clarinet Concerto
415

Clarinet Concertino
415

Konzertstück
357

Polacca brillante
493

Marcia vivace
505

Invitation to the Dance
190, 255, 318

Abu Hassan - overture
330

Euryanthe - overture
231, 321, 362, 448

Der Freischütz - excerpts
152, 175, 236, 291, 321,
324, 340, 357, 424

Jubel - overture
330

Oberon - excerpts
152, 163, 220, 291, 313,
321, 324, 326, 357, 376,
377, 477

Preciosa - overture
330

Ruler of the spirits
- overture
152, 330,

Ines de Castro - excerpt
504

F.Weber

Variations in F
505

Weigl

Ginerva di Scozia
- excerpt
478

Weill

Kleine Dreigroschenmusik
372

Weinberger

Schwanda the Bagpiper
- polka and fugue
235, 261, 270, 339, 361

Wieniawski

Violin Concerto No 1
302

Violin Concerto No 2
358

Violin Concerto No 2
- excerpt
431

Légende
431

Winter

Il ratto di Proserpina
- excerpt
478

Zaira - excerpt
490

Wiren

Serenade for strings
301

Wolf

Italian Serenade
148, 302

Morgenhymnus
404

Wolf-Ferrari

The Jewels of the Madonna
- intermezzo
230, 297, 300, 346, 509

Susanna's Secret
- complete
482
- overture
206, 248, 293, 297, 346,
367

The School for fathers
- excerpts
293, 297

Xenakis

Aroura; Antikthon;
Synaphai
455

Zandonai

Giulietta e Romeo
- excerpt
302

Zeller

Der Obersteiger - excerpt
311

Der Vogelhandler - excerpts
310

Ziehrer

Wiener Burger - waltz
318

Weaner Madln - waltz
318

Zito

Aja's Theme and
Divertimento
502

Zingaresi

Ines de Castro - excerpt
478

Appendix C: Recording Venues

A note on some principal Philharmonia recording venues

The problem facing most recording companies is to find a hall that is suitable acoustically as well as being located within easy access of both players and recording staff. Some of the big companies have their own purpose-built studios, such as EMI's Abbey Road Studios in St John's Wood, but the best acoustics are very often found in older buildings such as London's Kingsway Hall. Built in 1913, Kingsway Hall was used by EMI in the 1930s, and by both EMI and Decca from the 1940s until 1984.

Various town halls around London have been regularly used by the record companies over the years, at Walthamstow, Watford, Wembley and Hornsey, for example. When the Royal Festival Hall was opened in 1951, it was considered as a possibility for recording, but after some experiments during 1952 it was found to be unsuitable. The Church of All Saints, Tooting, proved to be a useful recording venue and has been in regular use since 1968; and the Henry Wood Hall, opened primarily as a new rehearsal hall in 1974, has also been used regularly for recording.

Kingsway Hall (extracts from an article by Denis Vaughan in "Wireless World", May 1982, reproduced with permission)
For several decades the most sought-after venue for recording orchestral music in England has been the Kingsway Hall in London: legend has it that Sir Thomas Beecham was the first to identify this hall as particularly suited for the purpose. Are there some identifiable reasons for its superior warmth and clarity ? ......
Looking at the Kingsway Hall, it is easy to see where it satisfies the main requirements. Its full width is at the upper limit 27 metres, with inner walls set on pillars at 19 metres width. But the width between the horseshoe balcony faces, with a very useful curved reflecting surface beneath them, is only 17 metres at its widest point. The balcony surrounds the orchestra at a height of 3.5 metres. To be honest, I think that such a horseshoe would bring any large symphony orchestra good acoustical luck. It gives all the players reflections back early enough, and at the right

angle, to allow them to obtain good ensemble. The unbroken surface allows early bass reflections to come back to the microphones (not too strong, mind you) because the long bass waves are refelected intact, and from a shape consonant to their own. It might be worth copying this reflecting shape in Abbey Road, Maida Vale, Henry Wood, Walthamstow, Brent and Watford, to name but a few London recording halls. The shape is reminiscent of those marvellous small Italian theatres.
In recent years, the Kingsway lease has been shared by EMI and Decca, also subletting it to RCA and other companies. Virtually all the seats have been removed downstairs, and many upstairs covered with cloth. At the moment its reverberation time with an orchestra present is about 2.5 seconds ......

Unfortunately, collaboration between EMI and London Underground is not yet such that the engineer's 'red light area' can extend to such nether regions. The rumble of the tube trains would not be so noticeable, were Kingsway not such a good hall. Moreover, the cavernous storerooms and airducts beneath the main floor, which undoubtedly contribute to the warmth of the sound there, develop the tube rumble with equal generosity - a sound which is cruelly revealed by digital recording techniques. The hall is very much alive at all frequencies, even when no-one is in it. The presence of 80 musicians is something which you not only feel there, but which gives the indispensible and audible human element to the music, with myriad small high-frequency extra-musical sounds.
(Footnote: Kingsway Hall was last used for recording by the Philharmonia Orchestra on 5 January 1984. It was then closed for rebuilding and refurbishing as a centre to be used by the Womens' Committee of the GLC)

Abbey Road (extracts from an article by Charles Reid in "Records and Recording", January 1966, reproduced with permission)

A bleak barn of a place, with parquetry floor as if for perpetual staff dances. On facing walls are prim looking clocks and red lights that come and go as 'takes' start and finish. Warning buzzers sneeze abruptly. The ceiling is a complex of ventilator trunks and catwalks. I am reminded vaguely of a 1930 airship hangar.

Such is EMI's No 1 Studio at Abbey Road, St John's Wood. Historically considered this is the ripest recording centre in the world, as well as one of the most active. It has been hard at work for 35 years. Before Abbey Road the company used, among other places, the Small Queen's Hall, on the upper floor of the old Queen's Hall, Portland Place; and before that, a fantastic top storey in a business block off Leicester Square, to which sound was piped by public telephone line from platforms as far away as the Albert Hall.

When Abbey Road opened (1931), HMV and all other labels were stuck - and destined to remain so for nearly 20 years - with the wax disc method. You kept a magazine of these discs, thickish, weighty objects, in heated cabinets, so that when put under the cutting head their surfaces would be malleable to just the right degree. You couldn't record more than $4\frac{1}{2}$ minutes of music at one go. As one wax ran out you transferred to another wax on a second machine, a process involving fade-out, fade-in, precise timing, deft hands, strong nerve. If somebody coughed towards the end of a take, the wax had to be scrapped and, cursing under your breath, you and your singers and players had to start all over again.

At Abbey Road, as elsewhere, tape recording long ago put an end to what must have been a technician's nightmare. Nowadays an intrusive cough can be snipped out and a couple of bars of corrective retake spliced in as easily as they pour tea in the canteen.

john hunt lecture recitals

- An established part of the recorded music scene.
- The presenter works in the classical music business and is Chairman of the Wilhelm Furtwängler Society UK, as well as being associated with the Elisabeth Schwarzkopf-Walter Legge Society.
- Specialises in illustrated talks on gramophone's past history.
- Presentations available include:
  Memories of Wilhelm Furtwängler
  Three Viennese Singers
  Maria Callas — supreme artist
  Vintage Philharmonia recordings
  The Art of Sviatoslav Richter
  Elisabeth Schwarzkopf
  — Her Masters Voice
  The Art of Herbert von Karajan
  Great Conductors of the Bayreuth Festival

Further details from:
**Flat 6, 37 Chester Way,
London SE11 4UR**

The Wilhelm Furtwängler Society UK

Our publications so far include:

The Furtwängler Sound
Complete discography; and
Furtwängler and Great Britain
Survey of the conductor's performances in UK, with press comments; full details of soloists, venues and programmes

In one volume price £6 (£10 overseas)

Furtwängler's New York Philharmonic Concert Programmes 1925-1927
Full programme details of all Furtwängler's US appearances

Price £5 (£7 overseas)

Berlin Philharmonic and its Conductors through changing times
by Gisela Tamsen
Survey of the orchestra's 100-year history under its four permanent conductors

Price £3 (£5 overseas)

Prices include post and packing. These publications, together with membership details, and information about recordings available exclusively to members, from:-

Wilhelm Furtwängler Society UK
Flat 6
37 Chester Way
London SE11 4UR

Music and Books published by Travis & Emery Music Bookshop:

Anon.: Hymnarium Sarisburense, cum Rubris et Notis Musicus
Agricola, Johann Friedrich from Tosi: Anleitung zur Singkunst. (Faksimile 1757)
Bach, C.P.E.: edited W. Emery: Nekrolog or Obituary Notice of J.S. Bach.
Bateson, Naomi Judith: Alcock of Salisbury
Bathe, William: A Briefe Introduction to the Skill of Song
Bax, Arnold: Symphony #5, Arranged for Piano Four Hands by Walter Emery
Burney, Charles: The Present State of Music in France and Italy
Burney, Charles: The Present State of Music in Germany, The Netherlands …
Burney, Charles: An Account of the Musical Performances … Handel
Burney, Karl: Nachricht von Georg Friedrich Handel's Lebensumstanden.
Cobbett, W.W.: Cobbett's Cyclopedic Survey of Chamber Music. (2 vols.)
Corrette, Michel: Le Maitre de Clavecin
Crimp, Bryan: Dear Mr. Rosenthal … Dear Mr. Gaisberg …
Crimp, Bryan: Solo: The Biography of Solomon
d'Indy, Vincent: Beethoven: Biographie Critique
d'Indy, Vincent: Beethoven: A Critical Biography
d'Indy, Vincent: César Franck (in French)
Frescobaldi, Girolamo: D'Arie Musicali per Cantarsi. Primo Libro & Secondo Libro.
Geminiani, Francesco: The Art of Playing the Violin.
Handel; Purcell; Boyce; Geene et al: Calliope or English Harmony: Volume First.
Hawkins, John: A General History of the Science and Practice of Music (5 vols.)
Herbert-Caesari, Edgar: The Science and Sensations of Vocal Tone
Herbert-Caesari, Edgar: Vocal Truth
Hopkins and Rimboult: The Organ. Its History and Construction.
Hunt, John: Adam to Webern: the recordings of von Karajan
Isaacs, Lewis: Hänsel and Gretel. A Guide to Humperdinck's Opera.
Isaacs, Lewis: Königskinder (Royal Children) A Guide to Humperdinck's Opera.
Lacassagne, M. l'Abbé Joseph : Traité Général des élémens du Chant.
Lascelles (née Catley), Anne: The Life of Miss Anne Catley.
Mainwaring, John: Memoirs of the Life of the Late George Frederic Handel
Malcolm, Alexander: A Treaty of Music: Speculative, Practical and Historical
Marx, Adolph Bernhard: Die Kunst des Gesanges, Theoretisch-Practisch
May, Florence: The Life of Brahms
Mellers, Wilfrid: Angels of the Night: Popular Female Singers of Our Time
Mellers, Wilfrid: Bach and the Dance of God
Mellers, Wilfrid: Beethoven and the Voice of God
Mellers, Wilfrid: Caliban Reborn - Renewal in Twentieth Century Music
Mellers, Wilfrid: François Couperin and the French Classical Tradition

Travis & Emery Music Bookshop
17 Cecil Court, London, WC2N 4EZ, United Kingdom.
Tel. (+44) 20 7240 2129

Music and Books published by Travis & Emery Music Bookshop:
Mellers, Wilfrid: Harmonious Meeting
Mellers, Wilfrid: Le Jardin Retrouvé, The Music of Frederic Mompou
Mellers, Wilfrid: Music and Society, England and the European Tradition
Mellers, Wilfrid: Music in a New Found Land: ... ... American Music
Mellers, Wilfrid: Romanticism and the Twentieth Century (from 1800)
Mellers, Wilfrid: The Masks of Orpheus: ...... the Story of European Music.
Mellers, Wilfrid: The Sonata Principle (from c. 1750)
Mellers, Wilfrid: Vaughan Williams and the Vision of Albion
Panchianio, Cattuffio: Rutzvanscad Il Giovine
Pearce, Charles: Sims Reeves, Fifty Years of Music in England.
Pettitt, Stephen: Philharmonia Orchestra: complete discography
Playford, John: An Introduction to the Skill of Musick.
Purcell, Henry et al: Harmonia Sacra ... The First Book, (1726)
Purcell, Henry et al: Harmonia Sacra ... Book II (1726)
Quantz, Johann: Versuch einer Anweisung die Flöte traversiere zu spielen.
Rameau, Jean-Philippe: Code de Musique Pratique, ou Methodes.
Rastall, Richard: The Notation of Western Music.
Rimbault, Edward: The Pianoforte, Its Origins, Progress, and Construction.
Rousseau, Jean Jacques: Dictionnaire de Musique
Rubinstein, Anton : Guide to the proper use of the Pianoforte Pedals.
Sainsbury, John S.: Dictionary of Musicians. Vol. 1. (1825). 2 vols.
Simpson, Christopher: A Compendium of Practical Musick in Five Parts
Spohr, Louis: Autobiography
Spohr, Louis: Grand Violin School
Tans'ur, William: A New Musical Grammar; or The Harmonical Spectator
Terry, Charles Sanford: Four-Part Chorals of J.S. Bach. (German & English)
Terry, Charles Sanford: Joh. Seb. Bach, Cantata Texts, Sacred and Secular.
Terry, Charles Sanford: The Origins of the Family of Bach Musicians.
Tosi, Pierfrancesco: Opinioni de' Cantori Antichi, e Moderni
Van der Straeten, Edmund: History of the Violoncello, The Viol da Gamba ...
Van der Straeten, Edmund: History of the Violin, Its Ancestors... (2 vols.)
Walther, J. G.: Musicalisches Lexikon ober Musicalische Bibliothec (1732)

Travis & Emery Music Bookshop
17 Cecil Court, London, WC2N 4EZ, United Kingdom.
Tel. (+44) 20 7240 2129

© Travis & Emery 2009

www.ingramcontent.com/pod-product-compliance
Lightning Source LLC
Chambersburg PA
CBHW060937230426
43665CB00015B/1978